On The Finland Watch

April 2019
ANN ARBOR,

For Judith Laikin Elkin

What a pleasure to meet a former Foreign Service colleague! I hope you will

On The Finland Watch

An American Diplomat in Finland During the Cold War

find familiar some of the vignetts of American Embassy life!

James Ford Cooper
U.S. Consul General (Ret.)

Sincerely

Ford Cooper

ISBN: 0-75961-769-4

This book is printed on acid free paper.

1stbooks rev. 6/21/01

Dedicated with profound love to my family,
who made this journey with me:
To my wife Magda
and to my children Lane, Carl and Vanessa

Contents

Foreword

No country challenged the capacity of American Cold War policy to find a place for it as did Finland—a nation of demonstrated wartime courage and democratic conviction which had, nevertheless, to devise and pursue a foreign and security policy based on an accommodation with the Soviet Union. And no American diplomat was as intimately involved with relations between the United States and Finland as the author of this book, Ford Cooper. For well over a decade, from the mid 1970s to nearly the end of the 1980s, Mr. Cooper held senior positions from which he played a central role in shaping U.S.-Finnish policy in Helsinki as the American embassy counselor for political affairs, heading up the political analysis team and, later, as the deputy chief of mission (the second in command at the embassy) and as charge d'affaires in the absence of the ambassador, and in Washington, where he headed the State Department team charged with the day-to-day oversight of the relationship. Indeed, as director of the office of Northern European affairs as the Cold War began to change and the dialogue between President Reagan and Mikhail Gorbachev began to create new opportunities for Finland in its relations with Western Europe, the United States, and the Soviet Union, Mr. Cooper was in a key position to develop and see to the implementation of political and economic policies that reflected new realities.

Ford Cooper has been able to record his unique insights on Finland and U.S. policy in a way that allows us to share the life of an American diplomat and, more important, leads us to an evaluation of the policies and perceptions that governed Finland's international relations during the Cold War. His broad experience in Finland helps him see issues as Finns saw them even as he was intimately involved in shaping the U.S. view of the same issues.

As Mr. Cooper points out, the "opportunities for misunderstanding" were large and various. The book examines a number of specific, often sensitive and controversial issues that manifested themselves in Finland during the Cold War. Luckily for us, Mr.

Cooper has had access to recently declassified diplomatic documents (a number of which he had written himself). He has spoken at length with an impressive range of important Finnish leaders and opinion makers who were his former professional contacts. While emphasizing events that took place when he personally was "On the Finland Watch," Mr. Cooper also reviews the relatively early post-World War II developments that were of pivotal importance in the evolution of Finnish policies during the Cold War.

Ford Cooper and I served together for many of the years represented by his book. We were in Finland together at the end of the '70s. My admiration for his work there, and his special skills of judgment and insight, led me to seek him out to serve as a special assistant when I became counselor of the Department of State after the ambassadorship in Finland. Half a decade later, when I was assistant secretary of state for Europe and Canada, Ford Cooper was the director of Northern European affairs. I can say with confidence, and I hope with credibility, that Mr. Cooper accurately reflects how, over time, the team of American diplomats in Helsinki and in Washington worked to understand the Finnish policy context and point of view. It is no easier now to capture the spirit of the then-Finnish positions and policies than it was throughout the post-World War II years. Nonetheless, Ford Cooper could do it then, when he was a player, and he clearly can still do it, as author and diplomatic historian. He appropriately reminds us that the United States did not place Finland at the center of its interests. NATO and the US/NATO policy context largely shaped official views of the developments in the High North. The actions and words of Finnish leaders sometimes led to very real uncertainties about whether there was any awareness of, much less sensitivity to, U.S. and NATO concerns. Put another way, many Americans who held Finland in affectionate regard, who admired Finland's ability to walk a difficult line, and who were prepared to make the case for Finland's place in selected Western councils appropriate for neutral Finland, often found themselves with a weak case. Ford Cooper takes on the challenge of dealing effectively and instructively with this tough, and nuanced, feature of the relationship.

It is fascinating to read of the degree to which a number of Finnish policy positions and attitudes during the Cold War–considered almost sacrosanct at the time–are now being questioned by many Finns, many of them the engineers if not the architects of those positions and attitudes. Some Finns now wonder whether Finland paid too high a price—an unnecessary cost—for its policy of neutrality. Mr. Cooper dares to enter into the evaluation of Urho Kekkonen and his presidency which is now taking place. Whether from courtesy or conviction, Mr. Cooper provides a balanced view of that controversial figure and his time.

Why courtesy? Because, as I can personally attest, Finland and its talented people always capture those who have the opportunity to live and work there for a few years. Additionally, Mr. Cooper learned and used Finnish, no mean accomplishment, which gave him even deeper ties and insight into the Finnish community with its astounding richness of arts, literature, music and its hardy sense of living life as reality. It is not easy to engage in a critical evaluation of such a hospitable country. Perhaps the most unusual feature of the book—at least from those expecting a straight-line, academic orientation in this record of Finnish political life and foreign policy—is the series of personal anecdotes and impressions shared with us about what it was like to be an American diplomat living in Finland during the 1970s and 1980s. Certainly, for my part I can agree wholeheartedly that years spent in Finland become memories of incredible warmth and vitality.

But the life of a diplomat is not about having a good time. American foreign policy is not about making other countries feel good. A diplomat must bring a clear and unforgiving eye to the issues and players of the country at hand, and foreign policy must yield a positive impact on the interests of the United States. Thus, despite his obvious fond regard for Finland, Mr. Cooper does not hesitate to reach conclusions about the nature of Finnish policies during the Cold War. While in general he praises Finland for the overall successes of its post-World War II and Cold War foreign and security policy, Mr. Cooper does not turn away from conclusions that are critical of specific Finnish developments and positions. In particular, and of great interest, he does not turn away from conclusions critical of some of the consequences of President Urho Kekkonen's long tenure. Like the Finns themselves, American diplomats associated with the relationship and the events are not of one mind in our judgments about Finnish policies during those difficult years. Certainly, we did have some concerns, as much for Finland's view of itself as for America's view of Finland, as I tried to make clear in my 1980 Paasikivi Society speech cited by Mr. Cooper. But I join in with him in the overall conclusion that the very fact that a democratic, open Finland survived its tough neighborhood and an out-sized neighborhood bully to now take its place quickly and comfortably in the post-Cold War European and trans-Atlantic world is evidence enough of a remarkably successful management of a difficult situation.

Mr. Cooper's book makes a valuable contribution to our understanding of a complex relationship conducted in a challenging time. It also provides unique insights into the processes of an American embassy, any time, anywhere, even as it lets us look into the assessments of the Helsinki embassy and those serving "On the Finland Watch" during the Cold War years. Mr. Cooper and I are together in being proud to have served the United States in Finland and to have had the privilege of getting to know Finland and Finns well. America has been (and is) well served by its career diplomats, who carry out these missions with skill, insight, and sensitivities and with a keen appreciation of where American interests lie. They (and most often their families) are the front-line representatives of our future abroad. One of the most skilled and well-regarded of them, Ford Cooper, has brought us a thought-provoking and valuable record of his mission in Finland and service to our country.

Rozanne L. Ridgway
U.S. Ambassador to Finland,
1977-1980

Preface

From the onset of the Cold War in the late 1940s to its demise with the collapse of the Soviet Union in the early 1990s, the primary United States policy objective in Finland was to support the independence and credible neutrality of a democratic and Western value-oriented Finland. This remarkably consistent and unchanging U.S. goal closely paralleled Finland's own vital national interest in the face of the ever-looming presence of her giant Eastern neighbor.

Ironically, the parallel nature of our shared interests was sometimes obscured because of Finland's overriding national policy imperative—the lesson drawn from its wars with the Soviet Union—to gain and maintain the confidence and good will of the Soviet Union as a precondition to preserving its independence. This made it awkward if not impossible for the Finns to acknowledge that it was the Soviet Union itself that constituted the only threat to Finland's independence and neutrality. In fact there were numerous occasions during the long Cold War period when Finland's independence appeared to be restricted, its neutrality questioned.

Even while attempting to support Finland's independence and neutrality, there were severe constraints on the United States' scope for acting in pursuit of that objective. Finland was too close to the Soviet Union and too peripheral to United States vital interests to be included under the US/NATO defense umbrella. Nevertheless, Finland clearly benefited from the policies of the NATO alliance which placed very real constraints on Soviet freedom of action anywhere in Europe, including in the Nordic area. Too blatant Soviet pressure on Finland would have risked broader Soviet interests in Europe and would have raised the risk of heightened Nordic ties with NATO, including closer cooperation with NATO by neutral Sweden.

That indirect benefit from NATO notwithstanding, Finland was basically on its own in dealing bilaterally with the Soviet Union.

United States support was largely diplomatic and moral. On the more practical side, U.S. economic assistance, particularly in the early post World War II period, was important when U.S. loans greatly helped Finland to find the resources to make war reparation payments to the Soviet Union. U.S. trade with Finland, while never huge, constituted a significant and continuing link between the two countries. However, the difficulty of the Finnish position, the United States' strong commitment to NATO, and the resulting differences between our world perspectives created occasional opportunities for misunderstandings between the two countries.

Throughout this long period, a small but dedicated band of United States career Foreign Service Officers served in "Amembassy Helsinki," the U.S. outpost for observing Finnish developments and pursuing U.S. objectives in Finland. Working variously under career or politically appointed ambassadors, these Foreign Service Officers, each in turn, with one "generation" succeeding the other, learned the Finnish language (some more, some less), studied the Finnish polity, observed Finland's domestic and foreign policies, and assessed how Finland was doing in pursuit of our shared interests. Above all, along with the ambassador and other members of the embassy "country team," they sought to maintain a close and supportive relationship between our two countries.

I was one of those embassy officers who served "On the Finland Watch," assigned to Helsinki for nearly six years: as political counselor from 1976 to 1979 and as deputy chief of mission (second in command) from 1984 to 1986. Moreover, I served in Washington as director of the State Department office of Northern European affairs from 1986 to 1988, continuing my professional responsibilities for Finnish and Nordic issues. Through these assignments, I was able to study and analyze Finnish developments closely and participate actively in US/Finnish relations.

The purpose of this book is three-fold. The first basic purpose is to describe how the United States embassy viewed key developments in Finnish national public life during the Cold War period. The primary perspective is from the point of view of U.S.

embassy reporting on and assessments of events as they developed. The source material for this information is a large number of diplomatic reports from the U.S. embassy in Helsinki (the great majority never-before published) which were declassified by the Department of State and released to me—and some to other researchers as well—for public use under the Freedom of Information Act (FOIA). While many documents are still unavailable, these declassified reports give an accurate flavor of United States diplomatic perceptions of Finland during long stretches of the Cold War. This book includes material covering the period before 1976 when I first arrived in Finland. Indeed, an awareness of Finnish history, including its wars with the Soviet Union during World War II and developments during the relatively early post-War years, is crucial to understanding Finland's actions throughout the Cold War period. However, the book also looks closely at the 1976-88 period during most of which time I was directly involved in Finnish affairs.

The reader will note that, while the United States was pleased with the overall obvious success achieved by Finland throughout the Cold War in maintaining its independence and a degree of neutrality, at various points along the way the U.S. embassy expressed concern about a number of specific Finnish developments both in domestic policy as well as in the security and foreign policy areas. There were concerns particularly regarding Soviet influence in Finland, Finnish positions on international questions of importance to the United States and our NATO allies, and what we perceived as some of the negative effects of President Urho Kekkonen's lengthy presidential tenure. Although the embassy rejected as inappropriate the term "Finlandization" and discouraged its use by U.S. government officials, the embassy was in fact concerned by some of the phenomena associated with the use of that term. The reader will also note that, just as among Finns there were and are differences of interpretation about political developments and Cold War events in Finland, different American diplomatic observers at different points of time also sometimes reached differing conclusions about the phenomena they were observing.

The second purpose of this book is to search for retrospective insights into how some of the Cold War events reported on by the embassy appear now in the light of additional information and the perspective of time. To provide context for this section, the book cites some recent articles and books relevant to this work. However, the objective of this retrospective section is not to present an exhaustive survey of the rapidly growing body of research on the Cold War period in Finland. Rather, my purpose was to go back to my most important former Finnish professional contacts from my diplomatic assignments in Finland and to exchange views with these Finns who were either involved in or observers of some of the most interesting developments discussed in this book. I am most pleased and honored to be able to draw on current observations on these past Cold War events by some of the more than thirty Finns who graciously received me during a six week research visit to Finland in May-June 1995. I am most indebted to these Finnish statesmen, military figures, politicians, diplomats, journalists, academics and economists who took time from their busy schedules to meet with this former American diplomat who had been their professional contact and interlocutor in the 1970s and 1980s. They proved correct the axiom that on a personal level, once you get to know Finns, they will never let you down. This remains a feature of continuity in an otherwise rapidly changing Finland.

Perhaps the major surprise I encountered in my interviews was the degree to which the Finns I met were prepared to express on the record for use in my book often highly controversial views regarding what many of them were prepared to refer to as the atmosphere of "Finlandization" that characterized Finland particularly during the 1960s and 1970s. It is clear that many Finns were more deeply disturbed by the negative dimensions of the political culture in Finland during those decades than they were prepared to disclose at the time. Many place most responsibility for these unhealthy developments squarely on the shoulders of President Urho Kekkonen and those around him, particularly on the latter during Kekkonen's waning years.

To be sure, President Kekkonen also had his defenders among my interviewees, and even his severest critics give him credit for his successful overall stewardship of Finland's foreign and defense policies during his tenure. But there is broad agreement among most Finnish observers that there was a damaging price to pay for this success. I myself have come to the conclusion that the extraordinarily long period of President Kekkonen's tenure introduced a number of dangerous and damaging dimensions into the Finnish political culture, particularly in the 1960s and 1970s. I have also come to the conclusion that his successor, President Mauno Koivisto—while he continued Finland's foreign policy practice of great sensitivity to Soviet foreign and security policy positions—deserves tremendous credit for removing many of the stultifying effects of the Kekkonen era on Finland's domestic political culture.

The foregoing personal observation provides a segue into the third basic purpose of the book: to describe what it was like to be an American diplomat and his family living in Finland during the 1970s and 1980s and to reflect on our experiences in and personal impressions of this fascinating country. It is also an opportunity to provide informed insights on the workings of the American embassy during those periods and to relate anecdotes from those interesting times. Actually, I discovered it would have been impossible for me to write a book about Finland without addressing the personal dimensions of the experiences in Finland of a then relatively young American Foreign Service family with children in the late 1970s and again in the mid-1980s. It is good to hold fast to such personal memories and to record them. It was a great time to have been in Finland, and we have many friends and experiences we will always treasure.

Finally, I know few, if any, American diplomats who concluded their assignments in Finland with anything less than high admiration for the Finnish people and their success in maintaining and strengthening their country's independence during the dangerous Cold War years. This admiration endured notwithstanding the concerns and policy differences that arose. There are important lessons to be learned from Finland's success in cementing its independence against seemingly great odds. However, there are also lessons to be drawn from the strains on Finland's constitutional institutions and foreign relationships resulting from the manner in which some of these crises were met.

This book discusses some of these controversial questions and policy issues because they were fascinating, they were what we studied, wrote and worried about, and they were important. These phenomena remain of deep interest to those generations of Finns who lived through that period, including those whom I was able to interview. These Cold War events are also of interest to Finland's many overseas friends and to those academics who follow Finnish and Nordic developments. It is important that current and future generations of Finns who did not personally experience those controversial years be aware of some of the issues and points of views discussed in this book.

But this book is comfortable in joining in the inescapable conclusion that in the final analysis Finland's post-World War II and Cold War performance represented highly successful long-term management of a precarious situation where her cherished independence and neutrality seemed often to hang in the balance. In the process, Finland's steadfast protection of her own vital and Western-oriented interests presaged the ultimate triumph in the final decade of this millennium of Western democratic, economic and moral values over the discredited values of the Soviet system.

The challenge now to Finland and the West–particularly, I would argue, to the United States as it gropes with domestic social issues and seeks guiding principles for it post-Cold War foreign and security policy—is to prove that we are worthy of the Western values we each in our own way so successfully defended during the long, twilight Cold War struggle.

James Ford Cooper
Punta Gorda, Florida

PART ONE

Learning of and Preparing for an Assignment to Finland

The unusually warm late May sun, still high in the sky at five o'clock in the afternoon, shone down on the grateful Finnish sun worshippers sipping their expensive drinks on the patio of the Kappeli Restaurant on Etelä Esplanadi in downtown Helsinki near the Market Square and South Harbor. The Kappeli patrons adjusted their chairs to receive the sunlight squarely on their faces on one of the first truly warm days of 1995 in Helsinki. Is there anyone, I wondered, more appreciative of warm sunshine than a Finn after a long, dark winter?

I was pretty satisfied myself, sitting there, nursing my draft beer, vaguely conscious that at 25 Finnmarks I had just blown almost $6 dollars on the admittedly sizable glass (the exchange rate that spring was about 4.20 Finnmarks to the dollar). What the hell, I thought, I'll probably have another anyway, it tastes so good and it's such a nice day. There were worse ways to end a day than having a beer at Kappeli.

It had been a good day all around. I had just come out of a long, two and one/half hour interview with former President Mauno Koivisto (president of Finland from 1982-1994) at his Bank of Finland basement office—he had referred to it humorously as his *korsu* (dugout), recalling his Continuation War experiences 1941-1944 when he had fought behind Soviet lines for many months. I had requested an appointment with President Koivisto as part of a series of similar requests with important Finns whom I had known professionally during my two diplomatic assignments to the American embassy in Helsinki.

The interviews, which had been going very well, were part of my research for this book into how Finland dealt with certain key political, foreign policy and security issues during the long Cold War years, as seen by the U.S. embassy at the time and as viewed now in retrospect. I had a most interesting interview with the former president in which we reviewed almost all of the important issues of Finland's troubled post-World War II period. President Koivisto had asked, however, that the interview be off the record, pointing out that he himself had written extensively about many of these issues in his own recent books in terms pretty much identical to those he had used in our interview.

I of course will honor his wishes, grateful, however, that all of my other interviews with key players and observers were on the record and usable in this book. In any case the interview with the former president provided me with many useful insights directly relevant to my book. Moreover, he of course emerges as a central element in the vigorous discussion over the proper use of presidential power in post-World War II Finland.

Sipping my beer in Kappeli that glorious May afternoon in 1995, I could not help but recall the series of events that had resulted in my life becoming inextricably linked with Finland, a country that until a fateful day more than twenty years earlier had scarcely penetrated my awareness. What a long and fascinating road it had been since Finland first came into our lives— surprisingly, unexpectedly. I could remember the unlikely beginning as if it were yesterday.

It had been in December 1974. We had limped into Popayan, Colombia from a long day's drive from Pasto, Colombia near the border with Ecuador. Our family, consisting of my wife Magda, sons Lane (9), Carl (5) and daughter Vanessa (2 1/2) were in a 1970 Jeep Wagoneer. The Rabinowitz family travelling with us was in a Toyota Landcruiser. We were on the return leg of an adventurous two-week driving expedition through the Andes mountains from Medellin, Colombia to Guayaquil, Ecuador and back again. It had been a marvelous adventure of great fun and no serious mishaps. However, our jeep's radiator had sprung a leak midway between Pasto and Popayan, and we had been obliged to stop every fifteen minutes to pour jerry cans of water into the boiling-over radiator. Upon finally arriving in Popayan, I dropped the jeep off at a radiator shop for repairs, and we checked into our lovely colonial hotel (destroyed a few years later by an earthquake, as was most of the rest of Popayan).

At the hotel front desk I was told I had a message from the American consulate in Medellín. I had been assigned to Medellín as principal officer of the consulate in March of 1973, and my family and I were anxiously awaiting news of my reassignment due sometime during the summer of 1975. Medellín had been a terrific assignment for us, my first opportunity to be responsible for my own post. The "Antioqueños," as the inhabitants of that area of Colombia are called, were charming, the city of Medellín was blessed with a perpetual springtime climate, and the drug trade that later ruined the city was only just beginning to be noticed.

However, I was anxious to get out of Latin American affairs, thoroughly disgusted as I was with our policy at the time of so-called "benign neglect" of Latin America and with our support of military and military-dominated regimes throughout the hemisphere. In fact, just prior to departing Medellín, I had submitted an official report through Department of State channels presenting a scathing criticism of U.S. policy toward Latin America at the time. Ironically, the author of our Latin American policy, or at least the man who presided over it, Secretary of State Henry Kissinger, was also the author of the personnel policy that afforded me the opportunity to escape Latin America. Kissinger had decided that America's Foreign Service Officers (FSOs, as we are called) were over-specializing in specific geographical regions.

The story goes that Kissinger, notoriously uninterested at the time in Latin America—except for Chile and Allende—had met some months earlier with a group of senior U.S. diplomats assigned to Latin America and found them insufficiently informed on his grand global foreign policy strategy. He thus ordered that personnel assignment officers henceforth give priority to providing FSOs with more varied geographical experience. That suited me just fine, and I asked my personnel counselor in Washington to get me an assignment as embassy political officer in a European post.

Sure enough, when I got through on the telephone to the consulate secretary in Medellín, she said that the State Department personnel office had called to inform me I had been assigned as political counselor of the American embassy in Helsinki, Finland. The terms of the assignment were that I would be transferred from Medellín to Washington in July 1975 for 44 weeks of Finnish language training at the Department of State language school, followed by transfer to Helsinki in the summer of 1976 for a three year assignment. I learned that my spouse Magda would also be able to take the Finnish language course.

I had not specifically asked for an assignment to Finland, and it came as a great but certainly not unwelcome surprise. While I had known some Finnish-Americans while growing up in Detroit, Michigan, and knew a few stray facts about Finland, I was pretty foggy generally about that part of the world. So David Rabinowitz of the Toyota Landcruiser and I walked over to the nearest bookstore to see what kind of information we could find about Finland. All we could locate was a map of Europe showing Finland tucked way up there at the top right side of the map between the Gulf of Bothnia and the Soviet Union. This, I felt instinctively, was going to be a fascinating assignment!

Upon returning to Medellín, I sent off to the Department of State library for some background books on Finland. *The Finnish Political System* by Professor Jaakko Nousiainen was the first book I read, and it was a great privilege to be able in June 1995 to interview Chancellor Nousiainen for my own book. We transferred to Washington in July 1975, enjoying *en route* a delicious nine-day boat cruise from Colombia to San Francisco followed by a four-day Amtrack railway trip across the United States. (Alas, those leisurely transfer trips are a thing of the past!)

After finding a house near Washington and otherwise getting organized, we commenced study of the Finnish language in August 1975. We immediately perceived that, notwithstanding my own fluency in Spanish and my wife Magda's fluent English, Spanish and French, learning the Finnish language would prove to be on a completely different scale of difficulty and challenge.

There were four of us in the class, and we would spend together six hours a day, five days a week for the next 44 weeks. Magda and I formed half of the class. Of course, for us it was not simply a question of six hours daily of class together, but rather, now, twenty-four hours a day for 44 weeks! Magda and I would often comment later that studying Finnish together was a challenge that most marriages perhaps had best not confront! One of the other students was Ward Thompson who was to be the Embassy labor-political officer and thus would work for me in the embassy political section in Helsinki. It quickly became clear that Ward was the star of the Finnish class. He had actually lived in Finland as an exchange student some years earlier and had a good head start on the Finnish language.

I considered it a stern test of my patience and maturity to participate in a class day after day while being out-performed in the Finnish language by some one who would later work for me. To his credit, Ward never wavered in his charge toward excellence in the Finnish language—and I, for my part, didn't exact revenge on him later for having excelled over me during the language course! Actually, Ward's excellence in the language made a major contribution to enhancing our own progress.

Our teacher throughout the great bulk of the 44-week course was Aili Bell, a Finn married to an American and a highly experienced teacher of the Finnish language. Over the years many American diplomats assigned to Finland studied the language under Aili Bell, attempting to understand what she meant on the difference between "dark-sounding" and "light-sounding" vowels as well as trying to penetrate the seemingly impossibly complex Finnish grammar and totally unrecognizable vocabulary.

The State Department's language school, a part of the Foreign Service Institute, has developed a language instruction system which—despite its critics—does a creditable job of providing well-motivated FSOs with the basic fundamentals of a foreign language in a relatively short period of time. We were pleased that by the end of 44 weeks we had gained a good knowledge of Finnish grammar, reasonably good pronunciation, and an elementary but useful knowledge of some basic vocabulary.

However, the real test of our ability to work in the Finnish language would come after we arrived in Finland. There are two kinds of students in the study of a difficult language: those who build upon the foundation of what they learned in language school to penetrate more deeply into the language once at post; and those who, through lack of effort or opportunity to actively use the language, see their language skills deteriorate during their assignments. We were determined to be among the former.

Also, during our 44 weeks at the Foreign Service Institute I attended one afternoon a week a course in regional European area studies with lectures by visiting professors and Nordic experts and State Department Nordic hands. These lectures, together with extensive background reading assignments, gave us a pretty solid grounding in Nordic affairs and U.S. policy objectives in Northern Europe. I supplemented this with independent study of Finnish history and politics. The Finnish embassy in Washington under Ambassador Leo Tuominen and Minister Arto Tanner also took an active interest in us American diplomats bound for Finland and insured that we began already in Washington to hear the Finnish point of view.

Finally, the long period of preparation in Washington came to an end. In July, 1976, after joining in the unique July Fourth American bicentennial celebration in Washington, we set out for Finland with our three kids (and a Colombian nanny) in tow. Little did we know then when we landed for the first time in Helsinki on July 15, 1976 that it would mark the beginning of an association with Finland that would spill over into three decades spanning the 1970s, 1980s and 1990s. Or that Finland would become a central feature of our Foreign Service career and, indeed, a major focus of our lives.

2

Getting Settled in Helsinki

Upon our arrival at Helsinki-Vantaa International airport that July day in 1976, our family of five was met by the U.S. embassy's administrative counselor, Marvin Brenner, together with support staff from his administrative section who assisted in clearing us through immigration and our luggage through customs.

One of the many positive aspects of serving with an American embassy abroad is that upon arrival there is a pre-existing support system to assist newcomers to the embassy in the settling-in process. Being met by representatives of the administrative section was always a big assist to new embassy personnel. Once we had completed the arrival formalities, we were taken in embassy vehicles to the hotel where we would be staying until the house we had selected as our residence became available.

We were fortunate with regard to housing. Ward Thompson had taken a preliminary trip to Finland several months earlier at his own expense to line up his housing arrangements. When he returned to Washington, he showed me a list of housing possibilities. Included among the housing becoming available was a house at Hietaniemintie 3 in the improbably named Helsinki suburb of "West End." This house was at the time occupied by Paul Hughes, the economic counselor of the embassy, who would be departing Helsinki for an onward assignment in August. From the description of the house and its setting, we decided that the Hughes' house sounded like the most attractive and suitable.

I wrote Hughes to ask that he advise his landlord we would be prepared to sign a three-year lease with him after the Hughes' departure. Hughes did so, and thus the house was ours to lease. However, the Hughes would not be leaving until about a month after our arrival, so we arranged temporary housing for the interim period.

With our three small children the idea of staying in a downtown hotel did not appeal to us. Consequently, in a move that proved to give us a major boost in getting off to a positive start in Finland, we arranged to stay at a "summer hotel" that we had heard about from some Finnish acquaintances in Washington before we left. The summer hotel in this case was a building used during the academic year as student housing at the Ottaniemi Technical High School (really a university) located in Espoo, a county adjoining Helsinki. Only twenty minutes by car from the embassy in downtown Helsinki, the technical school occupies a sprawling campus, beautifully wooded with the birch, pine and spruce trees characteristic of Finnish forests. On the campus was a stunning conference center called Dipoli that had been designed by the Finnish modernist architect Reima Pietilä. The Dipoli Conference Center had served as the site of preliminary meetings of the Conference on Security and Cooperation in Europe (CSCE) in which Finland played a key role.

We were to spend about a month at the Ottaniemi summer hotel. We had a suite of rooms at one end of a wing on the second floor. Our rooms shared a common area, including a kitchen, with other guests from an adjoining suite. Our rooms had no television set, but there was a lounge area downstairs where hotel guests could gather to converse or watch TV. During a good part of the time we were in the hotel, the 1976 summer Olympics were underway in Montreal, Canada. It was fun to go downstairs on those incredibly long summer evenings and watch the televised competition from Montreal.

Finland's Olympic team that year featured the brilliant but controversial long distance runner, Lasse Viren. Lasse was a national hero in the country that had produced one of the most famous long-distance runners of them all—the immortal Paavo Nurmi who, between 1920 and 1928, had won nine Olympic gold medals and three silver medals. Paavo Nurmi's long-distance running feats, Finland's payment in full of its post-World War I debts to the United States, and its heroic fight against the Russians in the 1939-40 Winter War are Finnish achievements many Americans have heard of, even if they know nothing else about the country.

The Finns worship their track athletes, and it was quite emotional to be sitting with a group from the hotel, mostly young Finns, while Lasse Viren was winning Olympic gold medals in both the 5,000 and 10,000 meter competitions, repeating his feat from the 1972 Munich Olympics. The Finns were less proud of Viren's victory laps in which he ostentatiously waved his brand-name track shoes, reportedly for valuable commercial considerations. The Finns backed Viren, however, when a Stockholm newspaper branded his publicity antics as outrageous.

Those evenings also provided Magda and me with a chance to practice our still struggling Finnish with other hotel guests and with the hotel staff. The latter were all Finnish students who, like college students most everywhere, were open and friendly. The university kids *cum* hotel employees were eager to practice their English. While this was not particularly helpful to our efforts to improve our Finnish, it was great for our three little kids who were practically adopted by the hotel staff. Eleven year-old Lane even earned a few Finnmarks in tips for carrying small suitcases for hotel guests.

Certainly, such unorthodox and less-than-private accommodations would not be everyone's cup of tea (and caused some raised eyebrows in the embassy). But in our case it gave us a sense from day one of sharing experiences with the people around us in a way that began to give us some insights regarding Finns and how they look at life. It was certainly a most pleasant transition into our new life.

We moved into the former Hughes house in mid-August. An important event in the life of every Foreign Service family is the day the moving truck pulls up to their new house in their new country of assignment. They watch eagerly as workers begin to unload from lift vans the furniture, household effects and other personal belongings that the family had seen loaded into the same lift vans some weeks or months earlier. Like most (unfortunately, not all) of our moves during our Foreign Service career, our things had arrived with no important breakage or damage, and we set about arranging our effects in our new house.

Our new house! It was charming! Hietaniemintie was a quiet *cul-de-sac* in the stylish West End just west of Helsinki. The house looked across a narrow road and over an old and ramshackle small summer cottage onto the Baltic Sea. Except for the house on our left that was the residence of Mrs. Catani, a very pleasant elderly Swedish-Finnish widow, our house had lovely nature views of the forest or sea from every window. From our Ottaniemi experience, and now in our new house, we could appreciate how close most Finns remain to nature, and how important the woods and the sea are to so many Finns.

A two-story, flat-roofed structure, our house had an unusual (to us) design. Entering the front door of the house, one was greeted by a flight of stairs leading up to the second floor that constituted the living area. On the second floor was a large living room dominated by a fireplace along the side wall, a separate dining room at the head of the stairs, a kitchen just to the right of the dining room, and a corridor to the right leading to three moderate-sized but comfortable bedrooms. Large, triple-pane windows and a narrow balcony ran along the entire length of the front of the second floor. The main feature of the first floor (which also contained the garage, furnace room and utility rooms) was a classic Finnish wood sauna and a sauna anteroom, which we also used as a television room.

To our great surprise and to the wonderment of our children, we discovered that some 100 yards back in the rough and forested ridges beginning right behind our house was an intricate network of military trenches, which had been blasted out of solid rock. The trenches zig-zagged methodically with larger square areas located at the intersections of some of the trenches, apparently machine gun emplacement sites. A bit further down Hietaniemintie, back from the road, was a cave that had also been dynamited out of rock, probably for an ammunition dump.

We were told that the fortifications dated from the World War I era when Finland was still a Grand Duchy of Russia, and that they apparently had never been used in warfare. However, the trenches somehow conveyed to me a vague sense of uneasiness and threat, a rock-hard symbol of living in a country which was itself living on the edge of almost palpable risk and danger.

A more real risk from the trenches for us as parents was their lure to our adventurous son Lane and his tag-along six-year old brother Carl. We admonished them not to play in the trenches but, boys being boys, they would sometimes sneak back there to play. One day a somewhat concerned and crusty Danish gentleman appeared at our door to advise us vigorously that he had seen the boys playing in the trenches near his house and on his property located at the end of Hietaniemintie road on a point looking south over the Gulf of Finland. The gentleman, Dr. Stefan Barnar-Rasmussen, and his Swedish-Finnish wife, Susan, became among our closest friends in Finland.

Stefan had come to Finland from Denmark in 1939 as a volunteer doctor to help out in a front-lines hospital during the Finnish/Russian Winter War. At the front he had met Susan, a young Finnish volunteer nurse. They married, and he never went back to Denmark to live. Later, in addition to his medical work for the Wartsila shipbuilding company and his own private practice, he acted for many years as physician to the American embassy. Thus, he also became our personal physician who took care of us then and during our subsequent assignment to Helsinki. We stayed in touch with Stefan and Susan until Stefan's recent death, and one of his sons visited us years later when I was the head of the U.S. embassy in Grenada and the younger Barnar-Rasmussen was sailing a yacht from Europe to the Caribbean.

One of the primary concerns to resolve in our settling-in process was the selection of schools for our children. Magda undertook to research the various possibilities, beginning before we went to Helsinki, making inquiries about what schooling options were available, particularly for the two school-age boys. The International School, where most parents from the American and British embassies had their children, in those days seemed too small and improvisational to us. The so-called English School specialized in teaching English to Finnish students, and the American nuns who ran the school offered us no encouragement in enrolling our children there. There were no other English language schooling alternatives.

Magda and I therefore considered enrolling our children in the local Finnish public school system. We were advised that the public school officials would be very pleased to receive our children at the local public schools. The question became, in the officially bilingual school system, should we send our children to a Finnish-language or Swedish-language school? Magda and I had thoroughly enjoyed studying the Finnish language. However, there was no gainsaying the fact the language was extremely difficult and of almost no practical use outside of Finland. We were happy to study it because of the professional requirements of our assignment to Finland. But for the children we asked ourselves whether it might not be more sensible and less stressful for them to attend a Swedish-speaking school. The Swedish language, after all, is so much closer to English and closely related to other Nordic languages. We decided that it made sense to send our children to the neighborhood Swedish-speaking school located in the nearby suburb of Matinkylä, or Mattby in Swedish.

The whole family still remembers the day that we dropped our two boys off at Mattlidens Skola. The boys spoke fluent Spanish but of course no Swedish. We heard our little boy Carl ask his older brother Lane how they were supposed to get along without knowing the language. Lane replied, "Don't worry, Carl, it's just like Spanish. At first you don't understand and then later you will!" That sage advice from an eleven year-old to his six year-old brother proved to be in fact exactly what happened.

The school officials, teachers and students could not have been more helpful in introducing the boys to their new surroundings and in helping them with the language. We in the meantime hired a Swedish tutor to help them at home after school. Within three or four months the boys became increasingly fluent in Swedish, and our home was soon filled with the blond-haired friends of our two dark-haired youngsters. Of all of the decisions we made in Finland, this was certainly one of our best. To a degree never approached by the children of other embassy families who attended the International School, our boys became thoroughly integrated into the local culture, even picking up passable Finnish language skills along the way. They formed friendships then that they maintain to this day.

3

The American Embassy: On the Finland Watch

In comparison with United States diplomatic relations with the older independent nations of Europe, formal ties with Finland are quite recent. Formal United States relations with Finland date only from the last century, and until 1919 were at the consular rather than diplomatic level.[1]

There of course have been close private and family ties between the United States and Finland ever since Finns formed an important part of the original Swedish colony of New Sweden established on the Delaware River in 1638.

The first official U.S. representation in Finland began in the middle of the eighteenth century when Finland was still a Grand Duchy of Russia after Finland was separated from Sweden in 1809. Dating from 1850, the United States had sporadic consular representation in Finland in the cities of Viipuri in Eastern Finland and Turku on Finland's Southwest coast.

It wasn't until 1917 that Thornwell Hayes became the first United States career diplomat to serve in Finland. He was U.S. consul in Helsinki beginning November 1, 1917, and was made "U.S. commissioner" with an interim rank of minister on May 24, 1919, following United States recognition of Finnish independence.

The United States was by no means the first country to recognize Finnish independence that was declared by the Finns on December 6, 1917. The Soviet Union, France and Germany recognized Finnish independence in January 1918 followed shortly thereafter by the Scandinavian countries. The United States and Great Britain withheld recognition because of the confusion of the civil war between "red" and "white" forces into which Finland was plunged upon independence. Germany, with whom we were still at war, supported the "white" forces in that civil war while the fledgling Soviet Union provided some support to the "red" forces. Unlike in the Soviet Union's civil war, the white forces were victorious in Finland. At one point a German prince was nominated to preside over a monarchical government in Finland, but the nomination was never consummated. In a policy statement May 28, 1918, President Wilson stated that the United States "shall be willing to recognize the Republic of Finland only when she shows that she is not controlled by Germany, as she now seems to be."

By 1919 World War I was over, Germany defeated and, according to Herbert Hoover who was at the time director of the U.S. relief effort in Europe, United States diplomatic non-recognition of Finland was delaying the delivery to Finland of much-needed food relief. After further deliberation, the United States announced its *de facto* recognition of Finnish independence on May 3, 1919. It was not until March 20, 1920 that the U.S. legation in Helsinki was formally opened. (At the time, the United States and Finland maintained "legations" in each other's capitals rather than embassies, and the chiefs of mission were called "ministers" rather than ambassadors. In 1954 by mutual agreement the two countries upgraded their diplomatic establishments to the level of embassies, and the chiefs of mission were given the title of ambassadors.)

A career Foreign Service Officer, Charles L. Kragey, became the first full-fledged United States minister to Finland in February 1922. Meanwhile, the first Finnish minister to the United States, Armas Saastamoinen, had presented his credentials to President Wilson in August 1919.

During the 1920's the U.S. legation was housed in offices located at No. 2 Etelä Esplanadi on the corner of Unioninkatu in downtown Helsinki. By 1931 the legation and consulate had been moved to the Stockmann Building, the site then and now of

Stockmann's, Finland's premier department store and a major Helsinki landmark. In 1935 a Michigan congressman, Frank E. Hook, stated in Congress: "I have been told that the American minister in Finland has his chancery in Helsinki on top of a department store. There have been many complaints that these conditions in which our minister finds himself are not only hopelessly inadequate and insufficient but also a shame to the United States."[2]

Perhaps in response to this friendly intervention on behalf of the State Department by a U.S. congressman (such congressional support for the Foreign Service is sadly lacking in today's Washington!), construction for a new U.S. legation building at the current embassy's site at Itäinen Puistotie 14 in the Kaivopuisto area of Helsinki was authorized in 1935. The building site chosen was on a lovely tree-lined street in downtown Helsinki between beautiful Kaivopuisto Park and Helsinki's South Harbor on the Gulf of Finland. The red brick Georgian-style embassy building houses both the offices of the embassy, known formally as the "chancery", as well as the "embassy" itself, popularly known as the ambassador's residence.

At the beginning of the twentieth century Kaivopuisto had been an idyllic area of wooden villas. During the first half of this century, however, most of the wooden villas were replaced by apartment blocks and embassy buildings. In addition to the American embassy, several other embassies, including the British, French and Belgian embassies, have been located in the Kaivopuisto area for years. In the past few years, the Italian and Brazilian embassies have also located on Itäinen Puistotie, and the newly re-opened Estonian embassy has returned to its original location on the same street.

Construction of the new U.S. legation building began in October 1938; completion was scheduled for October 1, 1939, but it was delayed by the slow arrival of equipment from the United States and then by the outbreak of the Winter War in November 1939. Finally, legation and consular offices were transferred to the new legation building in April 1940 and the minister took up residence there in May. In February 1944, the legation building suffered considerable damage from shell fragments and concussion as a result of a Soviet air raid on Helsinki.

When the initial building proved to be somewhat short on office space some time after the war, the embassy purchased an apartment building down the block on Itäinen Puistotie as well as the land between the two buildings. The apartment building was remodeled and used to house several embassy sections and offices.

Like most American embassies, the embassy in Helsinki is divided organizationally into several different components according to function. The basic composition of the embassy has changed little since the early post-World War II years. The organizational structure of the embassy is about the same as that of U.S. embassies in other countries of comparable size and importance. Several of the embassy components are staffed by Foreign Service Officers accountable to the Department of State. These are as follows.

Economic Section

The economic section is responsible for analyzing and sending reports back to Washington on Finnish economic developments and how they impact on U.S. interests. In the other direction, the economic section explains U.S. bilateral and international economic and trade policy positions to the Finns and seeks Finnish understanding and support for those policies. The section officers develop and maintain close contacts with the Finnish banking, industrial and commercial sectors as well as with key governmental economic officials. The economic section is headed by an experienced Foreign Service Officer from the State Department. The economic section chief is assisted by at least one economic officer and sometimes more, depending on budget and assignment vagaries.

Consular Section

The consular section is responsible for determining the eligibility of Finnish citizens and citizens of third countries residing in Finland for visas, i.e., entry permits into the United States. Depending upon the purpose of the intended travel to the United States, the consular officer issues the appropriate visa— tourist or business visa, residence visa, etc.—to qualified applicants and denies visas to applicants who do not meet the requisite qualifications.

The consular section is also responsible for providing statutory services to United States citizens resident in or visiting Finland. For example, the consular officer registers as American citizens children born in Finland of American parents, issues or renews United States passports of U.S. citizens, distributes social security checks, and assists American citizens in emergency situations— such as citizens who get arrested or become destitute. If an American citizen dies in Finland, the consular section will assist in notification of the next of kin and in the repatriation of the remains to the United States. The head of the consular section in the embassy in Helsinki has the title of consul.

Political Section

The political section consists of several officers, including a labor affairs officer. The chief of the political section, the position I held from 1976-79, had the diplomatic rank of "political counselor," although in recent years this position was "downgraded" to the diplomatic rank of "first secretary" (the economic section chief position suffered an identical downgrading). Perhaps the key responsibility of the political section is to become deeply knowledgeable about Finland's domestic political context and trends and about Finland's foreign and security policies. The section then analyzes and reports to

Washington on important developments in these areas and how they affect U.S. interests.

In pursuing these responsibilities, the section maintains close contacts with the Finnish foreign ministry, keeps the Finnish government fully apprised of U.S. positions on international political and security issues, and seeks Finnish understanding and support for our views. At the same time the section establishes close contact with Finland's political parties, the labor movement, the media, and intellectual and academic circles.

Administrative Section

The fourth traditional State Department Foreign Service Officer-staffed embassy section is the administrative section. This section is the key support ingredient without which an embassy could not go about its substantive business. The "admin section", as it is referred to, is responsible for the embassy's budget; for its communications, a highly sophisticated and absolutely essential component of a modern embassy; for its security and supervision of the U.S. Marine Corps security guard detachment; for maintaining embassy buildings, furnishings and office equipment, including now-a-days its information system; and for supervising the embassy motor pool.

Increasingly, the workload on the admin section has been expanding in many U.S. embassies around the world because of the need to provide administrative services to the other, non-State Department components of the embassy. In Helsinki these other components have been the following:

Defense Attaché Office

The "DAO" office represents in the embassy the Department of Defense and the three uniformed services. The DAO is headed by a defense attaché who is the ranking U.S. military officer in the embassy. In Finland the Department of Defense almost invariably assigns an Air Force officer as defense attaché, and that officer also doubles as Air Force attaché. There is also a Naval attaché, an Army attaché and, usually, an assistant Army attaché and a sizable support staff of lower ranking U.S. military personnel. The attachés usually hold the rank of colonel—commander or captain, in the case of the Naval attaché.

The attachés maintain liaison with their counterparts in the Finnish Defense Forces and report to the Department of Defense and their respective uniformed services on Finland's defense forces and capabilities. The assignment of military officers to embassies abroad to keep tabs on the doings of the host country military is a several hundred year-old tradition and is practiced by virtually all countries. It was a particularly interesting assignment for U.S. military officers in Finland during the Cold War period.

United States Information Service

An embassy component which became institutionalized during the post-World War II period is the United States Information Service. "USIS," as it is known, is the overseas arm of the United States Information Agency. It is responsible for working with the Finnish media to try to place information about the United States and to keep Finnish journalists well informed about U.S. policies and, more broadly, about the United States as a society. This they do through providing press feeds, backgrounders, TV material, electronic interviews with U.S. policy-makers, the texts of key speeches by U.S. governmental leaders, etc.

USIS also runs cultural, educational and exchange programs designed to promote closer ties between Finland and the United States. In addition USIS works closely with the Fulbright scholarship program, and arranges visits to the United States by upcoming young Finnish leaders in the various disciplines from politics to labor to business to the arts. Until quite recently, USIS operated an "America Center" and reference library on U.S. studies in downtown Helsinki. That site also served as the USIS office and general coordination point of USIS programs. However, in budget saving moves, the USIS offices were recently moved to the chancery complex, and the America Center closed. The reference library materials were transferred to the University of Helsinki.

USIS is headed by the public affairs officer and also includes a cultural affairs officer and an information officer. These officers are part of the USIA personnel structure, although a restructuring of the foreign affairs agencies in Washington will soon take effect, merging USIA into the Department of State.

Commercial Section

Finally, there is a separate commercial section in the embassy in Helsinki headed during the past twenty years or so until quite recently by an American citizen Foreign Commercial Officer of the U.S. Department of Commerce. Again owing to budget considerations the American citizen position was eliminated, and the section is today headed by a Finnish citizen commercial director, whose salary is paid by the U.S. Department of Commerce. The commercial section is under the general supervision of the chief of the economic section. The commercial section is responsible for promoting U.S. exports to Finland and for identifying trade and investment opportunities in Finland for U.S. private firms. Because of the growing importance of trade to the American economy, commercial promotion of U.S. goods and services has become an ever more important priority in U.S. foreign policy and among U.S. embassy objectives. That of course makes it all the more ironic that the commercial officer position was eliminated because of budget constraints.

Because I do not want to appear disingenuous to readers, I should point out that it is United States government policy not to comment on—neither to confirm nor deny—the presence, responsibilities or activities of U.S. intelligence services at United States embassies or other facilities abroad. However, it is widely known and has been publicly acknowledged by a number of former diplomats and intelligence employees that the United States government during the Cold War maintained Central Intelligence Agency (CIA) stations at most U.S. embassies around the world. Readers can draw their own conclusions with respect to the U.S. embassy located in Helsinki, capital of Finland with an 800 mile border with the then Soviet Union. Intelligence matters do not fall within the scope of this book, and I will not be commenting further on this subject.

In addition to the American staff assigned from Washington, the embassy employs a considerable number of Finnish employees in a myriad of functions. Included are economic and commercial specialists, skilled translators and interpreters, cultural and media specialists, consular assistants, administrative support staff, budget and financial specialists, maintenance workers, drivers, etc. In the 1970s and 1980s, the embassy staff was well over one hundred employees, almost evenly divided between American and Finnish staff. If anything, the embassy has grown somewhat over the past decade. This is in large part the result of administrative and supply responsibilities assigned to Amembassy Helsinki in support of U.S. embassies recently established in the newly independent states of the former Soviet Union. Another factor has been that the embassy has become a staging area for the long and ill-starred efforts to complete the construction of the new United States embassy in Moscow.

The average length of assignment of the American staff in Helsinki is between two and three years. Thus, while American personnel come and go, the Finnish staff provide invaluable continuity, some employees having been with the embassy for fifteen or twenty years and even longer.

At the head of the embassy and responsible for overall coordination of all United States agencies and departments with operations and responsibilities in Finland is the United States ambassador who is appointed by the president of the United States. United States ambassadors are selected either from the senior ranks of the career Foreign Service or from persons chosen from other fields, so-called non-career or "political" ambassadors.

The United States practice of appointing political ambassadors to anywhere from one-third to almost one-half of all ambassadorial positions is unique among the developed countries of the world with highly trained career diplomatic services, such as the United States Foreign Service. In fact the percentage of American political ambassadors assigned to the most prestigious American embassies, particularly in Europe and in the other most important countries in the world, is very much higher. In actual practice, the assignment of ambassadors from the career service to Western European countries has become more and more of a rarity, with a few happy exceptions. The Nordic countries have received more than their share of American political ambassadors over the years.

I will return to the subject of political ambassadors later in this book. Suffice it here to say that the role of the ambassador in coordinating and providing guidance to the activities of the complex group of U.S. agencies pursuing U.S. policies in Finland and in other countries is a vital one. This responsibility and authority to direct, coordinate and supervise all executive branch personnel and U.S. governmental operations in the country of his or her assignment is explicitly charged in writing to the U.S. ambassador as chief of mission by the president of the United States, whom the ambassador directly represents. [3]

In this oversight task and responsibility, the ambassador is assisted by a deputy chief of mission ("DCM" is the Foreign Service acronym). The DCM is the number two ranking U.S. official in the embassy and is the ambassador's *alter ego* and, in effect, a kind of executive vice president or executive director of the embassy under the authority of the ambassador. The DCM also becomes *chargé d'affaires* in charge of an embassy during the absence of the ambassador or between assignments of ambassadors.

The DCM is invariably selected from the senior ranks of the career Foreign Service and is in most cases personally selected or approved by the ambassador. The *sine qua non* of a well-administered embassy is a relationship of mutual confidence and trust between the ambassador and the deputy chief of mission. During my career I served as DCM under four ambassadors (one career and three political ambassadors) in Paraguay and Finland, and am pleased with and proud of my relationship with each one.

The ambassador and his or her DCM exercise, or attempt to exercise, this coordinating and oversight task of all U.S. government operations in country through formal coordination meetings or staff meetings of the heads of all key embassy sections and agencies present in country. Embassy recommendations to Washington will sometimes be referred to as "country team" recommendations, meaning that all embassy elements comprising the USG "team" at the embassy are in agreement with the recommendation. Under an effective, respected and energetic ambassador and DCM team, this coordination function can work quite well.

However, with modern technology bringing in FAX machines and computer-to-computer communications, it has become increasingly difficult for embassy management to be aware of, much less control, communications by individual agency representatives with their own headquarters in Washington. Increasingly, true team play and embassy-wide discipline are dependent upon the leadership qualities of the ambassador and DCM and upon the sense of honor and loyalty of their embassy colleagues. Alas, these qualities do not always abound, and it can sometimes require exceptional efforts on the part of the ambassador and DCM to assure themselves that all agency representatives at post are accepting their leadership and not engaging in unauthorized or unreported operations.

Most embassies of most countries in the world, including the embassies of Finland, are organized more or less along the same lines as United States embassies. In fact, it is really the other way around. The United States government in setting up its first diplomatic missions after U.S. independence organized its embassies on the older European models.

The principal difference between American embassies and those of most other countries (other than the question of political ambassadors) is that ours have tended to be substantially larger since World War II. This has been due largely to the Cold War and the position of the United States as a superpower with extensive world-wide interests. Our embassy in Finland was no exception. During the Cold War and until the collapse of the Soviet Union, Finland was considered a particularly interesting observation post for Soviet issues, in addition to our keen interest in Finland itself.

With respect to size, however, it is interesting to note that the Soviet embassy in Helsinki was always substantially larger than the U.S. embassy during the post-World War II period. This was no doubt a reflection of Finland's proximity to the Soviet Union and the importance that the Soviet Union attributed to its security interests in the Nordic region.

On the very first afternoon of our arrival in Finland, and not withstanding jet lag, I went to the American embassy to pay courtesy calls on Ambassador Mark Austad and the Deputy Chief of Mission Robert Houston. Mark Austad had been appointed ambassador to Finland in March 1975 by President Gerald Ford. We had already met in Washington. I knew he was a bit nervous over the changeover in two of his key political officers at the same time, the political counselor and the labor affairs officer.

My predecessor as political counselor had been Carl Clement, an excellent Foreign Service Officer with extensive Nordic experience, not the least of which being that he had been born in Finland and spoke fluent Finnish and Swedish. In succeeding Clement, I was indirectly following in the footsteps of a series of American embassy political officers who in my opinion did an outstanding job over the years—as chiefs of section or as labor/political officers—in analyzing and reporting on Finnish political developments. The ones whose work I am familiar with (there no doubt will be some inadvertent omissions) were, beginning in the late 1950s, Grant Hilliker, E.R. Cook, Harvey Nelson, Erik Fleischer, John Owens, Ted Sellin, Paul Canney, John Reinhardt and Alden Irons. Now it was my turn and Ward Thompson's. I was quite sure I would be able to win Ambassador Austad's confidence before long, although I obviously would never be able to gain the degree of language fluency possessed by Carl.

It is true that most foreign diplomats in Finland do not speak Finnish and rely instead on the English language skills of many Finns (virtually all Finnish Foreign Ministry officials speak English) in their conversations. They also count on translators to get a general sense of what is being said on television and in the newspapers. Few American ambassadors spoke Finnish, but we were able in the embassy through briefings and a daily press summary in English to keep them well informed about Finnish developments. Language fluency is, after all, only one of the various tools of diplomacy. Language skills serve for naught unless accompanied by experience, good political judgement, leadership qualities, negotiating, analytical and writing skills, and the ability to deal effectively and develop useful relationships with Finnish government, business and opinion leaders.

However, I am convinced that to be an effective embassy political counselor in Finland, good knowledge of the Finnish language is essential. I do not know how you can have a real sense of what is going on in Finland unless you are able to understand what is being said in the national dialogue. To be able to do that, at least at the intensive level required of a political officer, one needs to be able to talk to non-English speaking Finns, read the newspapers, understand what is being said on the radio, and follow television newscasts and interview programs accurately. To have to rely on third parties to convey this information to you through translation and interpretation adds a filter which moves the diplomat one step further away from the genuine dialogue and deprives him or her of the sense of immediacy and directness. It also isolates a diplomat from the vast amount of information which there is simply neither the time nor resources to translate. Without the language he sees only the tip of the iceberg, and even then only the tip which some one else chooses he should see.

It was a matter of importance to me (and, admittedly, of some pride) that almost every morning of my two assignments to Finland I read the Finnish newspapers on a regular basis. Virtually every morning I would read the powerful and independent *Helsingin Sanomat* from front to back and at least skimmed the political party-linked press: the Conservative *Uusi Suomi*, Social

Democratic *Demari,* Center Party *Suomenmaa,* Communist Party *Kansan Uutiset* and even the Stalinist-line *Tiedonantaja.* Moreover, I found during my assignments in Finland that a considerable number of Finnish political and labor leaders did not have a comfortable knowledge of English and were delighted to be able to converse with an American diplomat in Finnish.

It was not that my Finnish language skills were brilliant: I was painfully aware of my glaring grammatical mistakes even as I uttered them. However by drawing on my Washington language training, following up with weekly Finnish lessons, working hard every morning on the newspapers, and—importantly—deliberately seeking opportunities to speak in Finnish, within six months of my arrival I was able to communicate at a reasonably professional level in the Finnish language. It may not have been pretty or even close to being grammatically correct, but I was able to understand and make myself understood in conversing with non-English speaking Finns.

It was an anomaly that because of my professional responsibilities and interests I found I could do much better in discussions of rather esoteric national and international political, security and economic issues than on normal everyday matters. I had developed a rather specialized professional vocabulary in those areas that I used quite often, whereas when the conversation would turn to other subject matters, I could get quickly lost. And, in a hardware or general department store, I was often quite useless!

Of all the embassies in Helsinki, the Soviets by a long shot had the best (and the most) Finnish-speakers among their diplomats. It was proof of the importance they accorded to their Finnish neighbor that Soviet diplomats were apparently able to have a successful career dealing exclusively with Finnish and Nordic affairs. Consequently, it was quite common for Soviet diplomats, having studied the Finnish language in their own obviously first-class language schools, to have two or even three diplomatic assignments to Finland over the course of their careers.

It was quite decidedly **not** possible to have a successful career in the U.S. Department of State specializing in Finnish and Northern European Affairs. Therefore, it was rather unusual to have officers serving more than once in Finland, as I did. It was thus an added disincentive to a Foreign Service Officer's putting in the time and effort necessary to master the Finnish language to know that there was a high probability one would never be reassigned to Helsinki. And, as the record demonstrates, the selection process for U.S. ambassadors to Finland gives little or no priority to previous experience in the country or to Finnish language capabilities.

After the Soviets, the next best embassy for Finnish language skills was either the U.S. or British embassy, depending on your prejudices. Probably there is not a better facility in the world for teaching foreign languages to diplomats than the U.S. Department of State's language training school. However, as far as learning Finnish is concerned, the British system was to send certain officers to live in Finland for several months to study the language in country. This was superior to the State Department's system which I always thought would have benefited by providing six months of intensive preparation at the language school in Washington followed by four or five months of in country study at, let's say, the University of Jyväskylä. This observation notwithstanding, the U.S. system worked relatively well for the diligent student. The U.S. embassy also benefited occasionally from the presence of a Finnish-American diplomat who had learned Finnish as a child at home, or of a diplomat of the Mormon faith who had learned Finnish as a missionary in Finland.

In any case, I was confident that Ambassador Austad would soon be reassured that Ward Thompson, the new labor-political officer, and I would quickly get on top of things in Finland. And that he would be able to rely on us to maintain the high quality level of his previous political section team.

After my calls on the ambassador and DCM, I visited my office in the political section of the embassy. My office was situated on the second floor of the north wing of the chancery building with a view down onto the embassy garden between the north and south wings. The ambassador's residence facing east formed the base of the U-shaped building with the office and service wings of the building and the garden between reaching back to Itäinen Puistotie.

Ambassador Austad, always the jokester, used to kid about his long commute to work: through the door from the parlor room of the residence into his quite spacious and very comfortable ambassadorial office. My office was not very spacious but was comfortable enough. It was here that I would do my paper work and write my reports.

4

U.S. Understanding of the Finnish Context

As political counselor of the American embassy in the late 1970s, how should I interpret events in Finland? What reports should I be writing? What was the context within which the United States viewed Finnish developments? It is clear that to reach an accurate understanding about what is going on in any country requires an understanding of what has gone before. This is particularly true of Finland. Unlike the histories of, say, England, France and Germany which are relatively familiar to many well-read Americans, Finnish history and its Nordic context are quite unknown in general in the United States.

I set out to become knowledgeable about Finland and the Nordic area as rapidly as possible, building on what I had learned in my Washington reading and the area studies course. It is axiomatic that if one maintains his interest and diligence he becomes more and more experienced and knowledgeable about his subject matter, a strong argument for sending diplomatic officers back to the same country for follow-on assignments, as was to happen to me later in Finland. Meanwhile, I drew on information about Finland available in official Washington and embassy files and on what other American diplomats, as well as academics and journalists, had known and written about Finland.

It is beyond the scope of this book to delve very deeply into Finnish history. A number of English-language history and political science studies are available for those who wish to probe further into this subject. Suffice it to say, however, that an understanding of Finland's history and geopolitical setting and the way they have influenced the Finland of today is critical for a foreign diplomat's appreciation of the reality and motivations of modern Finland. In this context it is instructive to mention some of the dimensions of Finland's history and setting that struck us in the embassy as being particularly important in understanding modern-day Finland. It is also useful to refer to previous U.S. diplomatic reports on earlier noteworthy developments in Finland prior to my own experiences.

It is clear from the literature on Finland that even Finland's early history has direct relevance to the Finland of today. Any visitor who spends some time in Finland is struck by a sense that the country's geographical position, rugged physical setting and tumultuous history exercise a palpable influence on present-day Finland. A long summer evening in Finland's countryside or a crisp, cold January cross-country ski jaunt can easily transport one's mind back to that earlier Finland, traces of which are still clearly discernible today in the faces and features of modern Finland.

For instance, one becomes aware of the geologically short time that has passed since Finland emerged some twelve thousand years ago from under the massive weight of a giant ice cap, which, as it receded, allowed the earth slowly to rise—a process that continues to this day. Finland has literally risen up out of the sea. It is easy to see the legacy of the glaciers in Finland's rugged terrain and in the scores of thousands of lakes left behind. It is also easy to imagine in today's still heavily forested Finland the dark coniferous forests which, thousands of years ago when the first inhabitants arrived, covered almost all of what is now Finland.

It is important to understand that Finland's forests, though much changed over the ages, have exerted a tremendous influence on the Finnish people's lives and on the Finnish nation's psyche down to the present time. More than almost any other people, today's Finns remain deeply attached to the forests whence they came. Within living memory, even until well after World War II, a majority of Finns lived in the countryside. The rapid urbanization of the past fifty years has not erased the thousands of years of

Finnish links to their soil and forests. Moreover, throughout its history and right down to the present, Finland's forests, forest products, wood, paper, and machines to work and shape the forests and forest products have provided a major share of Finland's wealth and national income.

Another factor that I think important is to have an understanding of the unique place of Finns among the peoples of Europe. The continuing scientific investigation and debate as to where the first Finns came from and who they were is fascinating. Finnish historian Eino Jutikkala wrote the summary of a 1980 inter-disciplinary conference held at the Tvärminne research station in Finland to discuss whether a non-contradictory picture of the historical roots of the Finnish people could be reconciled from the findings produced by various disciplines.

Jutikkala concluded that the first inhabitants of Finland arrived some 10,000 years ago, long before the Finno-Ugrics, and he assumed that they had "eastern" blood group frequencies. Baltic Finns, themselves descended from a Finno-Ugric eastern people who lived by the bend of the Volga River in what is now Russia, are thought to have made their first appearance in Finland around 3200 BC.[4] According to Jutikkala, "western" genes were introduced into Finland with the "boat-axe" culture around 200 BC, and there is evidence that in subsequent centuries people of German and Scandinavian origin also moved in, making further "western" contributions to the Finnish population's gene pool.

Jutikkala notes that "...substantial and well-known Swedish migration to the Finnish mainland did not occur earlier than the period of the conversion to Christianity," perhaps around the thirteenth century. Jutikkala concluded from genetic evidence that repeated migrations into Finland from the south and the west have over time altered the original, eastern, genetic stock to such an extent that western features have become dominant. This process of assimilation was facilitated by the limited size of the population in prehistoric times—a small number of immigrants could produce relatively large changes—and by the fact that the mixing took place over five millennia.

Jutikkala's summary of available evidence gives a plausible description of the richness and complexity of the genetic heritage of modern day Finns. However, other researchers more recently have argued that modern day Finns have blood types quite identical to those of Central Europeans, thereby calling into question some aspects of the findings of the 1980 Tvärminne Conference summarized by Jutikkala. Thus, the debate over the genetic origins and influences on the Finnish genetic pool Finns goes on.

Regardless of their contribution to the genetic composition of the Finns and the impact of later western influences, clearly one lasting legacy of the early Finno-Ugric migrants to Finland was the Finnish language or at least an early version of it. The language introduced by the first wave of Finno-Ugric migration was the origin of the Finnish language that is the mother tongue of well over ninety percent of the Finnish people of today. The fact that the Finnish language belongs to the Finno-Ugric language group and is completely distinct from the Indo-European language family to which virtually all other languages of Europe belong has been of great historical importance to Finland.

Finland's unique present day language and its earlier dialects are and were well nigh impregnable to anything less than the most determined efforts by non-Finns to learn. Generations of American diplomats struggling to master the Finnish language can attest to this fact! The language barrier between the Finns and their neighbors has undoubtedly been an important factor in helping the Finns to maintain their identity and sense of community. This notwithstanding the fact that for hundreds of years—indeed well into the nineteenth century—the Finnish language was not regarded by Finland's politically dominant class as a suitable language for education or the conduct of official business. The uniqueness of the Finnish language has also served as a shield, helping Finland to resist outside influences that it did not choose to welcome.

Finland's extreme northern geographic position, in addition to influencing its climate, is also greatly important for other major effects it has had on Finland's development and history. Finland's location places it on the northern fringes of Europe and outside of the mainstream of European political, economic and social currents and activities. Moreover, it was important that as European events developed, Finland was frequently in a peripheral position between East and West, fought over and physically run through by forces from both East and West. Finland between East and West is a dilemma as old as history and as timely in the 1990s as ever, judging by many of the arguments presented during the 1994 electoral debate over entry into the European Union.

As Finnish sociologist Erik Allardt among others has noted, in historical terms it is extremely important that for about 700 years—from the Middle Ages until 1809—Finland was a part of the Swedish kingdom. Finland constituted the eastern "half of the realm" within that kingdom and as such was subject to the same legal and institutional principles and influence as all of the other parts of the kingdom.[5] During this enormously long period of time, Finland was fully absorbed institutionally by the association. It became indelibly a Nordic country with respect to social organization, education and religion. Like the other Nordic countries, the nobility in Finland during the Swedish period was relatively weak while the peasantry was able to exercise a degree of political independence and even influence during some periods. The weak position of the aristocracy has been regarded by some scholars as one of the major factors in the development of Nordic social democracy and the growth of the Nordic approach to a welfare state.

Moreover, when Finland became a Grand Duchy under Russia with the Russian Czar serving as Grand Duke, an agreed element of Finland's autonomous status as a Grand Duchy was that the Swedish legal system and law code of 1734 continued to apply in Finland. Thus, the Swedish structure was maintained. The social institutions of Sweden and Finland are so similar that Finland is usually grouped together with Sweden in the study of administrative history as comprising the "eastern Nordic system" in contrast with the "western Nordic system" consisting of Denmark, Norway and Iceland.

If the 700 year period of being the eastern half of the Swedish kingdom was definitive in fixing Finland as a Nordic society, the Swedish "loss" of Finland to Russian in 1809 marked a pivotal turning point for Finland. Finland was established as an autonomous Grand Duchy under the Russian Czars at Porvoo, Finland in March 1809 in a formal undertaking that "elevated [Finland] to membership in the family of nations."[6] Sweden had "lost" Finland to Russia during the upheavals of the Napoleonic Wars. After Finland was transferred as a Grand Duchy to Russia, the Diet meeting in Porvoo began 108 years of autonomy during which Finland had her own laws, Diet and administrative system. Russian citizens had no civil rights in Finland, and Finland bypassed the Russian bureaucracy, dealing directly with the Czars. The new capital of Finland was established in Helsinki.

Historians agree that the period of autonomy under the Russian Czars sparked a sweeping arousal of Finnish nationalism and culture that later became fundamental pillars of independent Finland. The Diet of Porvoo left unchanged the status of the Swedish language as the language of education and government— in short of the gentry—as opposed to the common people who, except in the relatively few Swedish-speaking areas, spoke Finnish. However, this began to change in the 1830s as Finnish nationalists, particularly Johan Snellman, commenced to underscore the importance of Finland's own national language. Surely, to understand today's Finland one has to be aware of the famous Snellman statement that proclaimed: "Swedes we are no longer, Russians we cannot become; we must be Finns."

In today's Finland one can appreciate the importance of Elias Lönnrot's compilation of the epic and heroic national poem *Kalevala* and the writings of Aleksis Kivi which further spurred recognition of the Finnish language as a language of culture. Proponents of the Finnish language vigorously promoted its increasingly wide use in home and school. It is significant that many Finns changed their Swedish surnames into Finnish names during this period. The prior low status of the Finnish language is underscored by the fact that the first Finnish-language secondary school was not founded until 1858! One can understand the predictable reaction among some Swedish-speakers against the "Fennomanians," and the emergence of a vigorous language debate—which often took on divisive cultural and even so-called "racial" overtones. An outside observer in Finland still today can note occasionally unpleasant remnants, fortunately much diluted, of the latent animosities between Finnish and Swedish speakers in Finland.

Of course one also cannot understand today's Finland without being aware of the history of the collapse of Czarist Russia, the Russian Revolution, Finland's seizure of the moment to declare its independence on December 6, 1917, and the tragic and bloody civil war in Finland that followed. The division of political thinking and loyalties in Finland between "red" and "white" remained politically significant at least until the 1970s and 1980s, notwithstanding the positive impact of the 1939-40 Winter War and 1941-44 Continuation War in ameliorating to a significant degree the hatreds spawned during the civil war. The supreme national struggle against the Soviet Union united Finns of all political persuasions, except a small number of extreme leftists, against the common enemy.

Finland's experiences leading up to and during its wars against the Soviet Union contributed critically and directly to the development of the Finns' basic attitudes, outlook and mind-set during the long Cold War era. Finland's very survival as a sovereign nation hung precariously in the balance during its military struggles with the Soviet Union during 1939-40 and 1941-44. Also important were the reactions of the West to Finland's circumstances during these wars with the Soviet Union and in their immediate aftermath.

To us in the American embassy, certain facts related to the war years seemed crucial to understanding the Finnish mentality during the Cold War period. It struck us as terribly important and of lasting significance that when Soviet troops first crossed the border into Finland on November 30, 1939, they established in the Finnish Karelian border town of Terijoki a so-called "Provisional People's Republic of Finland" under the long-time Finnish Communist leader Otto Ville Kuusinen.[7]

The Soviets claimed that this puppet government was the legitimate Government of Finland. They denied they had invaded Finland but, rather, argued that they had entered Finland at the request of the Terijoki Government. The fact that the Soviets later abandoned their support of this so-called government and negotiated a peace treaty with the duly constituted official Government of Finland in Helsinki in March 1940 did not erase the concern in Finland as to what Stalin might have had in mind for Finland's future. Also, it was not particularly comforting to know that the same O.V. Kuusinen whom the Soviets had temporarily installed in Terijoki remained as chairman of the Soviet Union entity the "Karelian-Finnish Soviet Socialist Republic" from 1940 to 1956. Some feared that this "Republic" could at some point become the embryo of a Soviet Republic that would physically incorporate Finland, making Finland an integral part of the Soviet Union. [8]

These developments are suggestive of a fundamental question of vital importance for the post-World War II years which has never been adequately answered and probably never will be. The question is: As World War II drew to a close, what *did* the Soviet Union have in mind for Finland for the post-war period. There is the precedent, discomforting to be sure, of the Soviet installation of the Kuusinen Government in November 1939.

On the other hand, one must recall that, as Finnish leaders themselves so often pointed out in the post-World War II period, it was Lenin himself who as head of the fledgling Soviet state recognized Finland's independence in January 1918. Invoking Lenin's name, as having personally recognized Finland's independence, was a device frequently resorted to by Finnish authorities in the post-war period in an apparent effort to impress Soviet leadership. If the legendary founder of the Soviet Union had recognized Finnish independence, it should not at some later date be lightly overturned by his successors.

However, the Lenin legacy and his intentions regarding Finland were by no means crystal clear. During Finland's short but brutal civil war in 1918, Lenin, despite having recognized Finland's independence, opposed the very government he had recognized and supported the "Finnish People's Commissariat" which was the executive authority of what was referred to as "Red Finland."[9] Indeed, he signed a treaty with the Finnish People's Commissariat in which at Lenin's behest the reference to the "Republic of Finland" in the treaty was changed to read "The Socialist Workers' Republic of Finland." It seems that Lenin's interpretation of what might constitute an independent Finland may well have been quite different from the kind of independence most Finns had in mind. However, as events demonstrated, the white forces under Marshal Mannerheim were victorious in the bitter civil war and Lenin's treaty with the People's Commissariat had no practical effect.

Other indications regarding Soviet intentions should be noted. It is now well-known that a secret provision of the infamous Molotov-Von Ribbentrop Non-Aggression Pact of August 3, 1939 assigned Finland and the Baltic countries to the Soviet sphere of influence and directly contributed to the Soviet invasion of Finland in November 1939. The pact also led to the subsequent Soviet takeover in the summer of 1940 of the Baltic states of Latvia, Lithuania, and Estonia and their physical incorporation into the Soviet Union. Was that what the Soviet Union had in mind for Finland?

The issue of Finland's future came up in the meeting of the Allied "Big Three" (Roosevelt, Churchill, Stalin) at the Tehran Conference in 1943. U.S. diplomatic reporting indicates that at the conference Stalin justified the incorporation of the Baltic lands into the Soviet Union on the basis that they had not enjoyed autonomous status during the final period of Czarist Russia. He pointed out that Finland in contrast had been a distinct state entity in Czarist times and that, therefore, it was not his intention to make Finland into a Soviet Republic but, rather, into a "People's Democracy."[10] That was a helpful clarification. On the other hand becoming a "People's Democracy" *á la* Poland and Hungary was not exactly an attractive alternative.

Incidentally, after the war, in March 1948, the Finnish Foreign Ministry inquired of the U.S. State Department whether at Tehran President Roosevelt had abandoned Finland to the Soviet sphere of influence. Secretary of State George Marshall responded that the

Department had "no, repeat no, knowledge of any agreement regarding Finland of this kind."[11] The Finnish Foreign Ministry made a similar inquiry to the State Department and received similar assurances in 1950. It is interesting that the Finnish authorities were discreetly making such inquiries at the same time they were publicly expressing their full confidence in relations with the Soviet Union.

A British expert and writer on Finnish affairs, Roy Allison, who was generally sympathetic to Finland's post-war policy toward the Soviet Union, observed that toward the end of World War II and in the immediate post-war period it seems likely that the Soviet Union harbored expectations that Finland would follow a pro-Soviet socialist course. He said that Red Army forward planning may have contemplated the occupation of part of Finland.[12] Soviet Colonel General Andrei Aleksandrovitch Zhdanov, the head of the Allied Control Commission (ACC) set up in 1944 to watch over Finland until the conclusion of a peace treaty, seemed to be particularly active in seeking to assure a pro-Soviet socialist Finland. In October 1944 he participated in the foundation of the Finnish People's Democratic League (SKDL) which won nearly one-quarter of the parliamentary seats in the March 1945 elections. In a speech to the Soviet-run international Communist organization the COMINFORM in September 1947, Zhdanov described Finland as having "firmly set foot on the path of democratic development alongside Rumania and Hungary."[13] The suggestion by Zhdanov of Rumania and Hungary as "democratic" examples for them to follow could hardly have been reassuring to the Finns.

Finnish historian Dr. Jukka Nevakivi recently was able to gain access to Soviet Foreign Ministry and Soviet Communist Party archives and to a collection of authoritative documents of General Zhdanov from his period as Chairman of the Allied Control Commission (ACC) in Helsinki. Nevakivi reports that the Soviets in 1944 appeared to have prepared themselves for the occupation of the whole of Finland. They later seem to have had second thoughts, particularly after the withdrawal and transfer to other fronts of half of the Soviet divisions that had been concentrated on the Finnish front.[14] The Zhdanov documents researched by Nevakivi indicate that Zhdanov frequently stressed that the Soviet Union would not take active measures to help the Finnish Communists take power in Finland during the 1944-47 period of the ACC presence in Finland. Rather, he indicated that it was up to the Finnish Communists to determine whether they should challenge for power in Finland; but they would have to do it on their own and could not count on the support of the Soviet Union.[15]

Some researchers have interpreted these attitudes as indicating a "soft" Soviet position vis-à-vis Finland during 1944-47. However, the Soviets and Zhdanov had ample reason to downplay tactically at that time the hopes of Zhdanov, at least, to see Finland eventually firmly placed in the so-called "democratic socialist" camp. As Nevakivi's article makes clear, the Soviets in the closing stages of World War II placed a high priority on promoting a popular front approach to the politics of neighboring countries in an effort to prevent the local Communists from endangering the war effort or joint cooperation with other anti-Nazi forces. In Finland particularly, there was the added incentive of not supporting the Finnish Communists' radicalization of politics for fear of endangering Finnish cooperation in throwing the Germans out and of undermining the internal order necessary to assure the payment of vital war reparations at a time when the rest of Europe was still at war or prostrate.

While these short-term but high priority considerations undoubtedly influenced the Soviets to take a somewhat moderate approach to dealing with Finland in that period, Nevakivi points out that even then Zhdanov had a "bi-level" approach to Finland. In his meetings with the Finnish Communists (who brought him reports directly from the private discussions of the Finnish government), Zhdanov did not refrain from giving advice and instructions to them on how to proceed—"forgetting" his assurances that he would not intervene in internal Finnish political affairs. He saw the Finnish Communists as the nucleus of the SKDL, the electoral front whose formation he had personally encouraged, and sought to create the conditions under which the Communist-dominated SKDL would direct Finland's ultimate political orientation. He advised the Communists to bear in mind that even coalition partners, like the Agrarians, were in fact adversaries. [16]

Nevakivi concluded that "the Zhdanov experiment along the lines of a people's democracy in Finland did not succeed, mainly because of the strength of democratic traditions in the country. In short, Zhdanov did not properly understand the Finnish culture or mentality." [17]

Not occupied by the Soviet Union, Finland was nevertheless bound from 1944 to 1947 by the decisions of the Soviet-dominated ACC that were not subject to appeal to any Finnish authorities. Meanwhile, in April 1946, a Finnish delegation went to Moscow to ascertain whether there was any possibility of receiving some relief from the severe territorial concessions exacted by the 1944 Soviet-Finnish armistice. The delegation was informed by Stalin himself that no changes would be made. For good measure, Soviet Vice Foreign Minister Vyshinski warned both the Finnish prime minister and foreign minister that if in the negotiations for a peace treaty the Finns were to attempt to side with other states against the USSR, then the Finns "would certainly see what will happen to them." [18] In 1947, Finland signed the Peace Treaty with the Soviet Union and the Western powers (not including the United States which had never declared war on Finland) which sharply limited the size of Finland's armed forces and weaponry.

In view of these Soviet constraints on Finland and Finnish independence, what can be said about the West's attitude toward Finland during the closing stages of World War II and at the beginning of the post-war and Cold War period? This is the other key dimension in understanding Finland's perception of its situation at the end of the war. Where was the West when Finland was facing all of these pressures?

The Allies approved at Tehran the main features of the conditions for peace with Finland which had been put forward by Stalin. The United States accepted that the USSR would require friendly governments on its Western borders. Before the end of the war against Germany and at a time when the U.S. wanted the Soviet Union to come into the war against Japan, the U.S.

representative in Finland in March 1945 told the Finnish foreign minister it was "especially important that Finland develop good neighborly relations with the Soviet Union."[19] The Western allies also went along with the 1947 Peace Treaty which sharply restricted Finland's security independence.

Meanwhile in the highest policy circles, the United States' position toward Finland was evolving with the course of events in World War II and in the immediate post-war period. As victory over Germany became more and more assured following the recapture of Stalingrad by the Red Army and growing Soviet and Western military strength, U.S. policy makers concluded that there would be little the West could do to influence Soviet activities in Eastern Europe and the Baltic. While policies to minimize Soviet influence were examined, there was general pessimism among U.S. policy makers. The State Department nevertheless considered Finland a special case. In a July 1947 review, the director of the office of European affairs cautioned that the U.S. should refrain from acts vis-à-vis Finland that could be regarded by the Soviet Union as a challenge to its interests. The idea was to support the Finns but to do so in an inconspicuous manner to avoid antagonizing the Soviet Union.[20]

Illustrative of the peripheral position of Finland in the post-War western view was a U.S. diplomatic report in July 1950, following the formation of the North Atlantic Treaty Organization (NATO). It stated that an understanding had been reached between the United States and Britain to the effect that "it was not anticipated that in the case of an attack by the Soviets action would be taken to assist Finland." The report also stated that Finnish ministers were told clearly in September 1950 that no United States "guarantees" existed for Finland in the event of such an attack.[21] A 1951 United States policy paper, taking into account the fact that the Soviet Union now possessed atomic weapons, stated starkly that "Finland does not constitute a strategically vital area and a Soviet attack on it would not be a valid cause for global war."[22]

This, then, was our understanding in the embassy of the cruel reality that Finland and Finland's leaders were faced with following World War II: heavy pressure from the Soviets and a clear indication from the West that Finland was on its own. It is vital to understanding the Finland of the 1960s, 1970s, 1980s—and the Finland of today—to recognize the situation that Finland found itself in at that time: a defeated, though unoccupied, small country on the border of one of the greatest military powers Europe had yet seen. It was absolutely clear to Finnish leaders, as the German retreat following Stalingrad gradually turned into a rout, that the old Finnish policy of balancing Germany and the West off against its "hereditary enemy" the Russians no longer held any validity. Finland had no one to turn to. It had been abandoned to its fate in 1939-40 at the hands of the Soviet Union in the Winter War and had survived by its own heroism as well as by possible Soviet concerns about great power movements as World War II neared. Once again after the war, the Western powers had made it clear to Finland it could not look to them for protection against the Soviet Union.

Finnish leadership drew the only logical conclusion: if Finland were to survive as an independent state it would have to establish a new relationship with the Soviet Union. A crucial part of that relationship would be to recognize that the Soviet Union had a legitimate security interest in assuring itself that Finland would not become a part of, or lend itself to the mounting of, any kind of security threat to the Soviet Union from or through Finnish territory. The embassy understood this fundamental premise of Finnish policy: Finland would provide those assurances to the Soviet Union while at the same time seeking to maintain its own way of life, values, institutional integrity and independence.

The leaders of this new and, to many Finns, bitter-to-swallow policy were Finland's two dominant post-war political leaders, J.K. Paasikivi and Urho Kekkonen. They had recognized late in 1944 the need for a policy of "national realism." They stressed that Finland's independence could be secured only "through winning [Soviet] confidence and the creation of good-neighborliness," to cite a 1944 speech by Justice Minister Kekkonen. Prime Minister Paasikivi, on Finnish Independence Day in 1944, said that to obtain Soviet confidence in this new basic tenet of post-war

Finnish foreign policy, "the term 'hereditary enemy' has to be forgotten once and for all." [23]

The Finnish strategy was to carefully manage its policies in such a way as to assure the Soviet Union that Finland was a reliable neighbor which would not let itself be used for any possible anti-Soviet maneuvering by Soviet enemies. In return, Finland would expect to maintain its own system of government, its democratic institutions, and its free-market oriented economy with a strong admixture of Scandinavian social welfare protection. Most observers would not have believed in the 1940s, or even in 1958 or 1962, that Finland would be successful in this policy, given the sad history of Eastern Europe throughout most of the Cold-War years.

However even as the overall policy was succeeding and was understood by the U.S. government in general and the U.S. embassy in particular, there were developments within Finland that raised disturbing questions about the price Finland was paying for its *modus vivendi* with the Soviet Union. These concerns focused on the Finnish positions regarding international and European security questions, as well as with respect to Finland's domestic political institutions and values. While there was an understanding of Finland's unique situation, there were also U.S. and NATO security concerns and interests that needed to be taken into account.

5

The U.S. and NATO Policy Context

Cognizant throughout the Cold War years of the "Finnish Dilemma" and sympathetic to the constraints on Finland's foreign and security policy resulting from this hard reality, the U.S. and its NATO allies nevertheless also had their own policy interests and goals in the Nordic area. It was not clear to us in the embassy that these policy interests were always widely recognized or fully appreciated in Finland.

This chapter reviews some of the principal policy concerns and strategic considerations governing the Western and NATO view of the Nordic region. These help explain why the alliance took certain positions and why, therefore, it would become concerned over Finnish positions that seemed to ignore NATO's deterrence policy and to echo or parallel Soviet positions.

Even before the end of World War II, the extraordinary importance of the North Atlantic region in the strategic balance with the one potential adversary that might emerge from the War—the Soviet Union—was already clear to the Western allies. In August 1944, British and American members of the Combined Chiefs of Staff agreed that, while it would be useful to the war effort for the Russians to harass German withdrawal from Norway:

...our long term requirement is to ensure that they should not permanently occupy Norwegian territory in view of potential threat to North Atlantic trade routes, Iceland and the northern approaches to the North Sea.[24]

At the same time, the Western Allies knew that the Soviets were also likely to be aware of the geographic and strategic importance of Norway. A 1944 study prepared for U.S. Secretary of the Navy James V. Forrestal noted that while the Soviets had given no indication of aggressive intentions in Northern Norway, nevertheless:

> ...the acquisition of...[Norway] in the Far North and the proximity of Norwegian territory to Murmansk, Russia's only ice-free port opening directly on the high seas, give Norway a very special place in Russian eyes.[25]

Nor was Norway the only country of concern to allied planners once the Cold War intensified in 1948. A 1948 U.S. National Security Council report noted that Scandinavia "lies astride the great circle air route between North America and the strategic heart of Western Russia." The U.S. Joint Chiefs of Staff argued that it was a major Western strategic interest in Scandinavia to deny to the Soviets air and submarine bases in Denmark and Norway and their island possessions.[26]

Concern over possible Soviet control of a section of the Norwegian coastline was a major factor in the calculations of the United States, Britain and Canada when they pressed for Norwegian membership in the embryonic Atlantic alliance in 1948:

> In the talks in Washington, Norway was often described along with Iceland, Portugal (the Azores), Denmark (Greenland), and Ireland as 'stepping stone' countries. They were stepping stones for communications between America and Europe and thus essential to an Atlantic arrangement.

And while Norway controlled egress from the Barents Sea, "Denmark and Sweden controlled an even more important waterway, the exit from the Baltic." Moreover, "Greenland was absolutely essential for the defense of the United States and for communications across the Atlantic."[27]

Thus, it could readily be seen already in the closing days of World War II and in the early Cold War years that the High North had all the potential for being an area of strategic "tug of war" between the Soviet Union and the western allies. For the West, it was essential that the Norwegian Sea and the long Norwegian coast not come under Soviet control or domination because of the threat that would pose to the Trans-Atlantic sea lanes and lines of communication that were critical for U.S. support and re-supply of its European allies. For the Soviets, the proximity of the North Cape and Norwegian Sea to Murmansk and the Kola Peninsula—

which were to assume ever-increasing importance as the Cold War progressed—led to a Kremlin concern not to permit these areas to be used for allied military operations against Soviet Kola-based military assets.

The U.S. was cool toward the prospect of a Scandinavian defense pact that was discussed in 1948-49 as an alternative to Nordic participation in NATO. There was initially some flexibility in the U.S. position, provided that Iceland and Greenland would be included in the NATO alliance and that any Scandinavian pact have some kind of links to NATO. Also, some credence was given to the Swedish argument that inclusion of Nordic countries in NATO might well serve to increase Soviet pressure on Finland. At one point, the influential State Department official George Kennan argued that "inclusion of Sweden in particular could quite likely lead to a strengthening of Soviet influence in Finland."[28]

It was clear to U.S. diplomats from the beginning that there was no possibility of Finland's becoming a part of NATO. There was also an understanding that Sweden was unlikely to abandon its traditional neutrality in favor of NATO membership. Despite the vague agreement regarding a Scandinavian defense pact reached in a January 1949 meeting at Karlstad, Sweden, it soon became clear that Norway and Denmark would not accept Sweden's insistence that there be no clear ties between the Scandinavian pact and the Atlantic alliance. Nor was a Scandinavian defense pact that lacked clear links with NATO seen by the Western allies as meeting their North Atlantic strategic concerns.

Consequently, Denmark, Iceland and Norway joined NATO as original signatories of the treaty on April 4, 1949.[29] As expected, Sweden remained outside of the Atlantic alliance. Showing an awareness of Soviet sensitivities and security concerns, Denmark and Norway each placed self-imposed restraints on their NATO memberships. They made it clear that they would not permit the establishment of foreign bases or nuclear weapons on their soil as long as their countries were not under attack or threat of attack. The unilateral nature of these pledges and the fact that they were deliberately applicable only during times of peace reserved the option for both countries of withdrawing those pledges if they considered that changed circumstances threatened the peace.

With the rapid advance of technology, the strategic importance of the northern region was increasingly acknowledged in the 1970s and 1980s. Added to the already recognized importance of the Scandinavian peninsula to the security of Atlantic supply and communication routes was the growing Soviet strategic build-up on the Kola Peninsula, the center of its strategic submarine fleet. "The control of northern waters is now critical to the balance of nuclear terror between the superpowers."[30]

The Soviet buildup in the Kola Peninsula began in the 1960s. Its bases comprised a complex of installations for sea, land, air and amphibious forces that were constantly expanded and improved through the 1980s. For the Soviets, the northern ports were essential to the role of the Soviet Union as a global sea power:

> From the Soviet point of view, the waters extending from the Norwegian mainland to Iceland and Greenland in the West, and from the Greenland-Iceland-UK line and Svalbard and the Barents Sea in the North will be equally important as a gateway for the projection of Russian maritime power/Soviet state sea power abroad, as they are as a protective zone for its strategic submarines and a barrier against enemy sea-borne threats against the homeland itself.[31]

A 1985 Norwegian Defense Ministry study detailed the magnitude of the Soviet build-up as measured by Western defense analysts. According to the study, since the mid-1960s the number of Soviet strategic ballistic missile submarines (SSBNs) in their Northern Fleet and the number of ballistic missiles carried by them had increased dramatically.[32]

Moreover, the Soviets had replaced many of their old Yankee class SSBNs—which had to penetrate the dangerous Greenland-Iceland-UK (GIUK) gap to get within range of the United States—with the giant Delta and Typhoon class SSBNs which could strike the U.S. from the Barents Sea and the Arctic Ocean. Intelligence analysts tended to agree that the main role of other Northern Fleet elements was to defend the Barents and Arctic bastions of the Soviet SSBNs. In the classic Russian style, however:

> ...the Soviets...interpreted bastion defense in aggressive operational terms, pushing out a 'defensive perimeter' which not only looks as if it would include Norway well behind its front line but which would also put Soviet

naval forces in a most favorable position to attack NATO's vital Atlantic shipping lifeline.[33]

The number of Soviet non-strategic submarines had held steady, according to the Norwegian study, but a larger proportion of these submarines now carried cruise missiles. Also, the total number of Northern Fleet surface ships almost doubled, and the number of aircraft, both fixed wing and helicopter, increased sharply and were upgraded in quality. BACKFIRE bombers began exercising from Kola bases in the early 1980s.

There were in the mid-1980s seventeen airfields on the Kola Peninsula. Soviet air defense capability tripled from the mid-1960s to the mid-1980s. The new (in the mid-1980s) AS-15 air to surface cruise missiles with an estimated range of 3,000 kilometers gave the Soviet BEAR-H bombers a formidable standoff capability. It was expected that BACKFIRE bombers exercising from Kola bases would also carry them.

In the Leningrad Military District (which included the Kola Peninsula) the number of army divisions was increased from the 1960s to the mid-1980s from eight to ten and their operating strength, fire power, armor, artillery and helicopter support enhanced. Although the divisions were kept in varying degrees of readiness, three of the divisions were considered capable of combat readiness in a matter of days. Two high-readiness, motorized divisions were based on the Kola Peninsula. A Soviet amphibious brigade was stationed on the Kola Peninsula with amphibious ships to move the brigade. A Soviet airborne division was based in the Leningrad Military District near Pskov, south of Leningrad. There was sufficient Soviet airlift capability to move the airborne division a moderate distance.

Among the information cited by John C. Ausland, upon whom much of this section draws, he makes an interesting point regarding Soviet nuclear forces in the Nordic area. Writing in 1986, he noted that:

> Soviet forces have a formidable array of nuclear weapons which they could use against the Nordic area. The locations and ranges of a number of those in the Leningrad Military District are such that they could only reach the Nordic countries. Let me take this one step further. There is an SS-12 regiment at the northern end of Lake Ladoga. The SS-22 is replacing the

SS-12. Despite its somewhat greater range (900 kilometers), the SS-22 could barely reach Norway from Lake Ladoga. One must assume, therefore…Either the Soviets propose to use the SS-22s to threaten Finland and Sweden, or they intend to move them forward into Finland at some point in a developing crisis.[34]

Another western analyst wrote that western security policy in the High North was shaped primarily by the Soviets' drive to extend their defense lines around the Kola Peninsula and to secure access to the Norwegian Sea and Atlantic Ocean. He cited large-scale Soviet naval maneuvers, which NATO referred to as SUMMEREX-85, held in the area in 1985:

It was the largest fleet maneuver ever to take place in the far north. Thirty surface combat ships took part, four of which were amphibious vessels from the Northern and Baltic fleets, with an exceptionally large number of submarines—perhaps as many as forty—and other vessels came from the Mediterranean to participate. The main Soviet battle force included an aircraft carrier group (the Kiev) as well as a modern missile cruiser (the Kirov); submarines were positioned for barrier defense and simulated attacks were launched against allied naval targets. At the same time there was a great deal of air activity from the Kola Peninsula, including long-range missions that simulated missile attacks on NATO naval assets.[35]

It was NATO's assumption that early during a European conflict, Soviet divisions would attack across Finnmark and northern Finland, assisted by Soviet amphibious forces. The objective would be capture of the airfields along the Norwegian coast that would then be used to dominate the North Sea.

Finnish military and security analysts have argued that such scenarios, projecting a Soviet thrust across northern Finland were unlikely, for several reasons. Finnish terrain in the region is unsuitable for military operations; the Soviets had more attractive options for airborne and amphibious operations that skirt Finnish territory; Soviet ground forces based on the Kola peninsula had relatively limited offensive capabilities; and, finally Finland is determined to vigorously defend its northern territory against any invader.

The Finns were greatly offended when in 1983, U.S. General Bernard Rogers, Supreme Allied Commander, Europe (NATO SACEUR), publicly questioned Finland's willingness and ability to defend its northern territories. During the 1970s and 1980s Finland progressively increased its military forces in the north precisely to demonstrate its intention to defend its northern territories. One Finnish security scholar has observed that:

> Finnish assessments concerning the Nordic region tend to emphasize the defensive nature of the conventional military buildup on the one hand and the strategic, non-regional character of the nuclear buildup on the other. In line with this Finland has argued that the military buildup undertaken by the two superpowers is principally connected to the central balance and does not pose a direct threat to the Nordic countries *per se.*[36]

NATO responses to the steady, long-term Soviet buildup on the Kola Peninsula dating from the 1960s were a long time in coming, in part owing to the United States' preoccupation with the Vietnam War. However, concern began to mount in the 1970s, and measures were studied to upgrade NATO's reinforcement capabilities. In 1974 a Collocated Operations Base agreement was signed covering bases in south Norway, north Germany, and the Danish belts. The agreement was gradually expanded to cover additional bases in north Norway.

In 1978 the Carter administration, belatedly alarmed by the steady Soviet buildup, agreed with its NATO partners on the need "to assure that the conventional improvements required by the evolving Soviet threat would be adopted throughout the alliance. To this end President Carter initiated a long-term defense plan (LTDP) 'to address selected deficiencies in forces, equipment and procedures.'" The NATO allies committed themselves to annual three per cent growth in real defense spending.[37]

Additional agreements were reached for pre-positioning plans covering eight Norwegian air bases and, in 1981, for the pre-positioning of equipment for a U.S. marine amphibious brigade. These agreements were integrated into NATO's Rapid Reinforcement Plan and given approval in 1982. By the mid-1980s reinforcements equal to several brigades and a significant number of aircraft squadrons had been assigned to the northern flank. These steps plus the pre-positioning of equipment and ability to airlift reinforcements strengthened short-term capabilities. However,

> Norway could not survive a crisis of any duration without reasonably safe lines of communication by sea to its western allies. Soviet naval strength in the Norwegian Sea constitutes a threat to Norway which can only be

counteracted by an allied naval presence in the area, and this is now [i.e. mid-1980s] being strengthened.[38]

In 1980 under the new American president, Ronald Reagan, and his secretary of the navy, John Lehman, the United States Navy adopted a more vigorous, "offensive" maritime strategy towards the High North. Under the new U.S. Sea Plan 2000, the Navy would have a major role in mounting a forward defense strategy. This plan would send NATO naval forces to attack Soviet submarines at the source and seal them off close to, or in, their own bases and place the Kola Peninsula at risk. The new strategy was to be based on a projected 600 ship U.S. Navy to include fifteen aircraft carriers, four battleships, and weapons systems that include cruise missiles, anti-aircraft and submarine capabilities and amphibious vessels. In the naval exercise Ocean Safari 85 in which both British and U.S. aircraft carriers took part, NATO forces demonstrated their willingness to carry their operations to the region.[39]

In summary, the importance of the High North in the military balance between the Soviet Union and the Warsaw Pact on the one hand and NATO and the U.S. on the other could not be underestimated. The strategic significance of the region steadily increased through the 1980s right until the collapse of the Soviet Union. Certainly, many of the Soviet naval assets based in the Kola Peninsula were strategic rather than regional in their implications. Nevertheless, NATO was aware that Soviet military doctrines were offensive in their construction and that the organization and equipment of Soviet forces as well as the presence of motorized infantry divisions and amphibious forces indicated offensive capabilities, if not intentions.

It has to be noted, however, and this was a point frequently stressed by the Finns, that the military potential of Soviet forces based on the Kola Peninsula was sufficient only for limited attacks on Nordic targets the modest military advantages of which seemed to be outweighed by the kind of countermeasures that could be expected from NATO. A more comprehensive attack that would strike the strategically more important Norwegian bases further to the south would require moving large numbers of Soviet forces, from elsewhere in the Leningrad Military District or from other military districts to the Kola Peninsula, an action which would give the West considerable warning that an attack was being prepared.

Nevertheless, the foregoing description of the balance in the far north underscores the critical importance of the region to NATO and the United States. It also explains why the U.S. and its allies were concerned that, from time to time, Finnish positions on military and security issues seemed to be inconsistent with NATO policies aimed at containing the Soviet Union. At the same time, it seemed to us that Finnish positions on some issues were also inconsistent with Finland's own long-term interest in an effective NATO counterweight against the Soviet Union.

At the core of U.S. and NATO policy concerns were any proposals that would seem in any way to constrain NATO's freedom of action in the North Atlantic or that might place limitations on the freedom of action of NATO members Denmark and Norway. These differing policy views between Finland and NATO, particularly the United States, would surface time and again throughout the Cold War as specific issues arose.

6

U.S. Perceptions of Some Early Cold War Finnish Crises

Three key relatively early post-World War II developments are frequently referred to as pivotal in the evolution of Finland's political and security position vis-à-vis the Soviet Union and the West. They were developments in 1948 concerning the Soviet demand for a security treaty with Finland and alleged efforts by the Finnish Communists to assume power through a *coup d'état*: the 1958 "Night Frost" government and political crisis; and the 1961 "Note Crisis" and its impact on Finland's 1962 presidential election. These crises were considered significant as they developed and were carefully studied by the U.S. government—albeit in an urgent and pressured manner based on the information available at the time. The U.S. sought to evaluate the extent to which these events reflected growing Soviet aggressiveness towards Finland and Northern Europe, which might adversely affect the strategic balance in the region and threaten the viability of Finland's independence and control over its own affairs.

All three of these developments have been extensively studied and analyzed and, indeed, continue to be subjects for research and lively debate as additional information becomes available from Soviet archives. Finnish researchers include Dr. Jukka Nevakivi and Dr. Hannu Rautkallio. There is also new information in the recent publication of the Paasikivi Diaries and Dr. Juhani Suomi's several volume biography of President Urho K. Kekkonen. These publications raise sometimes starkly contrasting viewpoints as to what happened and why during these pivotally important early post-war crises. (We will address some recently published viewpoints and other perspectives in Part Four.)

It is my purpose in this chapter to cite a sampling of U.S. official documents in order to give a flavor of what the U.S. embassy was reporting *as it happened*, without the benefit of information coming to light many years later.

At the U.S. National Archives and among State Department documents released to me under the FOIA process, I found an interesting (but apparently incomplete) collection of reports from the U.S. embassy in Helsinki—or from Washington agencies or other U.S. embassies—about the 1958-59 and 1961-62 situations in Finland. (I chose not to go back as far as 1948 in researching U.S. government documents, particularly inasmuch as another former U.S. diplomat from an earlier generation, Ambassador Raymond Ylitalo, wrote in 1978 on U.S. diplomatic relations with Finland during the late 1940s and cited numerous U.S. documents from that period.)[40] The above-mentioned researchers, Dr. Nevakivi and Dr. Rautkallio, among others, have also had access to these documents from the 1940s (as well as the 1950s and 1960s) and have cited various of them in their books and articles.

Embassy reporting, and Washington actions and reactions, give interesting insights into how contemporary Finnish developments were being reported and interpreted. They also constitute some precursor of U.S. and other NATO country concerns with respect to Finnish actions and positions later associated with the phenomenon termed "Finlandization."

The "Night Frost" Crisis

The 1958 Finnish parliamentary elections produced a Parliament that for the first time since 1916 had a majority for the socialist parties. The biggest winner in the elections had been the Finnish Peoples Democratic Union (SKDL in Finnish) the electoral front dominated by the Finnish Communist Party (SKP in Finnish). The SKDL went from 43 seats in the 1954 elections to 50 seats, making it the largest political grouping in the Parliament. Meanwhile, the radical minority "Skogist" faction of the Social Democratic Party (SDP), which had left the SDP the previous year, picked up three seats in Parliament under the banner of the Workers and Small Farmers' Social Democratic Union. It was believed that the SKP wanted to establish a popular front government consisting of the SKDL, the Agrarian Union and the "Skogist" SDP faction. Some within SKDL believed they had earned the premiership of such a popular front government.

Instead, on August 29, 1958, the Social Democratic Party put together a broad based majority government under the prime ministership of K.A. Fagerholm consisting of the Social Democrats, the Agrarian Party, the National Coalition or Conservative Party (Kokoomus), the Swedish People's Party and the Liberal People's Party. The Fagerholm government thus had the support of 137 of the 200 Eduskunta members. The formation of the Fagerholm Government elicited a highly negative reaction from the Soviet Union, producing the so-called "Night Frost" crisis.

The Soviet Union halted trade negotiations, slowed and then virtually stopped imports from Finland, turned back ships it had ordered from Finland, and announced that the Soviet ambassador to Finland had been recalled and transferred to other duties. The Finnish foreign minister, the Agrarian Party's Johannes Virolainen, resigned on December 4 followed later the same day by the other Agrarian Party members of government. Fagerholm was left with no choice but to ask for the dissolution of the government. President Kekkonen asked him to stay on until a new government could be formed. After negotiations over other government coalition combinations failed, Kekkonen proceeded in the new year to appoint an Agrarian Party minority government under the prime ministership of V.J. Sukselainen.[41]

While U.S. embassy records for this period—available from the National Archives in Washington—are for some reason still incomplete, it is clear from embassy reports that it had greeted the formation of the Fagerholm majority government with considerable satisfaction. The embassy's CONFIDENTIAL "despatch" No. 127 of September 4, 1958, written by embassy Second Secretary Grant G. Hilliker, saluted the government as Finland's "first political government since last winter and its first parliamentary majority government since the second Fagerholm cabinet fell at the end of May 1957."

While noting that the government's broad parliamentary support "superficially including all non-Communist Diet groups except for the opposition (Skogist) Social Democrats," the embassy report said the government was not actually as strong as it appeared. It pointed out that the exclusion of the Communist-front SKDL and the Skogist Social Democrats:

> ...effectively puts the bulk of trade union strength...in opposition to the government. Of possible equal importance depending on the course of events, the radical or small farmer wing which since the war has largely dominated the Agrarian Party, is weakly represented in the cabinet and could overthrow it if there arose a clear issue involving interests of small farmers/workers.

While noting that government support might not be as solid as it looked because of the factors just described, the embassy report said the new government "can be regarded as the first post-war union of conservative elements in all parties. It is thus a logical and constructive coalition..."

The U.S. embassy report noted, however, that sharp criticism of the government had come from the Communist and Skogist opposition press. The embassy also reported that Soviet reaction to the new cabinet was sharp. This reaction appeared first publicly in an *Izvestia* article distributed by the Soviet Information Bureau on September 1. According to the embassy,

> The article used the well-worn charges of resurgent reaction led by the Conservatives and Social Democrats and plans to change Finnish foreign policy. It even accused the Agrarians of a shift toward the right. Foreign Minister Virolainen, in a luncheon conversation with the counselor on September 2, commented that in general the Soviet reaction was just what had been expected, but that he still had been somewhat surprised at the foreign policy charge.

The embassy report cited another, unnamed Agrarian Party source, as being less sanguine about the extent of Soviet reaction to the new government. This source noted the sudden cancellation of a Soviet agricultural delegation expected August 30 and a negative *Tass* editorial on the Finnish "denial" of a visa to O.V. Kuusinen, and said these developments boded ill for Fenno-Soviet relations. The same source "speculated that difficulties might be encountered in connection with setting of prices in Fenno-Soviet commodity trade, on which negotiations begin this fall."

Embassy counselor Mose Harvey, whose luncheon with Virolainen had been noted in the report cited above, commented further on his luncheon meeting in embassy CONFIDENTIAL despatch 132 of September 5, 1958. He said that in commenting on the negative Soviet reaction to the government, based on fears that the new government intended to change Finland's foreign policy, Virolainen had "added that the Soviets 'are really incapable of appreciating realities in western countries'."

Harvey's report went on to observe:

Virolainen gave every indication that he personally was happy over the government setup and that he earnestly hoped it would prove successful. This, unless Virolainen was deliberately and effectively engaging in subterfuge, is significant since it runs counter to speculation that the aim of the Agrarian leadership is to insure failure of the government and then to secure its replacement with an Agrarian, or Agrarian-Skogist, minority government with Communist support.

Back in Washington, on October 28, the State Department bureau of intelligence and research (INR) prepared a five page CONFIDENTIAL analysis of the "Current Economic and Political Situation in Finland," drawing largely on previous embassy reporting. The report concluded rather optimistically, and as events proved, erroneously:

Although the Soviets have made it clear that they are displeased over the 'rightist' character of the present Finnish Government, they are not likely to make an open manifestation of their displeasure because of the unfavorable reaction any adverse development in Finnish-Soviet relations would create in the other Scandinavian countries...trade pressures, however, may be expected.

Thus, at the end of October 1958, Washington—or at least INR—was quite relaxed regarding the prospects for the Fagerholm Government. By early November, however, embassy reports began to reflect more concern. In a weekly political wrap-up report sent to Washington in CONFIDENTIAL despatch No. 308 on November 7, the embassy said it had noted,

> …a sustained flow of private speculation concerning how far the Soviets might plan to go in the critical aspect of their pressure campaign—foot dragging on renewal of existing trade arrangements…[A] Social Democrat told the embassy the Soviet embassy in Helsinki had…informed the Finns that the Finnish lists of commodities proposed for next year's trade agreement would require further study…Still other reports quoted President Kekkonen as having expressed great concern over the situation.

On December 5, 1958, an embassy report recorded the collapse the previous day of the Fagerholm government.

In a separate but related development earlier in 1958, the United States government had taken a presidentially-approved measure to waive with respect to Finland provisions of the Battle Act— legislation named after Senator Battle. This act was designed to deny all U.S. economic assistance to countries that knowingly permitted the export to the "Soviet bloc" of strategically important goods identified in the law. It was determined that some of Finland's exports to the Soviet bloc, particularly ships and copper cable, fell under the terms of the Act making Finland ineligible for U.S. assistance. However, the Eisenhower administration decided it was in the U.S. interest to proceed with the disbursement of the uncommitted portion (U.S. $14 million) of a previous U.S. loan to Finland. Therefore, on February 11, 1958 the administrator of the Battle Act, Deputy Under Secretary of State for Economic Affairs Douglas Dillon, sent a letter classified SECRET to the president requesting him to make a determination that the proposed loan disbursement be authorized, notwithstanding Battle Act provisions. The justification offered by the letter provides an insight into the administration's attitude toward Finland:

> Failure by the United States to take this opportunity to assist Finland in its attempts to reduce in some measure its dependence on the Soviet bloc, and thus its vulnerability to Soviet economic pressures, would clearly be detrimental to the security of the United States and the free world within the spirit of the Battle Act.

President Eisenhower approved the proposed action on February 15, 1958, and the U.S. Congress was subsequently notified of the waiver granted to Finland.

This action earlier in the year assumed new significance during the Night Frost crisis. Apparently at the initiative of the U.S. ambassador to Finland, John D. Hickerson, the United States put together a package of economic assistance which was subsequently offered to the Fagerholm government as a possible source of alternative economic support to offset the hardships imposed by the Soviet embargo of trade with Finland.[42]

In a radio-television speech to the Finnish nation December 10, President Kekkonen seemed to allude indirectly to this and perhaps other offers of assistance from the West. According to Helsinki telegram No. 287 of December 11 classified OFFICIAL USE ONLY to the Department of State:

> The [speech] referred [to] western advice 'in [the] press and otherwise' on Finland's relations with the Soviets including 'promises [of] aid and support...Any outside interference—however well intended' must be rejected because Finland itself 'in [the] final analysis and by its own efforts must manage its foreign policy. So we ha[ve] up to now; so we shall continue to do.'[43]

In another telegram later the same day, Helsinki No. 289 classified SECRET, a clearly unhappy Ambassador Hickerson wrote the Department in the first person that:

> While [the] president in his references to Western aid doubtless had in mind, among other things, the US offer (DEPTEL 231) and possible other offers including one reported from West Germany, his thinking was such as to place emphasis on [the] press with [the] result that only those officials who know of these offers would recognize the importance of the words 'and otherwise' following mention of [the] press.

> [The] statement clearly constituted rejection, under present circumstances, of [the] US contingency package program. [The] president appears [to] expect that government changes will satisfy [the] Soviets and bring alleviation [of] pressure. If this [is] not true and [the] Soviets demand unacceptable concessions, [the] president may decide or be forced [to] turn to [the] US although he certainly would insist that all appearances [of] political strings be avoided...I expect, however, that resort to [the] US will come, if at all, only after all hope [of] appeasing [the] Soviets [is] exhausted. I therefore continue to feel that [the] proper course for us for [the] time being is to sit tight...

> It goes without saying that I feel that there was an element of dirty pool based on partisan considerations in the president's airing [of the] aid issue, particularly the overtones on 'intervention.' HICKERSON[44]

Some months later, on July 15, 1959, Ambassador Hickerson had the opportunity for a private, after-luncheon conversation with President Kekkonen that he reported in embassy SECRET telegram No. G-8 of July 17 which was given limited distribution in the State Department. Ambassador Hickerson asked the president whether there was anything he would care to say about Finland's domestic political situation.

> I added that [my] inquiry was made out of friendly curiosity and with no desire to interfere, an example I wished would be followed by Finland's big neighbor.

> Kekkonen replied that he shared my wish, but said he found [the] situation very discouraging. As [the] situation now stands he saw no prospect of broadening [the] government to achieve majority support within [the] predictable future...He feared that any broadened government would encounter [a] fate similar to Fagerholm's last year.

In his conversation with Ambassador Hickerson, President Kekkonen discussed and defended his much criticized trip to Leningrad where he had met Khrushchev who had publicly lashed out against Finnish Social Democratic leaders by name.

> Kekkonen said that [the] atmosphere in Fenno-Soviet relations had improved for [a] time after [the] Leningrad visit, and then it had deteriorated again with [the] Soviets and Finnish Social Democrats exchanging charges in endless series. He felt [the] May Day speeches of Social Democrats were particularly unfortunate.

> In this connection I asked again as [a] 'friendly observer' and with [a] confession of diffidence whether he thought it reasonable to expect 'good Finns' to take abuse from Khrushchev without making reply. Kekkonen replied that he did not know, but that answers always complicated matters and that they could have been simpler. He made no comment on my warning that one could never know whom the Soviet might criticize next. I said this was [an] affair in which I could not take sides as among Finns, but had to say that I held Tanner and other Social Democrats condemned by Khrushchev in highest personal regard. He agreed [that] Tanner [is] 'one of [the] great men of Finland' but also one of the stubbornest he had ever known.

> As [a] parting thought Kekkonen said he knew we understood Finland's difficult position. Despite those difficulties he had every confidence [the] country can handle its relations with [the] Soviets and remain free, although this would from time to time require some 'adjustments.' HICKERSON

Repercussions in Washington of the outcome of the "Night Frost Crisis" continued to reverberate throughout 1959. Washington had received information from the U.S. embassy in

London that the British had also expressed concern about the Finnish situation. The State Department consequently sent a telegram to London and Helsinki providing guidance to the U.S. embassy in London for discussions with the Foreign Office regarding U.S. views on Finland. Telegram No. 01207, dated September 2 and classified SECRET, welcomed the opportunity to exchange views with the UK. It described U.S. concerns:

regarding unsatisfactory developments, which appear to arise from [the] following interrelated factors:

(1) Continued bad feeling between SocDem and Agrarian leadership which does not appear [to] reflect attitudes of [the] rank and file of either party.

(2) Deepening split among SocDems between regular SocDem party and left-wing opposition SocDem party (Skogists). Difficult [to] see how Skogists can avoid being penetrated, compromised and absorbed by Communists (SKDL). Friendly attitude and gestures of President Kekkonen toward Skogists have undoubtedly strengthened them at expense of [the] regular SocDems.

(3) Loss of control of central trade union federation (SAK) by regular SocDems to Skogist/Communist coalition and current purge of SocDem officials from SAK foreshadows eventual Communist takeover of SAK and has caused SocDem to initiate preparation for establishment of [a] new SocDem trade union federation.

(4) Kekkonen's excessive accommodation of [the] USSR, which goes beyond [the] Paasikivi line and which Kekkonen has consistently practiced is extremely risky in [the] US view. Even if he succeeds in cultivating [the] USSR without jeopardizing Finnish sovereignty and independence he is likely to establish a pattern of relations in which less clever Finnish leadership in future will be compromised.

(5) [A] sense of isolation among Finns and proximity of [the] Soviet threat, which leads many to regard [the] USSR as having balance of power if not in [the] world, at least in [the] Baltic area.

The State Department telegram suggested several areas in which U.S. and U.K. actions might help strengthen Finland's ties to the West and stiffen its resistance to the Soviets:

(1) Finnish membership or association with EFTA. US has already indicated to Finn Govt that it would favor such a move under circumstances outlined Deptel 507 March 1960. Initiative would have to come from UK and other EFTA countries, and US role would be purely passive. Sentiment in Finnish business and regular SocDem circles is favorable. Kekkonen's hesitation seems to stem from uncertainty about possible Soviet reaction and about [the] future of EFTA. On latter point, only [the] UK [is] in

position to assure him. Would also be useful [to] stress danger [of] isolation [of] Finland from western economic organizations…

(2) Step up contacts with Finns on all levels, including high-level visits, military visits, cultural exchanges, tourism, trade fairs etc. [US] election campaign and forthcoming UNGA make it impossible for US [to] consider any high level visits but we hope funds will be available to hold [a] large trade fair [in] Helsinki next spring, and we plan to intensify cultural exchanges and discreetly suggest military exchange visits. You may inform UK Govt in confidence that [the] US [is] negotiating [a] military sales agreement with Finland largely as [a] psychological measure against Sov attempts [to] penetrate and monopolize Finn military. [We] would welcome similar UK efforts to increase contacts.

(3) Promote closer ties between Finns and Scan countries in political and military fields.

(4) Support Finnish SocDem labor leaders in establishing [a] new trade union federation to compete with SAK now dominated by opposition SocDem/Communist coalition. US recognizes [a] likely consequence will be labor unrest with probable econ and political repercussions but believes [the] long run danger [of] Communist domination [of the] labor movement far worse.

(5) Seek [to] persuade Kekkonen that Finn independence depends in long run largely on keeping Finland at arms length from USSR regardless of how he sees balance [of] power between Free World and Sov Bloc in Baltic or world arenas.

It can thus be seen that the "Night Frost" crisis and its multiple ramifications for Finnish domestic and foreign policy had certainly gained Washington attention and a search for ways on the margin to try to assist Finland in maintaining a western orientation. The worries about President Kekkonen's "excessive accommodation" going "beyond the Paasikivi line" underscore that the Night Frost had begun a process of questioning in the United States and elsewhere in the West regarding Finland that presaged "Finlandization" concerns.

The "Note Crisis"

On December 1960, the United States National Security Council Planning Board issued a document updating a formal, officially sanctioned policy statement on Finland. Its purpose was to serve as the latest policy guidance to be implemented "by all appropriate executive departments and agencies of the U.S. Government." The document, "Statement of U.S. Policy Toward Finland" (NSC 6024, 30 December 1960) has been referred to by other researchers, but in this context serves as a useful bench mark in U.S. attitudes toward Finland going into the 1961-62 Note Crisis.[45]

The document in its General Considerations section discusses Finland's background and status in Europe vis-à-vis the Soviet Union and the West as seen from the U.S. perspective. Relevant excerpts are:

> Finland stands as an example of democracy on the Communist border, and...to the degree that Finland resists Communist blandishments and maintains its Free World orientation and trade, it serves as an example of what can be achieved by other countries in Eastern Europe. Complete Soviet domination of Finland would be a heavy blow to the posture of the Free World...In addition domination would put the USSR in control of advance air defense and early warning positions and additional naval bases on the Baltic. The continued denial of Finland to the USSR is thus psychologically and militarily important to the Free World.

> The capacity of the Finns to deal with this overriding problem is circumscribed by the influence of the USSR resulting from Finland's geographic proximity to Soviet power and its singular vulnerability to Soviet economic pressures, as well as by internal Communist influence and political dissension among non-Communist elements...On the other hand, any significant move by the USSR to capture Finland militarily or politically would have certain adverse effects for the Soviets...

> Finland's policy toward the USSR is to a great extent determined by President Urho Kekkonen, the country's leading political figure who believes that Finland's best interests are served by greater accommodation to Soviet pressures than a number of his countrymen believe necessary. He is apparently convinced that the world balance of power has shifted to a point where the Soviet Union is now in ascendancy over the United States and NATO and that...Finland cannot expect effective aid from the Free World should there be a crisis in its relations with the Soviets.

The document expressed concern that in their anxiety to draw closer to their Scandinavian neighbors:

> ...the Finns have shown periodic interest in the concept of a neutral Scandinavian bloc encompassing Finland and, by implication, involving withdrawal of Norway and Denmark from NATO...The Finns do not and would not deliberately serve Soviet interests. They have preserved their democratic institutions intact and, since 1948, when they courageously

removed the Communist cabinet ministers, they have joined forces to keep the Communists isolated from the Government...The ability of Finland to associate one way or another with [EFTA] is of such far-reaching importance that it may be a major determinant of Finland's fate as an independent country oriented toward the Free World.

The NSC paper expected that in the event of an East-West armed conflict the Finns would do whatever they could to preserve their independence and neutrality. Moreover,

A Soviet attack on Finland itself would probably meet armed resistance and Soviet occupying forces might even be subjected to intensive guerrilla warfare. Finland's independence contributes to the security of Scandinavia in particular and Western Europe in general. Although the Finns have thus far had success in staving off Soviet domination with little outside help, the threat of absorption into the Soviet orbit continues to persist...The extent to which the Finnish people are firm will depend in large measure on the strength of their Free World ties and on their confidence in...the Free World and in its ability and willingness to provide meaningful support.

The study conceded that the possibilities of taking measures in support of Finland are limited,

...because of the danger of Soviet counter-measures and Finland's determination to avoid the danger...[But] it is clearly in the interest of the United States, as well as the Free World in general, to continue efforts to strengthen Finland's independence and Free World orientation.

The NSC document concludes with a series of policy guidance points aimed at—within the above-acknowledged limits—strengthening Finland's political, economic, trade, cultural and informational ties with the West. Interestingly, among the various policy aims there is no mention in this document of seeking strengthened military ties.

The Note Crisis, to be properly understood, needs to be placed in both the international and domestic Finnish context within which the episode developed. Internationally, Berlin, long a bone of contention between East and West, began simmering on the front burner again in early 1961. The flow of East German refugees to the West through Berlin had by 1961 become an embarrassing flood. On February 17, the Soviets under Nikita Khrushchev "told the West Germans that unless a comprehensive peace treaty to terminate the allied occupation and four-power administration was signed, they would sign a separate peace treaty with East Germany. West Berlin would become a demilitarized 'free city,' and the East Germans would take over from the Soviet control of all air and land access routes to Berlin. The Allies would then have to negotiate with East Germany the new terms of access." [46]

At the Vienna summit meeting in June 1961, Khrushchev raised the Berlin issue with the new U.S. President John F. Kennedy in very harsh terms. U.S. Secretary of State Dean Rusk recalled:

> At one point Khrushchev said to Kennedy, 'We are going to negotiate a new agreement with East Germany, and the access routes to Berlin will be under their control. If there is any effort by the West to interfere, there will be war.'...Kennedy went right back at him, looked him in the eye, and said, 'Then there will be war, Mr. Chairman. It's going to be a very cold winter.' [47]

Khrushchev presented the U.S. delegation with a formal aide-memoir setting December 1961 as a deadline for a peace treaty. On June 10, as if to underscore their seriousness, the Soviets made public their aide-memoir. As a response to the ultimatum, President Kennedy that summer asked Congress for increases in the U.S. defense budget, called up some reserve and national guard units and strengthened U.S. forces in West Germany and West Berlin. Meanwhile, Secretary of State Rusk met with his allied counterparts, and they reached agreement on the importance of defending Berlin and standing firm. Meanwhile, in August 1961 the Soviets unilaterally broke an informal moratorium on nuclear weapons testing—that the USSR and the United States had been observing—when they began a massive program of testing dirty, high-megaton bombs in the atmosphere, producing massive fallout.

Allied foreign ministers met with Soviet Foreign Minster Andrei Gromyko in late September and reiterated that there were three non-negotiable elements in any Berlin settlement: West Berlin must retain its political freedom, the United States must retain its forces there and the West must have free civil and military access to the city. The Allies proposed that East Germany conclude an agreement with the USSR recognizing the four-power agreement on access to Berlin. They emphasized that allied rights in Berlin could not be given away by the Soviets.

Then, on October 17, the first day of the Twenty-second Congress of the Soviet Union's Communist Party, Khrushchev withdrew his deadline for a German peace treaty. The Berlin crisis was over, but the Berlin problem remained.[48]

Regarding the domestic Finnish context, 1962 was a presidential election year. President Kekkonen had already been named as the candidate of the Agrarian Union in 1960. He could also rely on the support of the Skogists and the SKDL. In the spring of 1961, an anti-Kekkonen coalition including the Social Democrats, the Conservatives, the Liberal People's Party and the Swedish People's Party formed and recruited retired Chancellor of Justice Olavi Honka as its candidate. Some observers believed that the "Honka Coalition" would be able to gain more votes than President Kekkonen in the election; others, including apparently the U.S. embassy, believed that Honka could not be considered a serious challenger to Kekkonen.

As the political battle lines were forming in preparation for the 1962 presidential elections, the U.S. embassy reported on developments with great interest and in considerable detail.

Embassy despatch No. 437 of March 20, 1961, prepared by Second Secretary Harvey Nelson, reported the early skirmishing between Kekkonen and Honka forces, the latter of which were still seeking to nail down multi-party support for their proposed candidate. Firm decisions were expected at the various party conventions scheduled for the spring and summer. Indications were that Honka enjoyed substantial support among the Social Democratic, Conservative, Liberal and Swedish parties, although there had also been expressions of opposition.

The despatch noted that foreign policy had

> top billing in the discussion and activity induced by the Honka candidacy. The Agrarian leadership is jealously seeking to retain its role as guardian of the Paasikivi Line, the principal ingredient of which is the assiduous cultivation of the best possible relations with the USSR.

The despatch reported that the foreign policy dimension had been given enhanced attention in the presidential campaign by an appeal by the Agrarian Union for "broad bourgeois support of the incumbent president, an appeal suggesting that Finland's international position can best be protected only by Kekkonen."

The Agrarian Union had addressed its appeal to the Conservative, Liberal and Swedish parties, calling for the most unanimous backing possible behind Kekkonen in order to "thus...best assure peace on our frontiers and continuation of our successful neutral policy." The appeal was denounced by elements of the media and political opponents as tantamount to saying, as expressed by the newspaper *Ilta Sanomat* that "the Agrarian appeal is a declaration that 'whoever denounces the Agrarian candidate opposes Finland's post-war foreign policy'."

The embassy report observed that the foreign policy controversy was "heightened by a March 5 *Izvestya* article in which Honka, the Socialists and the 'extreme rightists' were attacked for planning to alter Finland's foreign policy course. The Soviet article concluded that Fenno-Soviet relations might suffer a critical decline should Honka win."

In a follow-up despatch, No. 456, on March 30, the embassy reported the bitter debate and name-calling surrounding the use of the foreign policy issue in the election campaign. The report recorded that "the Conservative and Swedish parties had joined in an interpolation asking the government whether, as implied in the Agrarian appeal, a threat exists on Finland's borders."

Meanwhile, in the midst of these international and domestic Finnish developments, preparations went forward for an unofficial visit by President Kekkonen to the United States scheduled for October 1961. On October 14, 1961, the Department of State forwarded to McGeorge Bundy, President Kennedy's national security affairs advisor, a memorandum providing background material for President Kekkonen's visit to Washington beginning October 16. The memorandum had been prepared by the intelligence and research bureau (INR) of the State Department.

In general, the INR document, entitled "Trends in Finnish Foreign Policy," repeated the assessments and evaluations reached by the INR's earlier October 28, 1958 document and the December 30, 1960, NSC policy paper on Finland referred to earlier in this chapter. However, inasmuch as the paper was intended to prepare the White House for the approaching visit of President Kekkonen, it devoted considerable attention to President Kekkonen's policies and to comparisons between President Kekkonen and his predecessor, President Juho Paasikivi.

> The late President Juho Paasikivi initiated the so-called 'Paasikivi line' in Finnish foreign policy, an adaptation to the need to establish and maintain correct relations with the USSR and to avoid policies in international affairs unacceptable to the Soviets. The necessities embodied in this doctrine were recognized in Finland's reluctant acceptance of the Friendship and Mutual Aid Pact with the USSR in 1948.

> While Finnish policies have adhered to the basic principles of the 'Paasikivi Line,' they have fluctuated with the influence of pro-Western forces. These forces have been most influential when Finland's confidence in the US as a counterweight to the world power position of the USSR has been the greatest...

> President Kekkonen, the Agrarian leader who succeeded Paasikivi in 1956, reportedly estimates that the world balance of power has shifted in favor of the Soviet Union. This belief may account for the reinterpretation, adverse to the West, of the 'Paasikivi Line' brought about by Kekkonen in 1958. At that time, the president's failure, in the face of Soviet pressure, to back a coalition government including certain Social Democrats objectionable to Moscow, resulted in the fall of a government, which, from the Western point of view, was the most favorable of any in the postwar period...A serious weakening was indicated in Finland's sovereignty by the fact that the USSR was permitted for the first time to veto, in a sense, participation in the cabinet by persons unacceptable to Moscow.

The INR document further stated that Finnish association with EFTA had helped to counter negative foreign policy trends in Finland and that these gains were jeopardized by the British decision to negotiate entry into the EEC.

> Exclusion of Finland from the markets of the expanded EEC would be likely to bring about a significantly increased dependence on the Bloc for vitally important Finnish export markets, thereby increasing Finland's vulnerability to Soviet economic pressure.

The memorandum reviewed "important factors that will probably limit the extent to which Kekkonen and other Finnish leaders will go, or be called upon, to accommodate the Soviets," including the anti-Soviet bias of the majority of Finns, the fact that the Soviet Union would have more to lose than gain by pressuring Finland further, "the risk of undermining the position of Kekkonen, whose presidency has been advantageous to the USSR," and the adverse reaction of the Scandinavian countries.

Looking at the coming presidential elections in Finland, the memorandum stated that:

> Another element making for the continuation of present Finnish policies is the fact that opposition to Kekkonen is weak and likely to remain so; current efforts to prevent his reelection in 1962 are proving ineffectual. In the final analysis, most Finns will probably support him as the person best qualified to deal with the Soviets.

While President Kekkonen was in Hawaii following his consultations in Washington, the Soviet Union delivered the famous diplomatic note on October 30, 1961—two weeks after what Dean Rusk considered to be the end of the Berlin Crisis when Khrushchev on October 17 withdrew his ultimatum on Berlin. The Soviet note referred to the rearmament of the Federal Republic of Germany and increased West German activity in the Baltic region. In the note certain circles in Finland were alleged to be supporting NATO military preparations and distorting peaceful proposals made by the Soviet Union.

The note proceeded to call for consultations under Article 2 of the 1948 Treaty of Friendship, Cooperation and Mutual Assistance (FCMA). That Treaty obliged Finland to defend its territory by all possible means should there be an effort by a third party to invade the Soviet Union through Finland. Article 2 of the Treaty called for consultations between Finland and the USSR about military cooperation in the event of the threat of an attack that Finland could not deal with alone.

Because of the tension in Europe arising from the Soviet ultimatum over Berlin, there had already been some concerns expressed in Finland earlier during the year that the general situation could bring direct repercussions for Finland. On August 12, 1961 the chief of the Finnish general staff, General Tauno Viljanen, reviewed the international situation in a meeting of the Finnish cabinet. General Viljanen indicated the possibility existed that the Berlin Crisis could also affect Finland, for example, the USSR Government could propose military consultations with the Government of Finland under the FCMA Treaty.[49]

The Note Crisis hit the American embassy like a bomb. In selecting sparingly from the extensive flurry of embassy reports and back and forth communications with the State Department, I have chosen documents that: (1) reflect embassy efforts to find out and inform Washington what was going on as events developed and provide preliminary assessments; (2) describe the reaction in Washington, including some initial policy responses and efforts to be helpful; (3) and indicate longer term conclusions drawn in Washington regarding the meaning of the sudden resolution of the crisis after Novosibirsk.

One of the first embassy reports, Helsinki CONFIDENTIAL telegram No. 184 of October 31 to the State Department reported on a visit to the embassy earlier the same day by Social Democratic Party Secretary, Kaarlo Pitsinki who came to discuss the note. The report conveyed that:

> [Pitsinki] said representatives from all parties in [the] coalition supporting Honka for president had met this morning to discuss the note's implications. They discarded any idea [the] note [was] even partly motivated by Soviet desire [to] reelect Kekkonen. [They] concluded it was part of a larger Soviet plan in which Finland had a minor role. Impossible to say now what Russians might want of Finland.

> Consensus of meeting [was] that agreement to undertake discussions with USSR would in effect constitute acceptance [of] Soviet analysis of situation. Finland should not agree to this because contrary to facts. Group tentatively thought [that] coalition should recommend to Government that it not enter into negotiations on ground[s] that [the] present situation is not that envisioned by 1948 Treaty. Party discussions continuing.

On November 1, U.S. Ambassador Gufler called on the acting secretary general of the Foreign Ministry, Jaakko Hallama. He gave Hallama a copy of a press statement issued by the Department of State on the evening of October 31. That statement (sent to all posts by State Department circular telegram 810) read:

> The USSR note to Finland made public on October 30 by TASS is a typical effort by the Soviet Union to sow confusion and divert attention from its own activities. The explosion of the 50-megaton bomb in contempt of world opinion as expressed in the United Nations and the Soviet posture toward Germany and Berlin have made it abundantly clear that the Soviet Union is the source of the present world tension. In the face of those acts the Soviet Union has good reason to try to cover its own aggressive policies by false accusations.

> The old charges against the Republic of Germany and the NATO defensive alliance have been repeatedly exposed as false. The present allegations regarding Finland's Scandinavian neighbors are equally absurd.

We find it repugnant that the Soviet Union should seek to involve Finland in its diversionary propaganda activities, especially in view of Finland's chosen policy of neutrality.

Ambassador Gufler reported (Helsinki SECRET telegram No. 190 of November 1, 1961), that Hallama expressed appreciation for the statement. He indicated Hallama then said he had a proposal he would like to make that he thought would be helpful to Finland:

Hallama... asked me not to repeat [the] idea to anyone else in Helsinki, and added that [the] idea should not be attributed in any way to [a] Finnish suggestion. His idea is that NATO issue [a] reasoned refutation of contentions in Soviet note that it or any of its members have any plans or are taking any action that in any way menace Finland or Soviet Union through Finland and that NATO had every intention of fully respecting the desire of Finland to remain neutral.

In a separate message (Helsinki SECRET telegram No. 189) sent the same day as his conversation with Hallama, Gufler described information provided to him by Hallama. The latter said he had not had time to think out all of the implications of the Note, but believed it was motivated by something more than the accomplishment of Soviet aims in Finland:

Hallama does not think that [the] Soviets now mean to push for occupation of Finland or even for bases in Finland...Hallama thinks Finland should go slowly and play for time...He [had] advised President Kekkonen by telephone not to return immediately but to carry on [his] planned program.

Hallama is convinced that Finland cannot refuse [the] invitation to enter into conversations with Soviets, or it must do so within framework of policy of friendliness...Hallama believes however that accepting invitation to consult does not constitute automatic admission [of the] contentions of [the] Soviet note. Finns will insist that their territory is not menaced and that Soviet Union is not menaced through Finnish territory. They cannot however deny that war tension exists elsewhere.

Finland realized that it will have to handle its problem with Soviet Union alone and can hope for sympathy but can not count on material assistance from outside. GUFLER

Two days later Ambassador Gufler called on Foreign Minister Karjalainen, and sent the following report (Helsinki CONFIDENTIAL telegram No. 205 sent November 3) in which Karjalainen indicated:

The Soviet note came as [a] great shock but as more shock than surprise as Finns have feared some Soviet action of this sort. The [GOF]...will take several days to formulate its reply to Soviet note. It will have to enter into some sort of discussion with Soviets but does not yet know exactly within what framework these will be conducted. The [GOF] has no idea...what Soviets intend to demand from it.

Finland does not feel...menaced by NATO and does not accept the premises of Soviet note. It does not feel...menaced by West Germany...but the 'German problem has angles that must be considered in the light of history.'

He talked last night with the president, who is keeping cool and optimistic. He hopes that president's optimism will be justified...GUFLER

Over the next two days, the embassy sent two reports which included opinions picked up for the first time that the note crisis might be in part designed to bolster President Kekkonen's domestic position. In Helsinki CONFIDENTIAL telegram No. 207 of November 3, the embassy reported that Finns had been apprehensive since the beginning of the Berlin crisis earlier in the year that it might at some point involve Soviet invocation of Article II of the FCMA Treaty. President Kekkonen was reported himself as expressing such concerns. The message continued:

Speculation on Soviet intentions and Finland's future is met everywhere, and [the] most exaggerated rumors can be heard. These range from 'definite information' about specific bases and facilities [the] Soviets will request to allegation by some opponents that president [was] told in advance he would receive note. Local incidents related to Finnish fears over [the] Berlin crisis are cited by some...as 'evidence' of President Kekkonen's prior knowledge and as basis for assertions that he may be conniving with Soviets for his own personal profit.

Most Finns of all parties however seem to feel that because he is president they must put faith in Kekkonen and hope that he will somehow succeed in pacifying [the] Soviets without undue cost to Finland. GUFLER

The following day Ambassador Gufler reported on a conversation he had with the French ambassador. In Helsinki CONFIDENTIAL telegram No. 210 of November 4, Gufler wrote:

French ambassador expressed to me opinion on following lines; main motivations [of the] Soviet note were (1) desire to make absolutely certain Kekkonen reelection by frightening Finnish public and then permitting Kekkonen to 'save Finland' and (2) to frighten Scandinavia and if possible weaken Scandinavian allegiance to [the] West...

Ambassador Gufler commented:

French embassy views are out of line with other information received by this embassy, although some opponents of Kekkonen are circulating similar stories about Kekkonen's alleged advance knowledge [of] Soviet intention to act and Soviet intention to use [the] note to assist his reelection. GUFLER.

On November 6, Secretary General Hallama called Gufler to the Foreign Ministry to say "in strict confidence" he had received information from the Finnish embassy in Moscow that the US had been in touch with Scandinavian governments with a proposal that they should endeavor to influence the GOF to refuse to accept the Soviet summons to negotiate on the premise that there was a military threat from West Germany. Ambassador Gufler reported (Helsinki SECRET telegram 218 of November 6):

> Hallama disturbed over [the] possibility that this information might get to [the] Soviets and lead them [to] make trouble for Finland...He asked if I had any information that would throw light on this.

Gufler said he had told Hallama perhaps there had been some discussions based on the State Department's public statement, referred to above, but said he would report to Washington what Hallama had said and let him know what Washington responded.

On November 7, the day after Gufler's conversation with Hallama, the Department sent a telegram to the US embassy in Stockholm (Department telegram No. 03269) in fact asking US Ambassador Parsons in Stockholm to discuss with the Swedish prime minister the following:

> ...Department does not plan bilateral representation at this time in Helsinki with respect to Soviet note. This decision takes into account [the] views of other interested governments and reflects opinion that public and demonstrative support for Finland would not be helpful. We regard problem in first instance as [a] Scandinavian one in which Sweden has important responsibility and role. Suggest you invite comment on any official or unofficial discussion Swedes may have had with Finns...and if Swedes have any further thoughts this stage.

On November 8 the US embassy in Helsinki reported (Helsinki CONFIDENTIAL telegram No. 226) that Foreign Ministry deputy director [of] political affairs Max Jakobson told the embassy that:

> ...Finns wanted us to understand that Foreign Minister Karjalainen's trip to Moscow was for purpose informally exploring [the] basis for [the] Soviet request for consultations. Only after he reported back to Helsinki would [a] decision regarding formal consultations be made. GUFLER

The State Department, via Department SECRET telegram No. 03928 of November 8, sent instructions back to Ambassador Gufler regarding Hallama's query, saying:

FYI. Department had considered probability Finnish Government would become aware [of] US views as result [of] our consultations with Scandinavian Governments and on balance believes such knowledge beneficial in Finnish consideration of reply to Soviet note. Department gratified...over apparently cautious Finnish reaction as evidenced by Karjalainen's projected trip to Moscow apparently to obtain 'clarification' [of] Soviet intentions. If you consider it necessary to pursue with Hallama subject [of] US consultations with other governments which of course normal, suggest you comment along lines below. END FYI.

In public reaction to Soviet note which created wide-spread interest and concern in this country and elsewhere, US Government has confined itself to [its] statement of October 31. While diplomatic exchanges of views between friendly governments are normal in such circumstances, we [are] very conscious of Finland's delicate position and in [an] effort to prevent embarrassment have avoided any approach to Finnish Government. We particularly wished in this regard to refrain from expressing to [GOF] our views re implications of consultation under Article II 1948 Treaty.

A November 16 message from the US embassy in Moscow (Moscow SECRET telegram No. 1550 of November 16) reported that Finnish Ambassador Wuori in Moscow told US Ambassador Thompson that Hallama had inquired of the Soviet ambassador in Helsinki whether President Kekkonen's announcement of the dissolution of the Finnish Parliament and call for new elections satisfied the Soviet desire for political guarantees that Foreign Minister Gromyko had told Finnish Foreign Minister Karjalainen were necessary. Ambassador Wuori told Ambassador Thompson:

[He, Wuori,] was called to [the] Foreign Office by Kuznetsov today and told answer was no and Soviets expect qualified Finnish delegation to come to Moscow...Wuori said Soviets had indicated they were under pressure from Soviet military for guarantees of Finnish reliability but Soviets had given no indication as to what kind of guarantees were sought...He was inclined to think Soviet objectives were political. He thought pressure on other Scandinavian states was part of picture and that idea of keeping up tension generally possibly with Berlin crisis in mind was another factor. So far as internal Finnish politics were concerned Soviet action up to this last move would help Kekkonen but he was not sure how matter would develop now. THOMPSON

On the same day Ambassador Gufler sent a message (Helsinki CONFIDENTIAL telegram 246 of November 16) to the Department again reporting that:

Some persons have contended that [the] main initial purpose [of the] Soviet action initiated by October 30 note was to insure reelection [of] Kekkonen and [have] taken for granted that arrangements had been made by him with Soviets before he announced [parliamentary] elections...

Other persons have thought that elections were [a] clever move that would gain time for Finnish Government and have felt that Soviets had enough faith in Kekkonen to approve his action...

Wishful thinking has prevented most from facing possibility that Finland might be on way to satellite status, though some have expressed such fears.

...I believe, however, it unlikely that Kekkonen had advance agreement from Soviets for parliamentary elections. Soviets are notoriously and from their point [of] view rightly distrustful [about] such unpredictable things as free and uncontrolled elections.

Intention behind Soviet action may have included some small element of desire to help re-election [of] Kekkonen, though that difficult [to] believe in view [of] circumstance his re-election considered almost certain. Main intention must be to draw Finland closer into Soviet orbit.

...All Finns subscribe to Paasikivi line. If this proves insufficient [to] satisfy Soviets, there is in reality nothing for the Finns to do except realize that degree of independence, if any, that Finland will be able [to] maintain depends entirely on the Russians and not on anything they or the most skillful of Finnish leaders can do. GUFLER

Ambassador Gufler called on Hallama November 17 and reported the same day on his conversation (Helsinki SECRET telegram No. 248):

President and foreign minister both deeply shocked by latest Soviet action [Kuznetsov answer that Finns need to send delegation soon]. President apparently fears that calling of elections done too hastily...

Soviets had not given advance commitment to calling elections. Only discussion [of] elections in Gromyko-Karjalainen conversations had been [the] following. Karjalainen had said Finnish Government could give guarantee it would maintain present foreign policy up to time of elections. Gromyko had remarked with two elections coming up in Finland, one probably as late as next summer, Soviet Government felt that it was being asked to wait too long for definitive guarantee. Gromyko indicated in no way any desire, however, for speeding up elections.

Hallama feels latest Soviet action should disprove unfair rumors that have had wide circulation particularly in Helsinki that Kekkonen in any way leagued with Soviets or tied to them by some secret agreements. He believes it is high time for other parties to rally around Kekkonen and for Honka to withdraw his presidential candidacy.

Finns are faced with disturbing puzzle presented by enigmatic Soviet statement that 'if proper political guarantees are given' military consultations may be avoided.... GUFLER

It seems clear from the information that got back to the Finns about U.S. contacts with Scandinavian governments—the State Department's disclaimer notwithstanding—and from the Department telegram to Stockholm that the U.S. Government was very concerned about the implications of the Soviet note. Washington was anxious to consult with other friendly nations to see what could be done about it.

On November 17 the State Department sent CONFIDENTIAL telegram No. 08393 with the action copy going to Helsinki and information copies to Moscow, Stockholm, Oslo, Copenhagen, London and Paris, reporting on a request relayed to Secretary of State Rusk through the Finnish ambassador in Washington from Foreign Minister Karjalainen:

> Karjalainen had said he understands we wish to be as helpful to Finland as possible in its current difficulties and is very appreciative [of] this attitude. Karjalainen hoped we would not make any strong statement at this juncture. To do so would complicate Finland's efforts to resolve matters. We told ambassador we did not contemplate issuing any press statement. Report of secretary's comments on Finnish situation during press conference this afternoon by separate cable…
>
> Finnish ambassador was told US watching situation very closely and we would welcome keeping in close touch with both ambassador and Finnish Government.

The comment by Secretary Rusk at his press conference that day, as reported by State UNCLASSIFIED telegram, had been in response to a question about Soviet pressure on Finland that might result in Finland being absorbed into the Warsaw Pact and Sweden joining NATO. Secretary Rusk responded:

> I think sir, that it would not be…helpful for me to speculate on that point at the present moment. We have had great respect for the independence as well as the neutrality of Finland. As far as we in the West are concerned, we have not attempted in any way to embarrass Finland's neutrality. The Finnish are a very sturdy people and they have the respect of the American people. My guess is that they will have the strong support of people all over the world, neutral as well as those who are the so called aligned peoples, in their attempts to maintain their independence and their neutrality in this situation.

The State Department apparently sent out a request to several U.S. embassies for suggestions and ideas of how to proceed. The embassy in Helsinki responded on November 17 along lines that indicated the State Department had explored with NATO the idea suggested in Hallama's confidential request to Ambassador Gufler that NATO consider making a statement refuting the premises of the Soviet note. The embassy's CONFIDENTIAL telegram 250 of November 17 reiterated the proposal of:

...a reasoned and solemn refutation by NATO of charges set forth against it in Soviet note of October 30, for by 'Germany and its allies' NATO is most clearly meant and its hesitation to reply to these charges, dishonest and ill-founded thought they be, is regarded here as puzzling and of no assistance to Finland.

The embassy message went on to acknowledge that it could understand the complication in proceeding "without giving away [the] Finnish source of suggestion, in view [of] Danish-Norwegian conviction that nothing should be done and illusion that statement not wanted by Finns." The embassy worried:

We hope though that something can be done, all the more so because other Finns includ[ing] Diet members have suggested issuance of some statement refuting Soviet charges by France, UK, US and West Germany.... GUFLER

It is apparent that Hallama's confidential proposal did not enjoy the support of (and perhaps was not known by) his superiors who instead took the position that the Finns were concerned about the possible mounting of a Western campaign on their behalf which the Finns feared would be counterproductive. That would explain the Danish-Norwegian view that the Finns authorities did not in fact want NATO to issue a statement.

On November 18 the embassy in SECRET telegram No. 254 issued what can be considered its first report seriously critical of President Kekkonen's actions to date. While not directly expressing the embassy's own views, the despatch reported an:

Atmosphere of depression now prevailing throughout country has been deepened by disappointment over [the] actions [by] President Kekkonen since his return home felt by large numbers of thoughtful, non-Communist Finns, including members of his own party. [The] nature [of] this disappointment best shown by contrast between what has been done by him and what was hoped for or what is believed by his fellow countrymen might have been done.

The report stated that Finns felt Kekkonen's first speech should have appealed for national unity and an abandonment of partisan rivalries in the face of a national emergency and should not have included any comments regarding Germany that would appear to agree with the premises of the Soviet note. He should have consulted with other party leaders after Karjalainen's return from Moscow, requested a Diet resolution and formal party pledges committing Finland to the Paasikivi neutral foreign policy line regardless of the outcome of election and asked the "only other serious contender for presidency, Honka, to associate himself with president in similar declarations. The Soviet note should have been answered in a reasoned and temperate manner that stated Finland did not consider itself menaced and therefore does not agree that Article II of the Treaty applies..."

The embassy message said that instead of these hoped-for actions, the president's speech had been "partisan, attacked and ridiculed his political opponents, and tried unsuccessfully [to] please both sides by saying he knows NATO is [a] defensive alliance but that German rearmament [is a] source [of] anxiety." The telegram said that after Karjalainen's return, other party leaders were given almost no time to formulate their views, and the president...showed no real interest in hearing them nor were they and the Diet given any real chance to play a part in meeting the crisis. Instead the president hastily and after consulting with no one resorted to dissolution of the Diet and an announcement of new elections, "thus using in this international emergency [an event] that he is known to have planned prior to and independently of Soviet note for political purposes."

On November 21, President Kekkonen met with Ambassador Gufler who delivered to the president a message from President Kennedy (unfortunately, I came across no record of President Kennedy's message or its contents). The ambassador in SECRET embassy telegram No. 266 informed the Department of State of what transpired at the meeting. He explained that the numbered paragraphs were summary quotations of remarks made by President Kekkonen upon Gufler's delivery of President Kennedy's message:

> 1. I am very grateful for this expression of President Kennedy's consideration. I am also appreciative of fact that this is just between us two because if press were to get wind of your message my position in upcoming talk would be seriously damaged.

2. As I said in my speech on Sunday, I will leave with grave thoughts. We Finns are concerned about outcome of talks, but I do not personally believe that situation is as serous as President Kennedy thinks. Perhaps some of the press speculation about Finland's difficulties may have influenced him.

3. All Finn actions taken since receipt of note have had one aim in which so far we have been successful. We want to avoid military discussions according to Article II of the 1948 Treaty, because that would be tantamount to agreeing that threat mentioned in note actually exists. That was why we sent Karjalainen to Moscow. We wanted to have [a] civilian rather than military delegation, for latter would have been construed as tacit admission that threat exists. That was why we decided to dissolve parliament. I figured that in this way we could gain a 3-month breather. That breather lasted only 2 days. Now [the] only remaining alternative is to send me.

4. I hope that I have necessary arguments to use in my discussion with Khrushchev to convince them that it is in [the] interests of Soviet Union to permit Finland to retain its present position. If I can convince him of this and avoid discussion under treaty, then we will have come out on plus side. Worst would be if Khrushchev were to insist that Commies be put into positions of authority here in Finland. I do not think that this is realistic alternative, but in present situation all sorts of ideas go through one's head.

5. If this were to happen, though, and if my policy were to be shown as unacceptable to Soviet Union, then I will not continue in this position. One of the most difficult statements I ever have had to make was one in speech November 5 in which I said that if my policy is demonstrably unsuccessful, then I will resign. I have worked for fifteen years on assumption that my policy is right for Finland. If it develops that I have worked in vain, then I am not going to try to hold onto this job by hook or by crook. I would consider it my duty to resign and leave the area if my policy were to fail.

6. Regarding economic assistance offered by President Kennedy, I am grateful for his consideration, but do not believe that such assistance will in fact be required, because I do not expect any economic pressures.

7. My statement regarding the Strauss visit to Norway was part of effort to create favorable basis for negotiations with Khrushchev. I for my part don't care much what Strauss was doing in Norway, but I said what I did in order to create better atmosphere for talks with the Soviets. Number of statements made in my earlier speeches, if taken out of context, would be unsupportable, but I made with this same motive of creating favorable atmosphere and basis for discussing matters with Soviets.

8. Actually, you know there is genuine fear in Soviet Union regarding West Germany. They are afraid that if present development continues West Germany will be so strong that it will be able to do what it wishes without worrying about its allies. This is fear they have, and it is only being realistic to acknowledge its existence.

9. Once again, I appreciate discreet way in which President Kennedy's message has been delivered and am particularly grateful for wisdom and restraint shown by US Government in its attitude toward current crisis. Secretary Rusk's recent statement was most helpful.

10. Please convey to President Kennedy my warm personal thanks for his consideration in sending his message.

Ambassador Gufler said he was impressed by the "real warmth and sincerity with which President Kekkonen expressed his thanks for attitude of President Kennedy and Secretary Rusk." Gufler observed that at first glance:

President Kekkonen looked normal and reasonably cool. He began conversation in controlled, calm manner. When I looked at him more closely, however, I was struck with [the] deterioration [in] his appearance since I saw him at [the] airport when he returned here on November 3. He had obviously lost weight and his skin looked slightly yellow. He looked drawn and heavily burdened with care. As he unfolded his thoughts, particularly when he referred to possible failure policy for which he worked fifteen years, he revealed strong under-current of emotion and some sense of desperation.

He aroused in both me and Youngquist of our embassy, who served as interpreter, feeling of sympathy for sorely tried man, who though he has made mistakes, is nevertheless trying to do what he believes is best for his country.

President Kekkonen is apparently going on his mission intent on playing as his only card himself and his past record of dealing with Soviets and their leader. It is to be hoped that things go as he expects, but in the light of the rebuffs experienced by Finns within past two weeks it appears more likely that he may encounter situation beyond his control. GUFLER

The Department of State's persistent sense that active steps had to be taken by Finland's Western friends re-emerged in a SECRET Department telegram No. 09707 dated November 21 which was personally signed by Secretary of State Rusk.[50] The telegram was sent for action to the US embassies in Stockholm, Copenhagen, Oslo, London and Helsinki. These embassies were directed to raise the Finnish situation at high levels of the host country foreign ministries along the following lines (to be modified at posts' discretion to meet local circumstances):

In US view Soviet objectives in exerting pressure on Finland appear to fall in three general spheres: (1) to assure effective control of major internal Finnish policies and actions; (2) to weaken determination of Scandinavian countries [to] stand up to Soviets, in particular to reinforce neutral and pacifist sentiments and to increase anti-German feeling and acceptance of belief the FRG is becoming threat to status quo in Scandinavia; (3) to weaken free world resolve and generate increased pressure for negotiations on Berlin by continuation [of] policy of intimidation.

To accomplish its objectives in Finland Soviets are likely use variety of pressures similar to those applied in 1958 'Frosty Nights.' These include propaganda, diplomatic moves, economic pressure, play upon divisions between anti-Soviet political parties and in labor movement, and internal agitation and subversion by Finnish Communist Party. One apparent objective is inclusion [of] Communists in Finnish Government. We doubt Soviets would be prepared to use military force in Finnish context alone.

We believe especially in light [of] most recent Soviet moves it is no longer realistic to consider Finnish-Soviet problem as a bilateral matter which can be treated in isolation and disposed of through Finnish-Soviet negotiations. If Finland's Western friends continue hands off policy heretofore observed there is a grave risk that Soviets will achieve most of their objectives with serious consequences for entire position of free world. We realize disadvantages of confrontation with Soviets in Finland and further that Finns have indicated they would prefer Western powers not to involve themselves. However, our conclusion is that consequences for West of course which events now seem to be taking would be too serious to justify continuation of hands off policy...We believe that friends of Finland should now rally to that country's assistance.

In first instance ways should be found to reassure the Finns that they do not stand alone and that there is available to them feasible alternative to acceptance Soviet demands. Assistance might be given to Finland in political and public opinion fields, e.g. appropriately confidential bilateral démarches to Finns and public statements when opportune. Consideration should also be given to commercial and economic assistance in case of Soviet pressures in those fields. It would be particularly helpful if Scandinavian countries would now take initiative in support for Finland.

US policy toward Finland was expressed in joint communiqué issued by Presidents Kennedy and Kekkonen on October 16. In this statement we expressed understanding of Finland's policy of neutrality, our firm intention scrupulously to respect that chosen course, and the necessity for all nations to avoid interference in affairs of Finland. In all our actions we would plan to make clear that our only purpose is to assist Finland in following its freely elected course. In turn, we have right to expect Finland will in fact be truly neutral.

As a part of its follow-up on the policy initiative, the State Department, at the level of Deputy Under Secretary Johnson, called in separately the Nordic ambassadors to make presentations along the lines indicated in the message to the embassies. The results of these discussions were reported to the field in the Department SECRET telegram No. 10541 of November 22, 1961.

Swedish Ambassador Jarring's reaction was:

a) great care must be exercised in any public statements (as GOS is doing) to avoid prejudicing Finland's position; b) Secy Rusk's press conference statement [was] extremely well balanced and widely appreciated in Scandinavia and Finland; c) GOF already knows it could count on Scandinavian and US support; and d) Swedish thought is to leave further course of action to Finnish judgement.

Norwegian Ambassador Koht noted that authoritative comment by the GON must come from Oslo. He thought that:

On [the] question of possible economic support for Finland [he] was not sure Norway could help as in [a] sense their two economies were competing ones. Surely there could be no doubt among Finns they had support of their Scandinavian friends. Norway felt that up to this point [the] GOF had stood up quite firmly to [the] Soviets and GON has had [the] feeling [the] Finns themselves could best handle [the] matter. Ambassador Koht confirmed [the] fact that [Norwegian Foreign Minister] Lange had [a] long talk with Gromyko and also seeing Khrushchev in Moscow Dec. 2. [He] assumed his foreign minister would...put forward well-known Norwegian views on [the] defensive character of NATO.

Danish Ambassador Knuth-Winterfeldt said although he had not received comments from Copenhagen:

...he thought one Soviet objective in Finnish situation was to hinder NATO developments such as formation [of] Baltic Command by frightening Denmark out of participation. Broader objective was to frighten Scan countries generally into compromise on [the] Berlin problem. [He] quoted Danish UN PermRep to effect [that] Danish Govt decision would remain firm re Baltic Command despite obvious Soviet effort. As to Finland itself he thought Soviets seeking inclusion [of] Communists in key govt posts for purposes [of] working from within to weaken Finnish neutrality policy. He considered objectives of bases in Finland and Finnish signature [of an] eventual GDR peace treaty as lesser possibilities. [He] reacted favorably on need...[to] reassure Finns confidentially of support and said [he] would inform his Govt re US views and suggestions.

Finnish Ambassador Seppälä said the Finns were aware of the deep American friendship:

Nevertheless [it was a] comfort [to] have specific assurances of friendship and assistance. [He] said his own assessment [of the] situation [was] very similar to Department's. However, [the] Soviet démarche of November 16 following Kekkonen's announcement [of] dissolution [of] Parliament suggested [the] Soviets [were] more interested in military rather than political matters. Seppälä asserted there is no...political deterioration in

Soviet-Finnish relations, and expressed hope problem could be solved. [He] said Finnish-Soviet trade was only one of…points on which Soviets could bring pressure, and not necessarily the most important. [He] states he would report US views…

The United States also consulted with the British through the U.S. embassy in London. The British expressed themselves in general conformity with Washington's assessment but cautioned against any approaches to the Finns before the Novosibirsk conversations. The British also indicated some uneasiness over what Washington meant in saying that it was "no longer realistic to consider Finnish-Soviet problem as bilateral matter."

On November 24, the US ambassador to Sweden reported on a testy meeting he had with Swedish Foreign Minister Unden based on the US démarche (embassy Stockholm SECRET telegram No. 380). Ambassador Parsons had apparently earlier raised the matter with one of the Foreign Ministry's senior officials (Belfrage). Ambassador Parsons reported Unden said that:

After consultations with his colleagues he wished [to] state that [the] Swedish Government fully supported remarks made by Belfrage here and Jarring in Washington regarding the line set forth [in the] Department's [message] to Stockholm. Government found 'change of policy' by US rather disturbing, as it was very anxious to follow here whatever course Finland considers desirable about possible 'interventions.' I [Parsons] interrupted to ask if minister meant 'interventions' from Soviet Union to which he replied that he had meant possible interventions or démarches from Western side. Swedish Government's view was that Finland should be left [to] negotiate with USSR without interference from outside. Government was inclined to think actions pursuant our démarche not helpful and would make Finland's position in negotiations more difficult. Unden was sure Kekkonen sought to fulfill neutrality as far as possible. Furthermore, he was sure Kekkonen was conscious of support Finland enjoyed from outside world and also of limits of that support. Accordingly Swedish Government considered it more helpful from Finland's point of view for foreign powers not to consider any joint action.

Ambassador Parsons observed that the meeting was conducted "in the normal quiet but cool Unden manner. Regrettably his response comes as no surprise."

Following the Novosibirsk meeting, the US embassy in Helsinki on November 26 submitted via UNCLASSIFIED despatch the complete translated text of the Finnish-Soviet communiqué issued November 25 on the Kekkonen-Khrushchev talks in Novosibirsk, Siberia. The embassy summary of the communiqué stated that: (1) Khrushchev explained to Kekkonen the Soviet Government's motivation for proposing military consultations in light of the German 'threat' in the Baltic; (2) Kekkonen proposed that in order to avoid a war psychosis in Scandinavia, the Soviets not insist on military consultations; and (3) Khrushchev expressed confidence in Kekkonen, agreed to "postpone" military talks and asked Finland to watch the situation in northern Europe with a view to recommending "appropriate measures" if necessary.

The communiqué said Khrushchev "placed great value on the political experience of the president of Finland and…relied on his good will and ability to uphold and strengthen the Paasikivi-Kekkonen line of foreign policy, the line of Finnish neutrality which the Soviet Union supports."

Meanwhile, before President Kekkonen had departed for Novosibirsk, former Prime Minister Fagerholm recommended that the parties supporting the Honka coalition abandon their support in favor of the reelection of President Kekkonen. While Kekkonen was meeting with Khrushchev in Siberia, the Liberal People's Party and the Swedish People's Party announced they were leaving the Honka coalition. Soon thereafter Olavi Honka announced that he was withdrawing as a presidential candidate 'in the interest of the fatherland.'[51] In the 1962 presidential elections, President Kekkonen was easily reelected over a splintered and demoralized opposition.

The initial reaction in the State Department to the *denouement* of the 1961 Note Crisis can perhaps best be characterized by the comments of Foy D. Kohler, assistant secretary of state for European affairs, in a meeting with Swedish Ambassador Gunnar Jarring on November 27. It was recorded in a memorandum of conversation of the same date:

> Mr. Kohler said that he thought the Russian move had been blatant interference in Finnish internal affairs, and not for the first time. The danger, he suggested, is that each time it happens the Finns may become a bit more supine. He recalled that in 1959 when Khrushchev sent out invitations to 21 nations to attend a peace conference the Finns reacted quite properly by saying that if the Big Four decided to have such a

conference they would comply. But the Finnish reaction and performance this time were not as straightforward. Does this mean, he asked, that the Finns are slowly going down?

Ambassador [Jarring] suggested that Finnish fear of a Soviet request for military bases, or at least tying the Russian and Finnish radar system together, could be a reason. Mr. Kohler then said he thought the Finnish-Soviet conversations had demonstrated that the Soviet main objective, at this time, was political, as shown by the fact that the conversation concluded with Khrushchev apparently forgetting the 'German threat.'

Mr. Kohler's negative reactions characterized the U.S. government's concern over the Finnish handling of the note crisis. Nor was the United States alone in its concerns. A CONFIDENTIAL message from the U.S. embassy in Paris (Paris telegram No. 2805 of November 28, 1961) reported on French reactions to the outcome of the note crisis as follows:

In aftermath [of] Kekkonen-Khrushchev communiqué, French considerably worried over situation [in] Northern Europe, according Froment-Meurice (chief, Eastern Europe Foreign Office). Although military conversations staved off, Khrushchev has not really withdrawn demand. Froment-Meurice said he disagreed with [the] line taken yesterday by influential *Le Monde* stressing *détente* after Kekkonen trip. French analysis is that Khrushchev has already achieved certain objectives, first, in bringing about internal changes in Finland, such as elimination [of] rival of Kekkonen and pressure on Finnish conservatives (though Froment-Meurice said no evidence Khrushchev had made any moves [to] get Finnish Communists in Government.) Second, Khrushchev has served notice that Finland is [a] kind of hostage for good behavior of [the] Scandinavian countries. Subsequent steps in Scandinavia re military build up and NATO developments will be utilized by Soviets to keep heat on Finns and weaken Scandinavian ties to West. [He] said disquieting factor was Kekkonen's...failure [to] understand consequences for Finland and for other Scandinavian countries of communiqué agreed to at Novosibirsk.

FYI: As to Western policy, Froment-Meurice gave personal view that first task was to make sure that Norway and Denmark were not deflected from intended courses of actions, such as creation [of NATO] Baltic command, by Soviet pressure on Finland. Second task was to reassure Finland, when Soviets reacted to these steps, that country could count on support [of] Atlantic powers.... GAVIN

The US embassy in Helsinki reported on March 30, 1962 in "airgram" No. A-75 classified SECRET on a meeting in Helsinki between Counselor Melbourne of the U.S. embassy and Finnish Foreign Ministry political director Max Jakobson. (As an aside, an airgram was a "modernized" successor State Department reporting format to the despatch. Both forms, which were mailed in diplomatic pouches, virtually disappeared from use when technological advances permitted the automatic encryption and decoding of telegrams resulting in almost all State Department and embassy messages being transmitted electronically.)

In the meeting between Melbourne and Jakobson, the new-format "airgram" reported that Jakobson:

> ...at a luncheon meeting he had requested, told Counselor Melbourne that during the Nordic Council session he had been informed by his Swedish and Norwegian colleagues that U.S. was concerned over trend it saw in Finland toward greater Communist influence and Soviet control...Jakobson wanted [to] raise matter informally to learn if there were any U.S. apprehensions and to try to allay them.

> Jakobson remarked that since last November the trend of editorial comment in Western press, including U.S., had been pessimistic regarding Finland's independent future and, in some significant instances, seemed to take for granted that Finland was bound to come under Soviet control. He added this distinctly unhelpful to Finland if indicative [of] Western state of mind since Russians read [the] same press.

> Counselor reminded Jakobson that Western interest in November and after Kekkonen's talk with Khrushchev at Novosibirsk had been high. It obvious that Western countries were concerned that [the] Soviet move then forecast infringement on Finnish independence.

Mr. Jakobson proceeded to give a lengthy defense and explanation of Finnish policy and of President Kekkonen's attitude toward the Soviet Union and offered in the future to try in an informal manner to clear up any uncertainties that the U.S. embassy might have.

The same subject came up again the following month when Counselor Melbourne referred in a meeting with Jakobson to a conversation that had taken place in Washington between Ambassador Seppälä, Deputy Under Secretary Johnson and Assistant Secretary Kohler. The embassy reported the exchange with Jakobson in SECRET airgram No. A-252 of April 15, 1962. Jakobson said he was aware of the Washington conversation. He expressed concern that Kohler had apparently stated to Ambassador Seppälä that President Kekkonen "had gone quite a ways in his public statement on his return from Novosibirsk toward accepting [the] thesis of German menace and agreeing to being responsible for keeping his eyes on these developments."

[Jakobson] admitted in response to counselor that it could be subject to misinterpretation abroad. Jakobson said Finns, however, thought [the] president had successfully evaded acceptance [of the] Soviet thesis of German menace and any obligation to Soviets to watch developments in this connection...Significantly, although Jakobson showed himself aware of our belief that Soviets had flagrantly interfered in Finnish internal affairs, he did not endeavor to refute it. Nor did he argue with counselor when he reiterated it. Again as on other occasions Jakobson, who is undoubtedly pro-Western, gave signs of feeling that he had a difficult case to justify...

Finally, to drive home the seriousness of United States interpretations of the 1961-62 Note Crisis and its consequences, Ambassador Gufler called on Foreign Ministry Secretary General Hallama a few days later to assure that "Hallama correctly understood the nature of our concern about Finnish policy toward the Soviet Union." In embassy SECRET airgram No. A-254 of April 18, 1962, Ambassador Gufler reported that in his meeting with Hallama he had referred to the meetings in Washington between Ambassador Seppälä and senior State Department officials and to Counselor Melbourne's meetings with Max Jakobson in Helsinki. Gufler said he told Hallama that one might be led to assume that the Foreign Ministry was surprised by the reports of U.S. views about Finland's recent policy. His message was that the Finns should be under no illusion that this was some kind of misunderstanding or miscommunication. The Finns were correct when they thought they were hearing about U.S. concern and unhappiness, and they should not be surprised by these reports.

We will look further at later assessments of some of these developments in the retrospective section (Part Four) of this book. However, it was clear at the time that whatever reasons and purposes that President Kekkonen may have had in dealing with the Soviet Union and his domestic opposition the way he did in 1958-59 and in 1961-62, his actions raised serious questions in the West which later merged with other developments to contribute to the gradual emergence of the "Finlandization" epithet. Whether this was fair or not will be examined further. That the epithet emerged should not have come as a surprise.

Part One Notes

[1] This section on U.S./Finnish diplomatic relations draws heavily on Robert Rinehart, ed., *Finland & The United States—Diplomatic Relations through Seventy Years*, Washington D.C.: Institute for the Study of Diplomacy, Georgetown University, 1993.

[2] Information on the early legation sites and the construction of the new legation is taken from an informal U.S. embassy document "History of the American Embassy—Helsinki" which in turn drew from a consular log or notebook kept occasionally by the U.S. consul from 1937 until the early 1950s.

[3] Each U.S. president sends a letter of instruction to all U.S. chiefs of mission (ambassadors and chargé d'affaires) updating letters of instruction issued by his predecessor. For example, when I was chief of mission and chargé d'affaires of the United States embassy in Grenada 1988-1991, I received via official cable such a letter from President Bush dated July 10, 1990.

[4] Description of the origins of the Finns are drawn from Eino Jutikkala. "The Colonization and the Roots of the Finnish People," in *Finland: People, Nation, State*, ed. by Max Engman and David Kirby (Bloomington: Indiana University Press, 1989): 16-37.

[5] Erik Allardt, "Finland as a Nordic Society," in Engman & Kirby, pp. 212-243.

[6] Eino Jutikkala, with Kauko Pirinen, *A History of Finland*, 4th rev. ed. (Finland, Weilin & Goos, Espoo, 1984): 168. References here to developments in the period of autonomy depend heavily on *A History of Finland*, pp. 174-201.

[7] Jukka Nevakivi, "Independent Finland Between East and West," in Engman & Kirby, p.135.

[8] Ibid.

[9] Ibid.

[10] Osmo Jussila, "Finland from Province to State," in Engman & Kirby, p. 85.

[11] J. Raymond Ylitalo, *Salosanomia Helsingista Washingtoniin* (Otava, Helsinki, 1978): 268. Cites diplomatic reports.

[12] Roy Allison, *Finland's Relations with the Soviet Union 1944-84* (New York: St. Martin's Press, 1985): 13. While Allison tends to assume benign Soviet motivations and is sympathetic to most Finnish policy decisions, his well-written book is an excellent source for Cold War events and how they affected Finnish/Soviet relationships.

[13] Rush, ed. The International Situation and the Soviet Union, p. 130. Cited by Allison, p. 131.

[14] Jukka Nevakivi, "A Decisive Armistice 1944-47: Why Was Finland not Sovietized?" *Scandinavian Journal of History* 19:2 (1994): 95, 114.

[15] Ibid., p. 96.

[16] Ibid., pp. 108-9.

[17] Ibid., pp. 113-4.

[18] Hannu Rautkallio, *Suomen Sunta, 1945-48* (Savonlinna, 1979): 67-70. Cited in Allison, pp. 12-13.

[19] *Foreign Relations of the United States, 1945* (Washington, DC, 1969): IV:685. Cited in Allison, pp. 12-13.

[20] Allison, p. 26.

[21] Ibid., pp. 65-66.

[22] Citation by Jukka Nevakivi, in Engman & Kirby, p.70

[23] Kekkonen and Paasikivi quotes in Allison, p. 17.

[24] The Conference at Quebec, 1944, joint chiefs of staff to secretary of state, September 12, 1944, enc. 1, pp. 399-401, quoted in Geir Lundestad, *America, Scandinavia, and the Cold War, 1945-49* (Oslo: Universitetsforlaget, 1980): 38. Lundestad provides a comprehensive examination of U.S./ Scandinavian relations during the early Cold War years. Finland is not a specific focus of his book.

[25] Ibid., pp. 39-40.

[26] Ibid., p. 250.

[27] Ibid., p. 251

[28] Ibid., p. 261.

[29] Lundestad has an excellent detailed review of the delicate negotiations regarding Scandinavian participation in NATO, pp. 235-328.

[30] Finn Sollie, "The Significance of the Northern Region," in *Clash in the North*, ed. by Walter Goldstein (Washington, D.C.: International Defense Publishers, 1986): 136.

[31] Finn Sollie, "The Soviet Challenge in Northern Waters—Implications for Resources and Security," in *The Arctic Challenge*, Kari Möttölä, ed. (Boulder and London: Westview Press, 1988): 95.

[32] Except where noted otherwise, these figures and the data on Soviet military strength in the Northern Region presented in the following paragraphs are cited by John C. Ausland, *Nordic Security and the Great Powers* (Boulder and London: Westview Press, 1986): 100-110.

[33] Eric Grove, "The Norwegian Sea—NATO's First Line of Defense," in *NATO's Defence of the North*, ed. by Eric Grove (London: Brassey's, 1988): 2.

[34] Ausland, p. 109.

[35] Nils Morten Udgaard, "Norwegian Foreign Policy and Regional Security," in *Clash in the North*, p. 154.

[36] Kalevi Ruhala, "Finland's Security Policy: The Arctic Dimension," in *The Arctic Challenge*, p. 119.

[37] Tonne Huitfeldt, *NATO and the Northern Flank* (Oslo: Research Center for Defense Studies, 1986): 20-21.

[38] Udgaard, p. 155.

[39] Ibid., p. 165.

[40] See Raymond Ylitalo.

[41] Martti Häikio, *A Brief History of Modern Finland* (University of Helsinki, Lahti Research and Training Center, 1992): 44-45.

[42] Jukka Nevakivi, "Postwar Finnish Neutrality and U.S. Interests," in Rinehart, p. 71. Nevakivi cites a National Archives document which I did not myself see in the files in 1995.

[43] Words considered unessential to understanding the meaning of U.S. embassy telegraphic messages were usually eliminated in the drafting and transmission of telegraphed texts in the days when encryption and decoding of telegrams was a labor intensive endeavor. This was the case in the1960s and well into the 1970s. "Telegraphese" was not always easy to follow, so I have taken the liberty of inserting in brackets missing words that I think contribute to easier reading of the messages.

[44] See Chapter 25 below for an account by Dr. Juhani Suomi of how outraged President Kekkonen was that the U.S. would offer economic support to Finland.

[45] For example, see Nevakivi in Engman & Kirby, p. 143.

[46] Dean Rusk, as told to Richard Rusk, *As I Saw It* (New York: W.W. Norton & Co., 1990): 219.

[47] Ibid., p. 221.

[48] Ibid., pp. 221-226, 253-54.

[49] Raimo Väyrynen, Conflicts in Finnish-Soviet Relations: Three Comparative Case Studies (Tampere: Tampereen Yliopisto, 1972): 92.

[50] It is sometimes forgotten that of the thousands of diplomatic telegrams sent out annually from the Department of State over the name of the secretary of state, only a relative handful are actually seen and personally approved by the secretary. All of the others are assumed to be telegrams that are sufficiently within U.S. policy guidelines as to permit their authorization by lower levels of the State Department hierarchy.

[51] Häikio, p. 53.

PART TWO

1976-79:
ON THE FINLAND WATCH
AS NEW U.S. EMBASSY
POLITICAL COUNSELOR

7

Ambassador Mark Austad's Embassy

The American ambassador to Finland when I walked into the embassy in July 1976 to assume my responsibilities as chief of the political section was Mark Evans Austad, a non-career ambassador who had been appointed by President Ford in February 1975. Ambassador Austad had experienced a long and multi-faceted career, including having been a radio personality in Washington, D.C. under the name of Mark Evans. He had come to the Republican Party and President Ford's attention for having organized some of the events at President Nixon's second inauguration. His reward was to be appointed United States ambassador to Finland. That's how these things work in the U.S. political system.

Ambassador Austad, despite having never before served in a diplomatic or foreign policy capacity, brought some real strengths to his new position. He was, above all, a master communicator, indeed, a communications professional from his media days and from his lecturing experience. By the time I arrived, he had become a celebrity in Finland who was much commented on in the media and in official circles. Not a trained diplomat, he successfully endeavored to turn his media skills and celebrity status to his advantage. He reveled in being a highly public and outspoken promoter of the United States in Finland and in promoting United States/Finnish ties. A big, good-looking, hearty man who turned sixty while serving in Finland, Ambassador Austad became the darling of the trendy and popular "general" magazines and tabloid newspapers.

The ambassador was assisted in making a considerable public impact in Finland by his formidable speaking skills. While he spoke no Finnish, he developed a highly effective speaking technique, in the execution of which he relied on one or two favorite Finnish interpreters. He would get up before a Finnish audience (word of an Austad speaking engagement would usually assure a sizeable crowd) and would begin speaking about U.S./Finnish ties and shared values. His technique would be to speak movingly in English for three or four short sentences. The excellent interpreter would then repeat the phrases in Finnish, accurately reflecting the mood and emotion that Ambassador Austad had imparted. Austad would then proceed to the next few sentences, which would then be repeated in Finnish, and then to the next, and so on. Before long the audience would get caught up in the emotion of Ambassador Austad's deep-voiced delivery, and the almost hypnotic rhythm and sequencing as the ambassador and his interpreter would bounce their phrases back and forth.

The rhythm and emotion of it reminded me of what one could hear from a first-class American preacher in full stride. His standard stump speech (and that is essentially what it was, the diplomatic equivalent of a U.S. political campaign speech) invariably would end with a tribute to Finnish/American ties, veiled references to the dangers to Finland from the East, a stirring assertion that Finland could always count on the United States, a hand gesture from the podium toward the American and Finnish flags flanking the speakers table, and a closing rhetorical question. "Don't they look beautiful standing side-by-side; let's forever keep them together!" Sustained and boisterous applause would almost invariably follow.

Official Finland and the "serious" media scarcely knew what to make of Mark Austad. They considered him a substantive lightweight who was not particularly well read and who had little specific expertise on the key issues of the day nor on the Nordic region and the Soviet Union. It is difficult for me to take serious issue with these judgements, which were right on the mark, so to speak. These "serious" Finnish observers were highly concerned over his "take it to the people," unorthodox, non-traditional diplomatic style. They were taken aback by his vigorous, unrelenting protests over what he considered, rightly in the view of the rest of us in the American embassy, was a slanted and biased portrayal of American society and foreign policy by important segments of the Finnish media, particularly the government-owned radio and television stations.

The government-owned but quasi-independent TV and radio stations run by the government public broadcasting corporation *Yleisradio* would often run highly critical documentaries about the United States, produced in other European countries or, even, self-critical pieces produced in the United States. Seldom were these negative reports balanced by more upbeat reporting on positive accomplishments. We used to joke wryly in the embassy that *Yleisradio's* idea of balance was to run a highly negative documentary on the United States produced in France, and follow that with a highly negative documentary on the United States produced in America!

Ambassador Austad complained bitterly that the Finnish people were getting an unfair and inaccurate view of the United States from the Finnish media, which was at the same time almost totally uncritical of the Soviet Union and often laudatory of Soviet policies.

Before my arrival in Finland, he was once invited to appear on an *Yleisradio* television news program in which the TV current events directors must have expected they would show Austad up for being the inexperienced and uninformed amateur they undoubtedly believed him to be. Instead, Austad went right over the heads of his interviewers, looking straight into the TV camera and speaking directly to the Finnish people, telling them they were not receiving an accurate picture of the U.S. society from much of the Finnish media, citing examples and correcting the record.

The television appearance from the embassy's perspective was a complete success. In what must be considered as a major miscalculation by Austad's Finnish media critics, the interview had the effect of making Austad an even bigger celebrity in Finland than he had been before. Even "serious" Finns would come up to him and to other embassy officers to congratulate Austad for having put down so effectively the haughty leftists who dominated *Yleisradio* during those years. Moreover, Austad's intervention on TV seemed to have had a modest moderating influence on editorial decisions by *Yleisradio* on what kinds of programs about the United States to show on Finnish television. However, it wasn't until sometime later, after the departure from *Yleisradio* of its director Eino S. Repo and of his successor Erkki Raatikainen, that some semblance of objectivity began to be noted in *Yleisradio* programming.

Many representatives of the Finnish media deeply resented Austad's criticism of them. At the same time, however, it seemed clear that Finnish governmental officials recognized they were dealing with someone who had established an unusual rapport with the Finnish public, and they treated Ambassador Austad with considerable tact, even with kid gloves.

Ambassador Austad and President Kekkonen developed a cordial, even warm, "man-to-man" relationship, and the ambassador had frequent access to private meetings with the president. Unfortunately, not a lot of substance came out of such meetings. While there was much manly camaraderie and good-natured joking, not much business was transacted nor serious issues discussed. I accompanied Ambassador Austad on a call on the president on November 3, 1976. The meeting had been scheduled for some time, but by coincidence it took place the day after the U.S. presidential election in which Jimmy Carter defeated President Ford. Ambassador Austad knew that being a political appointee, he soon would be replaced following Carter's inauguration, and he was in a down mood.

In his meeting that day at Tamminiemi, the president's official residence, with President Kekkonen, the two chatted about the U.S. elections, joked about each other's neckties, and shared some morning liquid cheer. While the meeting with Kekkonen produced little of substance, it was evident to me that the two men simply liked and respected each other. The meeting cheered Austad up considerably.

President Kekkonen's fondness for Ambassador Austad was dramatically demonstrated a few days later on November 8 at a reception in the Soviet embassy celebrating the Bolshevik Revolution. The annual Soviet embassy reception was a virtual command performance for important Finns. To receive an invitation was an indication that the Finn was seen to be on good terms with the Soviet embassy, a vital factor for the prospects of one's political career in the Finland of those years.

President Kekkonen almost invariably attended the annual Soviet embassy reception (in contrast, he seldom attended the annual United States embassy's July 4th reception or the receptions of other countries). On this occasion, as was his custom, President Kekkonen did not make an appearance until at least one hour into the reception. The large and ornate Soviet embassy on *Tehtaankatu* street was jam-packed with most of the guests on the upper floor in a huge ballroom awaiting Kekkonen's arrival. I was there along with two or three other senior U.S. embassy officers and, of course, Ambassador Austad. Austad was standing well into the ball room with his back to the entrance chatting with other guests when President Kekkonen entered the ball room, accompanied by Soviet Ambassador Vladimir Stepanov.

Austad did not at first notice Kekkonen's arrival. Upon entering the room, the president spotted Austad, left the official receiving group, including Ambassador Stepanov, and strode some thirty feet over to Austad, who by now from the hush of the crowd knew something was up and was turning around toward the entrance. The Finnish president reached Austad's position, and, standing there in the Soviet embassy with all eyes fixed on him, proceeded to slap Austad on the back and give a hearty "Mark, nice to see you, how are you" greeting. There was a brief exchange, following which President Kekkonen returned to the unhappy-looking Soviet ambassador leaving behind a beaming Ambassador Austad. The incident speaks volumes for the relationship that existed between the two men. It no doubt also reflected a deliberate Kekkonen intention to slap down the arrogant Stepanov whose heavy-handed interventionism into Finnish internal affairs was notorious and increasingly obvious.

The ambassador for his part was very high on President Kekkonen, and he strongly discouraged negative reporting from the embassy calling into question any of Kekkonen's positions or actions. This caused no little difficulty within the embassy as President Kekkonen, as commented on in the previous chapter, undertook a number of actions over his unprecedented twenty-six year presidency that were not necessarily viewed well in the West. Intellectual honesty, objectivity, balance and judgement are essential ingredients of responsible embassy analysis and reporting which in turn is a principal information source for Washington in the formulation of United States foreign policy. These principles required that all of the gray areas of the Finnish reality be examined and reported along with the good and commendable. This should include reporting on questionable domestic political developments as well as Finnish foreign policy positions at odds with U.S. interests.

This issue remained a problem throughout Ambassador Austad's tenure as ambassador. It was aggravated by continuing tension between the ambassador and his deputy chief of mission, Robert Houston. Houston had a rather negative outlook on Finland's foreign policy and domestic political situation. The word soon got out among the Finns that Houston was not as sympathetic as most Finns thought he should be to their situation. As political counselor, I soon found myself caught between the personal and philosophical differences between the ambassador and his DCM. My own views of the Finnish scene were still in the process of formation, but instinctively I was not as blue-eyed and positive as the ambassador nor as negative and pessimistic as DCM Houston.

It became awkward for me professionally when, at one point, the ambassador called me in and directed me not to take DCM Houston's views on political matters into consideration as I prepared my political analyses. The fact that it was Bob Houston who prepared my annual "efficiency report" did not make my position any easier. Ambassador Austad meanwhile apparently proscribed Houston from sending in substantive political reports of his own. I learned from that experience that an embassy cannot function effectively unless there is a close and mutually supportive relationship between the ambassador and DCM.

The relationship between Austad and Houston was never resolved. In retrospect, Houston deserved more credit than he received for pointing out some of the negative dimensions associated with the term "Finlandization" which Austad did not want reported. On the other hand, as events have shown, Houston seems to have been unduly pessimistic about Finland's being on the "slippery slope to socialism," as some of us in the embassy jokingly but with some exaggeration characterized his general outlook.

The tendency of Ambassador Austad to ride roughshod over his staff was also demonstrated by his poor relations with the embassy's information officer, Richard Gilbert, whose responsibilities brought him into daily contact with those in the Finnish media whom Austad considered the enemy. Gilbert's efforts to rein in some of the ambassador's more egregious efforts to teach the Finnish media a lesson earned him a kind of "guilt by association" label and a high position on Ambassador Austad's enemy list. The fact that Gilbert's personal political views were more liberal than those of the staunch Republican ambassador exacerbated their professional disagreements. Austad went so far as to question Gilbert's patriotism and to lodge criticisms of Gilbert with personnel authorities in Washington in a clear and grossly unfair effort to damage his career. All in all, it was not an easy time within the embassy.

Notwithstanding such difficulties, the embassy under Mark Austad was always interesting. Among his many talents was his experience as a producer of travel documentaries, and he had a long association with the National Geographic Society and its magazine. In what may have been a "first" in diplomatic history, Ambassador Austad undertook to record on film his adventures in Finland with the intention of hitting the American lecture circuit with his film presentation upon the conclusion of his ambassadorship.

However, it was clear he was in no hurry. Austad loved being the U.S. ambassador to Finland and was loath to leave. He even came to hope that his popularity in Finland would lead to President Carter's asking him to stay on despite the fact that he was a Ford appointee. I have been told that Austad organized the sending of messages to the Carter White House from certain high level Finns urging that Austad be kept in place. Notwithstanding these efforts, he was soon recalled by President Carter.

Prior to his departure, Ambassador Austad gave a few private and public showings of his highly laudatory documentary on Finland, not incidentally placing himself and his efforts in a most positive light. The Finns, once again, did not quite know how to deal with the Austad film. It was so complimentary and favorable as to be almost embarrassing to sophisticated Finns. On the other hand, the film clearly was a highly positive public relations coup for Finland, given that Austad intended to take his show around the United States, which is what he did.

Most Finns were not about to look a gift horse in the mouth and, despite their embarrassment on one level, they were pleased to have such a flattering picture of their country given such high visibility in the United States. In addition, Ambassador Austad undertook to work in favor of Finnish interests back in the United States, for example promising to use his influence on the perennial issue of trying to convince the United States Coast Guard to purchase a Finnish ice-breaker. It is my understanding that he was to be compensated for his lobbying efforts on Finland's behalf in Washington, although I have no specific information on this aspect.

And so, Mark Austad departed Finland in April 1977. He was later to re-emerge in the Reagan administration as the U.S. ambassador to Norway. I had several occasions to see Ambassador Austad in those later years. He was quick to offer that, even though he was of Norwegian descent, he was never as comfortable or happy in Norway as he had been during his ambassadorial tenure in Finland. Somehow, his personality and talents seemed less pleasing to the Norwegians than to the Finns. Austad did not seem to be able to achieve the celebrity status in Norway that he had in Finland. For whatever reasons, Ambassador Austad always spoke nostalgically about his heady days in Finland. I can certainly sympathize with him on that perception.

8

Getting Started as Political Counselor

Having settled my family into our new house and our children into their new schools, I turned my attention to getting on top of my new assignment as political counselor. It was a position I took most seriously. In the U.S. Foreign Service there is a certain rank ordering of geographical areas of the world in terms of prestige of assignments. Latin America was fine for those who like political turmoil and enjoy, as we did, the Latin American culture and society. The Middle East had strong appeal to a certain group of self-styled Arabists who fought over assignments to Damascus or Amman. The Far East had its loyal group of specialists who would ponder the mysteries of oriental inscrutability. North Africa had its devotees who thrived in places like Casablanca and Tripoli and other cities that conjured up images of old Humphrey Bogart movies. Sub-Sahara Africa probably was the least sought-after area of specialty, but it did attract a number of dedicated Africanists.

However, there was no doubt that Europe stood highest in the Foreign Service order of preference, considering its importance to United States interests during the Cold War years as well as its desirability from the point of view of overseas living. Within Europe there were, of course, gradations of desirability. Eastern Europe was considered the preserve of dedicated cold warriors who thrived on the deprivations of living behind the Iron Curtain and doing daily battle with the "Evil Empire". Soviet specialists, of course, competed mightily for assignments to Moscow, given the centrality of the Cold War in United States policy considerations.

For most Foreign Service Officers, however, Western Europe was clearly the most desirable and prestigious place to be, particularly in one of the major capitals like London, Paris, Rome or Bonn. The Nordic area was considered a part of Western Europe but somewhat removed from the mainstream. Nordic countries thus did not place as high as some of their Western European neighbors as a desirable career option for most FSOs. This was particularly true of Finland with its easterly location and seemingly indecipherable language.

However, Finland was Western Europe as far as I was concerned and offered me the opportunity to prove I could hold my own with the Europeanist FSOs who looked somewhat askance at those who had spent most of their careers, as I had, on Latin American assignments. I was determined to prove myself. My top priorities, in addition to working on the Finnish language, were twofold. First, to develop my Finnish contacts in the Finnish Ministry for Foreign Affairs (MFA) and among Finnish political and opinion leaders; and, second, to establish a work program and reporting schedule that would give a sense of direction to the political section's reporting and analysis efforts and provide a framework within which individual reports could be placed in perspective.

In an August 1976 memorandum to the ambassador and DCM, I proposed that from then until the summer of 1977 the political section—with particular focus on Ward Thompson and myself—should aim at preparing reports focusing on parliamentary developments, the coming municipal elections and their significance, Finland's incomes policy, Finnish/Soviet relations and Finland's performance in international agencies. I also proposed that we continue a series of analyses of Finland's political parties, one-by-one. Also, we would prepare two reports required annually by Washington, the yearly labor report and the embassy's annual policy assessment. In addition to these scheduled analyses, the political section would also prepare "spot reports" on significant developments as they occurred. The ambassador and DCM approved my proposed reporting program. It proved to be a bit more than we could fully deliver on, but it helped to focus our priorities and to keep us from being diverted from our principal reporting targets.

As political counselor, reporting in the embassy to the DCM and the ambassador, I had to carefully select my Finnish contacts. I had to be sensitive both to what my superiors in the embassy would consider to be appropriate contacts as well as to what level of contact would be considered suitable by the Finns. Cabinet ministers and the most senior MFA officials, for example, considered themselves as meriting the direct attention of the ambassador or DCM rather than a political counselor.

Initially, therefore, I concentrated in the Foreign Ministry on those levels I could reach comfortably without offending anyone. It was my hope and expectation—which proved correct—that I would soon be able to extend my contacts up the line in the foreign ministry while retaining good contacts at the practical working level. The question of with whom I would take contact depended upon the issues that were to be discussed. As the embassy's political counselor, I often would ask for appointments with the MFA to discuss European security issues—particularly questions relating to the Conference on Security and Cooperation in Europe (CSCE) and arms control matters. Additionally, there were multilateral political issues, such as pending UN votes about which we would explain our positions to Finland and urge that Finland vote this way or that.

Officials of the Finnish MFA were invariably well informed on the issues under their responsibility. I often would be raising issues under instructions from the Department of State and would sometimes have no information on the subject at hand, for example the latest UN issue coming up for a vote, beyond that which had been provided me in the cable of instructions from the Department. I would frequently learn more from my MFA interlocutor about the matter under discussion than I had been informed about in my instructions. As time went on, I developed excellent relationships and even friendships with my MFA colleagues. Contacts were for the most part easy and comfortable. However, it was always clear to me that the Finnish officials strictly adhered to Finnish positions that had been agreed within the MFA, friendship or no friendship.

This, of course, was as it should be and was true of my positions as well.

One of my first official calls in Helsinki was on foreign policy advisor to President Kekkonen, Jaakko Kalela. I was aware that Kalela's appointment by the Center Party (formerly Agrarian Party) veteran President Urho Kekkonen had been greeted with some surprise, even concern, because of Kalela's background in Social Democratic intellectual circles which had been quite critical of Finland's security policy. He had been associated with a school of thought that had urged less reliance on Finnish military preparedness in favor of closer security cooperation with the Soviet Union. Within two weeks of my arrival in Helsinki I invited Kalela to lunch at the attractive Bellevue restaurant in Helsinki, beginning what was to prove to be a series of frequent, most agreeable and informative get-togethers, both formal and informal, that lasted throughout both of my assignments to Finland.

In addition to developing my MFA and other official Government of Finland contacts, I set about getting to know the appropriate people in the Finnish political parties. In this regard I was determined to reach anyone who would be prepared to meet with me. I began by calling on political party secretaries and general secretaries. Among my earliest contacts were Ulf Sundqvist and Paavo Lipponen of the Social Democratic Party, Vilho Koiranen and Veikko Tavastila of the National Coalition (also called Conservative) Party, Mikko Immonen of the Center Party and Kalevi Viljanen of the Liberal Party. Sundqvist and Lipponen were to remain close SDP contacts during both of my assignments to Finland. Immonen was also one of my closest contacts, and we held many an interesting discussion over lunch or after tennis. I also made it a point to call on Veikko Vennamo, chairman of the Rural Party; Raino Westerholm, chairman of the Christian League; Georg C. Ehrnrooth, chairman of the Constitutionalist Party; and Henry Wiklund, secretary of the Swedish Party.

In short order I was able to develop a good relationship with Harri Holkeri, chairman of the National Coalition Party, which has endured over the years. I also made a formal call at the parliament on Prime Minister Kalevi Sorsa who was also chairman of the Social Democratic Party. Over the years I was to see Mr. Sorsa from time to time usually in connection with his meetings with U.S. ambassadors. I accepted that owing to his high positions in government (usually during my assignments he was either prime minister or foreign minister) his usual contacts in the embassy were with the ambassador. I also found that the Center Party leaders above the rank of party secretary Immonen were difficult to reach. I would see three of the party's top leaders, Johannes Virolainen, Ahti Karjalainen and Paavo Väyrynen, from time to time to time mostly in conjunction with their meetings with the U.S. ambassador or at other official dinners or receptions.

I will never forget my first meeting with Ahti Karjalainen, one of the handful of Finnish politicians considered to be a potential successor to President Kekkonen. It was at an October 20, 1976 reception at the East German embassy, some three months after I had arrived in Finland. I noticed at one point Karjalainen standing alone, so I walked up to him and introduced myself as the new political counselor at the American embassy. We chatted pleasantly for a few minutes, and I complimented him on his English. He shot me a quizzical look, which I noticed but did not understand, and then resumed the conversation normally. It was only sometime later that I learned of the standard Finnish jokes circulating poking fun at Karjalainen's rather limited English skills. Karjalainen had obviously wondered if I was pulling his leg when I had complimented him on his English. In fact I wasn't, not being aware at the time of the jokes about Karjalainen's English. I had simply wanted to flatter him; I was always flattered when some Finn complimented me on my Finnish, notwithstanding its limitations!

One of the proposals in my August memorandum to the ambassador and DCM on political section priorities was that the section establish contacts with the Finnish Communist Party (SKP) and with the broader electoral front, the Finnish Peoples Democratic League (SKDL), as we did with the other political parties. I had concluded shortly after my arrival in Helsinki that the embassy political section did not have adequate direct contact with the SKP, even though developments within the party, by then a frequent partner in Finnish coalition governments, were considered important and closely watched by the embassy—from a distance. There was a sense in the embassy that direct contact with members of the SKP might be construed as constituting embassy endorsement of the party as a government partner or in some other way imply U.S. approval. This was at the time when the question of a political "opening to the left", i.e., to the Communist parties in Italy and France, was being hotly debated in Washington.

My embassy superiors told me that my proposal could not be authorized without prior Washington approval. Somehow, I was able a short time later to get an unofficial green light from the State Department's office of Northern European affairs, and I initiated some contacts. I proceeded to call on Aarne Saarinen, chairman of the Finnish Communist Party. I also met and kept periodic contact with Jorma Hentilä, then secretary of the SKDL.

With respect to my first appointment with Saarinen, I recall being somewhat nervous upon arriving at the Communist Party offices and being greeted with curious glances when I announced myself as the political counselor of the American embassy. When I was ushered into Mr. Saarinen's pleasant office, he greeted me—in Finnish—in a professional but friendly manner. In my crude Finnish, I said that I understood there had not been much contact between the American embassy and the SKP in the past. I then explained why I thought it important that the embassy be able to hear directly from the SKP about its positions on matters of national and international significance.

He agreed that we get together occasionally to exchange views, even though there would undoubtedly be many points upon which we would disagree. From that point on we met from time to time which I found very helpful and informative. As with a number of other friends and contacts mentioned above, I was pleased when I returned to Finland in 1995 to do research on this book to be able to have a lengthy interview with Mr. Saarinen.

I also made it a point to get to know a good number of members of Parliament from the various political parties and established periodic contacts with many of them.

Outside of the political arena (narrowly interpreted), I was anxious to establish useful contacts with key media observers and opinion leaders. My two most important contacts in this regard were Dr. Jan-Magnus Jansson, then the distinguished editor-in-chief of Finland's leading Swedish-language newspaper, *Hufvudstadsbladet,* and a leading Finnish political figure in his own right, and Ambassador Max Jakobson, then head of the Finnish business organization known as EVA which served as a think tank for the Finnish private sector. Jakobson had earlier been Finnish ambassador to the United Nations and a principal Foreign Ministry policy-making figure. I was very pleased to be able to meet regularly with both of these keen observers of the Finnish and international scene, establishing relationships that have lasted to this day.

Among other outstanding "non-political" relationships that I was able to establish early, and which I have highly valued over the years, was with one of my best friends, Per-Erik Lönnfors of *Hufvudstadsbladet* and later of the Finnish News Service (STT). Additionally, my contacts included Simopekka Nortamo and Olli Kivinen of *Helsingin Sanomat,* General Aimo Pajunen, Kari Nars, then of EVA and now with the Ministry of Finance, Juha Sipilä, then of EVA and now with the Helsinki Metropolitan Council, Paavo Laitinen, former diplomat and then with Union Bank, and Aarno Laitinen, journalist and author. These contacts helped broaden my understanding of Finland and Finnish current events.

As the holder of a Master's Degree in Political Science from Cornell University who had considered a university teaching career before joining the Foreign Service, I made it a point to get to know members of the Finnish academic community, particularly those interested in international relations. Among the numerous contacts I made in this area were Kari Möttölä, Osmo Apunen, George Maude, and Göran Von Bornsdorff. A number of other Finnish academicians had already found their way into important official government positions in Finland, such as Klaus Törnudd, Juhani Suomi, Keijo Korhonen, Jaakko Blomberg, Pauli Järvenpää and Jaakko Kalela.

Another dimension of my responsibilities and activities as political counselor was to represent the American embassy at periodic meetings of embassy counselors of NATO countries represented in Helsinki. At these meetings we would exchange information about developments in Europe and in Finland relevant to NATO's interests. We would also compare notes and exchange gossip about political developments in Finland. In and outside of these meetings I maintained particularly close contacts with my counterparts from the British, French, West German, Canadian, Belgian, Danish, Norwegian and Italian embassies. These meetings and contacts outside the meetings were very agreeable socially and most useful professionally. I also maintained close contact with my counterparts in the always well-informed Swedish embassy.

It might well be asked, what was the significance of my frequent contacts with a cross-section of politically significant Finns? What would we talk about? Why would Finns from the political parties, the media, academia and others want to sit down and discuss issues with an American diplomat? Was I acting as some kind of a spy, trying to pry national secrets out of them? What were they attempting to learn from me? These questions get at the very core of the diplomatic function and of the value of well-qualified professional diplomatic presence in each other's countries.

Diplomatic exchanges—whether formal exchanges between embassy officers and officials of the Finnish Ministry for Foreign Affairs or informal discussions between embassy officers and representatives of Finnish political parties or the media—present the opportunity for an exchange of information. To sit down at a leisurely lunch with Harri Holkeri or Paavo Lipponen provided me with an opportunity to learn their personal views and the official views of the organizations they represented regarding national or international developments of the day.

They or Mikko Immonen or Jorma Hentilä would tell me what they thought of the current government situation or of the latest tension between East and West. I would give them my own assessment of how the United States government viewed an emerging crisis in the Middle East, or why we were concerned with the latest initiative regarding a Nordic Nuclear Weapon-Free Zone. I would discuss with them political developments in the United States, who Jimmy Carter was and why he might have a chance to defeat Gerald Ford in the 1976 elections. Maybe I would ask what was behind the latest resignation of the Center Party minority government or why the Social Democrats had decided to go into opposition. Maybe Holkeri would describe how the National Coalition Party was preparing for the 1979 parliamentary elections. I might give the U.S. view on the 1979 NATO two-track decision regarding the deployment of INF intermediate range nuclear missiles in Europe.

It was a two-way street. Unless my counterparts left a meeting feeling that they had effectively explained their perspectives and had learned something from me about U.S. positions, the get-together would have been a waste of time and they would "not be available" the next time I requested a meeting. Occasionally I would find a meeting so unproductive and the interlocutor so unresponsive that I would cross that person off my list of persons I wanted to meet with.

I loved this part of Foreign Service work. The idea that my government would pay me—and even cover the cost of lunch—to have an interesting conversation with a knowledgeable Finn struck me almost as receiving unfair benefits! Modesty aside, my meeting partners also seemed usually to find our meetings and luncheons entertaining and informative as well, judging from the way I was able to strike up relationships that continued over the years.

I made an effort to stay in touch with all of the above friends and contacts, both Finns and foreign diplomats through meetings, business luncheons and social events. Magda and I would have frequent dinner parties, small receptions and occasional larger receptions to be able to entertain our friends and to maintain contacts. It was part of our job, Uncle Sam paid for it, and we enjoyed it! We began to receive numerous invitations as well. It was through these kinds of contacts, supplemented by the meetings and social events hosted by the ambassador or DCM and by periodic trips outside of Helsinki, that I attempted to learn what was going on in Finland politically and to keep abreast of trends in Finnish society.

Maintaining relationships with my numerous Finnish professional contacts, supplemented by the personal and professional contacts made through my wife, created a very heavy schedule. Staying in touch with friends and contacts and learning about and understanding what was going on in Finland was only part of the process. The task was incomplete without analyzing this information and reporting to Washington political and foreign policy developments in Finland and their implications for United States interests.

It was demanding work but, as I say, fun and fascinating at the same time. I laugh to myself when I hear the know-nothings in Washington and in the American political parties who consider embassies and diplomats unnecessary and irrelevant in this age of instant communication and CNN. Or those who still believe that you can put any political ambassador into an embassy and that magically he or she will produce informed and accurate assessments about what of importance is going on in a country.

How can this, I would like to know, substitute for having trained and professional observers living in a country like Finland over a period of years, developing trusted contacts, digging into the country's history and society, understanding its processes, its political culture and assessing significant developments and providing policy recommendations for Washington decision-makers? We may not have been always right in the embassy in our assessments (I would assert that our record was pretty good) but we certainly knew what we were trying to do and how to go about doing it. And the Finnish embassy is doing the same thing in Washington that we tried to do in Helsinki, although having to operate within a far less manageable and coherent political universe. That is what diplomats do—provide the diplomatic reporting and expertise that constitute the fundamental building blocks in foreign policy formulation.

9

Important Issues Leading Into the Late 1970s

In the years following the Night Frost and Note Crisis episodes, embassy reporting continued to closely follow a number of thematic issues in Finland's foreign and domestic affairs. Internal developments and divisions within the Social Democratic Party (SDP) and the Finnish Communist Party (SKP) were frequent and predictable recurring themes. Another subject was the struggle for control of the Finnish trade union movement between the traditional Social Democratic Party, on the one hand, and the "Skogists" or "Simonists" and Communists on the other hand. Selections from a handful of the hundreds of embassy reports over the following years give an accurate sense of embassy views of developments in these and other areas leading up to the mid-1970s when I arrived on the scene.

Regarding the Social Democratic Party, in 1962 and 1963 the embassy submitted a series of reports examining the breach in the SDP and in the labor movement. Several were written by political/labor officer Ted Sellin who later returned to Helsinki as political counselor. In CONFIDENTIAL embassy despatch No. 620 of April 15, 1962, Sellin reported a conversation with Olavi Saarinen, Secretary of the Confederation of Finnish Trade Unions (SAK), in which Saarinen commented favorably on the prospects for re-unification of the Social Democratic and Skogist parties but thought that such reunification would not prompt a similar re-merger of factions in the trade union movement.

Later in 1962, Sellin reported in CONFIDENTIAL embassy airgram No. A-424 of November 25 that:

efforts to achieve some kind of *modus vivendi* between the Social Democratic Party and the Social Democratic Opposition (Skogist) Party are continuing. The desire for some kind of reconciliation and eventual reunion of the two groups appears to stem largely from the Skogist Party. A scheme for reunion has been drawn up by Director of Schools Raino Oittinen...[who is] close to the Skogists...Among other things, Oittinen's plan does not call for the deposition of any of the so-called right-wing elements of the Social Democrats. The reunion proposals were given to Social Democratic Party Chairman Vaino Tanner...who has decided to ignore the proposals completely.

The embassy prepared a long and thoughtful analysis of the 26th Congress of the SDP in 1963, calling the congress, which marked the retirement of party chairman Vaino Tanner, "one of the most significant milestones in the history of the party" (embassy A-21 of July 16, 1963, written by political officer Harvey Nelson.) In the embassy's view, "in light of the party's misfortunes," the congress focussed on building the party's unity, improving its organizational efficiency, and giving it a more radical image. Addressing the SDP's image problem with the USSR, the report noted that in addition to Tanner's retirement because of age, "it seems highly likely that implacable Soviet opposition to Leskinen was partially responsible for the decision to leave Leskinen out of the leadership.... [The] "mild-mannered and conciliatory Rafael Passio...easily won election as Tanner's replacement."

Subsequent embassy reporting over the years recorded the steps in the Finnish Social Democratic Party's ultimately successful quest for acceptance by President Kekkonen and the USSR as a suitable party for government responsibilities. Paasio led the party back into government in 1966. The embassy reported on Prime Minister Paasio's historic visit to Moscow in November 1966 and his decision not to meet with officials of the Commust Party of the Soviet Union (CPSU).

The embassy also reported (embassy A-338 of February 7, 1967, written by political officer Eric Fleisher) on SDP Secretary Erkki Raatikainen's speech in Tampere on January 30 in which, according to the embassy:

Raatikainen (1) called for the re-election of President Kekkonen, preferably by passage of a special law in Parliament; (2) emphasized the importance to the Social Democratic Party of maintaining the present [popular front] coalition in office; (3) stated that the Social Democratic Party's relations with the East are not entirely satisfactory; and (4) said that the Finnish Social Democratic Party would take the lead in the Socialist International in proposing that relations be established between western social democratic parties and the Communist parties of Communist countries.

A February 21, 1968 CONFIDENTIAL airgram (Helsinki A-303 drafted by political/labor officer Paul Canney) assessed the situation within the SDP following the January 1968 presidential elections in which SDP voter support plummeted. Citing party sources, the embassy report said that factors in the poor SDP turnout were: that the SDP supported Kekkonen in the campaign and did not put up its own candidate; the unpopularity of Kekkonen among SDP voters; an element of protest against growing unemployment and the government's economic policies; dissatisfaction among many Social Democrats "over party secretary Raatikainen's policies, particularly his efforts to move the party to the left and his advocacy of increased government control over the Finnish economy;" and a belief among some Social Democrats that a vote for the Kekkonen electoral alliance would mean endorsement of communist participation in government.

On March 14, 1968 the embassy submitted a lengthy report, "Evaluation of the Social Democratic Party and Its Policies" (embassy A-339, prepared by Eric Fleisher). It took as its point of departure the fact that on January 31 the SDP party council announced the party had received an invitation to send a delegation to Moscow:

The Social Democrats have been waiting for this invitation for more than a year. Paasio's visit at the head of a Finnish Government delegation in November 1966 had failed to establish a satisfactory relationship between the Social Democratic Party and the Soviets.

The airgram analyzed the SDP's relations with the East and Secretary Raatikainen's initiative to establish relations between the Finnish SDP and the communist parties of Eastern Europe. The embassy report noted the Social Democrats believed that in the long run such a direct relationship with the Soviet CPSU would break the monopoly that the Center Party had in this field through President Kekkonen. The embassy message observed there was a strong feeling at all levels of the party that:

> Paasio can handle relations with the Soviets and prevent party-to-party relations from deteriorating into a chain of command from Moscow...[and] that such a relationship with the Soviet Communist Party would be valuable to the Social Democratic Party in its efforts to obtain support from those left wing elements who are uncomfortable with what they consider the Finnish Communist Party's and the Finnish Peoples Democratic League's undue subservience to Moscow.

The embassy report said that the "domestic corollary" to the SDP's opening to Moscow was its political cooperation with the Communists, the "opening to the left," of which Secretary Raatikainen was the most "vociferous advocate." In the critically important trade union arena, the SDP Party Congress adopted a resolution restating that the principal objective was trade union reunification of the SDP Federation of Finnish Trade Unions (SAJ) and the Confederation of Finnish Trade Unions (SAK) led by the left-wing "Simonist" Social Democrats and Communists. However, the report stated, the SAJ was reluctant to make the concessions required of it by the SDP in order to achieve unification, and no concrete measures had been taken in that direction.

The report stated that the SDP gave the prime ministership to Mauno Koivisto, about whom the embassy noted:

> Koivisto is highly respected in the Social Democratic Party and in Finnish political circles as a top-flight economist and administrator. He had an excellent record as minister of finance, which position he left to become governor of the Bank of Finland on January 1, 1968. Although a long-time Social Democrat, Koivisto has never been involved in internal party politics, is not identified with any faction in the party, and has no known enemies in the party. He has been a consistent advocate of Finland's official foreign policy of friendly relations with the Soviet Union, and of austere domestic economic policy.

The embassy analysis concluded that the SDP could be expected to continue its policy of opening to the East, which "has found acceptance in the party as a logical extension of the...Paasikivi-Kekkonen line" and to "continue to strengthen its ties with the Social Democratic and labor parties of Western Europe...those of Scandinavia in particular." With respect to a domestic opening to the left, the embassy pointed out this policy was not popular with many party members. Moreover, "…it has become quite clear that because of Center Party opposition [the SDP] has virtually no prospects for realizing any significantly increased government control over the economy under a coalition government that includes that party."

Over the years the embassy also devoted considerable energy and effort to reporting on developments within the Finnish Communist Party. Particular attention was paid to the growing rift between the "moderate" majority and "Stalinist" minority. The embassy reported February 18, 1967 in SECRET airgram A-361:

> Since mid-1965 the Communist movement has been split by factionalism. It has been under strong pressure from younger liberal elements to drop the trappings of outworn Marxist dogma particularly as regards the use of force in the transition to socialism and as regards the concept of the dictatorship of the proletariat…The 14th Party Congress held in January 1966 showed that factionalism could no longer be contained.

> Losses in popular support for the communist-front SKDL were evidenced in the March general election, and the losing trend continued in the municipal by-elections in October. Participation in government has been a mixed blessing that has produced considerable frustration…A Soviet attempt to bolster the morale of the Finnish Communist Party through the visit of Mihail Suslov showed the importance the Soviets attach to the Finnish Communist Party as the only communist party in government in Western Europe, but brought no tangible rewards for the party…

In another analysis of the situation within the SKP (Helsinki CONFIDENTIAL airgram A-226 of December 15, 1967, drafted by Eric Fleisher), the embassy reviewed the draft text of a new party program and the status of the internal schism. The embassy said that the draft party policy reflected the clear influence of party liberals. It reported that release of the draft program was preceded by "the strongest public attack yet made on the old guard Stalinists by a top Finnish Communist Party official," party Vice Chairman Erkki Salomaa. The embassy reported that the vice-chairman charged:

> …the Stalinists were splitting the party by arguing that they have a monopoly on relations with the Communist Party of the Soviet Union. Salomaa stated…that the Finnish Communist Party needed to cleanse the atmosphere with a de-Stalinization congress such as Khrushchev conducted

at the 20th Party Congress of the Communist Party of the Soviet Union in 1956.

The embassy took note of the significant changes in communist doctrine contained in the new draft program. Regarding the transition to socialism, the new program stated:

The Finnish Communist Party aspires to achieve socialism in Finland by peaceful and democratic means, and believes in a transition to socialism through a series of progressive reforms...Socialism cannot in this country be achieved by violent means undertaken by a single minority group against the will of the majority of the people.

The embassy predicted that the Stalinists would attempt to water down the program and believed that "a bitter internal struggle is shaping up which will trouble the Finnish Communist Party for the next few years." In fact for the next twenty years the embassy reported on the seemingly endless turmoil within the SKP, the repeated interventions of Soviet ambassadors and CPSU representatives and the foreign and domestic policy ramifications of the schisms.

The Center Party, under firm Kekkonen control throughout the late 1960s and the 1970s, lacked the internal contradictions and upheavals of the SDP and SKP and, therefore, was not often the subject of close embassy scrutiny. However, the Center Party was almost constantly in office during this period, and contacts between the embassy and leading Center Party officials were frequent. The main concerns in the embassy with the Center Party were not over domestic programs—where the Center Party was a force for moderation—but rather with the manner in which the party, under the direction of its real leader, Urho Kekkonen, managed its relations with the Soviet Union to promote its own interests.

On May 7, 1976 the embassy submitted a report, "The Center Party at the Crossroads," (embassy CONFIDENTIAL airgram A-57 drafted by labor/political officer Alden Irons) which examined the Center Party. The report stated:

The Finnish Center Party, which...can be said to have dominated the Finnish political scene for the past 30 years, is at a crucial point in its history. The continuing decline in its rural base, the internal conflict over its future leadership, the leftward shift by President Kekkonen and his not-too-distant departure from the...scene pose basic questions for the future shape of Finnish politics.

The report observed that the Center Party—formerly Agrarian Union—had enjoyed a unique ascendancy in Finnish politics. This was due in part from its position in the center of the Finnish political spectrum and as a buffer between the Social Democrats and communists on the left and the representatives of business and capital on the right. With the decline in the rural population and notwithstanding the Center Party's efforts to broaden its base, the embassy saw the party as soon being in danger of "becoming too small to be a credible middle force in Finnish politics". (Note: I might wryly observe that two decades later in 1999 this political obituary still seems a bit premature!)

Regarding the Center Party's future leadership, the report discussed the "subterranean rivalry for advantage in the presidential sweepstakes." The report described the then party chairman Johannes Virolainen as:

a highly sophisticated politician, skilled in foreign languages...[who] enjoys solid support from the party rank-and-file...[He] is in the paradoxical position of having a reputation for getting along with the Social Democrats while at the same time being criticized by his own left-wingers for retarding the modernization of the Center Party. Virolainen, however, was first elected party chairman on a program of modernization and it was under his leadership that the party changed its name. A greater problem for Virolainen is that he has long been in disfavor with President Kekkonen...[which] stems in part from the fact the he is one of the rare men in Finland who refuses to agree on all points with the president...[Also] his relations with the Soviets, as with Kekkonen, are not of the best...he is not perceived as representing the faithful continuation of Finland's post-war foreign policy line.

This mantle has been appropriated by Virolainen's arch-rival within the Center Party, Ahti Karjalainen...a Kekkonen protege, brought as a very young man into positions of senior responsibility by his mentor.... With his academic background, Karjalainen has never been close to the grass roots of the Center Party and had never even aspired to the party chairmanship...Karjalainen has been one of the chief interpreters and a faithful executor of what is now called the Paasikivi-Kekkonen line in foreign policy. He is viewed favorably by the Soviet Union and is well acquainted with much of the senior Soviet leadership.

But Karjalainen too has weaknesses. Just as Virolainen as a teetotaler is considered unable by many Finns to establish the necessary rapport with the hard-drinking Russians, so it is feared that Karjalainen with his reputation for...over-indulgence might give too much away. Karjalainen is also considered by many too ready to sacrifice principle for tactical advantage. His courting of the minority (hard-line) faction of the [SKP] is only one example.

The embassy May 1976 report identified the young Paavo Väyrynen as "the only really open challenge to Virolainen's leadership." The report continued:

Väyrynen is bright and thinks analytically and philosophically about the Center Party's role in Finnish politics. Väyrynen's strategy has been to hitch his star to Karjalainen. If Karjalainen should succeed to the presidency, Väyrynen's future in the party would be assured. But even if Karjalainen should fade, Väyrynen figures he would be in position to lead the party into the future...[His] major handicap is his youth.

Meanwhile, the embassy was keeping a close eye on Finland's foreign policy and relations with East and West. On the positive side, embassy reports during the difficult years of the Vietnam War frequently noted that Finland and Finnish governmental officials usually showed considerable restraint in addressing U.S. involvement in the war, particularly compared to the outcry in other countries (not to mention within the United States itself). In a "U.S. Policy Assessment" of Finland (co-drafted by political officer J.P. Owens and economic officer M.Y. Hirabayashi, submitted via SECRET airgram A-191 of July 18, 1970) the embassy noted:

The Finnish record on Vietnam has been relatively good from the U.S. standpoint; despite leftist agitation, the government has generally refrained from public criticism of U.S. policy in Vietnam. As on the case of the two Germanies, the government has maintained its policy of non-recognition of both Vietnam governments....Although there were several anti-U.S. Vietnam policy demonstrations during the year...the level and intensity of the demonstrations was considerably lower than in the other Scandinavian countries, and in general the Vietnam question has not been a source of contention between the two governments.

The same report, and a number of others submitted over the years, also counted as positive that:

On the international scene, Finland's activist policy has enabled it to exert an influence greater than its size would indicate. The Finns have taken the initiative in proposing a conference on European security to be held in Finland, have successfully pushed Helsinki as one of the sites for the SALT talks, and in the U.N., have proposed regularly scheduled meetings of the security council.

The report also identified what it considered to be "negative aspects" regarding the maintenance of Finland's independent policy. One was the failure of NORDEC, a Scandinavian effort in the late 1960s-early 1970s to create a Nordic economic entity:

> After carrying out serious negotiations for many months with the other Scandinavian countries on Nordic economic cooperation (NORDEC), the Finnish Government announced in March—following the elections—that it would not sign the Nordec agreement. Although the reason given was the intention of the other Nordic countries to begin negotiations with the Common Market, it is generally believed that Nordec was abandoned because of Soviet objections—either implicit or explicit.

The embassy report also counted as negative that:

> Other indications of Soviet influence and/or pressure in Finnish political life appeared following the [1970 parliamentary] elections. Although the election results would have seemed to suggest popular support for a government based on a clear non-socialist majority and which included the country's second largest party (the Conservatives), it was clear to observers that President Kekkonen never seriously considered the appointment of a government which excluded the former government parties. On the contrary his main effort since the elections has been to seek ways to reconstitute the popular front government which had been in power for the last four years, although with a Center Party figure—Ahti Karjalainen—as prime minister instead of a Social Democrat. The Soviets in various ways had made clear their wish to see a continuation of the popular front, and Kekkonen appeared willing to satisfy this Soviet desire...[These events] reflected unfavorably on Finnish independence of action.

The embassy further complained of the continuing "leftist bias in radio and TV" but hoped that the new supervisory parliamentary board "will act to lessen the amount and degree of slanted programming." The embassy report observed "a degree of ambivalence" among the Finnish leadership regarding the projection of Finland's policy abroad. On the one hand, the Finns believe they know how to deal with the Soviets and that they can gain much in substance if they cater to the Soviets on matters of form. On the other hand, they worry about impressions in the West that Finland is not really independent and does not follow a truly independent policy.

The embassy pointed to articles in the *New York Times* charging that Finland cannot make a foreign policy move without consulting Moscow, and to the coining of the "Finlandization" term in

Germany and its subsequent use in U.S. publications as causing concern in Finland. The embassy observed:

> On the other hand, it could be pointed out that to the degree the Finns actually do give in to Soviet pressures, even on matters of form, they must expect such conclusions to be drawn, and they must be prepared to accept an image of lessened independence.

The report suggested that perhaps Finland had become "overconfident" regarding the degree of "understanding" for its positions that it could expect from the West.

The just-cited report referred to "media" concerns—both U.S. embassy concerns about the leftist, anti-American bias of Finnish TV and radio, and Finnish concerns about Western media perceptions of Finland. The issue of "self-censorship" in the media in Finland was a frequent subject of embassy reporting. It is generally agreed that the Finnish people came out of the wars with the Soviet Union with hostile attitudes toward their eastern neighbor. Both Juho Paasikivi and Urho Kekkonen, as has been noted, perceived the need to change Finnish attitudes toward their "hereditary enemy" if Finland were to be able to maintain its independence in the unfriendly geopolitical power reality in the Baltic region following World War II.

In the late 1960s and into the 1970s, the Soviet Union manifested great sensitivity toward Finnish news articles in any way critical of any aspect of Soviet life. President Kekkonen lay heavy stress on the responsibility of the media even during the 1958-59 and 1961-62 crises in relations with the Soviet Union. As noted below in this chapter, references to the responsibility of the media in maintaining good relations between Finland and the Soviet Union began to be included in joint Finnish/Soviet communiqués issued following visits of important officials.

In an excellent analysis written by embassy political section chief John Owens upon his departure from his assignment in Finland (embassy CONFIDENTIAL airgram A-257 of August 6, 1971) he *inter alia* assessed the impact of the Kekkonen policy on the media:

> If the Soviets were to be presented in a favorable light to the Finnish people (as well as to avoid giving offense to Moscow) Kekkonen's policy required that the media adopt a 'positive' approach to the Soviet Union, which meant

that by and large, comment on the USSR should avoid emphasis on the unfavorable aspects of Soviet life. As a result, particularly in recent years, the Finnish press has developed a double standard in its handling of news and political commentaries; while the Western countries, and particularly the United States, are frequently subject to criticism, only on rare occasions (as during the invasion of Czechoslovakia) is the Soviet Union taken to task. And when individual Finnish papers violate this 'understanding,' the Soviets are quick to take offense...

The net result of the presidential pressure has been an unbalanced picture of world affairs presented to the Finnish public by the press and particularly by radio/TV. Fortunately, the Finnish public seems to be deeply distrustful of the radio and television as indicated by the heavy criticism of the media through the country.

The above reference is only one of the many such observations that appeared frequently in embassy reports and assessments over the years.

As mentioned, one of the favorable developments noted in the 1970 U.S. policy assessment of Finland was Finland's initiative in proposing a European security conference, which it proposed to host. This endeavor, which gradually became known as the "CSCE process" was one which, perhaps more than any other single foreign policy development, enabled Finland to burnish its neutral credentials in both East and West. The embassy made many references to CSCE developments in its reporting during the years leading up to the 1975 CSCE Conference.

In the embassy's "1972 U.S. Policy Assessment of Finland" (embassy SECRET airgram A-125 drafted by Owens and Hirabayashi) the embassy again referred in favorable terms to Finnish efforts on behalf of the CSCE:

Through most of 1971 the Finns followed up on their 1969 proposal to serve as host to a European security conference with low-key soundings in European and North American capitals by roving Ambassador Enckell. While seeking to find some sort of consensus regarding the conference, the Finns attempted to make clear that their role was largely passive and dependent on the willingness of all interested parties to convene a conference. A certain euphoria in early 1971 arising out of hopes for rapid results from West Germany's *Ostpolitik* gave way to a more balanced appraisal of the actual speed of *détente*...

Further Finnish contacts and efforts began to pay off. The gradual development of the CSCE process towards fruition was repeatedly acknowledged by the embassy as a favorable and ultimately successful Finnish initiative.

An initiative that was certainly less well-received by the United States than Finland's CSCE efforts was an announcement in September 1971 by the Finnish Foreign Ministry that it proposed to negotiate two identical treaties with East and West Germany to normalize relations with both. As recorded in the embassy's May 1972, U.S. policy assessment:

> The announcement of the Finnish plans was somewhat premature as a result of a press leak. The Finns had reportedly planned to float their trial balloon after the Berlin agreements were signed. U.S. displeasure, which focussed on the unfortunate timing of the initiative while sensitive negotiations were underway, was registered with the Finns. They replied...that any negotiations between Finland and the Germanies would be separate but parallel...They also reasoned that the form of the proposal...permitted either of the two Germanies to postpone indefinitely the negotiations...East Germans early indicated a willingness to open negotiations. West Germany, unhappy about the idea, has informed the Finns only that the proposal is under study...The West Germans are fearful, however, that total disregard for the proposal will ultimately prompt the Finns to begin talks with the East Germans alone...The Finns are becoming impatient. Finland wants to be among the first to recognize East Germany once the logjam breaks...

In an April 8, 1971 report (CONFIDENTIAL airgram A-116 drafted by John Owens) the embassy described what it considered to be the highly visible Soviet role in the government "crisis" during the winter of 1970-71 which ultimately resulted in the withdrawal of the SKDL from the Karjalainen Government:

> It is an axiom of Finnish political life that in periods of crisis, the Soviet role in Finnish affairs becomes more evident. The recent crisis created by the withdrawal of the communists from the popular front government of Prime Minister Ahti Karjalainen was not an exception to this maxim. The secret visit of Soviet Deputy Foreign Minister Kuznetsov to Helsinki in December, the hurried trip in February of President Kekkonen to Moscow to consult with the Soviet troika, the calls of senior Finnish officials at the Soviet Embassy and a visit by a Soviet official [embassy counselor V.M. Vladimirov] to President Kekkonen during the height of the recent political crisis, all illustrated the intense Soviet interest in Finnish political events. Alert reporting by the Finnish press, including photographs of some of the visits, brought home clearly to the Finnish public the Soviet role in Finnish political life.
>
> This is not to say that the Finns do not frequently resist Soviet pressures; they do, often successfully. But in the most recent crisis, there was a

disheartening abundance of indications that the Soviets were playing some kind of active role, as reflected by the steady traffic of high-ranking figures moving between a triangle whose three corners were the president's residence at Tamminiemi, the prime minister's home at Kesaranta, and the Soviet embassy on Tehtaankatu.

After I arrived in Finland in July of 1976, the embassy continued to watch closely those issues which we considered could affect Finland's political direction and which, thus, had real or potential implications for U.S. interests in Finland. Included in these themes were some of the standard items for most embassies in most countries, such as political party developments, labor issues, elections and government changes. In addition we looked closely at a variety of other issues.

One such recurring issue was the periodic issuance of Finnish/Soviet official communiqués. The Finns were devotees of "meaningful communiqués," particularly as far as the Soviet Union was concerned. It was a Finnish conviction, which we shared, that the joint communiqués issued following visits by senior Soviet officials to Finland or by senior Finnish officials to the Soviet Union were extremely important in taking the temperature of Finnish/Soviet relations.

An excellent example of a close study of a Finnish/Soviet communiqué was the embassy analysis of the communiqué issued following a visit by President Kekkonen to the Soviet Union in May 1977. This visit followed by a few weeks a visit of Soviet Prime Minister Aleksy Kosygin to Finland in April. The embassy's telegram (Helsinki 01230 of June 14, 1977) analyzing the Kekkonen visit communiqué thus contained numerous cross-references to the embassy telegram (Helsinki 0643 of April 11, 1977) analyzing the Kosygin visit communiqué. I was the principal drafter of both messages. The Kekkonen visit message was approved by, and went out over the name of Robert Houston as chargé d'affaires, Ambassador Austad having departed Finland and Ambassador Ridgway having not yet arrived.

The cable on the Kekkonen visit was classified CONFIDENTIAL and directed to the Department of State with information copies sent to U.S. embassies in the Nordic countries and Moscow. The telegram noted that the joint communiqué after the Kekkonen visit was "the longest Soviet/Finnish communiqué in years," owing to:

considerably more attention than in previous communiqués on economic cooperation and measures; more emphasis than in [the] Kosygin communiqué on [the] 1948 treaty of Friendship, Cooperation and Mutual Assistance (FCMA) and related issues...and generally heavier emphasis than in previous communiqués on CSCE, *détente*, disarmament, international questions and references to world trouble-spots.

Regarding economic matters, the communiqué referred to economic agreements signed during the Kekkonen visit. Turning to political aspects of the communiqué, the embassy telegram first addressed the question of how Finnish neutrality was treated, which was:

...always the most important part of [any] communiqué as far as Finland is concerned. Because of satisfactory treatment of this question in [the] Kosygin communiqué earlier this year, Finns expected no difficulties and were not disappointed. Communiqué language was exactly the same as used in recent years, although as noted in [Helsinki 0643 of April 11, the] wording now being used in this regard does not refer as directly to Finnish neutrality as did [the] formulation used in [the] late 1960's and up until 1971.

It should be noted that in the April 11 embassy message on the Kosygin visit communiqué, the embassy had spelled out its understanding on the changed wording with reference to Finland's neutrality that had first occurred some years earlier. The April 11 message had noted:

[The] language used in [the] Kosygin/Kekkonen communiqué is consistent with language used since 1971 on similar occasions in that such communiqués have referred to Finland's endeavor (or desire or aspiration) to apply a peace-loving policy of neutrality. Communiqués issued in the late 1960's, however, and upon Kekkonen's visit to [the] Soviet Union in July 1970, used a more direct formulation about Finland's neutrality. [The] official communiqué used in Kekkonen's 1970 visit stated: 'both parties have again noted...Finland's peace-loving policy of neutrality and the friendly relations it maintains with all countries...' Thus, language of [the] new communiqué reaffirms formulations used in recent years without, however, returning to the more direct reference to Finnish neutrality used in [the] earlier period.

Returning to the Kekkonen visit communiqué, the embassy's June 14 telegram looked at references in the communiqué to the FCMA Treaty and Finnish/Soviet relations:

As always, [the] FCMA [is] described as [the] foundation of Finnish/Soviet relations. As in [the 1974] Podgorny visit communiqué, [the] FCMA is considered also to have [a] significant role in consolidating peaceful conditions in Northern Europe and strengthening security in Europe in general...[The] communiqué states [that the] FCMA continues [the] course of Finnish/Soviet friendship and cooperation which was begun by [the] Lenin decree recognizing [the] political independence of Finland. This course also holds clear and secure prospects for [the] future. Thus, [the] FCMA [is] seen as [a] source of continuity and permanence in Finnish/Soviet relations. Communiqué notes Finnish/Soviet relations have become [a] 'convincing manifestation' of [the] realization of peaceful co-existence between states of different social systems.

Regarding the section of the communiqué referring to the responsibilities of the communications media, the embassy noted:

In describing growing friendship and cooperation between [the] two countries, [the] communiqué states [that] both parties note [the] significant task of [the] communications media in [the] continued strengthening of such relations, and note 'the feeling of responsibility and objectivity required by this important matter, without damaging the favorable development of relations between the two countries.' This [is the] first time [a] reference to [the] responsibility of [the] media [is] included in [a] Finnish/Soviet communiqué since [the] Podgorny visit in October, 1974 when [the] same language was used.

In noting a reference in the communiqué to the importance of regular personal contact between President Kekkonen and Soviet leaders, the embassy observed:

[The] communiqué states that such contact is [an] expression of [a] high level of trust and one of [the] most efficient forms of political cooperation. [The] embassy considers it interesting that this reference for the first time has been personalized with [the] use of Kekkonen's name; similar expressions in past communiqués referred to [the] 'President of the Republic of Finland.'

Analyzing references in the communiqué to the Nordic Nuclear Weapon-Free Zone (NNWFZ), the Embassy message said:

In addition to usual language on [the] importance and topicality of [the] Finnish proposal for [a] North Europe Nuclear Free Zone, [the] new communiqué makes an important addition: 'The Soviet Union for its own part confirmed its readiness to participate in a constructive discussion of these proposals and jointly with other nuclear powers to act as a guarantor of the status of the nuclear free zone in North Europe, should the states possibly participating in this zone express interest in this matter.' While there was a reference of [a] similar nature made in [a] speech by Podgorny during his October 1974 visit, to embassy knowledge, this [is the] first time concepts of nuclear power guarantee of [a] Nordic Nuclear Free Zone [have been] included in [an] official communiqué.

The message declared that, regarding the Brezhnev all-European conference proposal that the Soviets had earlier put forward, the "communiqué edges [a] step closer to (but stops short of) Finnish endorsement of Soviet proposals by agreeing that they 'could provide useful impulses for implementation of relevant provisions of [the] final act of [the] CSCE.' [The] Kosygin communiqué merely expressed interest that such proposals receive consideration in [a] constructive spirit."

The embassy telegram pointed out with respect to the then pending Warsaw Pact non-first use of nuclear weapons proposal that, as in the Kosygin communiqué:

[the] parties express hope [the] proposal will be considered in [a] constructive spirit. [The] new communiqué, however, goes another step by suggesting [a] preliminary exchange of views at an agreed level between states participating in CSCE.

After its detailed analysis of the Kekkonen visit communiqué, the June 14, 1977 embassy message concluded with the following comment underscoring the communiqué's significance:

COMMENT: [The] GOF, Finnish media and virtually all informed Finnish observers have expressed considerable satisfaction with [the] Kekkonen visit and with [the] communiqué. Reference[s] to [the] Finnish neutrality endeavor, [the] Kostamus project, and [the] long-term economic agreement [are] all considered to be favorable to Finnish interests. Also, few Finns appear [to] see any points in the communiqué negative to Finnish interests.

However, on a number of points in [the] communiqué [the] GOF has agreed to language which appears to represent some movement towards positions more supportive of apparent Soviet views. Movement can be noted particularly in: slightly tighter linkage of [the] October revolution and Finnish independence in Kekkonen's reference; [the] view of [the] 1948 Treaty on FCMA as [a] 'convincing manifestation' of peaceful co-existence, thus edging closer to the concept of Finnish/Soviet relations as an example to be followed by other states of differing social systems; re-inclusion of provisions emphasizing the responsibilities of the mass media in promoting good Finnish/Soviet relations; wording on CSCE hinting at support for the Soviet political concept approach to Belgrade; introduction for [the] first time in [a] communiqué of [the] possibility of [a] Soviet guarantor role in any future Nordic Nuclear Free Zone; and [a] more affirmative posture on Brezhnev all-European proposals and Warsaw Pact proposal for no-first use of nuclear weapons by CSCE countries.

[The] degree of movement in communiqué language in these areas [is] not, perhaps, startling, and new formulations [are] still…qualified in one way or another and stop short of straight-out GOF endorsement of Soviet positions. Most Finns would probably argue that none of the changes adversely affects important Finnish interests, or that on some…questions language reflects pre-existing agreement with Soviet positions. It is also possible that the changes were suggested in such a way that the GOF considered them to be a *quid pro quo* for economic agreements…Embassy recognizes that [the] GOF in its relations with the Soviet Union prefers not [to] dig in its heels unless important Finnish interests [are] at stake. Whatever the pressures or motivations, objective analysis makes clear that compared to previous communiqués there has been movement—however slight—and [that the] direction of that movement seems to be helpful—however marginally—to Soviet positions on various international issues. HOUSTON

While I was the principal drafter of the embassy message, and was in full agreement with its main points and overall interpretation, the content and tone of the message reflected a clear input from the interim chargé d'affaires Robert Houston. The message with its direct and implied criticism of Finnish positions probably would not have made it out of Mark Austad's embassy without considerable watering down. Nevertheless, some of the concerns expressed in the June 14, 1977 message are precisely those which during the Cold War years were recognized as raising questions about the character of Finland's relationship with the Soviet Union and, more importantly, the way in which some Finnish leaders used that relationship.

One of the most enduring issues from the 1960s through the 1980s was the Kekkonen proposal for a Nordic Nuclear Weapon Free Zone (NNWFZ) and later variations on that proposal. The Finnish proposal, adapted from earlier Swedish and Soviet nuclear weapon free zone ideas, surfaced time and again over the years. The objective of a NNWFZ was one which the United States and NATO sharply opposed, no matter in what guise or with what wrinkles it was put forward. As discussed in the chapter on the NATO policy context, the U.S. and NATO were concerned over any measure that would constrain the defense options of any NATO member. The concern over the NNWFZ was that it would freeze into a formal treaty-like arrangement the informal and unilateral assurances by Norway and Denmark that *in peacetime conditions* they would not permit the stationing of nuclear weapons on their territory.

In was the U.S. and general NATO view that such an undertaking would dangerously limit Norway and Denmark's flexibility during a time of crisis or war and would seriously undermine the equal responsibility, equal risk principles underpinning NATO solidarity. Moreover the scant likelihood, in our opinion, of the Soviet Union's accepting credible limitations on its nuclear weapons in the Kola Peninsula or the Baltic Sea meant that a NNWFZ affecting only the Nordic countries would be patently asymmetrical and would result in USSR wartime nuclear predominance in Northern Europe.

These clear and strongly held U.S. and NATO positions notwithstanding, the U.S. was consistently tolerant toward, and understanding of, Finland's position on the NNWFZ concept. As is indicated in the message cited directly below and in other citations in this book, we considered that the Finnish authorities consciously used the NNWFZ as a tool in managing Finland's relationship with the Soviet Union. It was our view that when Finland was feeling pressure from the Soviet Union for one reason or another, Finnish authorities would trot out the latest version of a NNWFZ proposal. The initiative would founder from the opposition of the other Nordic countries, through no fault of Finland, and Finland meanwhile would have demonstrated to the Soviets that it had done its best to push a proposal in which the latter were very interested.

We realized that some Finnish government officials, academics and politicians took the NNWFZ seriously and were dedicated to making it a reality. Nevertheless it was our assumption that key government policy makers, including President Kekkonen, were more interested in the NNWFZ as a *process* than as an objective. After all, if a NNWFZ were achieved, the Finns would need to find another policy issue to use in managing the Soviet relationship.

During the autumn of 1978 the Finns once again moved the NNWFZ issue to the front burner. As noted below, the resurgence of active Finnish interest in the NNWFZ was in our view related to Finnish uneasiness over the proposal in July 1978 by Soviet

Defense Minister Ustinov for joint Finnish/Soviet military maneuvers (see Chapter Twelve). Again, this view was consistent with our theory that the Finns used the NNWFZ as a useful process in managing their relationship with the Soviets.

On September 25, 1978, I called upon MFA Under Secretary Keijo Korhonen to request information from him concerning recent Finnish government activities with respect to the Kekkonen NNWFZ proposal. I made reference to Korhonen's consultations on the subject in Copenhagen on August 28 and to a statement by Soviet Premier Aleksei Kosygin in support of a NNWFZ during President Kekkonen's recent visit to the Soviet Union.

Korhonen responded that my call on him was a timely one, because he had only just returned from a two-day visit to Moscow the main purpose of which had been to discuss the Kekkonen plan. I reported on my conversation with Under Secretary Korhonen in an embassy telegram to the State Department on October 3, 1978 (Helsinki 3212).

Korhonen said he had been formally received at the Soviet Foreign Ministry by Deputy Foreign Minister Zemskov but that his substantive talks had been with Ambassador Viktor Israeliyan. Korhonen described his talks with Israeliyan as "businesslike and constructive" and free of ideological bombast. Korhonen said the Soviets had expressed great interest in information learned by the Finns in their previous contacts with other interested parties. However, Korhonen said he had told Israeliyan that in this process Finland was not carrying messages but "rather attempting to identify, through a series of specific questions, what each party might consider possible or impossible with respect to a Nordic NWFZ." Korhonen did not further characterize his meetings in Moscow or in Copenhagen, saying with respect to the latter he assumed the U.S. had been informed on the contacts of those talks by the Danes. (My telegram noted parenthetically the "the Danish embassy in Helsinki has told us the Danes had given a negative response to Korhonen, more negative, according to the Danes, than the responses of Sweden and Norway.")

Korhonen said that he had now formally discussed the Kekkonen proposal with each of Finland's three Nordic neighbors and with the Soviet Union. He said he would like next to discuss formally the Kekkonen proposal with the U.S. in Washington. He reiterated that he considered that his previous contacts with U.S. officials on this subject had been preliminary and unofficial. What he was now seeking was a formal exchange of views with U.S. authorities on the subject. Noting he would be in the U.S. from October 23 to November 3 in conjunction with the UN General Assembly, he asked that the U.S. embassy inform the Department of State of his request for a meeting on the Kekkonen proposal sometime during that period. He said he would also appreciate a schedule of other appointments with appropriate officials of the Washington foreign affairs community to discuss general European and Northern European political questions.

The embassy message conveying the substance of the foregoing, reviewed and approved by Ambassador Ridgway, closed with the following comments and recommendations:

> In his previous contacts with U.S. officials in Washington and Helsinki, Korhonen [had been] careful to emphasize that he was not expecting an official reaction, that he considered such contacts preliminary, and that Finland would seek further opportunities to discuss the matter again. As Korhonen made clear, the Finns consider that their [requested] discussion in the U.S. would constitute the last step in their current round of bilateral discussion on this matter. The embassy realizes that after Ambassador Ridgway's presentation to Korhonen in July...there should be little doubt in the Finnish Foreign Ministry as to where the U.S. stands on this proposal.

> The Finns, however, clearly consider it very important to be able to carry the process of bilateral discussion of the Kekkonen proposal through the step of formal discussion with the U.S. We are preparing an evaluation of the current effort by the Finns on behalf of a Nordic NWFZ in an effort to understand their motivations and their possible objectives. While this remains a very difficult area in which to reach firm conclusions, we are leaning increasingly to the view that Finnish efforts in pushing the Kekkonen proposal may in part be the result of Finnish concern over increased Soviet interest in Northern Europe in general and in Finland in particular, as evidenced by the recent Ustinov proposal for joint Soviet/Finnish military maneuvers.

> The Korhonen visit offers an excellent opportunity for Washington officials to explore current Finnish views on Northern European security with the MFA's highest ranking political affairs official (and former foreign minister). We recommend that Korhonen be received at an appropriately high level in [the Department] for a meeting on the Kekkonen proposal at which the USG could officially hear out the Finnish presentation and give

authoritative Washington views. We also urge that a full schedule of appropriate appointments be made for Korhonen for discussion of the general European and Northern European political issues.

As is noted in Chapter Twelve, a full and useful schedule was in fact arranged for Under Secretary Korhonen in Washington.

10

The Charms of Finland (I)

My family and I were asked innumerable times during my career—and are still asked after having retired from the State Department—what was our favorite overseas assignment. Independently, each of us has invariably answered: Finland.

Why is that? How does one explain to other Americans who have never been to Finland—or indeed, even explain to Finns themselves—what it is about Finland that charms those foreigners who have the chance to live and work there and to get to know the country well? It isn't easy to explain. Our own positive attitudes toward Finland, which grew into a deep fondness, developed from the mosaic of our experiences in Finland and from a predisposition to like Finland dating from our excitement upon first learning of the assignment.

Part of the explanation lies in the fact that, from the point of view of my profession as an American diplomat, I found Finland most challenging and interesting. As I have already indicated, the assignment to Finland first of all meant a welcome change after serving in Nixon and Kissinger's Latin America. Unhappy over U.S. policy in Latin America, I was very comfortable with and supportive of our foreign and security policies in Europe. Moreover, as I have said, the Finnish assignment gave me the opportunity to compete in the Foreign Service's most prestigious area of operation—Europe.

In addition, for me as a "political scientist" and political officer, Finland was intrinsically a fascinating country to serve in, particularly during the Cold War. Finland's history during the twentieth century was eventful, fascinating and precarious. Its heroic struggle against the Russians in the 1939-40 Winter War, its desperate efforts during World War II to save itself from disaster and, after the war, its struggle to survive as an independent state while the Soviet Union's other neighbors slipped into satellite status, all fascinated the outside observer.

Finland's ambiguous relationships with the Soviet Union and with the West, its complex domestic political situation and the anomaly of a democratic country being presided over by a strong-man president well into his third decade of power were features that made Finland an intriguing country in which to work as an American diplomat. So, professionally, Finland offered an unusual and interesting challenge.

On a more personal political level, I have been fascinated by Finland, and by the other Nordic countries, as a very decent social model that balanced and combined political democracy, social justice and economic equity, on the one hand, with that essential motor of economic growth, a largely profit-motivated, free enterprise economic system on the other. Throughout the entire Cold War period and my professional relationship to Finland, the Finnish version of the Nordic model performed admirably well. This certainly added to my fascination. Recent trends in advanced countries, including Finland, are raising very serious questions as to whether the Finnish or Nordic political/economic model is sustainable into the next century. But the Nordic "third way" continues to fascinate and—if it is sustainable—continues to remain a very attractive model.

Finland's physical and climatic characteristics deriving from its geographical location high in Europe's northeast corner also—by its very uniqueness—constitute a fascinating feature. I remember that during our first autumn in Finland, in November of 1976, the embassy received a U.S. congressional delegation from the important House of Representatives Foreign Affairs Committee. The delegation had come to Finland on its way to the Soviet Union to monitor CSCE human rights developments in the light of the previous year's Helsinki Accords. During the committee's brief mid-November stay in Helsinki the skies were dark and overcast.

At that time of year it frequently was not possible really to see the sun at all in Helsinki, just a kind of twilight from around 10:00 in the morning until 3:00 in the afternoon when the city was once again plunged into darkness. The snows had not yet come. It was pretty miserable.

I was control officer for the visit. Members of the congressional staff asked me, how in the hell can you stand living in this climate? I could only answer, I don't know, I just got here a few months ago. I couldn't really explain to them that I was watching the steadily shrinking days with something like fascination. The period of daylight each day seemed not just shorter but *dramatically* shorter than the day before. I had the sensation of going into some kind of new dimension. I knew intellectually that the winter solstice would arrive around December 21 and the days would then begin to lengthen. But for that first winter in mid-November I was not entirely convinced this would happen. On some kind of strange emotional level I could half believe it would simply continue forever to get darker and darker. I would look forward to each new day to watch the darkening process continue. There would occasionally be a relatively cloudless day; then, walking in downtown Helsinki at mid-day, the winter sun would cast its side-long rays at strange angles, giving off a quality of light that is somehow different from what is known in more temperate climes.

And finally came the first snows! It really is true what Finns say, that the light then comes from the ground, not from the sky! Or at least so it seemed in those years of the late 1970s when Helsinki seemed to enjoy ample snow cover from late December until late March or April, unlike in several recent years. I remember one May 4 when we were celebrating our daughter's birthday on the lawn in front of our house on Hietaniemintie overlooking the Baltic Sea. We had to wear heavy jackets, and huge chunks of ice were still floating in the bay. For me April and May were almost the worst months of the year in Finland, even worse in their way than the dark and snow-less months of October and November. Because by April and May, the rest of Europe was already experiencing spring, whereas winter seemed reluctant to release its grip on Finland. But even bad weather in Finland perversely seemed to add to its unique charm.

I had never been on skis before Finland. None of my family had; we had come straight from the tropics. We had never been downhill or cross-country skiing. That first year, with winter approaching, I took the whole family to Stockmann's department store and we outfitted ourselves with ski equipment. We had made reservations to spend December 28-January 4 at a popular ski lodge in Kuusamo. We drove up with the whole family and our gear packed into (and on top of) our 1974 Chevrolet Nova sedan.

We had reserved a separate cabin for the family, away from the main lodge and only a few yards from one of the cross-country ski trails. Situated seemingly in the middle of the woods, our cabin was surrounded by a landscape that looked like a fantasy Christmas card of snow-covered hills, ravines and trees. That was, when you could see it, because Kuusamo, some 750 kilometers north of Helsinki, was almost up to the Arctic Circle, and in late December there were barely four hours a day of twilight.

That is where we learned to ski—more or less. The two boys, Lane and Carl, picked it up almost immediately and soon were looking for steep inclines on or off the trail on which they could work up some real speed. I started soon to get the hang of it as well and Magda also could begin to make her way along the easier trails. Little Vanessa too began to get used to her tiny skies. Before long, the boys and I were skiing several kilometers a day; it wasn't, at least in my case, very pretty or efficient, but the miracle was that I could stand up on those slippery slats and move along over the trails.

We enjoyed having dinner every night at the lodge and, on New Year's Eve at the stroke of midnight, the downhill ski instructors in full view of the lodge dining room snaked down the mountain carrying torches, ushering in the New Year 1977. That week of learning cross country skiing in the classic and unique beauty of Northern Finland, in the dead of winter, remains indelibly imprinted upon our memories as one of our favorite experiences in Finland. From that time on, we eagerly anticipated the arrival of winter in Finland and became devotees of the cross-country ski paths in Helsinki and its environs. I become more ambitious about cross-country skiing when I came back on assignment to Finland some years later, older but—with regards to skiing—not wiser.

Summer in Finland also brought its charms. Just as the clutch of darkness in winter could awe, the brightness of summer could delight. The sparkling waters everywhere to be seen in and around Helsinki give the city a rustic, maritime character befitting the Daughter of the Baltic. Although fair summer weather was by no means guaranteed, it came often enough most summers to reward the patient. As a jogger, I would enjoy running along the Kaivopuisto waterfront from the embassy through Kaivopuisto Park and towards the Wartsila shipbuilding plant. Or in the evenings or on weekends in West End, I would run on paths through woods, which could trick you into believing you were miles from a bustling capital city. We would be invited to visit friends at a summer cottage or to go for a boat ride in the Baltic. We would go to the zoo on Korkeasaari or take the ferryboat to Suomenlinna, the island site of an historic fortress in Helsinki harbor. Outside of Helsinki, we went to the opera in Savonlinna and to the jazz festival in Pori.

We went each year to the Mid-Summer's celebrations on Seurasaari, an outdoor living museum of ancient Finland. We would observe the folk-craft exhibits, enjoy the folk-dancing exhibitions and gaze in awe at the huge Mid-Summer's Eve bonfire. The endless mid-summer days, barely interrupted by a two or three hour period of quasi-twilight, were as dramatic and mysterious as the opposite almost complete lack of daylight in mid-winter. The violent contrasts of Finland's seasons intrigued and entertained.

Winter or summer, I had a favorite routine that I would follow several times a month on some of my frequent calls on the Foreign Ministry, then located on Ritarikatu off of the Senate Square, or calls on Jaakko Kalela at the Presidential Palace. I would have an embassy car take me to my scheduled appointment and send the car back. Then, following my appointment, I would stroll back to the embassy. The ritual was, however, to stop at the Market Square in front of the Presidential Palace on the South Harbor. There I would enjoy the colorfully dazzling produce stalls with their fruits and vegetables attractively presented and their rustic owners hawking their wares. I would check out the fishermen selling their fresh catches right off the rear of their boats. I would stop in one of the semi-permanent tent-cafes and purchase a steaming cup of coffee and a *pulla,* a delicious Finnish pastry.

When both my visual and gastronomical appetites were sufficiently sated, I would continue my walk back to the embassy in Kaivopuisto, strolling along the waterfront past the Silja Lines whose large ferryboats carried passengers and their cars back and forth between Helsinki and Stockholm. Next my stroll would take me past a strange statue of a large bronze lady, obviously suffering some kind of caffeine fit, presented by the people of the Soviet Union to the people of Finland. I greatly valued these periodic sojourns and did not feel at all guilty about the hour or so of Uncle Sam's time that I wasted. What a delightful working environment, what a nice life style Helsinki offered!

Another charming dimension of our life in Finland was the frequent official trips we were able to make around the country. I occasionally accompanied the ambassador on some of his or her speaking trips around Finland. However, even more interesting were the speaking engagements that I fulfilled. Magda and I saw these latter trips as opportunities to get outside of Helsinki and to see the other dimensions of Finland. The invitations to speak that we received were usually from chapters of the League of Finnish-American Societies, which are scattered throughout Finland. On such visits, working with the local Finnish-American Society organizer, I would make arrangements not only for the speaking engagement at the society's meeting but would also organize a call on the provincial governor, if applicable, on the mayor and city council, and on the local newspaper. Frequently, the city authorities would offer a luncheon in our honor, and we would usually have dinner with members of the Finnish-American local chapter.

With the invaluable assistance of the U.S. embassy translators, I would have the text of my speech prepared in Finnish. Magda and I considered these trips as opportunities to submerge ourselves in the Finnish language and culture for two or three days, depending on the length of the trip. Among the cities I visited during my 1976-79 assignment, either with the ambassador or on my own or with my wife, were Lahti, Rauma, Savonlinna, Lieksa, Joensuu, Kouvala, Turku, Lapeenranta, Rovaniemi, Oulu, Tampere, Mikkeli, Kuopio and Kankaanpää. We were always overwhelmed by the warmth of the reception that we received on my official calls as well as by the friendliness of the Finnish-American Society members. We invariably had marvelous experiences on our trips, talking about U.S.-Finnish relations, getting to know various parts of Finland, practicing our Finnish language skills and enjoying being together with our hosts.

This brings me to the most closely held secret about the charm of Finland, namely the warmth and friendliness of its people. In fact, it is more than a secret. There exists an inaccurate but widespread perception abroad—abetted by the self-perceptions of many Finns themselves—that Finns in general are dour, aloof, stand-offish and even unfriendly.

Maybe some Finns are; some people in every society are. It is true that Finns in public places tend to be reserved, don't make eye contact with strangers, nor smile at people they don't know nor engage routinely in syrupy casual greeting and farewell expressions. I hasten to add that I do not myself disdain the American trait of breezy greetings, "How're ya doin?" or farewells, "Have a nice day." I see nothing phony about these kind of friendly messages which I think accurately reflect the outgoing nature and casualness of the American personality.

Finns don't do that. They are shy and reserved with strangers, with other Finns as well as with foreigners. In fact, it has been my experience that they are quicker to warm up to a foreign visitor than they are to each other. Admittedly, to be introduced or to be known as a diplomat from the American embassy helped, I am quite sure, in being taken seriously and greeted courteously, at least in most circles. However, time after time we found that any demonstration on our part of personal warmth and sincere interest in Finland and its culture and language would quickly be reciprocated by a return warmth and friendliness that went far beyond the formal and the courteous. And here I am referring to Finns that we would meet casually in our travels or in department stores or bookstalls.

On quite a different level is the warmth and responsiveness that would not infrequently develop from an initially professional relationship. Most of my professional contacts with Finns—there were of course exceptions—were from the very outset courteous, informative and enjoyable. I am proud to say that almost all of the Finns I have known professionally over the past twenty years seemed sincerely happy to see me and were most willing to be interviewed when I returned to Finland in 1995. Colleagues and counterparts, I consider many of these professional acquaintances to be "friends." Beyond that, my wife and I are privileged to have developed what we consider to be close friendships with a small number of Finns with whom we have maintained contact over the years. Several of them have visited us in the United States and the others are welcome.

There is a cliche in Finland that it is not easy to make friends with a Finn, but once you have done so, you have a friend for life. That is, I think, a fairly accurate description of reality as far as making "deep" friendships. But I would argue that anyone who is prepared to take the initiative and to demonstrate his own warmth and interest will find a reciprocal response from many Finns. That is my perception. My wife and children had similar experiences in Finland. That is why we reacted with indignation a few years ago to the U.S. TV program "Sixty Minutes" distorted portrayal of "Last Tango in Finland." For most Americans, that will be their only insight into the Finnish personality (and it is amazing how many Americans mention that program when they hear we have lived in Finland). On the other hand, many Finns seem to recognize a part of themselves in that TV piece. I guess that points up another Finnish trait: self-deprecation. I for one do not buy that portrayal.

Of course not all Finns were friendly to all foreigners. There were limits. I remember one marvelous insight into this dimension during an "election watch" hosted by the Finnish Foreign Ministry at the Marski Hotel on Mannerheimentie Avenue in downtown

Helsinki. I believe it was following the 1978 presidential elections, although it might have been after the 1979 parliamentary elections. It was one or the other. The Foreign Ministry would organize an election returns center on such occasions where foreign diplomats could observe the results of Finnish democracy in action. Representatives of most of the countries with a diplomatic presence in Finland were in attendance along with numerous Foreign Ministry officials and some Finnish and foreign journalists. Groups would gather to chat and discuss the election results.

On November 25, 1977 I had received at the U.S. embassy a Soviet "diplomat" named Mikhail K. Makarov. When he had telephoned earlier requesting an appointment I had checked him out and learned that our specialists considered him to be a KGB agent. When he called on me, I made it clear to him that I had no interest in his business or in having any follow up contacts with him. In later discussions with colleagues from NATO embassies, I learned that Makarov, a young hard-charger, was making a nuisance of himself with his blunt and heavy-handed efforts to establish relationships with NATO diplomats in what we assumed was a crude effort on his part to "recruit" us. His reputation quickly spread, and we all avoided him.

At the Marski reception, a small group of Western diplomats, including myself, were chatting amiably with Ambassador Ilkka Pastinen, who held at the time a senior position in the Foreign Ministry. To our surprise, Makarov unexpectedly walked up and boldly introduced himself to Ambassador Pastinen, holding out his hand for a handshake. Pastinen glared at him and did not respond to the proffered hand. Instead, he said sharply, "I know who you are," turned on his heel and walked away. We were stunned, and Makarov looked as though he would like to find a hole to crawl into. It was a heartening reminder that official Finland, and in this case Pastinen specifically, did not always strictly adhere to a "good neighborly" approach to Soviet officials, at least not when it was considered that an impertinence had taken place. It certainly warmed my own attitude toward Pastinen who on an earlier occasion shortly after my arrival had none-to-gently rebuked me for a comment I made which he construed as my comparing Finland's relationship with the Soviet Union to Nicaragua's relationship to the United States. Pastinen apparently didn't suffer fools lightly, no matter from which super power! You can be sure that I steered clear of any further pairing of those examples!

Other pleasurable memories of Finland from my first assignment stemmed from the relationship the embassy had with the Finnish private sector research and promotional organization EVA. Of course Ambassador Jakobson became one of my most valued Finnish interlocutors with whom I would meet quite frequently over the years. However, I am thinking right now of Kari Nars and Juha Sipilä, both advisors to Jakobson at EVA, Nars on the economic side and Sipilä on the political side. Matt Lorimer as the embassy economic counselor and I both maintained contact with EVA. In January 1977, Nars and Sipilä invited Lorimer and me to a sauna in a downtown hotel followed by dinner and many drinks. How far U.S. and Finnish political and economic relations were advanced that night is debatable. However, we all had such a good time that the foursome repeated the sauna night two or three times during the course of the next two years, including a memorable farewell sauna shortly before my departure in July 1979. We became close friends with the Nars and Sipiläs. In another spontaneous gesture of friendship, Juha Sipilä the next two Christmases came by our house as "Joulupukki," (Christmas Goat) the Finnish version of Santa Claus to delight and amuse our children. Yes, those aloof Finns!

Another unforgettable experience occurred when I was invited to Lapeenranta in the fall of 1977 for a moose hunt by a group of men some of whom were associated with the Finnish-American Society chapter of Lapeenranta. It turned out the group was a veterans club. I learned as the day wore on that the moose hunt was a good excuse for these Finnish war veterans to get together and remember their war experiences in fighting Russia whose border now, after the imposed loss of Karelia, reached to only a few miles east of Lapeenranta. It made a powerful impression on me, being on the Soviet border among a group of Finnish men who felt no ambiguity or ambivalence regarding who were Finland's friends and who were Finland's enemies.

The straightforward patriotism and honesty of these good Finns, as well as their friendship and admiration for the United States, was touching and clean. Their hatred for their big eastern neighbor was exposed to me like a raw, unhealed wound. It was an honor to be welcomed as a friend and to share their good cheer and their vodka. I must in all honesty confess that I was not the last man left standing by the end of the night, as best as I can blearily recall. It was indeed an emotional and deeply moving experience.

At the same time, however, I gained an unexpected insight into the profound psychological obstacles within the Finnish population that had to be confronted by other good Finns who were faced with the responsibility of trying to guide Finland in the hard reality of Finland's post-war situation. It was a cruel twilight zone where the harsh but simple and honest attitudes of the 1939-1944 period no longer seemed relevant. The challenge was how to soften the hard edges of bitter wartime experiences without, however, snuffing out the very spirit that one day, whatever the odds, Finland might need to call upon again. I could see the dilemma. And I mean it when I say I could see good Finns on both sides of the issue.

Another dimension of the charm of Finland is "Vapunpäivä" or May Day. This holiday is a particularly interesting one in Finland in that it combines several purposes: celebration of graduation from high school, an occasion where Finns of all ages will wear their traditional high school graduation caps; a welcoming of spring, although May 1st can often be a blustery day in Helsinki; and the traditional internationally observed socialist celebration of labor day. We had the good fortune to be among close Finnish friends during at least two of our Vapunpäivä days in Finland. One we spent with the Per-Erik Lönnfors family and other friends at the Adlon Restaurant in downtown Helsinki. Another we spent at the Haikon Kartamo, an historic manor house on the Baltic coast east of Helsinki, where we invited good friends Tapani and Lysa Brotherus and Jaakko and Mikki Jahnukainen to lunch. Both occasions were wonderful Finnish experiences, which we felt privileged to spend with Finnish friends.

It is a marvelous sight to see half of Helsinki parading the streets proudly in their white graduation caps, many after attending May Day political speeches. It was a less inspiring sight to see so many school children on "Vapunaatto," or May Day Eve, including even many pre-teenagers, getting falling down drunk in the streets of Helsinki. I have never quite understood why parents in a country with a serious alcohol problem could permit their children to participate in such a destructive festivity. It was as if a new generation was consciously learning to drink to excess. This was a less charming aspect of Finnish culture. This observation comes of course from someone whose own society is free of all such excesses!

11

From Ford to Carter:
From Austad to Ridgway

A change in presidencies in the United States, particularly when there is a change from one political party to another, brings major personnel changes in Washington. Such changes are far more sweeping in the American political system than in the other advanced democracies, notwithstanding the fact that the vast majority of the 3 or 4 million federal government career employees are protected from arbitrary dismissal by their civil service status. They are covered by laws developed in the late nineteenth century aimed against the "spoils system" under which virtually all government employees were sacked and replaced by the new president.

A new president nevertheless is able to name a couple of thousand key officials at the top of the various government departments and agencies as well as to replace most of the White House and executive office officials of the previous administration. The objective of this practice, the purpose of which I support, is to assure that the new president is able to place in key policy positions people who are loyal to him and who support his policies.

However, it is clear to any serious observer of Washington that this process often goes too far. Too many new and inexperienced people are brought in—in recent decades mostly, it seems, from remote state capitals—who have no idea of how to function in Washington and whose only criteria seem to be to do things differently from the outgoing administration. This is particularly true when the incoming president has based his campaign running against "Washington" and against the "Washington bureaucrats," as has been the case in recent years with Presidents Carter, Reagan and Clinton.

The result is predictable and inevitable: a period of intense politicization and distrust of inherited officials and policies; change for change's sake; a need to vilify previous policies and those career people remaining behind who assisted in implementing them; and an insistence on re-inventing the wheel. It makes little difference whether the change is from a Republican president to a Democratic president or vice versa—the mindless wheel-spinning, the counter-productive policy flip-flops, and the victimization of career officials associated with the previous administration take place over a period of approximately two years. Usually by the end of that period, the new officials will be more comfortable, more knowledgeable and less defensive. They will come to appreciate that the career government employees are for the most part dedicated public servants who want nothing more than to be supportive of the new administration and to help that administration succeed.

For the State Department and the Foreign Service, there is the added wrinkle of the constitutional right of presidents to appoint ambassadors and the fact that the use of ambassadorial appointments to reward political allies or campaign contributors is a practice endorsed and shamefully utilized by both political parties. There are individual differences, however, between presidents. During my career, the most relentlessly "political" presidents in their naming of ambassadors were Ronald Reagan and Bill Clinton. The most willing and most likely to appoint career diplomats as ambassadors were Jimmy Carter and George Bush.

And so it came to pass that following his recall of Ambassador Austad in April 1977, President Carter appointed Rozanne L. Ridgway as the new ambassador to Finland. Ambassador Ridgway arrived in Finland in late July 1977 and presented her credentials to President Kekkonen on August 5.

With Ambassador Ridgway came important changes in the U.S. embassy. Robert Houston acted as chargé d'affaires of the embassy during the interim and stayed on briefly as DCM during Ridgway's initial weeks in Finland. However, Ambassador Ridgway had chosen to designate a new DCM, Samuel E. Fry, who arrived later in the fall. It was part of her overall plan to put her own stamp on the embassy and to bring a new, more collegial spirit and approach to it than had been the case under the gregarious Austad who enjoyed being alone in the limelight.

Rozanne Ridgway was a career Foreign Service Officer who had risen through the ranks to become the United States' first woman ambassador to Finland at the young age of forty-one. The lot of a female Foreign Service Officer was not an easy one when Ridgway joined the Foreign Service right out of college in the late 1950s. There was still active prejudice against the idea of women Foreign Service Officers. While this attitude was breaking down, there was still a sense that women FSOs were more suited to consular, personnel and administrative work than to the substantive work of political, economic and security affairs. How could a female officer expect to run around a country and establish political contacts with male politicians, military officers and economists?

During the first part of her career, Ridgway had labored under those traditional attitudes. Gradually, however, through sheer talent and perseverance, she was able to establish herself not only as a female FSO but also as one who would be called upon to tackle difficult substantive issues. At the same time, the department began consciously to address the imbalances that had prejudiced the careers of women officers. Ridgway parlayed her expertise on international fishing issues gained from serving as State Department desk officer for Ecuador—at the time a notorious "troublemaker" on international fishing issues—to become the leading official in the State Department on setting and implementing U.S. policy on international fisheries questions. She traveled the world negotiating fishing treaties for the United States, attaining the personal rank of "ambassador" in the process. Her friends called her "Tuna Roz." Earlier, she had also developed a reputation as a European security specialist with credentials in working on NATO and other security matters.

It was with this background that Roz Ridgway arrived in Helsinki as the new United States ambassador. There had been some grumbling in the mostly-macho embassy that our new ambassador was a woman. Some Finns asked whether sending a woman ambassador to Finland meant that the United States was not taking Finland seriously. I was asked if it bothered me to work for a woman ambassador. My reply was, not at all, although I did admit to some discomfort in—for the first time—working for an ambassador who was younger (slightly) than I!

Ambassador Ridgway quickly established the kind of team spirit and collegiality that she sought for her embassy. In this process she was assisted by the fact that she, her new DCM Sam Fry, Matt Lorimer the economic counselor, and myself the political counselor were all virtually the same age, forty-one or forty-two. We were all career officers who had begun our careers within a few years of each other. The fact that she had risen rapidly through the ranks to become ambassador was not for us other three a problem. She deserved it. And we still had time to make it, we thought: as it turned out, none of us did!

The embassy became more professional, better organized and better focussed under Ambassador Ridgway. She had a clear understanding of U.S. interests and sought to have a more consistent and less flamboyant presence in Finland. To her credit, she learned quickly and fully acknowledged that Ambassador Austad had made some important contributions to promoting U.S. interests in Finland, particularly with respect to calling attention to the bias in the Finnish media, especially *Yleisradio*. But she wisely proceeded to project her own more intellectual and more professional style. She immediately won the respect of "serious" Finns in the Foreign Ministry and in literary, cultural and intellectual circles. At the same time, she showed other dimensions of her personality, becoming a familiar face at the hockey games of the Finnish hockey league and on the local golf links.

As far as I am aware, President Kekkonen did not permit a close professional relationship to develop with Ambassador

Ridgway. She did not see him as often as Ambassador Austad had. That was a pity, because she would have been able to deal with the president more productively on an agenda of issues of common interest than had Mark Austad. Whether President Kekkonen did not personally relate to the idea of a woman as the American ambassador I do not know. I do know that ultimately President Kekkonen came to recognize Ambassador Ridgway's capabilities and the respect with which she was held within Finnish official circles. When Ambassador Ridgway gave her memorable "farewell address" before the Paasikivi Society shortly before her departure in 1980, President Kekkonen personally attended.

While Ambassador Ridgway's February 11, 1980 speech gets us a bit ahead in our account, it is important for the insights it provided into her professionalism and into what she believed, based on her tour in Finland, were the key aspects of the state of U.S./Finnish relations which Finland might bear in mind.

Taking note of President Kekkonen's presence in the audience as well as that of numerous representatives of the Finnish foreign policy establishment, Ambassador Ridgway noted (speaking in English through a translator):[1]

> I am especially honored by your presence here this afternoon, Mr. President. I consider myself today, therefore, a professional among professionals, and I would like to offer my remarks to you in that same collegial spirit.

She noted first her belief that the two countries' bilateral relations were warm and favorable. She said that one reason why the relations were healthy and warm was that each side was aware of our different although compatible roles on the world stage:

> ...one a large nation with global responsibilities and global power, the other an independent neutral state with strong regional ties and interests, in addition to a well-defined voice in international affairs. We each approach the other with an awareness of our differences but with a genuine respect for our separate roles...

Taking note that it is normal for two such countries not always to be of the same view on all issues, Ridgway stated:

> I believed when I arrived, and continue to believe now, that the relationship between our two countries should be so broad and so deep that no single aspect of trade or politics becomes symbolic of the total relationship. We cannot escape, however, the reality that the relationship between Finland

and the United States today takes place in the context of the often conflicting and troubling demands of a world disturbed by resort to force and violence. I would like to take a few moments to comment on what is required from foreign policy in that world.

Getting diplomatically at one of the concerns that emerges several times in this book as an issue that bothered the United States over the years, Ambassador Ridgway asked rhetorically:

I believe that the United States, in its relations with Finland, acknowledges and understands the unchanging principles of Finnish foreign policy which have been articulated with clarity by Finnish representatives for more than three decades. This belief raises a corresponding thought which I would pose as a question: Does Finland, for its part, recognize the essentially unchanging principles and objectives on which the foreign policy of the United States is based?

I raise this question because the times are such that it is important that we evidence toward each other a mutual awareness of, and a mutual respect for, the international posture and policies of each nation. I must, as I take my leave of Finland, confess that I have a sense of uncertainty that there is full understanding here of the principles from which American policies flow and the objectives toward which they are directed. Without such understanding, the essentially unchanging character of post-war American foreign policy may not be fully recognized and fully appreciated.

The ambassador then laid out the broad outlines of U.S. post-war foreign and security policy beginning with President Truman's intention to build and preserve a lasting peace. She cited some constants in United States policy over the post-war years: support for the United Nations, belief in a strong NATO Alliance as a corner stone of U.S. policy, the creation of a world-wide economic and trading structure, the projection into our foreign policy of the basic human rights principles on which the United States was founded, and a search for arms control. She added:

The world today is a quite different place from the world of which President Truman wrote in 1946. Yet complex events and challenges to peace are still with us.

Recent events in Afghanistan have challenged the directions in foreign affairs which both Finland and the United States, each from its own perspective, have charted for ourselves during the past decade. These directions were intended to contribute to a permanent relaxation of East-West tension, to create a system for the peaceful resolution of international disputes, to foster communications and exchanges of ideas across borders, and to preserve the rights of sovereignty and territorial integrity of all nations, large and small. Let me be clear and direct. Our response reflects our belief that the violation of the codes which govern international conduct should not be cost-free. No nation which prefers to wage war to impose its views on how a smaller neighbor shall be governed should expect to continue to partake of the benefits of a cooperative relationship with the United States.

Then in a direct and unmistakable reference to the fact that Finland alone among the world's democracies failed to vote in the United Nations in favor of the resolution condemning the Soviet invasion of Afghanistan (Finland abstained) the ambassador said:

> More than one hundred nations have stepped forward in the United Nations to record their recognition of and support for the principle that there must be protection for all nations in the world before any nation can be considered secure.
>
> For those of us who have made East-West reconciliation a matter of national policy there are difficult times. There can be, however, no division of the world into small, mutually exclusive areas where no relation exists between behavior here and behavior there. There are obligations implicit in a cooperative relationship. When these obligations are ignored, the consequences must be confronted.

The ambassador went on to make an observation on another area which crops up in U.S. embassy reporting time after time as a concern: the media and its place in a democracy:

> In the past, citizens of both our nations have been troubled by the quality of comment which exists in the media regarding the policies and institutions of the other. We both recognize, however, that societies which seek to exercise a constant control over the media cannot be called truly free.

Ambassador Ridgway closed her remarkable and much commented upon speech by putting her above comments into the perspective of someone who had greatly valued and appreciated her two and one-half year assignment to Finland, saying:

> I leave Finland with an admiration for this nation and for its people. Its success is its own recommendation...I am confident that the relationship between our two countries which I leave with you and my successor is one from which we can all take satisfaction and of which we can all be proud.

Thus concluded Ambassador Ridgway's speech and her assignment to Finland. Fortunately, before that moment came, I had the good fortune of working for her at the embassy for almost two years. She was most supportive of our efforts in the political section to try to bring some clear long-term objectives to our reporting plan. Meanwhile, Ambassador Ridgway also put an end to the informal discouragement of any negative reporting that we had felt during the Austad years, thereby restoring a better balance to embassy reports.

12

The Ustinov Proposal: Uneasy Finland

In July 1978, Finland and outside observers of Finland received an unexpected and unwelcome reminder that Finland still lived on the border of a powerful and enigmatic superpower whose processes were opaque and actions often unpredictable. During a visit to Finland in that month, the Soviet Minister of Defense Dimitri Ustinov made a proposal that even though it was immediately rejected, shocked Finland in a visible and dramatic way. Details of exactly what happened are hard to come by even today, because the official Finnish response at the time was to deny that any proposal had been made or rejected.

However, it is clear that during his July visit to Finland, Defense Minister Ustinov proposed enhanced military cooperation between Finland and the Soviet Union under the 1948 Treaty of Friendship, Cooperation and Mutual Assistance (FCMA Treaty). Specifically, it is now recognized, Ustinov in a meeting with President Kekkonen proposed joint peacetime military exercises between Soviet and Finnish forces. President Kekkonen reportedly immediately rejected the Ustinov proposal out of hand, and it was not again raised during the Ustinov visit or thereafter.

Nevertheless, the fact that the Soviet Union would as late as 1978 propose such an undertaking has to rank as one of the most shocking developments of the entire post World War II Finnish/Soviet relationship. President Kekkonen had frequently described the establishment of a credible Finnish neutrality as his "life's work." That the Soviet leadership had come to an interpretation placing clear limits on their understanding of

Finland's neutrality has already been discussed above. But it was mind-boggling—and a denial of everything Kekkonen had striven for—that the Soviet Minister of Defense would propose the one act that would absolutely and irrevocably undermine any credibility of Finnish claims to neutrality—the holding of joint military maneuvers with the Red Army.

The U.S. embassy had first gotten word of the Ustinov proposal through "sensitive" channels. This information came from sources who were not direct witnesses of the proposal but who were considered by our embassy "specialists" to be reliable. As political counselor, I set about attempting to confirm the proposal and to obtain additional information clarifying the proposal and the circumstances surrounding it.

On August 25, 1978, the embassy sent a telegram to Washington (Helsinki message No. 2737) under the subject heading "More on Soviet Defense Minister Ustinov's Proposal for Joint Soviet/Finnish Military Maneuvers." The message, classified CONFIDENTIAL, was sent to the Department of State with information copies sent as well to the U.S. embassies in Moscow, Copenhagen, Oslo and Stockholm as well as to the U.S. mission to NATO in Brussels. I wrote the message and got the clearances and inputs of other elements of the embassy before submitting it to the chargé d'affaires at the time, Sam Fry, who approved its sending (Ambassador Ridgway was out of the country when the cable was transmitted). Highlights of the message follow:

> The embassy has been attempting to develop additional information concerning the proposal by Soviet Defense Minister Ustinov during his recent visit for joint Soviet/Finnish military maneuvers…Our task has been made more difficult by the fact that the government has adopted a policy of flatly denying that Ustinov made any such proposal…Two ranking MFA officials have told the political counselor that no such proposal was made. They supported their assertions by arguing the Soviets would never make such a proposal, because it would…undermine Finnish neutrality…against the Soviets' own interest.

> Despite disclaimers from Finnish Government officials, there can be no doubt that Ustinov did in fact make the proposal. In addition to the reliable-source information [previously reported] the embassy has in recent days received additional confirmation separately from two important private sector Finns close to the government defense and foreign policy community. Both stated they have information that Ustinov proposed joint

military maneuvers during his visit…[and] that President Kekkonen firmly rejected the Soviet proposal.

With respect to possible Soviet motivations in putting forth such a proposal at this time, the first of these two sources said, almost wistfully, it would be nice to assume that Ustinov—being a military man—did not realize the political complications of what he had proposed and had not cleared his proposal at the political level of the Soviet Government. The source went on nevertheless to categorize this hypothesis as a highly unlikely one…

The same source referred to what he characterized as two schools of thought in the Soviet Union about Finland, one supportive of Finnish neutrality and the other hostile to the concept. He speculated that the Ustinov proposal was the work of proponents of the latter school. He said the hard line position on Finland is usually identified with the CPSU (Communist Party of the Soviet Union) because of its ideological approach, whereas the Soviet military has usually tended to be more pragmatic and willing to see the Finnish point of view. Thus, according to this source, it is somewhat surprising that Ustinov would make this proposal. The source went on to speculate that Soviet motivation may be…a…reaction to the general rising level of tension between East and West or may reflect…the impending change in Soviet leadership.

The second source also tended to explain the Soviet proposal in terms of rising Soviet concern over East/West relations. This source, however, was inclined to place much of the blame for the proposal on Soviet Ambassador to Finland, V.S. Stepanov, whom he believes has been recommending to Moscow a firmer Soviet policy toward Finland. Whatever the Soviet motivation, both sources expressed the belief that the Ustinov proposal was a very troubling Soviet step which the Finns are taking seriously. Both expressed satisfaction that Kekkonen by his firm rejection…had effectively defended Finnish interests…

Neither source was surprised by the efforts of the Finnish Government to hold very closely information concerning the Ustinov proposal and to deny in fact that it had been made…One source implied that it might become an embarrassment to Ustinov if it became known that he had made a proposal which the Finns had so firmly rejected…

After this straight-forward reporting on what the embassy had been able to find out about the Ustinov affair, the telegram closed with its own assessment as to what the whole matter meant, labeled under the heading of "Comment."

COMMENT: The fact that MFA officials are unwilling to admit to us that Ustinov made his proposal for joint military maneuvers closes off at this time any possibility of exploring with them questions about possible Soviet motivation or about implications for Soviet/Finnish relations. We are inclined at this point to the view…that the Ustinov proposal is perhaps best explained in terms of Soviet objectives and concerns in the Nordic area. It may well also be related, as some Finns appear to suggest, to Soviet anxieties generally concerning the evolution of East/West relations and the China challenge.

As far as the specific implications for Finland, the most disturbing aspect for the Finns must surely be that the proposal underscores Soviet insensitivity to Finnish aspirations for a credible neutrality. President Kekkonen in the past termed Finnish neutrality as his life's main work, and it must be very disturbing to Finnish foreign policy makers that the Soviet leadership would be willing to undermine Finland's already somewhat embattled neutral image by proposing joint military maneuvers. This implication of the Ustinov proposal more than any other aspect may explain the Finnish Government's efforts to keep the proposal from becoming widely known. In this regard it is significant that the Stalinist-line Finnish newspaper *Tiedonantaja* again raised the desirability of joint Finnish/Soviet military maneuvers in an editorial August 22, still without mentioning the Ustinov proposal. Since it is unlikely that *Tiedonantaja* would return to this…subject without guidance, the…latest editorial may indicate the Soviets do not intend to let the concept of joint maneuvers die regardless of the Finnish Government's rejection of the Ustinov proposal…

The embassy's final comment regarding the possibility that the Soviets perhaps did not intend to let the proposal for joint maneuvers die fortunately proved to be inaccurate. However, it was a reflection of the deep concerns picked up from all Finnish observers regarding the seriousness of the Ustinov proposal and the fears and uncertainties that it had aroused.

As a couple of references in the telegram just quoted from make clear, I was extremely frustrated by the hard line followed by my official contacts in the MFA denying even that the Ustinov proposal had been made, insisting that the alleged proposal was an entire fabrication. I was particularly upset with the highest ranking MFA official that I had been able to reach, Under-Secretary for Political Affairs Keijo Korhonen, who had recently served briefly as foreign minister. In my meeting with Korhonen, he looked me straight in the eye and told me it had never happened. It was a bizarre meeting. I knew that he knew what had happened, and he knew that I clearly had information about what had happened. And yet he looked me in the eye and lied to me.

I recalled then the supposedly facetious adage that a diplomat is an honest man sent abroad to lie for his country! I knew that official dissembling was nothing new in diplomacy or in Finnish statecraft. I could imagine how the Germans felt, sitting across the table from President Risto Ryti in 1944 and accepting his solemn promise that Finland would never sue for a separate peace with the Soviets, only to have Ryti resign shortly thereafter and be followed by Marshal Mannerheim who reached a separate peace agreement with the Soviets!

I could appreciate the Finns' not wanting the matter to become public. I could even appreciate their not wanting to go officially on the record as admitting that Ustinov had made his proposal. However, there is a line between a formal, on-the-record official denial which protects the position of the government and maintains credible deniability for the official involved, and a posture or gesture which conveys to the other guy—who is representing a friendly country important to Finland's neutrality—look at me, I am denying that this ever happened but draw your own conclusions. Korhonen didn't give me the latter. He even went on to argue why the Soviets could not have possibly made such a proposal because it would harm Finnish neutrality. I never forgot that.

Some weeks later Ambassador Ridgway was finally able to achieve what I had been unable to do: get confirmation (from Foreign Minister Paavo Väyrynen) that the Ustinov proposal had, as everyone knew, been made. Väyrynen told the ambassador that Finland could hardly expect to receive honest information and assessments from its diplomatic partners if Finland was not itself prepared to be open and candid with them. The ambassador told the foreign minister that indeed it was difficult for friends of Finland to have an informed and constructive relationship if it could not rely on the information it received from Finnish authorities in response to its inquiries. She said that such situations could even call into question the quality of the professional relationship between the embassy and the Foreign Ministry. Väyrynen explained that at the time the embassy had made its inquiries, it was not clear whether the Ustinov offer had been made with the knowledge of the Soviet leadership, and spokesmen for the government felt they had no choice but to deny the event. He said that he, Secretary General Tuovinen and Under Secretary Korhonen understood the value of candor with us.

Well, it had been one of those three who had decidedly not been candid with me. Maybe two out of three is not bad.

MFA Under Secretary Korhonen's request, mentioned in Chapter Nine above, for discussions in Washington in late October on the Kekkonen proposal for a Nordic Nuclear Weapon Free Zone combined with an unofficial visit planned during the same time-frame by Prime Minister Kalevi Sorsa motivated me to draft a "think piece" message to the Department of State to put these pending visits into perspective for the Washington audience, particularly in light of the recent Ustinov proposal. I remember thinking how terribly important it was to step back and look at the Finnish situation. I spent an entire weekend at home writing a draft telegram that I entitled "Troubled Finland: Implications for US Policy Approaches."

On Monday morning I gave the draft report to Ambassador Ridgway for her consideration. She reviewed it and agreed with its general thrust but had a number of changes and additions that she wanted to see included. She called me in for a meeting, and we discussed the message. It was clear that we agreed basically on where we wanted to go with this message. I went back to my office, incorporated her changes, redid the message and brought it back to her for another meeting and discussion. She made some final adjustments, approved it and had the cable room send it off to the State Department with information copies sent as well to our embassies in the other Nordic capitals and Moscow and to the US NATO Mission in Brussels. Reading the message again now, twenty years later, I do not remember exactly which points were hers and which were mine. It doesn't matter, because we were in complete agreement; as was usually the case with Roz Ridgway, it was a collegial and team effort, this time between her and me.

The telegram, Helsinki 3367 of October 17, 1978 provides some excellent insights into embassy perceptions on Finland at that time. It also in my opinion represents an embassy at the top of its game: sizing up a specific situation, citing both Finnish concerns and embassy judgements on those concerns; putting the situation into a longer-term context and relating it to US interests; indicating the timeliness and relevance of the issues raised, given the pending visits to Washington by Finnish officials; and putting forward policy considerations and recommendations for use by Washington officials. This is how an embassy can influence policies in positive directions, bringing to bear an expertise and depth of knowledge about a subject or issue—in this case the existing Finnish situation—that a busy Washington simply does not have the time or the specialized knowledge to produce.

The telegram, bearing the classification of "SECRET" stated:

1. SUMMARY: In view of the forthcoming visits to Washington during the next three weeks by Finnish Prime Minister Sorsa (travelling unofficially) and MFA Political Under Secretary Korhonen, we believe that a brief update of the Finnish security and foreign policy situation would be timely. A fresh assessment is particularly relevant at this time because the Finns appear somewhat concerned about their current situation and because they are moving ahead with their revival of President Kekkonen's Nordic Nuclear Weapon Free Zone (NNWFZ) proposal. The causes of Finnish concern and its effect on Finland's current attitudes and policies have important implications for US/Finnish relations and how the USG should approach them. This message analyzes the Finnish situation (Paragraphs 2-6) and recommends appropriate US responses (Paragraphs 7-10). END SUMMARY

2. Three years ago Finland could look out at the world—toward both East and West—with a considerable degree of satisfaction and equanimity. The 1975 CSCE summit meeting in Helsinki—to an important degree the result of tireless Finnish efforts—seemed to have demonstrated clearly to East and West the constructiveness and utility of Finland's unique role in the European community. In a broader context, the Spirit of Helsinki seemed both to reflect and to further a flourishing process of détente between the United States and the Soviet Union. Since it is axiomatic in Finland that Finland's degree of national well being and security is positively correlated to the fortunes of the US-Soviet relationship, Finnish satisfaction and optimism at that time can be readily understood. In that context it was not difficult for Finland to remain relatively unconcerned about…signs that the Soviet leadership did not fully share the Finnish interpretation of neutrality, that the…strategic importance of Northern Europe was attracting increasing attention from East and West, and that in the West use of the term Finlandization was on the increase.

3. As Finland looks out upon the world today it sees quite a different prospect than in 1975. The CSCE process clearly is going to be long and difficult, and as a forum it is not immune to the stresses and strains of the broader East/West relationship; for the Finns this means that instead of

being able to play a showcase role in the CSCE process, they must for the time being adopt the low-profile posture they tend to assume on issues in controversy between East and West. Meanwhile, a number of incidents in Northern Europe have demonstrated that East/West interest in the area continues to grow, along with the potential for rising tension. These developments, along with several other indicators, provided clear evidence to the Finns of a downward trend in East/West relations. Consistent with the Finnish axiom, this trend signaled trouble for Finland.

4. The trouble has arrived. In the East, Soviet reservations about Finnish neutrality became clearer and more blunt, culminating (thus far) in Soviet Defense Minister Ustinov's proposal last July for joint Finnish/Soviet military maneuvers...In the West there has been an upsurge in the disparaging use of the Finlandization term in ways that appear almost to assign Finland to the Soviet camp. The Finns have been particularly upset by the fact that Finlandization has become a political issue in West Germany between Social Democrats and Free Democrats on the one hand and the Christian Social Union and Christian Democrats on the other...

5. Times of tension between East and West bring into sharper focus the dilemma inherent in Finland's efforts both to maintain the confidence of Soviet leadership—the overriding imperative of Finnish policy—and to nurture Finland's standing in the West and third world as a credible neutral. In trying times such as these the Finns believe that the Finnish national interest dictates paying special attention to maintaining the good will of the Soviet leadership. We believe this was a major factor in the Finnish decision to revive and put forward the modified version of the Kekkonen Nordic NWFZ proposal...The Finns continue to rely heavily on the assumption that Finland's foreign and security policy as it is now constructed best serves both its own interests and the legitimate long-term Soviet security interest in Finland. A basic cause of Finland's current concern is the indication in Ustinov's proposal that the Soviets may not see it that way.

6. The Finns apparently expect that in this situation the West should show understanding for the difficulty of Finland's position (even though they are reluctant to take us into their confidence). It is our impression that the Finns consider the increase in references to Finlandization as evidence of a lack of understanding in the West and even as a sign of possible hostility toward Finland in some Western press and official circles. The Finnish press has hinted at an alleged link between the Finlandization campaign in West Germany by the Christian Social Union and Christian Democrats and US Government officials reportedly concerned about neutralist tendencies within the German Social Democrats. Also, a prime offender in Finnish eyes as a propagator of Finlandization is...the Research Council of the Center for Strategic and International Studies in Washington. Finnish suspicions about Western attitudes...have been further raised by the rather dramatic handling in the Western press of the Ustinov incident which

Finnish officials had hoped (against logic) would not become public; some Finns suspect the news leaked from Western diplomatic sources. The problems and issues we are addressing with Finland on economic and commercial matter further complicate matters for Finnish policy leaders.

7. Even taking into consideration all of the above, we would describe the Finnish mood as concerned rather than alarmed. The Finns are calm, and there is no sense of impending crisis. They have been there before. There is a sense that their difficulties are temporary and that this phase too will ease with an upswing in US/Soviet relations. Nevertheless, we believe that their present concern is real and that how the US reacts to this situation will be very important to the Finns and to US/Finnish relations. Rather than any change in the basic US policy toward Finland, what is required is to place the current situation into longer term perspective and to pay special attention to the tone and style of our approach in dealing with the Finns. While they remain as taciturn as ever, they appear to us to feel on the defensive and in need of some reassurance. They resent Western insinuations that on some policy issues they either do not know what they are doing or are deliberately acting as a Soviet stalking horse. The Finns believe they deserve recognition for having successfully managed their relations with the Soviet Union since World War II in a way that has preserved their independence and maximized their neutrality. They want Western understanding that their policies and proposals today are based strictly on their perception of Finland's own national interest.

8. While the survival and independence of Finland today constitute powerful evidence of the essential success of Finnish foreign policy since World War II, we also see disturbing elements in Finland's approach to foreign affairs. There is a tendency for Finns to downplay the constraints inherent in their situation and to protest rather too loudly the even-handedness of Finnish neutrality; but when outside observers point out that there are constraints which do affect the balance of Finnish neutrality, the Finns tend to react sharply and defensively. We believe the Finns are not always as careful as they should be about the impact [on] Western interests and sensitivities of some of their policy statements and proposals designed to maintain good relations with the Soviet leadership. It seems to us that the Finns sometimes go further than would appear necessary in assuaging the Soviets and that within the confines of their relationship with the Soviet Union there is margin for more maneuverability than the Finns are currently utilizing. We also believe Finnish leaders need to make more of an effort to explain to representatives of some friendly western governments the background, context and motivations for some of their decisions. Because of these kinds of shortcomings, it is no accident that Finland has been unsuccessful in counteracting the negative connotations often associated in Europe and America with the term Finlandization.

9. Despite these reservations on some elements of Finnish policy, we believe that under Finland's present circumstances it is important for USG

officials in their contacts with high-level Finns in coming weeks to reassure them that a solid base of mutual respect and understanding underpins US/Finnish relations and to emphasize the continuity of our relationship. It is important that the Finns not fall into a pattern of thinking that begins to assume lack of understanding or vague hostility from the West. US officials should explicitly (perhaps publicly) disassociate the USG from the term Finlandization on the grounds that the Finnish/Soviet relationship has its own historical and geopolitical context which is completely different from the Western European/Soviet relationship. Using these general reassurances as a point of departure, US officials in their contacts with Finnish leaders should go on to (1) state that while the West understands the need for Finland to manage its relationship with the Soviet Union with great care, Western interests and sensitivities can also be taken into consideration so that Finnish positions or initiatives do not appear to detract from Finland's reputation in the West, thereby feeding the Finlandization discussion; and (2) acknowledge in policy discussions with the Finns our acceptance that their positions or proposals are based on Finland's perceptions of its own national interest; (3) point out that in the same spirit and with the same obligation to advance our own policy goals and objectives, on some important issues the national interest of the US and our allies will lead us to take positions different from those taken by Finland. On economic and commercial matters, we must be...alert to see that our decisions are perceived to be fair and not [lacking in]...concern for...[their] importance...to the whole fabric of Finnish policy, as seen by Finns.

10. There is little we can do for Finland to relieve whatever pressure the Finns are receiving from the Soviet Union. We are certainly not going to jeopardize our security interests or those of our allies in an effort to be helpful, nor is it in our interest to attempt to distort Finnish neutrality in our direction...Our best contribution in support of our own and Finnish national interests during this difficult period for Finland is to be patient, reassuring and understanding while...calmly but firmly protecting our and our allies' interests. RIDGWAY

The embassy message was well-received in Washington, and Robert Funseth, director of the Department of State's office of Northern European affairs, helped arrange excellent schedules for both Sorsa and Korhonen. Both were, as I recall, quite satisfied with their Washington visits. As noted earlier, there was simply no bridging of the substantive gap between the U.S. and Finnish positions on the Nordic Nuclear Weapon Free Zone issue, and Korhonen could have received no encouragement on that score. However for the Finns, we were convinced, the process of discussing and negotiating about a NNWFZ was at least as much of a Finnish objective as the NNWFZ goal itself. Korhonen could in any case come back from Washington pointing out that the Finns had raised this issue with the United States, thereby continuing the process.

The references to Finnish concerns over the "Finlandization" epithet in the embassy's message served to reinforce an effort by the Department of State to discourage the use of the term by U.S. officials. The difficulty of fine-tuning this message was amusingly conveyed in an anecdote related to me in 1995 by Bob Funseth, who had been in charge of the Department's Nordic affairs for some years in the late 1970s and early 1980s. Funseth recounted how he and his office were preparing Vice President Walter Mondale for a trip to Norway and Finland in April of 1979.

Funseth said he had personally briefed Mondale, and when it came to Finland he said, "Look, Mr. Vice President, there is one thing. You are going to get asked about this, but whatever you say, do not use the word 'Finlandization.'" Funseth explained why and then reiterated to the vice president, "Sir, that term should not pass from your lips." The vice president indicated that he had understood the advice. Then they had a press briefing session with American and foreign reporters at the National Press Club before Mondale went off on this trip. Sure enough, someone raised his hand and asked the Vice President something about Finlandization. And Mondale looked over at Funseth, and turned back to the questioner and said, "Well, I have to tell you that I have been told that the word Finlandization should never escape my lips." Then he turned back to Funseth and said, "Did I do that right?" Now that Mondale has had the experience of serving as the United States ambassador to Japan, he perhaps might in retrospect wish he had been a little more sympathetic to Funseth's diplomatic effort at spin control of a sensitive issue!

13

My 1979 Assessment of Kekkonen and the Presidential Succession Issue

For over two years I had intended, prior to completing my assignment to Helsinki in July 1979, to prepare a detailed assessment of the Kekkonen presidency and the implications for Finland and for U.S. interests of the eventual transition to a post-Kekkonen period.

The "Presidential Succession Issue" was a very hot topic in those years. President Kekkonen's long domination of the Finnish political scene was an unusual phenomenon in Western European politics, and there was real interest in Washington as to what would happen after his eventual departure. Although there were fundamental differences in their respective situations, an analogous case had been the interest in what would happen in Yugoslavia after Tito's departure.

President Kekkonen was clearly aging. The diplomatic community spent a considerable amount of time assessing how Kekkonen had looked in their most recent encounters with him. Highly classified reports were sent analyzing every head cold or other perceived health weaknesses noted in the president. It was becoming quite obvious that he had good days and bad days, and that the bad days seemed to be coming with more frequency. These latter were the days when the president would seem somewhat confused or out of touch in conversations with visiting foreign officials accompanied by diplomats from their respective embassies in Helsinki. We foreign diplomats would compare notes on how the president had performed in his meetings with "our" visitors from home.

Increasingly the reports were not encouraging regarding the president's appearance and performance. Many of us wondered how much of the day-to-day work of the presidency was actually being done by the president, and how much was being done by aides in his name. Finnish officialdom was hermetically discreet and protective of the president. There were no published reports of the president not being in good health, and few Finns who had access to the president would discuss his health.

However, interest in the succession issue was natural. By 1979 Kekkonen had been president for twenty-three years or an incredible thirty-eight percent of his country's existence as an independent country since December 1917! He had over his long presidency built up enormous authority and had come to dominate the Finnish political scene. He personally managed relations with the Soviet Union, and he and his Center (formerly Agrarian) Party had for years claimed that only he could successfully handle the Soviets. How would Finland survive without Kekkonen? What would the Soviets do to Finland after Kekkonen? Would a novice president be able to manage relations with the Russians? Didn't Finland need Kekkonen to keep the Soviets at bay?

With these concerns in mind, Ambassador Ridgway had approved my proposal that the embassy prepare a comprehensive study of the "Finnish Presidential Succession". As political counselor, it was my baby, although the analyses benefited from suggestions by the ambassador, DCM Fry, and my political section sidekick, Ward Thompson. The final reports were reviewed by the DCM and the ambassador and thus reflected the collective judgement of the embassy. The six-part analysis was submitted in a series of four "airgrams" between March 1 and June 29, 1979—the latter date three days prior to my July 2 departure from Finland.

At the time I considered the messages comprising my reports of the Finnish presidential succession issue (embassy airgrams A-8, A-27, A-29 and A-42) to be the best analytical work I had done in the Foreign Service up to that point. Even now from a perspective of 20 years, and knowing what I know now, I think the reports were remarkably on target in most important respects. I would only add that in today's more outspoken and objective Finland, my reports if anything look a tad cautious and guarded with respect to their assessment of President Kekkonen.

The first report "Finnish Presidential Succession—Part I: The Process" (embassy airgram A-8 of March 1, 1979) introduced the theme of presidential succession by noting that President Kekkonen was beginning his twenty-fourth year in office and the second year of his latest six year term. It remarked that President Kekkonen would be 83 years old if he completed his term in March 1984. The report noted the possibility that, although he was in "fair health for a man of his age," it could not be excluded that he might not be able to serve out his term.

> Because of the overwhelming political authority that Kekkonen has built up during his twenty-three years in office, the passing of the presidency from his to another's hands will rank as a political development of central importance and significance.

I noted that the method of selecting a president in Finland had been clearly established in the basic legislation at the beginning of Finnish independence sixty years earlier. (Until the most recent presidential elections in 1994, Finnish presidents were elected indirectly through an electoral college quite similar to the United States' system. Beginning with the election of President Martti Ahtisaari in 1994, Finnish presidents are now elected by direct vote of the electorate.) However, I emphasized that in fact there had been numerous occasions in which the president had been selected by vote of the Finnish Parliament—most recently in 1973—under "exceptional procedures" authorized under Finnish law.

The report stressed that whether a new president were selected by electoral or exceptional means, "the role of the prime minister in his selection process can be a critically important one, which helps account for the current lively political interest in who will be the prime minister following the 1979 parliamentary elections."

Part I concluded that:

> In an unscheduled presidential succession situation resulting from the incapacitation of the president, the political position of the prime minister/acting president would become very powerful indeed, Because of

the authority that would be wielded by the prime minister/acting president as political leader, head of government and chief of state, he would immediately be considered the most likely presidential successor.

The next report "Part II: The Aging Incumbent and the Finnish Presidency" (airgram A-27 of May 10) assessed the long Kekkonen presidency, its significance and its probable legacy. The report analyzed the place and powers of the presidency in the Finnish Constitution. The constitution places supreme power with parliament: legislation once approved by Parliament is not subject to judicial review, and Parliament can rewrite the constitution itself by two-thirds majority, over the opposition of the president, if necessary.

The message explained that, while the constitution deposits ultimate supremacy theoretically with Parliament, it also places unusually significant powers (by Western European standards) in the presidency. The president can appoint and dismiss cabinets and individual cabinet ministers as well as other leading officials. He can dissolve Parliament or call it into extraordinary session. He can veto legislation (subject, however, to being overridden by Parliament). Perhaps the most significant powers placed in the presidency by the constitution are that he is responsible for directing foreign affairs and is commander-in-chief of the armed forces and responsible for Finland's national security.

The May 10 report reviewed the rise of the Finnish presidency. In the post-World War II period real political power in Finland tended to flow away from the Parliament, the political parties and the cabinet towards the presidency. While this trend was already noteworthy during the ten-year presidency of J.K. Paasikivi (1946-56), it became far more pronounced under Urho Kekkonen. By 1979, the report observed, President Kekkonen had "come to attain virtually unchallenged authority over all aspects of Finnish politics."

The Part II report analyzed how this concentration of power in the hands of the president had come to pass.

The reasons for Kekkonen's enormous influence derive in varying degrees from basic political realities, from his long incumbency and from his own powerful personality. The most important political reality fostering the power of the presidency is the interrelationship between two key factors: (1) the constitutional authority vested in the Finnish president for the conduct of Finland's national security and foreign policy and (2) the fact that relations with the Soviet Union are absolutely central to Finland's national survival. Since all other national issues must be subordinate to Finland's survival as an independent state, meaning the successful management of relations with the Soviet Union, there is a strong tendency that the person or institution responsible for managing that relationship will assume primacy in national political life.

I observed that other factors also served to reinforce the president's management of foreign and security affairs.

Particularly, the relative instability, fragmentation of power and lack of continuity which characterize other Finnish political institutions (the political parties, Parliament, government cabinets) render these institutions incapable of providing the continuity necessary for steady management of foreign affairs, in sharp contrast to the extraordinary stability of the presidency (only two presidents since 1946) [up to 1979]. Moreover, given the well-known preference of Soviet leaders for dealing with established statesmen whom they know personally, the longstanding relationship between President Kekkonen and the Soviet leadership further reinforces Kekkonen's position in Finnish politics as the one man able to manage the all-important relationship with the Soviet Union.

The fragmentation of power among the numerous Finnish political parties (eight parties are currently represented in Parliament) and the relative instability of Finland's usually coalition governments (some 60 different governments—cabinets—in 61 years of independence) have contributed to the accretion of presidential power also in domestic political affairs. Because of the relative weakness of the other political actors, the stability of the presidency...resulted in the president's assuming more responsibility and authority over domestic affairs than was probably anticipated by the constitution. The length of Kekkonen's incumbency and his strong personality have undoubtedly reinforced the...power of the presidency in domestic affairs as well as in foreign relations.

The report then dealt with the important issue of "Kekkonen and His Critics." I noted that while in the 1978 presidential elections Kekkonen had the support of all of the traditional political parties representing over eighty percent of the Finnish electorate, Kekkonen had by no means always enjoyed such support.

Throughout his political career he [had] been a highly controversial figure. He was first elected president in 1956 by the narrowest of margins (by a 151-149 vote of the 300 presidential electors). His current unchallenged position is more a tribute to the tremendous authority he has slowly built up and to Finnish acceptance of foreign policy realities than to his personal popularity.

I stated that there had been two broad and partially overlapping areas in which the president had sometimes been attacked by both domestic and foreign critics: his management of relations with the Soviet Union and his contribution to the relative eclipse of Finland's other domestic political institutions. I presented the arguments as follows:

Management of Relations with the Soviet Union—No responsible Finn challenges the foreign policy imperative of maintaining good relations with the Soviet Union. Most Finns probably accept that Finland (i.e., Kekkonen, since 1956) has done an effective job of managing its foreign relations: Finland has prospered economically, maintained its basic independence, developed a credible though somewhat restricted neutrality and maintained its Western values and institutions. Such accomplishments notwithstanding, some observers have criticized Kekkonen's management of relations with the Soviet Union on three counts. One charge of the critics is that Finland under Kekkonen has been unduly solicitous towards the Soviet Union in the formulation of Finland's positions on specific foreign policy issues. They say Finland's neutrality has been too timid or that it is unbalanced in favor of Soviet interests. Critics cite, for example, Finnish positions on some European *détente* and disarmament issues which seem closer to Soviet positions than to Western views and, recently, awkward Finnish maneuvering to find an official position on Southeast Asia and the China/Vietnam conflict that would not conflict directly with the Soviet position.

A second criticism of Kekkonen's management of Finnish/Soviet relations is that he...permitted undue Soviet interference in Finnish domestic politics and, even, that he...used Soviet interference to further his own political interests at the expense of political rivals. The classic cases cited by critics are: 1958 when Soviet pressure resulted in the resignation of a Finnish coalition Government accused of containing anti-Soviet elements; 1962 when Soviet pressure resulted in withdrawal of the strongest presidential candidate opposing Kekkonen, allegedly because he was being supported by anti-Soviet elements; and 1973 when Parliament extended President Kekkonen's term of office to 1978, allegedly because the Soviet Union insisted on Kekkonen's continuation in office as a *quid pro quo* for Soviet acquiescence in Finland's signing a free trade agreement with the EEC...

A third area of criticism of Kekkonen's management of Finnish/Soviet relations relates to the tone of the Finnish approach to the Soviet relationship under Kekkonen...Critics are unhappy with a tendency of the Finnish government towards fulsome praise of the Soviet Union and Soviet leaders, with Kekkonen's continuing encouragement of Finnish self-censorship, meaning avoidance of criticism of the Soviet Union, and with the tendency of Kekkonen to portray Finnish/Soviet relations as a model worthy of emulation by other states in their relations with the Soviet Union.

With respect to these criticisms, I said in the May 10 report, the embassy believed that "within the constraints imposed by history and geopolitics, Finland under Kekkonen has done an effective job in preserving basic Finnish interests while at the same time complying with the foreign policy imperative of maintaining good relations with the Soviet Union." However, I went on to point out that:

> ...while we recognize the essential success of Finland's foreign and security policies under difficult circumstances, we have also noted some disturbing elements in Finland's approach to foreign affairs. It seems to us that under Kekkonen's leadership the Finns have not always been as careful as they might in weighing the impact of Western interests and sensibilities of some of their policy statements and proposals designed to maintain good relations with the Soviet leadership. It also appears to us that the Finns sometimes go further than would appear necessary in assuaging the Soviets and that within the confines of their relationship with the Soviet Union there is margin for more maneuverability than the Finns are currently utilizing both with respect to position-taking on foreign affairs issues and to limiting the degree of Soviet influence of domestic Finnish affairs.

Readers will note that some of the phraseology here repeats similar observations in the earlier embassy message on "Troubled Finland" quoted in the previous chapter. With respect to criticisms of Kekkonen on his management of relations with the Soviet Union, Part II concluded that:

> In short, then, President Kekkonen is not completely invulnerable to the criticisms of his detractors, although the latter often appear to ignore the fact that the realities of Finland's relationship with the Soviet Union impose definite constraints on Finland's freedom of action.

Concerning the criticisms of Kekkonen's relationships with other Finnish political institutions and players, the May 10 report offered the following assessment:

> *The Eclipse of Other Political Institutions*—In addition to criticizing Kekkonen for his management of relations with the Soviet Union, some observers tend to blame him for the gap that has developed between the powers of the presidency and that of the other political institutions, i.e. parliament, the political parties and the cabinet. While, as described above, the fact of the fragmentation of power within these other institutions was itself an important factor in the accretion of presidential power, there is both a cause and a result effect at work; the increased power of the president has accentuated the fragmentation of the other organs of government. Critics of President Kekkonen charge that through his political elimination of potential rivals over the years, his use of the foreign policy weapon to

buttress his own political position, and his apparent determination to stay in office as long as he is physically capable, Kekkonen has systematically contributed to an unhealthy distortion in the balance of political power in Finland. His worst detractors fear he has even undermined the very foundations of Finnish democracy.

Regarding Kekkonen's critics on domestic grounds, Part II concluded that:

...here, as with their criticisms of Kekkonen's management of relations with the Soviet Union, his critics have considerably overstated their case and have tended to ignore the factors beyond Kekkonen's personal control which have resulted in the strengthening of the presidency. On the other hand, their can be no gainsaying the fact that Kekkonen's exclusive grip on real political power in Finland and his long tenure in office now well into its third decade, have combined to emasculate—at least temporarily—the other Finnish political institutions.

Finally, the May 10, 1979 report raised "A Basic Question: The Durability of Kekkonen's Impact on the Presidency". The report said in this regard that:

...there may be some aspects of the Kekkonen presidency that even most Kekkonen supporters will not wish to see perpetuated. For example there is broad support among political circles for taking steps to redress the balance between presidential power and the power of the other political institutions. Impossible even to contemplate while Kekkonen is in office, the question of curtailing presidential power will probably become a major political issue in Finland after he leaves office. After a quarter century of Kekkonen domination of Finnish politics, the period immediately following his eventual departure will almost surely be one of a searching evaluation of the impact of his long presidency on Finnish democratic institutions and on Finland's relations with East and West.

The next report in the series on the Finnish presidential succession (Helsinki A-29 of May 17, 1979) included "Part III The Potential Candidates" and "Part IV The Domestic Politics of Succession". This report named the Finns that the embassy considered the most likely candidates to succeed President Kekkonen and analyzed the multi-party context in which their selection would take place. The apparent front-runners in the presidential succession sweepstakes were identified in alphabetical order as Ahti Karjalainen (Center Party), Mauno Koivisto (Social Democratic Party), Kalevi Sorsa (Social Democratic Party) and Johannes Virolainen (Center Party).

Part IV emphasized that a winning candidate would have to enjoy the backing of at least two of the major parties, plus additional support, in order to win a majority of the 300 presidential electors and speculated that probably no candidate could win enough votes in an initial round of presidential elector voting. I observed that for historical reasons and because of party dynamics, the Center Party seemed to be most favorably placed to provide the winning candidate. Although the logic of the arguments appeared to be sound, as events turned out this prognosis proved to be considerably off the mark! To be fair to myself, however, I did point out the "rivalry within the Center Party between Karjalainen and Virolainen could result in a mutual blocking of each." I also noted that in Mauno Koivisto the SDP had "...the hottest political property in Finland. All public opinion polls show the charismatic Koivisto as by far the people's favorite candidate; in fact he is the favorite candidate among the voters of all parties."

However, the report noted:

Koivisto's popularity notwithstanding, his prime difficulty would appear to be gaining his party's nomination, given Sorsa's control over SDP party machinery and presumed intention to obtain the SDP presidential nomination for himself. In this regard Koivisto's position would be considerably strengthened should his designation May 11 by President Kekkonen as government formateur result in his becoming prime minister (still unclear as of this writing). As noted in Part I of this series of reports, the prime minister enjoys important advantages in the presidential succession sweepstakes which could more than offset Sorsa's influence within the SDP. Moreover, a successful prime ministership by Koivisto would have the effect of reducing Sorsa's influence within the SDP itself.

As it turned out, Kekkonen did make Koivisto prime minister, Koivisto's performance as PM was indeed highly successful, and he did in fact become acting president when President Kekkonen had to submit his resignation because of poor health in the autumn of 1981. Thus Koivisto did in fact obtain the SDP's presidential nomination for the 1982 elections. In those elections his remarkable popularity, commented upon in the May 17, 1979 embassy report, continued to hold sway, and he won an easy first-round majority of the presidential electors. But that gets us ahead of our story.

In the final report of the presidential succession series, Helsinki A-42, submitted June 29, 1979, I presented "Part V The Soviet Role" in Finnish Presidential politics and "Part VI Conclusions." Part V reviewed embassy judgements on what interests motivated Soviet policy toward Finland. This is an issue that recurs throughout the post-World War II period and is discussed frequently in this book. In the 1979 report we asserted that:

The trend of post-World War II developments in Finnish/Soviet relations indicates that the basic Soviet interest in Finland has been essentially a military/security interest: the Soviet leadership no doubt considers it essential to guarantee beyond question that the area of Finland will never be used as a gateway through which enemy forces might threaten or invade the Soviet Union. The Peace Treaty of 1947 was intended *inter alia* to assure that Finland itself could never pose even a limited military threat to Soviet territory; the 1948 Treaty of Friendship, Cooperation and Mutual Assistance (FCMA) was intended to assure that Finland would oppose—with Soviet assistance if necessary—any effort by an enemy to invade the Soviet Union through Finnish territory. This basic Soviet policy concern that Finland and Finnish territory be completely secure militarily [was] probably...re-enforced in recent years by the strategic buildup in the Kola Peninsula.

The fundamental shift in Finland's own security and foreign policy in the wake of World War II and its tragic lessons for Finland was to recognize and accept the Soviet security interest in Finland. While maintaining security contingency plans to resist an invader from any direction, particularly from the Soviet Union, Finland has based its post-World War II security and foreign policy on the conclusion that Finland was considered expendable by the West and the belief and expectation that the Soviet Union has no objectives in Finland beyond its understandable security interest.

The June 29 report went on, however, to point out that the Soviet Union had not if fact limited itself solely to defensive military/security interests with respect to Finland:

It is true that by refraining from satellizing Finland—which militarily it could have accomplished at any time over the past forty years—the Soviet Union has a continuing *prima facia* case that its interest in Finland [was] benignly defensive. This impression was further nourished by apparent Soviet acquiescence, particularly in the 1960s, in Finland's aspiration to follow a neutral foreign policy. However, Soviet tolerance of the concept of Finnish neutrality appears to have narrowed in recent years...In any case, it has long been evident that the Soviet Union has considered not only Finnish security and foreign policy but also Finnish domestic politics as legitimate areas for wielding influence and exerting pressure.

In discussing precedents of Soviet behavior, I noted in the report that "The Soviets have shown particular interest in the selection of Finnish presidents:"

The classic case of Soviet interference occurred in 1940 when Finland was preparing to select (in the electoral college) a successor to the gravely ill President Kallio who had submitted his resignation. Six names were prominently mentioned as presidential candidates: Marshal Mannerheim; ex-President Svinhufud; former Prime Minister Toivo Kivimäki; incumbent Prime Minister Risto Ryti; Social Democratic Party Chairman Vaino Tanner; and Ambassador to the Soviet Union J.K. Paasikivi. On December 6, 1940 in Moscow, the Soviet Foreign Ministry presented Paasikivi with a diplomatic note stating that selection of Mannerheim, Svinhufud, Kivimäki or Tanner as President would signify that Finland did not wish to fulfill its (Winter War) Peace Treaty with the Soviet Union. Inasmuch as Paasikivi was considered by Germany as pro-Soviet, Risto Ryti—the only candidate acceptable to all foreign powers concerned—was elected. In Part II [Helsinki A-27 of May 10, 1979] we have already referred to alleged Soviet pressure that caused Olavi Honka to withdraw his candidacy against President Kekkonen in 1962 and to reported Soviet insistence in 1973 that President Kekkonen's term (due to expire in 1974) be extended to 1978.

Against this background the June 29 report argued that it was clear the Soviet Union, if it considered it necessary, "would not hesitate to exert pressure on the coming presidential selection process." The paper went on to speculate that much would depend on how the Soviets related to the various contending candidates and its assessment of the likely electoral outcome:

Of the four leading candidates, it is believed—on admittedly skimpy evidence—that the Soviets have in recent years favored Ahti Karjalainen (Center Party) and have tended to look with disfavor on Johannes Virolainen (Center Party). It is also considered that Kalevi Sorsa (Social Democratic Party - SDP) would probably be acceptable to the Soviets, given his key role in leading the SDP to a far-reaching accommodation with the Soviet Union. Mauno Koivisto's (SDP) standing with the Soviet leadership is unclear; there is a feeling that the Soviets might consider him too independent-minded and maybe even too popular. It is certain that the Soviets will be watching very closely Koivisto's performance as prime minister.

The report went on to speculate that how strongly the Soviets felt about the various candidates and how the Soviets assessed the candidates' chances would importantly influence Soviet behavior. I noted that Soviet influence wielding in Finland had generally become more indirect and subtle over recent years, "particularly when compared to their crude—but effective—intervention in the 1940 selection process."

However, there are still occasional examples of heavy-handed and unsubtle approaches, such as the 1978 brusque proposal by Soviet Defense Minister Ustinov for joint Soviet/Finnish military maneuvers and the 1979 election-eve *Pravda* article attacking the Conservative Party. Finnish reactions to both of these incidents would appear to argue to the Soviets the merits of a more indirect approach. Moreover, direct, blatant Soviet intervention in the presidential process would also tend to ring alarm bells in the other Nordic countries and to have a potentially negative effect on broader Soviet interests. Nevertheless, the possibility of direct Soviet interference in the selection process cannot be discounted.

The report went on to speculate that:

It is very likely that the Soviet Union will attempt early in the term of the new president to assure that he pursues policies that maintain if not strengthen Finnish/Soviet ties. A perhaps apocryphal story in Helsinki is that during the first six months of every new Finnish foreign minister's tenure, Soviet diplomats can be observed shaking their heads and expressing grave doubt about the new minister's sincere dedication to good neighborly Finnish/Soviet relations; this results, so the story goes, in the new foreign minister's leaning over backwards to demonstrate his good neighborly spirit. This type of attitude could constitute one possible Soviet approach to the new Finnish president. More serious would be a Soviet move to attempt to extract important concessions from or simply intimidate the new Finnish president who they may feel will lack the experience or courage to resist.

In the final Part of the series, "Conclusions: Implications of Finnish Presidential Succession," the report again emphasized how during the long Kekkonen incumbency the power of the presidency had come to dwarf the powers of the Parliament, the political parties, the prime ministership and the cabinet.

Regardless of why this...happened—many blame President Kekkonen—it is almost certain that there will be a major effort undertaken upon Kekkonen's departure to redress the balance between presidential power and the power of the other political institutions.

I predicted that such efforts would probably include amendment of the Form of Government Act of 1919 to limit the President to two-six-year terms. Another frequently mentioned reform would be a change in the manner of electing the president, either by direct election, as favored by the center and center/right parties or by making the president more responsible to Parliament, as favored by the Communists and Social Democrats. The report suggested that:

Regardless of what reforms are approved, the simple fact of Kekkonen's departure will in itself result in an instant redressing of political powers, because much of Kekkonen's power is personal, the result of his extremely long incumbency, his elimination from influence of potential rivals, his taste for power and his willingness to use the foreign policy weapon to buttress his domestic...position. A new president would begin on more even footing with the other political institutions, as did Kekkonen 23 years ago.

The report concluded that structural factors, particularly the president's responsibility for the conduct of foreign and security policy, would assure that the presidency would continue to be the locus of considerable political power, given the importance of relations with the Soviet Union for Finland's continued viability as an independent country.

Moreover, most Finns would probably agree that the Finnish president must continue to be endowed with sufficient authority to manage effectively Finland's foreign relations.

Nevertheless, reform efforts following President Kekkonen's eventual departure from office will likely result in an improved balance of power among Finnish political institutions; probably many of President Kekkonen's warmest supporters would share in the sentiment of 'never again.' His departure is likely to introduce a period of re-invigoration of Finland's democratic processes with all of the inherent advantages and disadvantages that that implies.

Regarding implications of the presidential succession for Finnish/Soviet relations, the paper speculated that the succession and transition period would likely to be a time of considerable uncertainty in Finnish/Soviet relations with a very real possibility of some form of Soviet interference.

With respect to the selection stage of the succession process, it is not at all clear that the Soviet leadership will have serious objections to any of the potential presidential successors identified in Part III. Certainly, none of the prospective successors has evidenced any indication of favoring alteration of the essential features of post-World War II Finnish/Soviet relations. In a sense Soviet influence on the Finnish political system is already reflected in the fact that no Finn critical of Finland's current foreign policy would be given serious consideration for the presidency. Moreover, all potential candidates, including the one eventually chosen as Kekkonen's successor, will no doubt attempt by word and deed to assure the Soviet Union of their strong support of continued good Finnish/Soviet relations. With no challengers of the Paasikivi/Kekkonen line in sight, Soviet attitudes toward the various presidential prospects will have to be based on rather vague subjective considerations difficult at this time to predict. Because of these factors, it remains to be seen whether the Soviet Union will consider it necessary to intervene in the selection stage of the succession process.

Regarding Soviet attitudes toward a Kekkonen successor the report concluded that:

...in the current world context...dramatic, high pressure Soviet moves against the new Finnish president would raise the question of whether the potential gains from such an approach would be outweighed by costs to broader Soviet policy interests. A harsh Soviet move against Finland would probably have serious negative implications for the Nordic security balance, for Soviet *détente* policy in Europe and for Soviet influence and prestige in the Third World. Moreover, the gains to the Soviet Union in terms of its relationship with Finland are highly questionable in that all of the old Finnish suspicions and hatreds, never far below the surface, would be revived for no visible practical advantage to the Soviets in return. In our view these factors place important constraints on how far the Soviets may be willing to go in attempting to extract concessions from a new Finnish president. Rather than any dramatic new initiatives, we consider more likely continuing, steady Soviet pressure, perhaps marginally increased in an effort to establish credibility with the new president.

The success of Soviet efforts—dramatic or otherwise—to influence the Finnish presidential succession/transition process will, in large measure, depend on the integrity of the Finnish political system, on the country's determination to resist unjustified interference and, very importantly, on the character of the new president. In our view it would be a mistake to over-exaggerate the danger to Finland's basic interests posed by the succession and transition period or to assume that the new Finnish president will necessarily be less able or willing to resist Soviet influence than has been President Kekkonen.

As pointed out in Part II, it is our opinion that Finland under President Kekkonen has not always taken full advantage of the admittedly limited room for maneuverability that exists in the Finnish/Soviet relationship as a result of broader Soviet policy concerns. It is not inconceivable to us that the leadership style provided by the new president could result in subtle but significant attitudinal changes in the Finnish approach to relations with the Soviet Union that would tend to correct some of the impressions and connotations associated with the concept of 'Finlandization,' without of course affecting the substance of Finnish/Soviet relations. As with domestic Finnish political institutions, there will be opportunities as well as challenges in Finnish/Soviet relations as the presidency changes hands from Kekkonen to his successor.

The concluding section of the overall six-part report was entitled "Implications for U.S. Interests." It attempted to relate the lengthy analysis of the Finnish presidential succession question to U.S. interests and policy objectives in Finland. This section began by stating U.S. interests:

Maintenance of a democratic and Western-oriented Finland is strongly in the U.S. interest, Existing U.S. policy underscores the importance of the mission's staying very close to the groups and individuals likely to play an important role in the selection of the next Finnish president…This should remain an important mission objective during the remaining period of Kekkonen's presidency. While opportunities for the U.S. to influence the course of events in Finnish succession and its aftermath are extremely limited, we enjoy the enormous advantage that fundamental Finnish interests are in basic consonance with our own. Only a Soviet decision to intervene in Finnish succession in a particularly heavy-handed fashion would be likely to pose a serious challenge to basic Finnish interests. Such a Soviet decision, as we have noted, is not in our view likely, given the negative implications it would entail for the Nordic balance, Soviet *détente* policy in Europe and Soviet world prestige: our expectations are for Soviet probing and pressure, not for direct intervention. Under this scenario, the current U.S. policy supportive of Finnish independence and neutrality will remain appropriate.

In the event of a serious Soviet effort in the succession/transition period to alter the character of the Finnish state and Finland's place in the world, the U.S. should consider at that time in consultation with its allies and with Sweden appropriate actions to encourage Finnish resistance to Soviet efforts at intimidation and to signal to the Soviet Union the disproportionate costs of direct interference in Finnish domestic affairs.

Our overall conclusion is that Finnish presidential succession will reveal a great deal about the underlying strength of Finland's Western values and institutions and about Finnish commitment to meaningful independence and neutrality. While the succession and transition period may pose serious challenges to these values, institutions and commitments, it may also provide opportunities…to redress distortions and imbalances that have built up over the past two decades. It is our judgement that Finnish democracy and independence will emerge intact—perhaps even strengthened—from the approaching trial.

These judgements on the Kekkonen presidency and Finnish presidential succession, written in May-June 1979, reveal embassy perceptions at the time of the critical relationships among Finnish domestic politics, Finnish/Soviet relations and U.S. interests and objectives in Finland. Later in this book we will review the post-Kekkonen period and how the embassy views of 1979 have stood up to the test of time. We will also look at later embassy assessments of the Kekkonen presidency that differed considerably in tone from the one just presented. Moreover, we will also hear further assessments of the Kekkonen era by Finns reflecting in 1995 on that period.

~14~

Our Sad Departure from Finland

The Cooper family had been amazed at how rapidly our time in Finland had passed. However by July 1979 our three-year assignment was coming to a close. In that sense as well, the series of reports on the Finnish presidential succession consciously reflected a kind of summing up of a lot of what I thought I had learned in Finland.

After having spent almost ten of the previous twelve years in overseas assignments, it was clear to me that the time was long overdue for a transfer back to the Department of State and a full "home office" assignment. I had hopes of being selected as the deputy director of the office of Northern European affairs, which would have been a logical onward assignment in the department following Helsinki. However, Bob Funseth, the then office director had another officer in mind for that job. Fortunately, I was able to draw on my previous contacts within the bureau of Inter-American affairs and was offered the position, which I accepted, as deputy director of the office of Caribbean affairs.

So, my transfer from Finland would take me away from European and Nordic affairs for what appeared to be an indefinite period. We left Finland with considerable reluctance, even sadness. We had come to appreciate Finland greatly. Not only had we made some firm and long-lasting friends among the Finns, but we also had been proud to work with Ambassador Ridgway and with what we considered to be an outstanding team of professional diplomats at the American embassy.

We were invited to a number of farewell parties and dinners by embassy colleagues and diplomats of other embassies whom we had come to know. Ambassador Ridgway offered an elegant black tie farewell dinner in our honor, which was featured in an article in one of Finland's social magazines. In a particularly gracious gesture, Ulf Sundqvist, then Secretary General of the SDP, and his wife had Magda and me over to their country home for a small farewell dinner, for which we were most appreciative.

On another nostalgic note, Kari Nars and Juha Sipilä invited economic counselor Matt Lorimer and myself for one last sauna evening together which finished many drinks later in the wee hours of the morning at the M Club in the Hotel Marski.

On our final weekend in Helsinki, the Cooper family spent one entire glorious July 1 summer day wandering around Helsinki and taking photographs of the city that had treated all of us so well and in such a friendly fashion. We were sad to be leaving, and had no clue that we would be destined one day, some years later, to return to the Daughter of the Baltic.

Part Two Notes

[1] The Finnish text of Ambassador Ridgway's speech can be found in the archives of the Paasikivi Society. A copy of the English text was provided to the writer by Ambassador Ridgway.

PART THREE

1984-88:
ON THE FINLAND WATCH
AS DEPUTY CHIEF OF MISSION AND
DIRECTOR OF THE STATE DEPARTMENT
OFFICE OF NORTHERN EUROPEAN AFFAIRS

15

There is Life between Helsinki Assignments

Upon our return to Washington, we moved into the colonial-style home we had purchased in the Chevy Chase section of Washington D.C. just prior to our assignment to Finland. We had never lived in the house, and it had been occupied by tenants for the past three years, so we had a lot of repainting and redecorating to do.

Our oldest boy Lane entered the private (Catholic) St. John's College High School located nearby. Carl and Vanessa entered the local public primary school, which had been able to maintain good standards in an otherwise deteriorating public school system in the District of Columbia. The adjustment to the U.S. educational system was not an easy one for the children. The boys were fluent now in two foreign languages, Spanish and Swedish, but that did not particularly help them in English grammar or American history.

In September, I began what proved to be a hectic year as deputy director of the office of Caribbean affairs. The first week I was on duty a hurricane devastated the island of Dominica in the Caribbean and severely damaged several other islands. This created an around-the-clock emergency situation in our office as we set up a task force to provide assistance.

Having been thoroughly disillusioned with the Nixon/Kissinger policy towards Latin America and the Caribbean, I now expected to fit nicely into the new policies of the Carter Administration. However, I soon discovered that the pendulum of U.S. policy toward the area had swung from the excessive concern over stability and support for authoritarian regimes that marked the Nixon and Ford Administrations to an excessive naiveté and lack of organization and focus among the Carter foreign policy team. Having served in Finland, I thought I understood social democracy and the vital link between its social and economic policies on the one hand and a commitment to democratic processes on the other. However, important elements in the Carter administration saw little difference in Latin America between Leninism and social democracy and appeared to accept that Cuban and Soviet-assisted left-wing movements in the region deserved U.S. support or at least tolerance.

The phrase "ideological plurality" as a worthy U.S. objective in Latin America and the Caribbean was often heard from Carter appointees in the National Security Council's Latin American team and among the Carter political appointees in the State Department. The idea apparently was that Leninists in the region had the right to compete without U.S. interference. Needless to say, revolutionary movements in Central America and the Caribbean were greatly encouraged by the strangely tolerant American approach, and Cuba redoubled its efforts to support, directly and with Soviet aid, its co-religionists in the region.

While correctly disassociating the United States from the corrupt and dictatorial Somoza regime in Nicaragua, the Carter administration was unsuccessful in its efforts to promote its succession by a moderate, democratic regime. Instead, the Marxist/Leninist Sandinistas took over. Meanwhile, the guerrilla movement in El Salvador, which Fidel Castro had helped to unify and to arm, made strong inroads in that country. Grenada fell to a Marxist *coup d'état* in 1979. A radical group of dissident police took over Surinam in 1980. Across the West Indies, bearded "revolutionaries"—appropriately attired in combat fatigues, *à la* Castro—challenged the existing parliamentary regimes of the islands. Revolutionary Grenada's role was to encourage such movements in the English-speaking Caribbean.

In addition to this ideological muddiness towards the region, Secretary of State Cyrus Vance counted among his virtues a stirring commitment in principle against the use of force or the threat of the use of force. This later led Vance to resign over the ill-fated effort to rescue the American hostages being held in Iran. In the meantime it precluded, for example, possible joint American/Dutch action against the police mutineers in Surinam who overthrew the democratically elected government there. On top of that, budget constraints led to an extreme shortage in assistance funds for the region in support of democratic governments.

On the positive side, the Carter administration, following the lead of the Democratic party in Congress, formally introduced human rights as a major consideration in formulating foreign policy. The Carter team initially tended to apply this policy as a sledgehammer sometimes with little regard for other U.S. interests. However, the Carter administration's human rights commitment gradually became a permanent feature in U.S. policy that was continued—with differences in nuances and application—by the Reagan, Bush and Clinton administrations, generally with positive results.

In the midst of my daily struggles in Caribbean affairs, Rozanne Ridgway was rewarded for her outstanding performance as ambassador to Finland and called back to Washington to become the counselor of the Department of State, on paper the fourth-ranking position in the Department. Ambassador Ridgway was the first woman to hold that position. Upon her return, she looked for staff to replace those who would be transferring out in a normal rotation of assignments. I sought Ambassador Ridgway out to express interest in working for her as a special assistant. She was able to get the personnel system to make the change, and I transferred to her office in the summer of 1980.

The duties of the counselor of the department are not formally established by regulations and have traditionally depended upon the wishes of the secretary of state. Edmund Muskie had become secretary of state in May 1980 after the resignation of Mr. Vance. Ambassador Ridgway received a wide and varied array of oversight responsibilities as counselor of the Department. She was the senior officer in the Department, for example, in overseeing its interests in an immigration reform effort then underway, negotiations with the islands of Micronesia regarding establishing a new relationship with the United States, and U.S./Mexican border matters.

Because of her past assignment to Finland, she was also eagerly contacted by the Nordic ambassadors and visiting delegations. In this capacity, both Ambassador Ridgway and I had frequent contact with Finnish Ambassador Jaakko Iloniemi and Finnish official visitors. One such visit was by a delegation of the foreign affairs committee of the Finnish Parliament in September 1980. The group was comprised by Jutta Zilliacus of the Swedish People's Party, Orvokki Kangas of the Center Party and Aarne Saarinen, still Chairman of the Finnish Communist Party. Ambassador Iloniemi and Finnish embassy political officer Pasi Patokallio accompanied the group in their calls. Earlier in the day the group had met with Assistant Secretary of State for European Affairs George Vest and with David Aaron of the National Security Council.

The meeting was like old home week for Ambassador Ridgway and me, sitting there in the counselor's impressive office high in the State Department with some of our old friends from Finland, including the friendly adversary Saarinen, and discussing current issues. However, the visit took place in the chilly climate of the recrudescence of the Cold War due to the Soviet invasion of Afghanistan, severe disagreement over arms issues (particularly the 1979 NATO dual track decision to deploy intermediate range nuclear missiles in Europe if the Soviets refused to pull out its recently deployed SS-20 missiles), the growing "Solidarity" upheaval in Poland which at the time appeared to be leading toward some kind of Soviet action, and disagreement on the CSCE follow-up process.

The dialogue with the Finnish delegation reflected some of these concerns. These discussions were reported in a telegram from the Department of State to the U.S. embassy in Helsinki on October 12, 1980 (State 272105, classified CONFIDENTIAL). Finnish members of the delegation expressed several concerns: Saarinen questioned the U.S. contention that there was an imbalance of forces in Europe favoring the Soviet Union or that the Soviet Union foreign policy could be considered as aggressive taking into account historical factors. He asked why the West was making such a fuss over Afghanistan. Kangas noted there was concern in Finland over the pre-positioning of military materiel in Norway. Zilliacus expressed concern over the impact of the chill in the East/West relationship on the CSCE process.

These and other questions were dealt with as they arose by Ambassador Ridgway and the other U.S. officials with whom the Finnish delegation met. Once again, however, the special sensitivity of Finland to tension in East/West relations became apparent by the nature of the concerns expressed by members of the Finnish delegation. It reflected the differences in perspectives of the world as seen from Helsinki and Washington.

While Ambassador Ridgway was as always highly effective in accomplishing the many varying tasks assigned to her in her senior role as counselor of the Department, I had the impression that she felt somewhat under-utilized and shut out of the Muskie inner circle. However, any uneasiness on that score ended following the election of Ronald Reagan in November 1980 and his inauguration on January 20, 1981. With the appointment of Alexander M. Haig, Jr. as secretary of state, Ridgway was unceremoniously shoved aside and replaced as counselor by Robert (Bud) McFarlane, a retired Marine Corps colonel who had worked with General Haig in the National Security Council during the Nixon administration. Ridgway spent a brief period in near oblivion before, once again, by sheer force of talent she soon emerged as a key foreign policy player on the Reagan team.

Meanwhile, Counselor McFarlane inherited me as a part of his staff when he took over his new office. Much to my surprise, I was drawn into a very confidential, closely held effort by the new Reagan administration to reverse the declining U.S. position in Central America. As the Reagan administration was taking office, the El Salvadoran Marxist insurgents had launched their self-styled "final offensive" against the Salvadoran government. The Reagan administration and the combative Secretary of State Haig were determined to carry the fight in Central America "to the source," i.e., to get directly at Cuban and Soviet support for the Central

American insurgents. Haig directed that Bud McFarlane head up a secret top-level inter-agency team to suggest policy recommendations.

As the only person on McFarlane's staff with Latin American and Caribbean experience, I was thrown into the thick of planning and drafting sessions together with the staff representatives of McFarlane's counterparts on this project from the State Department political-military bureau, the CIA and Department of Defense. I would not want to exaggerate my importance in this process, because I was only a staffer. However, I do believe I played a significant role in proposing that the policy effort include more than a military/security focus in dealing with the Central American insurgencies—which was the initial thrust of the planning. I argued successfully that it be expanded to include the equally necessary elements of economic and social assistance and strong support for democratic processes.

These initial policy drafts were subsequently incorporated into a sweeping Reagan administration policy review towards the region, which was brought into focus by the famous Kissinger Commission report. It was an exciting time to be working for Bud McFarlane, whom I came to respect highly, a respect that I still maintain, notwithstanding his subsequent difficulties as National Security Advisor in the "Irangate" affair.

My two-year Washington assignment was due to come to an end in the summer of 1981, and I had been keeping my eyes open for possible new assignments. At one point, the ambassador to Finland who had succeeded Ridgway, James Goodby, asked me to come back to Helsinki as his deputy chief of mission. My family and I were extremely excited about the prospect. Unfortunately, just as my assignment as DCM in Helsinki was about to be formalized, Ambassador Goodby was notified that he himself was being replaced by a political appointee, notwithstanding the fact that he had been in Finland barely a year.

Therefore, the question of who would be the DCM in Helsinki would be postponed pending the confirmation of a new ambassador. Fortunately for me, I was offered another assignment as deputy chief of mission, this time in the South American country of Paraguay. Ambassador Lyle Lane, an outstanding career Foreign Service Officer, had asked me if I would come to Asunción to serve as his DCM. Coincidentally, the confirmation of this appointment was telephoned to my wife one evening as I was on my way home from work, the same evening that Magda and I had a dinner date with Rozanne Ridgway and her fiancée, Coast Guard Captain Ted Deming. Magda withheld the news until dinner when she astounded me with the development. It was nice to be able to toast my new assignment with Roz and Ted.

My assignment to Paraguay was for three years. It was a most interesting period. After the first year, Ambassador Lane was himself replaced with a political appointee, Ambassador Arthur Davis. The long-term president and dictator of Paraguay, Alfredo Stroessner, was well into the third decade of his reign. I am pleased to be able to say that the U.S. embassy deliberately adopted a policy of distancing our government from the undemocratic regime and of openly associating with the democratic process. This involved frequent contact with Paraguayan opposition groups, both those tolerated by the regime as well as those being persecuted. We also identified ourselves with freedom of the press and protested vigorously every time the Stroessner regime moved to infringe press freedom—a not infrequent happening.

President Stroessner had expected a warm embrace from the conservative Reagan administration and was pleased when the non-career, Republican party activist Arthur Davis was named ambassador. He could not, therefore, understand why the embassy under Ambassador Davis took high profile positions that were critical of Stroessner's harsh domestic political policies. After all, the Stroessner regime pointed out, it was strongly anticommunist and always voted with the United States in the United Nations. What more could a Reagan administration want?

When the embassy under Ambassador Davis did not see things Stroessner's way, the latter looked around for a reason and found one in me. The president and his advisors concluded that in some way as the embassy's number two official and highest-ranking career officer, I had "turned" Ambassador Davis against his regime. In fact, all that had happened was that Ambassador Davis happened to believe in democracy and limited government. He believed governments should obey the law and permit a free press. He therefore was determined to carry out the Reagan administration's policy of supporting democratic governments and not supporting undemocratic governments of either left or right. I perhaps helped Ambassador Davis determine how best to pursue such a policy, but the Stroessner Government was mistaken in fingering me as the instigator of it.

Coincidentally, about the time that the Stroessner regime was increasingly critical of me, I received a telephone call in December 1983 from the personnel division in the State Department saying there had been a sudden and unexpected vacancy in the deputy chief of mission position in Helsinki and asking me if I would be interested. I reminded them that it had long been my ambition to get back to Helsinki as DCM, but pointed out that I still had some ten months to go in my assignment to Paraguay. Nevertheless, the Department asked me to come up to Washington to be interviewed by the U.S. ambassador to Finland Keith F. Nyborg, who had replaced Ambassador Goodby in 1981. I went up to Washington and had a very good interview with Ambassador Nyborg.

Ambassador Nyborg then asked the Department to assign me to Helsinki. The Department for its part was anxious to get a qualified DCM with prior experience in Finland to Helsinki as soon as possible. The Department promised Ambassador Davis in Paraguay that they would assign a replacement for me very shortly, and Ambassador Davis graciously approved my early departure from Asunción for Helsinki in March 1984 via one week of consultations in Washington. And so it was that, having been frustrated in my desire to return to Finland as DCM in 1981, I was able to make that dream come true three years later.

16

Finland Presents Big Changes: From Kekkonen to Koivisto

Following my departure from Finland in July 1979, the embassy had of course continued to follow closely the Finnish presidential succession. In October 1980, the embassy under Ambassador Goodby submitted several telegrams regarding the maneuvering which had already begun for the scheduled 1984 elections. In an October 27, 1980 telegram (Helsinki 6022) classified "CONFIDENTIAL" the embassy reported that lively speculation was underway in Finland about whether President Kekkonen would aspire to yet another presidential term and, if not, who his successor might be. The embassy noted that Prime Minister Koivisto, according to a public opinion poll released October 15, was favored by fifty-five per cent of the electorate.

The embassy noted, however, that there had thus far been very little comment by political party leaders themselves. Koivisto had stated it was "far too soon" in 1980 to speculate about the 1984 elections. However, the telegram noted that an editorial a week earlier by Jan-Magnus Jansson in *Hufvudstadsbladet* had deplored the lack of focus on the presidential candidate issue, dismissing arguments that a:

protracted debate about presidential candidates would cause domestic 'anxiety'—which he thought a strange argument in a democracy—or call into question the president's foreign policy 'authority'—which he saw equally odd since 'there can be no question of a new president departing from Kekkonen's line.'...Jansson suspected that the real reason for political party reluctance to discuss the issue was the fact that, with one exception, no party has a presently viable candidate to propose: instead they assert continued fealty to Kekkonen's running again as a way of postponing the debate until Koivisto, they hope, slips.

Acknowledging previous recourse to special legislation to extend a president's term of office, Jansson was cited in the embassy report as arguing against such measures in the next period, stating that such procedures should be reserved for instances where elections are not possible. The embassy message went on to note that:

> this…discussion escalated on October 18 when SKP Chairman Saarinen told an interviewer that a candidate Koivisto would not receive the backing 'of a united left.' He ascribed Koivisto's popularity to 'growing rightism' in Finland and said that 'rightist groups' are backing Koivisto 'for foreign policy reasons'.

The embassy credited Jansson for an apparently "sincere wish on his part to get party officials and the public used to the idea that there should be elections—not 'special legislation'—the next time around, and that the candidates should be widely acceptable to the public, not just party officials." Noting "…it is widely believed that Koivisto is regarded warily—if not quite considered 'unreliable'—by the Soviets," the embassy message said Saarinen had in effect called into question "both Koivisto's loyalty to the 'Paasikivi-Kekkonen line' and his more general ability to handle foreign policy." In a subsequent TV interview, Saarinen defended his criticism of Koivisto on foreign policy grounds by noting that Koivisto himself had earlier been "quoted as saying that his 'relations with the Soviet Union are nothing to brag about'."

Incidentally, the embassy telegram observed wryly that when SKP Chairman Saarinen visited the U.S. ambassador's residence a few days later, he had mentioned to Ambassador Goodby it was the first time he had been there since, as a construction mason, he had helped construct the embassy building in 1939-40! Regarding the debate over presidential candidates, Saarinen "told the ambassador ruefully that 'by poking around with my stick, I've stirred up an ant-hill.'"

Two days after filing the above report, the embassy sent in another message (Helsinki 6060) classified "SECRET" which had obviously been under preparation for some time. Referencing the series of messages I had submitted eighteen months earlier on the presidential succession issue, this embassy telegram was intended to appraise "the current dynamics powering the search for Kekkonen's successor." The telegram predicted that 1981 would be a year of intense political activity and speculation with national conventions scheduled by the Social Democratic Party, the Finnish Communist Party, and the Finnish People's Democratic League, and with the annual meetings of the Conservative Party and the Center Party. The embassy message noted the Social Democrats had in Koivisto:

> ...a candidate who in any popularity contest could easily defeat any candidate that any of the parties could put forward...The alternative for Conservatives, Centrists and Communists, therefore, is to find a way of neutralizing Koivisto and of developing a viable substitute. In this it is not inconceivable that they would have the support of the president of the Republic. The vested interest in trade with the Soviet Union on the part of major Finnish metalworking and construction industries, in particular, is such that a blocking effort on the part of these industrial leaders and the political leaders of the Communist Party, the Center Party and the Conservative Party would be a formidable combination to contend with. Finnish democracy faces an unusual test in whether a transition from Kekkonen to another leader sometime in the next few years can be accomplished within the normal electoral process.

The embassy message updated its assessment on some of the key factors surrounding the presidential succession issue:

> In Finland, the special role of the president of the Republic has been to handle almost on a monopoly basis Finnish relations with the Soviet Union, by establishing personal rapport and a close working relationship with key senior figures in the Soviet Government. Although we have no reliable information to indicate whether the Soviet Government has expressed a preference among the presidential candidates, it is arguably clear that their first choice would be Center Party politician and present acting governor of the Bank of Finland, Ahti Karjalainen...But, although some recent articles in the press have begun to play up Karjalainen as an able Finnish leader, his personal reputation among the people is somewhat unsavory, and he would have very little chance in a straight one-on-one race with Koivisto, or even with most other possible contenders.

> President Kekkonen...is not known to be a strong supporter of any of the present leaders in the various parties. Former Center Party Chairman Virolainen is said, in particular, to be unacceptable to him, and he would probably go out of his way to prevent the Center Party from developing any groundswell of support for Virolainen. Kekkonen may see Foreign Minister

Väyrynen as a possible successor, but not a serious contender in the next few years...Koivisto['s] relations with Kekkonen are correct and free of apparent friction, but not notably cordial.

Reviewing a number of other possible candidates, the embassy message...mentioned Jan-Magnus Jansson, noting that "of all of the...'dark horses,' Jansson is probably best qualified to be president, and there has been a good deal of speculating in recent days about his reasons for triggering the current debate about successors to Kekkonen." Calling him a "highly respected figure," the embassy speculated that his best chance might be as a compromise candidate in the case of a deadlock in the electoral college. The report also mentioned Harri Holkeri...but added that "any viable Conservative Party candidate for president is still extremely unlikely."

Regarding SDP Chairman Kalevi Sorsa, the embassy report pointed out that he represented another potential Social Democratic candidate. The embassy described him as a former prime minister and foreign minister, and a man who has been active in the Socialist International:

> In terms of his foreign policy credentials, he would probably be more acceptable to the Soviet Union than Koivisto, but his support among voters is meager compared to that of the present prime minister. Some argue, however, that in the end, the SDP will dump Koivisto in favor of Sorsa. In contrast to Sorsa's well-publicized views on foreign affairs, Koivisto's Moscow connections are not well developed and his leadership roles have been essentially economic. [Koivisto's] major foreign policy thrust during his first prime ministry was...enhanced Nordic cooperation, and his interests still seem to lie in that direction.

Further regarding Koivisto, the embassy report pointed out that he would be facing serious tests in coming months in dealing with a more intractable Communist Party, growing economic problems as Finland's economy was beginning to slow, and possibly difficult labor negotiations. Nevertheless, the embassy said "he has heretofore been viewed as an honest man who has told the people the hard facts and who is dealing with those facts as best he can." In assessing Koivisto's place in the succession picture, the embassy noted that between 1980 and 1984 his popularity could drop and saw uncertainty as to whether this "...essentially private man who occasionally expresses weariness with his public duties—wants to be president of Finland at all. We believe he is sorely tempted, however."

The embassy then discussed some concerns about Koivisto and foreign policy:

> Koivisto's critics indeed have a point when they say he suffers from a lack of clearly understood views on foreign policy. His only foreign policy speech of recent memory was given earlier this year and attracted widespread comment because he 'seemed'—in his typically delphic way— to be giving praise to the Soviets' wish for peace and *détente* while failing to mention any similar aspirations on the Western side. His attitude towards arms control and on East-West relations generally has been ill defined, except that he has tended to accept the vaguely pacifist tendency of a large part of the Socialist movement.
>
> Because of this lack of definition on Koivisto's part, it would not be surprising if during the coming year he sought to burnish his image and aspire to a higher posture than he normally prefers on foreign policy matters. The problem from the U.S. standpoint will be that in order to curry favor with the Soviet leadership and with those critics in Finland who feel that he could not deal with the Soviet Union effectively, he may tilt towards the Soviet Union on issues where U.S. interests come into play.

In the conclusion of the October 29, 1980 message, the embassy acknowledged the uncertainty of President Kekkonen's health and "the possibility that he might attempt to fix a succession in advance of the normal elections…Our guess is that he would try to stay in office until 1984 but his strength is obviously declining and…it is possible that he could think of stepping down while he still has a strong role in arranging his own succession."

The embassy accorded high significance to the events of April, 1981 when it was believed that President Kekkonen tried but failed to force Prime Minister Koivisto's resignation. The embassy reported on its understanding of events in two messages, Helsinki 2103 of April 7 and Helsinki 2184 of April 10. Both messages were classified CONFIDENTIAL.

In its first message, with the heading "Finnish Domestic Politics: Koivisto's Serve," the embassy reported that on April 3 the presidential palace had issued a statement saying Kekkonen had 'summoned' Koivisto to the residence the previous day and told him to speed up the process of achieving agreement within his government on an incomes policy. The embassy message reported: "Koivisto, according to the statement, said he would do so and submit not later than April 10...any unresolved issues to the president along 'probably' with his resignation." The embassy reported the Finnish media had read a great deal into the presidential statement, and the press had concluded that Kekkonen had "toppled" the prime minister or at least "reprimanded" him and imposed a deadline for resolving the situation.

The April 7, 1981 embassy message said President Kekkonen had received two other visitors that week, Kalevi Sorsa and Aarne Saarinen. According to the message, Sorsa after meeting with the president "volunteered that Kekkonen had not been 'optimistic' about [the government's] survival." The message said Saarinen for his part emerged from his meeting with the president:

to say that even if the cabinet didn't have to go, Koivisto did. He said that Kekkonen had agreed that Koivisto could not continue, because both the SDP and the Center Party wanted him replaced. Saarinen also said that he and the president agreed that the successor government should be a political one, not a 'civil servant' cabinet.

Saarinen went on to quote the president as 'complaining' that the prime minister did not consult him on government business. Saarinen judged that relations between the two were 'very bad, with no real contact between them.' Saarinen said the Communists agree that Koivisto is 'too independent' and does not maintain sufficient close relations with the parties making up his government.

The embassy's April 7 message reported on the varying reactions to these developments from Finnish political circles, with attention focussed on what kind of government should succeed the Koivisto government. According to the message, Center Party Chairman Väyrynen said the present government should be replaced by a political cabinet of about the same party make-up, by a minority government if that proved impossible, and by a civil servant government only as a last resort. SDP Chairman Sorsa said his party had tried to compromise with the Communists who, however, had showed no flexibility. He "suggested a new government composed of the SocDem and Center parties..."

The embassy report said that:

Perhaps the strongest reaction came from an SDP member of Parliament and columnist, Arvo Salo, who said in an April 5 speech that the real problem came from the excessive power held by the president's 'messenger boys.' 'Old rulers,' Salo said, have a tendency 'to become nervous when somebody else appears capable of running the store.' He suggested that

Kekkonen's response was to try to cut such promising individuals down to size, 'Sorsa two years ago, Koivisto now.' Salo identified Foreign Minister Väyrynen as a Kekkonen 'messenger' and referred to Saarinen as 'vice president.'

The embassy said that initially Koivisto's attitude toward "predictions of his government's demise did appear passive." (Note: In an August 7, 1995 interview Ambassador Goodby told the author that Koivisto had described himself at that time to Goodby as a "dead man" politically.) According to the embassy April 7 message, however, Koivisto's attitude changed:

On April 6...[Koivisto] unexpectedly announced that he had no intention of resigning. Looking perkier than he has in many months, the prime minister announced that recent political maneuvers were 'a volleyball game in which we are all free to play.' He said that the issues being contended were not worth the life of any government, and warned that his resignation could bring about 'premature parliamentary elections.' He emphasized he would not dissolve his cabinet even if the communists vote against the incomes agreement in Parliament; but commentators noted that...the communists had agreed not to vote against the package in Parliament in exchange for being permitted to attach a dissent from it. Kivisto *[Note: Leader of the communist front electoral group SKDL]* and (surprise!) Saarinen were quoted as saying...that they found the most recent twist of events 'positive.' Koivisto stressed that he had not discussed his decision with Kekkonen, observing that while cabinets are appointed by the president they can only be dismissed by Parliament. He said he would place his fate in the confidence of the latter and that meanwhile 'I'm the one who makes decisions.'

In the concluding section of the April 7 report labeled COMMENTS: the embassy added its assessment of the series of events described in the message:

COMMENTS: The events of recent days have sparked considerable local interest, and some amusement. The outlook is not yet certain, but several aspects may deserve comment now:

(A) The President and his Men: Open conflict between Kekkonen and the most popular choice to succeed him would be the hottest political story in Finland in years...While Kekkonen has never felt personally comfortable with Koivisto, we are told, the prime minister has been able to get along with the sometimes devious and irascible president all right, largely by masking his own considerable political ambitions...[Also] the president continues to see no better alternative to this cabinet on the immediate horizon and will not make a definitive move until he does. Under this theory, Kekkonen's 'ultimatum' was just what it professed to be: a tactic to get things moving toward intra-cabinet agreement which would preserve the

Koivisto Govt...This, however, is not to say that persons close to the president aren't operating behind the lines...[Although] the general opinion is that [Head of the Presidential Office or Chancery Juhani] Perttunen is a devoted anti-Koivisto wheeler-dealer, we believe that the picture of Kekkonen as a captive leader deserves to be treated with the utmost caution.

B. Why Saarinen? Even assuming that the president or his aides were trying to discredit Koivisto, why would they choose the chairman of the Communist Party as their mouthpiece?...Saarinen has felt before the repercussions of 'ill-timed' remarks about Koivisto, so another question on the present occasion is, did he fall or was he pushed? I.e. was he misled about the president's view, or did he jump to unwarranted conclusion about his April 3 conversation? That may never be known, but it seems reasonably clear that the communists have more reason to dislike the idea of dissolving this coalition...than any other coalition member. For that reason, their cautious support for Koivisto's vow to stay in office is understandable, although Saarinen himself may have to consume more crow.

C. Kekkonen-Koivisto Consultations: We have heard various reports over recent months that the president is increasingly withdrawn from daily domestic politics, and that when Koivisto has gone to him with problems, Kekkonen often responds that the prime minister should find solutions himself...The president may have sought to stop such allegations by turning the tables on Koivisto, as well as by publishing an ultimatum which may be perceived as the tactic which 'saves' Koivisto.

The second embassy message, Helsinki 2184 of April 10, classified CONFIDENTIAL was entitled "Finnish Domestic Politics: Game, Set and Match, Mr. Koivisto." The summary section of the embassy report stated:

Prime Minister Koivisto has achieved a striking victory in resolving the issue most immediately threatening the continuation of his coalition government. On April 10 it was announced that the incomes legislation over which coalition partners are squabbling would be tabled in Parliament that same day as a unanimous government proposal, without the dissents which communists and others had said they would attach.

The embassy characterized as "only minimal face-saving for the communists" the announcement that a "team" of government leaders will monitor the progress of the incomes legislation. The embassy cautioned, however, that:

...despite jubilation among Koivisto supporters, longer-term prospects for intra-government cooperation are not unclouded, however, because of the events of the last two weeks. Communist Chairman Saarinen is the obvious loser in this compromise outcome, but there are those who wonder whether the president hasn't been embarrassed as well and, if so, whether it wouldn't be a good idea for Koivisto to publicly mend fences with Kekkonen—and quickly.

In the body of the message the embassy reviewed some of the specific developments, including uncertainty among some politicians whether constitutionally a prime minister can refuse to resign "even if major elements of his coalition vote against his policies." The embassy agreed with the general view that, while there were ways the president could still force the prime minister to resign, it would require courses of action (dissolving Parliament, refusing to sign government legislation) which were viewed as too extreme under present circumstances.

The embassy message noted a belief among some that

...the basic problem is caused by maneuvering for position in the race for presidential succession. SDP Chairman Sorsa, often accused of leading an anti-Koivisto fifth column within the party, left Helsinki and toured Northern Finland where he spoke of peace and *détente*—on the international scene.

The embassy noted that Saarinen had taken some raps for his remarks "purporting to express President Kekkonen's displeasure with Koivisto," being publicly criticized by both SDP Secretary General Sundqvist and Center Party Chairman Väyrynen for his "unheard of" indiscretion in presuming to speak for Kekkonen. Saarinen for his part defended his account of what he had heard from Kekkonen. The embassy report noted:

On the other hand, he said that someone had been feeding the president 'false information.' When asked who the president's mis-informer was, Saarinen responded that 'everyone in politics knows who' (i.e. Chief of Chancery Perttunen, although [note our previous telegram] for our skepticism about casting Perttunen as the malevolent power behind the throne). With a blandness which we are told delighted Koivisto, Saarinen said to reporters that he thought his criticism had the happy result of energizing the prime minister to stand up to the president.

The embassy's concluding comment to the April 10 message was:

COMMENT: Koivisto seems the clear winner in all this. Not only, as we have noted, has his personal popularity soared among the populace who viewed the situation as one in which the lonely prime minister was being attacked by devious politicians before whom he stood his ground; but his reputation for political savvy has also received a strong boost. The question remains, who lost? Saarinen almost certainly did...There are also those who believe the president himself has lost face. Whatever the authoritative inside story, Kekkonen is widely perceived as having failed. That perceived failure is something most think that wouldn't have happened at earlier and more vigorous stages of Kekkonen's career, a reflection that could suggest to the president that he had better try to achieve a perceived success in the same direction soon—a reflection that may give the prime minister some pause. END COMMENT.

Although it is difficult for me to put myself in the embassy's shoes of April 1981, it strikes me from the advantage of hindsight that the embassy's assessment of this pivotal event in Finland's post-war history did not quite grasp its importance. The president, with or without the encouragement of those around him (almost certainly, the former was true) tried to force Prime Minister Koivisto out, as he had successfully done to many other prime ministers before him, and was unable to do so. This marked an important turning point in the way the political game was played in Finland. As the embassy report noted, this indeed was the interpretation of many Finnish observers of the day. The embassy curiously seemed to resist this conclusion, referring to it as a "perception" which the president had better try to reverse with a later "perceived success" and wondering whether it might not be a good idea for Koivisto "to publicly mend fences with Kekkonen—and quickly." Of course, as events proved, President Kekkonen would have no further successes, perceived or real. Finnish politics would never again be the same after the events of April 1981.

A couple of months earlier in 1981, in February on the occasion of the twenty-fifth anniversary of President Kekkonen's assumption of presidential power, the embassy submitted a thoughtful assessment of President Kekkonen's achievements and place in Finnish history. To my knowledge, it was the first comprehensive look at the Kekkonen presidency since my own assessment prepared almost two years earlier. The embassy report was personally approved by Ambassador Goodby, and thus probably reflected his views.

The report was embassy telegram 0939 of February 19, 1981. Bearing the classification SECRET, it had the title of "Anniversary of Kekkonen's Accession to the Presidency of Finland." The report was sent to the Department of State with information copies sent to U.S. embassies in Oslo, Copenhagen, Stockholm, Moscow and

Leningrad and to the U.S. Mission to NATO in Brussels. The introduction to the report explained that President Kekkonen was receiving considerable public tribute for the approaching March 1 date at which time he would complete twenty-five years as president, "which will probably set a record never to be repeated in Finnish history." The message stated that although there had been occasional rumors that Kekkonen might step down from office, most indications were that he planned to stay in office until the completion of his term in 1984.

> To the Finnish people, Kekkonen is a man who is still deeply respected. His views on basic policy questions are still likely to prevail when he chooses to flex his political muscle. But he has also become a figure obviously about to make an exit from the stage and whose apotheosis has already begun.

The embassy report placed the Kekkonen period in the historical perspective of Soviet policies that had absorbed or given USSR control over virtually every other territory lost during the Bolshevik revolution and had placed continuing pressure on Finland. The embassy report noted:

> That Finland has added under Kekkonen twenty-five years of independence to its brief history is in itself a notable achievement. Finns—and the rest of the Western world—can take satisfaction in the fact that Finland has done much more than merely survive, however. Kekkonen deserves credit not only because of his crafty—and occasionally courageous—handling of the Russian connection, but also because of his stewardship of Finland's internal economic and political scene.

The embassy report stressed Kekkonen's responsibility for foreign policy successes and the establishment of Finland's neutrality which he himself had described as his 'life's work.' The report continued:

> One may reasonably ask whether the incessant Finnish litany of praise for Soviet-Finnish friendship, as repetitious as the message of a Tibetan prayer wheel, is really necessary. Probably, in Kekkonen's eyes the Soviet hunger for predictability and Moscow's concern for its security interests in Northern Europe justify this rhetoric. Kekkonen's European policies may also seem questionable at times, but his basic view is that tensions in Europe limit Finland's possibilities while good East-West relations increase the margin for maneuver...
>
> Kekkonen's foreign policy has not given us real practical cause for complaint. This is especially so against the background assumption, which virtually all Finns share, that neither the United States nor any other Western power would do anything more than shed a tear or two if the Finns

got cross-wise (once-again) with the Russians. Kekkonen's best known initiative—the Nordic Nuclear Weapon-Free Zone—has a potential for mischief, but the Finns have done little to promote it and seem to regard it as a distraction which keeps Moscow from taking up more serious ideas. In the meantime, and without fanfare, Finland has gone about building close political, economic and social ties with the other Nordic countries. Such ties were foreseeable, but far from inevitable, twenty-five years ago. Likewise, the relationship with the United States is virtually problem-free...

Despite all the attention to his foreign policy line, whose appellation he how shares with his predecessor President Paasikivi, Kekkonen's contributions to Finland's internal structure may be even more significant. Politically, Kekkonen has favored a center-left coalition in recent years and he has managed to keep such a government in power. While doing this he has fostered a climate of conservatism rooted in traditional Finnish values and including a rather self-centered dedication to exclusively Finnish national interest...he has helped to give centrists an unduly high proportion of ministerial positions and has kept the Foreign Ministry's top echelons almost entirely in the hands of Center Party adherents. The president of the Finnish Republic has a hand in nearly every major appointment in the country, whether in government, universities, government-owned corporations, etc., and, while not an 'anticommunist' as such, Kekkonen has used his authority to build a power structure dominated by conservative-minded people. No leftists occupy senior positions in the armed forces. Those leftists who are appointed to high office, with few exceptions, are people who have strong incentives for working within the system. As in France, an important part of the social fabric is the farming community, which, with Kekkonen's discreet support, is maintained at a high level of subsidies, both for strategic and social reasons. Wage earners are, increasingly, technicians or white collar workers whose interests focus on bread-and-butter issues and who are made keenly aware of the vital importance of Finland's exports' remaining competitive in the world market.

During Kekkonen's quarter-century domination of the Finnish scene, the country has firmly established itself as a highly industrialized western-oriented market economy country. The economic framework follows in most respects the Scandinavian model of a 'mixed-economy' with a high degree of private participation. Finland's largest trading area is the European community, followed by the Soviet Union, Sweden and the United States. Roughly eighty percent of its trade flows Westward.

A further legacy of the Kekkonen era is that for the foreseeable future the Communists (through the Finnish Peoples' Democratic League—SKDL — Front) have no chance whatever of dominating the government or of being any more than they already are—one party in a government coalition faced with the choice of cooperating with a non-communist majority or of going into the political wilderness. In fact, the Kekkonen era has seen a steady decline in voter support for the SKDL Party. In Finnish political life, where a person's political affiliation is more often than not most strongly influenced by which side his grandfather fought on in the 1918-19 Civil War, the decline of Communist Party and SKDL strength represents an erosion not only of voting strength but more importantly in the decline of public appeal and youth attraction for the Far Left. The prospect is for more of the same. At the same time, the Conservative Party has steadily increased in strength having become Finland's second-largest political party. In fact, in the last decade the overall political tide has been flowing to the center and right. All of this has occurred despite a massive and sustained Soviet campaign to tilt public opinion to the left. Youth, teachers, cultural leaders, the press, as well as the labor movement, have been the targets of Soviet attentions. Some Soviet successes, it must be said, have resulted from this unremitting pressure, but the trends are still running against Moscow. One…indication of this is that the number of Finnish exchange students going to the United States has greatly increased in recent years [and] in some programs…is exceeded only by much larger countries such as the FRG and Japan.

The message concluded:

During Kekkonen's presidency, Finland has moved with great circumspection to establish its place firmly in the Western world. The art of statesmanship in the Finnish condition is to do that which the country wants done quietly and without notice, while ostentatiously paying tribute to Finland's good relations with 'the big neighbor.' This has been Kekkonen's role and it is likely to be the role model of any future successful Finnish leader. The ambiguous actions such a role demands are not conducive to creating heroic figures. Yet no less than the larger-than-life Finnish hero Mannerheim, Kekkonen has helped to create a modern, prosperous Finland which is independent and basically Western.

While not referencing or referring to the earlier assessment of the Kekkonen presidency done in the series of reports submitted at the conclusion of my assignment to Helsinki in 1979, the above message presents a quite different focus and emphasis than did the earlier reports. The 1981 embassy report stressed President Kekkonen's positive achievements in expanding Finland's links and commercial ties with the West and in maintaining Finland's independence and neutrality and successful management of Finland's internal political affairs. It raised only mild complaints about his relationship with the Soviet Union and did not address at all issues such as his attitude toward Soviet involvement in Finnish internal affairs, his playing of the "Soviet card," and the impact of the tremendous, almost exclusive authority of the Kekkonen presidency on Finland's other political institutions and players.

The 1981 report thus represented a sweeping reinterpretation of the Kekkonen presidency compared to the earlier messages. In a curious way the contrast between these two differing U.S. embassy interpretations of the Kekkonen presidency anticipated by almost a decade the debate in Finland about the meaning of the Kekkonen period. In my August 7, 1995 conversation with Ambassador Goodby, he reiterated many of the views expressed in the February 1981 embassy report. We will discuss these views in the retrospective section of this book below, along with the present day views of other observers regarding the real meaning of the Kekkonen legacy.

However one viewed it, the long Kekkonen presidency came to an end in the autumn of 1981. As noted, he had been in failing health for several years. During a fishing trip to Iceland in August 1981, his condition worsened noticeably. President Kekkonen went on sick leave on September 11. He presented his resignation as president on October 26, citing ill health as the cause. He lingered, completely out of public sight, until his death on August 31, 1986. A U.S. delegation headed by National Security Advisor Bud McFarlane flew to Finland to represent the U.S. government at the funeral rites. Ambassador Ridgway and I were on the delegation.

Meanwhile, as noted, Prime Minister Mauno Koivisto assumed the position of acting president upon Kekkonen's departure from office and was overwhelmingly elected president in the special elections of January 1982. A new era had dawned for Finland.

Ford and Magda Cooper in front of their
West End home, October 1976

Magda and children at U.S. embassy entrance
with Marine Security Guard, July 1979

Daughter Vanessa as Santa Lucia sitting on Ambassador
Mark Austad's lap December 1976

U.S. embassy in Helsinki July 1979

Ambassador Rozanne Ridgway, DCM Fry and Coopers June 1979

Celebrating May Day 1978: Mikki Jahnukainen, Magda Cooper, Tapani Brotherus, Lysa Brotherus, and Jaakko Jahnukainen

On a moose hunt near Finland's eastern border with group of Finnish war veterans, Fall 1977

Prime Minister Kalevi Sorsa and U.S. Vice President Walter Mondale, Helsinki-Vantaa airport, April 29, 1979

Family friends Pearl and Per-Erik Lönnfors and Ford and Magda Cooper, Summer 1985

4th of July reception 1986. Foreign Minister Paavo Vayrynen shakes hands with DCM Cooper after having greeted Marna Schnabel and Ambassador Rockwell Schnabel.

Deputy Chief of Mission residence in West End, a Helsinki suburb

DIPLOMA

COOPER FORD
has completed XIII Finlandia Ski Race
on February 23, 1986

10.30,45   8656
Time   Placing

Mr. Mauno Koivisto, President of the
Republic of Finland, was the honorary
patron of the race.

Lahti, February 1986
FINLANDIA-HIIHTO

Toivo Lehtovuori
President of the
road Committee

Risto Rytökoski
Chairman of the
Organizing Committee

Tappu Määttänen
Secretary General

Juhani Honkaniemi
Chief of the Finish Area

landia hiihto
Hämeenlinna → Lahti 75 km.

Cooper's far-back
placement in 1986
Finlandia ski race

Ambassador Keith Nyborg
presents Meritorious
Performance Award in
August 1985 to DCM
Cooper

Frost-covered Finlandia skier

Secretary of State George Shultz greets new Soviet Union Foreign Minister Eduard Shevardnadze on Steps of the U.S. embassy in Helsinki July 31, 1985

U.S. negotiating team for meeting with Shevardnadze: from left Max Kampelman, Paul Nitze, George Shultz, Arthur Hartman, Rozanne Ridgway, interpreter, and Jack Matlock (back to camera).

Cooper and Secretary of State
Shultz June 1988

Ford Cooper chats with Finnish
President Mauno Koivisto at
Finnish Embassy reception in
Washington April 1991

17

Taking a Reality Check:
A 1984 Update of Embassy Assessment
of Finland and U.S. Interests

Arriving back in Helsinki in March 1984 directly (via one week in Washington) from sizzling Asunción, Paraguay, where temperatures in February and March would frequently reach well over 100 degrees Fahrenheit, surely presented a dramatic contrast. I had been away from Finland for five years, although while special assistant to Rozanne Ridgway in the Department in 1980 I had been able to follow Finnish affairs to a degree. Nevertheless, I felt somewhat out of touch. Also, the embassy in Helsinki had been through some unexpected personnel changes in the DCM position and had been in somewhat of a leadership vacuum below the ambassador's level. Moreover, there had been dramatic changes in Finland in recent years, particularly the withdrawal of President Kekkonen and the election of President Koivisto in 1982.

I had not seen embassy assessments of the situation in Finland since the assumption of President Koivisto. In fact, in my research for this book I was unable to get the Freedom of Information Office in the State Department to volunteer reports from this period. All of the reports discussed in this Part (Part Three) of this book are those which I myself had kept copies of and which I submitted to the FOIA Office for review and declassification.

In any case, I had gained the impression that the various components of the embassy "country team," described above in

Part One, were not working particularly closely when I arrived in March 1984. Consequently, I proposed to Ambassador Nyborg that I chair a review by the embassy country team of U.S. policy toward Finland and that, once the ambassador had approved our findings, we would submit them in a message to Washington. It was my thinking that by going through a comprehensive analysis and review with all elements of the country team, we could achieve a consensus about the situation in Finland and what the United States should be trying to achieve. I also saw it as a way to bring the country team closer together through participating in a joint exercise. Moreover, I thought it would establish myself with all country team elements as a knowledgeable DCM who enjoyed the full confidence of the ambassador and as the person they would want to go to in order to get to the ambassador or to get decisions.

The fruit of our effort was a lengthy forty-three page (triple spaced) telegraphic message (Helsinki 2305) of June 6, 1984 bearing the awkward but descriptive subject line of "The Finnish/Soviet/NATO/Nordic Equation and Nordic Security." The report was classified SECRET/NOFORN (the caption NOFORN signified that the report was not to be divulged to any foreign diplomatic, military or intelligence colleagues). Given the unusual length of the message, the embassy also submitted a separate nine-page message that we called an EXECUTIVE SUMMARY of the fuller report (Helsinki 2316) which summarized the conclusions and recommendations of the main report. Both reports were addressed to the Department of State with information copies sent to the Department of Defense, our embassy colleagues in the Nordic countries, our embassies in Moscow, Berlin and Bonn, the U.S. mission to NATO in Brussels, and various U.S. military commands with European responsibilities. Ambassador Nyborg was the approving officer for the main telegram, and he initialed the final report authorizing transmission of the telegram. I was listed as the editor, and the separate contributors to the telegram were acknowledged: Katherine Croom and Paul Petty of the political section; Thomas Carter of the economic section; Max Ollendorff, the commercial attaché; Col. Ralph Miller, USAF, the Defense attaché; and Col. Jay Mumford, the Army attaché.

I think it is informative to review the analysis in some detail, because it presents in a single report the most comprehensive U.S. embassy assessment of Finland's overall situation of which I am aware. Incidentally, the message refers to a "study underway in Washington." I have no knowledge whether that study was ever finished or, if finished, whether it was distributed or subsequently declassified and released. I doubt the latter. I do recall that we in the embassy had noted a number of areas in the terms of reference for the study that we did not agree with. To get across the embassy points of view on these issues represented another important reason behind our decision for this embassy perspective.

Major excerpts from the text of the message follow:

INTRODUCTION AND CONCLUSIONS

This message assesses Finland's position and posture within the broader context of Nordic security. A joint country team message, it is inspired by and hopes to contribute to the study currently underway in Washington on NATO and Nordic security. This analysis is also intended to help focus our thinking for the forthcoming Nordic chiefs of mission conference to be held in Helsinki June 14-15.

Our principal conclusions and observations are as follows. Finland's foreign and security policy has its roots deep in its World War II and immediate post-war experiences. Its overriding goal has been to consolidate and strengthen Finnish independence and credible neutrality by (1) accepting the Soviet defensive security interest in Finland and assuring Soviet leadership of Finnish goodwill and confidence; and (2) balancing to some degree the disparities of the Finnish/Soviet relationship by developing its Nordic associations and broader international relationships. That policy has served Finland well, and its fruits of Western democracy, economic prosperity and reasonable security are readily apparent to all...Within the constraints of treaty-enforced limitations, Finland has developed a foreign and security policy designed to minimize the chances that its super power neighbor would have any cause to fear developments in Finland and, should disaster strike and that effort fail, to raise the costs of any attack against Finland to a level incommensurate with any potential gains that could possibly accrue.

There has been a remarkable continuity and stability in Finland's foreign and security policy. National consensus behind the policy remains overwhelming; with only the far communist left seriously disputing any important aspect of that policy. Concerns are occasionally raised...whether the 'liturgy' of Finland and the Soviet Union's 'good neighborly relations' might not be weakening the understanding...of the underlying realities of Finnish/Soviet relations. While...such concerns should be carefully monitored, we see no threat to continuing Finnish resolve for the foreseeable future…Certainly, we see no domestic-originated circumstances that could cause Finland to veer from its path. Sudden and unprecedented Soviet pressure on Finland could force a re-evaluation by Finland of its policy. However, we are convinced that Finland would be prepared to pay an extraordinary price to maintain its independence, integrity and Western values. Military redeployments toward Northern Finland and increased defense funding in recent years have underscored Finnish determination to clearly demonstrate its defense commitment.

The foregoing notwithstanding, it should be understood that Finland's foreign and defense policies are designed to serve its own national purposes. There is little altruism left in Finland after its World War II experiences of being abandoned by Nordics and other Western democracies, and little interest in serving as a Western first line of defense against the Soviet Union. Therefore, Finnish perceptions on vital Northern European security issues are essentially parochial and not overly sympathetic to questions relating to maintaining the integrity of the NATO alliance. Despite the great importance to Finland of her Nordic relationships, Finland's security perceptions and policies may differ considerably from those of most of her Nordic neighbors. For the same reasons, US and Finnish views, perceptions, and policies on some Northern European security issues will continue to differ, and Finnish positions on some general disarmament issues important to the Soviet Union are likely to be opposed to US positions.

While Finland's foreign and security policy has remained essentially unchanged, there may have been…some policy shifts in other Nordic countries toward Finnish positions on some issues, such as on a Nordic Nuclear Weapon Free Zone. To the extent that this trend continues with a consequent weakening of the 'Nordic balance,' we believe Finland's own interests are to that degree undermined, although the Finns might not agree with or acknowledge such a conclusion.

With respect to implications for US policy, we believe that traditional US goals and objectives in Finland remain fully valid: US support for Finnish neutrality and independence, continued Finnish commitment to Western institutions and values, and maintenance of a credible and Western-oriented Finnish military establishment….[W]e have no illusions about the ability of US policy approaches to effect important changes in basic Finnish policies and perspectives. However, US interests in Finland coincide closely with Finland's perceptions of its own basic interests: the Finns know and value this fact. Where policy differences arise, we should understand and take into account Finnish policy views while…firmly protecting the interests of ourselves and our allies.

Following this section of introduction and summary conclusions, the long message proceeded to its analytical sections,

Sections II through IV. It is in these sections that the embassy lays the groundwork of analysis that makes the case for the conclusions drawn and recommendations put forward.

Section II on the Background of Fenno/Soviet Relations was a conscious effort—on my part with respect to the embassy staff, and on the embassy's part with respect to Washington—to remind everyone of how Finland got to where it was at that point in 1984. I was very conscious of the fact that there were few people in the embassy and probably even fewer in Washington who had given any serious attention to Finland's history and to its relationship to Russia and the Soviet Union. Therefore, it was necessary every couple of years to "educate" the current regional analysts and policy makers in the Washington foreign affairs community on the background of this part of the world which they could not be expected to be exposed to in the normal course of events. It is not necessary here to detail the points made in the background section most of which have been described in this book and which draw on previous assessments done during my earlier assignment where I felt they continued to reflect the Finnish reality.

After the Background Section, the report continued on to the analytical sections:

III. CURRENT FINNISH CONTEXT

A. DOMESTIC POLITICAL DEVELOPMENTS

...Since the signing of the [1948] FCMA Treaty [with the Soviet Union] much of Finland's national security effort has been devoted toward insuring that the Soviet Union has no reason to invoke the FCMA Treaty and to come to [Finland's] 'assistance' or demand consultation about providing such assistance. While Finnish defense expenditures are thus justified publicly by citing the need to maintain defense capabilities sufficient to meet its FCMA Treaty obligations, the real, largely unspoken, purpose of Finnish defense is to maintain a credible deterrent against Soviet attack...

Except for the Communists and a minority element among the Social Democrats, all Finnish political parties are committed to a strong defense policy. And except for the Communists, there is general agreement that the direct potential military threat to Finland comes from the East. Most political party and even civilian/military differences over Finnish defense policies have been fought out in three formal Finnish Parliamentary Defense Committee reviews...the political parties...[thus] have little room for subsequent political maneuvering on these issues. In addition, an all-important public consensus is thoroughly committed to a firm defense policy and has remained extremely high over the years. A 1982 Gallop public opinion poll showed that a higher percentage of Finns (about 75 percent) expressed their willingness to defend their country than did the citizens of any of the other twelve countries polled, including the USA, UK, West Germany and France...

Concerns are raised from time-to-time in Finland, and by outside observers of Finland, as to whether there has been or might develop an erosion of national consensus of Finland's basic objectives of independence and neutrality, or a weakening in Finnish understanding of the Soviet threat....Certainly, intellectuals have emerged on the left, including some within the Social Democratic Party, who seem to have lost a grasp of the underlying, unspoken realities of the Finnish/Soviet relationship. Some youth group representatives back from youth festivals in Eastern Europe seem to echo the Soviet propaganda line, as do some peace groups which find some favorable response in Finland to their often one-sided positions on disarmament.

While such concerns warrant monitoring...it would be inaccurate to exaggerate their significance. There are few Finns who see much to envy in the Soviet Union and fewer still who would lend themselves to the weakening of Finnish independence and neutrality. Press self-censorship is markedly less evident today than it has been over the past two decades, and public debate and discussion including by GOF officials, more vigorous. Youth are, if anything, more conservative and more nationalistic than a decade ago. And rejection of Soviet tutelage, as in the 1981-82 presidential maneuvering and as in last week's Finnish Communist Party Congress, remains a healthy Finnish national trait.

Because of the enduring nature of public support for a strong defense posture, and the multi-party character of Finnish politics which almost invariably produces coalition governments composed of several parties, it seems highly unlikely that a government would soon appear that might attempt to weaken Finland's defense posture. Despite pacifistic tendencies among some Social Democratic Party   intellectuals, shared with other European SDP's, it is probable that political competition and public opinion will keep a large majority of the SDP firmly committed to the Finnish defense policy under foreseeable circumstances, leaving the Communists pretty much isolated on the left on this issue. Therefore, we see no domestically motivated REPEAT domestically motivated change in Finland's continued commitment to a firm defense policy over the next 3-5 years...

B. THE ECONOMIC PICTURE AND PROSPECTS

A strong upswing is now taking place in Finland's business cycle—simultaneously with signs of economic recovery among the other Western democracies. Finland should enjoy healthy growth levels as recovery proceeds—real annual growth levels in the range of three percent are likely over the next two years. Growth rates beyond 1985 will depend in large measure on performance of the world economy....Over the past five years, when Finland grew at an annual rate of four percent the other European OECD nations grew at less than 1.5 percent...Much of the growth Finland will enjoy will occur in the modern, urban sector. Rural areas will probably be 'left behind' somewhat...and rural to urban population shifts will continue to take place.

Over the next five years, Finland's economy will be stronger, more diversified into fields like electronics, and more strongly integrated with the other Western democracies in terms of trade and capital investment. Finland's relatively 'open' trade regime, coupled with its trade pacts with EFTA and the EEC, will all militate in the direction of closer integration, barring an upsurge of protectionism among the Western democracies. Finland's trade ties with the Soviet bloc are expected to shrink correspondingly...to some 20 percent or less...

Finland's trade with the bloc will continue to be carried out within the strait jacket of a soft-currency trade pact which calls for symmetrically balanced trade. We see no indications that the USSR seeks to shift its trade arrangement with Finland into more flexible hard currency trade. The GOF appears to be of the same view because of the advantages that have flowed from the requirement for balanced trade. The advantages result from the fact that, for every Finnish import from the USSR, the Soviets agree to buy Finnish goods of equal value. Some four-fifths of Soviet exports to Finland consist of oil. The bilateral trade pact's call for balanced trade means that the Soviets agree to corresponding levels of imports from Finland. This is particularly helpful in time of OPEC-inspired oil price shocks. The Finns could never get a 'deal' of this sort from the OPEC oil-exporting nations, even taking into account the disadvantage that a somewhat unrealistic ruble/Finnmark exchange rate tends to favor the Ruble.

The questionable ruble exchange rate is not the only factor which makes Finland's trade with the Soviet Union a not unmixed blessing for Finland, despite its obvious benefits. An overarching bothersome aspect of Finland's trade with the Soviet Union is that political considerations must and inevitably do enter into the management of the trade relationship. Finland has accumulated a very substantial surplus (officially put at 350 million rubles but perhaps fluctuating up to twice that level) in its trade with the Soviet Union: i.e. Finland has exported more to the Soviet Union than it has imported, meaning that there is an overhang of exports to Finland which the Soviet Union 'owes' Finland in order to balance what it has imported from Finland....While the Soviet Union agreed in November, 1982 to paying interest on 300 million rubles of the balance, it did so only most reluctantly. Rather, the Soviets tend to pressure the Finns to buy products or projects which might serve to lower the surplus balance but which otherwise may be of little interest to Finland...

The magnitude of these troublesome aspects of Finland's trade with the Soviet Union should not, however, be exaggerated...Finland's dependence on the USSR for nearly all petroleum requirements suggests a corresponding 'vulnerability' to politically inspired supply interruptions. The current international 'buyers market' for oil tends to lessen that vulnerability over, at least, the medium term. Alternate oil suppliers are not currently lacking. The GOF also strives to minimize any vulnerability through the maintenance of underground oil reservoirs with a capacity equal to at least three months of normal (un-rationed) consumption...Likewise, Finland is dependent on the USSR for all of its natural gas requirements, but regulations are in place that require all natural gas consumers to maintain the capacity to switch to alternate fuels in the event of any supply interruption.

Individual sectors of the Finnish economy may be more dependent on Soviet trade than is the economy as a whole. For example, a considerable part of the Finnish shipbuilding industry specializes in icebreakers and ice-capable merchant ships...Nevertheless, given the apparent high Soviet priority on development of remote areas of ice-bound Siberia, any politically inspired cut-off of Soviet orders for such ships would probably entail a heavy cost to the USSR itself. However, it would unquestionably represent a disastrous blow to the Finnish shipbuilding industry, a vulnerability widely recognized in Finland.

C. FINNISH DEFENSE CAPABILITIES AND POLICIES

1. FINNISH PERCEPTIONS OF SOVIET INTERESTS AND AIMS

It has been a cardinal political assumption of Finnish foreign and security policy in the post-World Was II period that the USSR harbors no further territorial designs against Finland and politically is not seeking to impose Soviet-sponsored communism on the Finnish people. This Finnish assumption holds that the Soviet security interest in Finland is essentially a defensive one, i.e. to assure that Finland does not constitute a security threat to the Soviet Union and that Finland or Finnish territory is not lent to the purposes of third countries that could threaten the USSR. This optimistic political assumption of Soviet policy towards Finland has not always been accurate, as there have been numerous post-war incidents of heavy Soviet pressure on Finland or meddling in Finland's internal affairs...In any event Finland seeks to address the Soviet Union's defensive security interest in Finland by assurances that no threat to the USSR will emanate from, through or over Finland.

On the broader question of Soviet strategic interests in the Nordic area, Finnish military leadership shares the NATO evaluation that the basic Soviet strategic interests are the war-time neutralization of Northern Norway and the use of the Norwegian sea for naval egress of the Kola based Northern Fleet. The Finns, however, view the increase of the Soviet Naval fleet and buildup on the Kola Peninsula as based on strategic superpower considerations and not aimed primarily at Finland or at the Nordic area. The Soviet ground forces on Kola are judged to be primarily for local security of the massive naval and air complex. However, the Finns recognize the offensive capabilities of the Soviet ground forces on the Kola and are concerned over their potential for use in a strike across Finnish terrain against Northern Norway.

2. FINNISH DEPLOYMENT CHANGES

In the post-World War II period, and notwithstanding Finland's assumption that the USSR security interest in Finland is essentially defensive, Finnish military planning has in fact focused primarily on defending against a possible independence-threatening invasion of Southern Finland where the only possible aggressor state could be the Soviet Union. The bulk of Finnish ground forces have been stationed there, and the Finns have invested considerable resources in fortifying their southern shores. Because of treaty limitations on the size of Finland's active duty armed forces (a total of about 40,000 for all services) Finland would rely on its reserves in case of an attack. Finland has a reserve of some 700,000 men. A fast deployment force of 250,000 could be mobilized within a few days. Finland's well-trained and well-organized reserves, its pre-positioned weapons caches, its rugged terrain (only 10 percent of Finland's terrain is suitable for armored operations) its severe climate, its hardy population and its demonstrated fighting skill and will combine to insure that a Soviet invasion would be a most costly undertaking indeed. While no Finnish military leader would believe that Finland could prevail over a determined and sustained Soviet onslaught, virtually all are convinced that the price would come so high as to outweigh any advantages that an aggressor could derive: that in essence is the strategic objective of the Finnish Defense Forces (FDF).

A secondary security concern over the post-war period has been to prevent air and ground transit of Finnish Lapland, either to interdict Western forces heading for the Soviet Union (as Finland is enjoined to do by the 1948 FCMA) or of Soviet forces transiting in the other direction. The Soviet Kola buildup beginning in the 1970's and the NATO response drew increased attention to the weakness of Finland's defense capabilities in Finnish Lapland.

The FDF had been painfully award of [the] growing strategic importance of and inadequate defense capability in Lapland since at least the late 1960's and early 1970's when a steady, but limited upgrading effort was begun. In 1976 the Second Parliamentary Defense Committee formally recommended permanent shifting of additional forces to the zone. The Committee's deliberations were influenced by a 1975 Finnish-Norwegian dispute on the viability of FDF Arctic zone defense capabilities, wide spread public attention to the alleged 'military vacuum' there and a Nordic strategy think-piece by two FDF War College officers.

The interim years before the 1981 III PDC findings were ones of slow but continued growth of military capabilities in Lapland. The III PDC expressly identified Lapland as one of two 'key areas' requiring appropriate defense policy. The Committee's findings in large measure mirrored the FDF viewpoints and in practice provided the 'stamp of approval' of parties in Parliament and the commitment of required funding. The last three years have seen a speed up—or perhaps better stated—culmination of the upgrade plans that had their origins in the early 1970's.

Specifically, the following concrete steps have been taken by the FDF to increase military capability in Lapland:

(1) Upgrading the Lappi Infantry Battalion to a Brigade, which would under mobilization doctrine, be the core for expansion to division strength in wartime;

(2) Contracting for US ITOW anti-tank missiles for deployment in the Arctic Circle invasion belt;

(3) R&D, and letting of an initial production contract to SISU Inc. for a domestic armored personnel carrier which was designed to meet cross-country mobility requirements in Northern Finland;

(4) Procurement decisions made to improve night visibility for ground troops in Lapland;

(5) Placement of over-snow Swedish 'BANDWAGEN' tracked prime movers in the three most Northern brigades;

(6) Marked increase in the number of reserve forces (from Southern Finland) trained in the Lapland environment. This has included testing of the transportation (primarily rail and highway) system to move forces in mobilization conditions to the Northern zone;

(7) Establishment of the Lappi Air Wing. The Hame Air Wing was moved North to Rovaniemi and re-designated the Lappi Air Wing. Housed in rebuilt and upgraded facilities, the most modern in Finland.

The military importance of Lapland and increased FDF attention thereto should not, however, mask the focal point of Finnish strategy. Superpower infringement in Lapland would destroy Finland's claims to neutrality and lead to a Finnish military response; but a successful attack on the demographic political and economic center of Southern Finland would spell the end of Finnish national existence. Thus, the bulk of the FDF effort is directed towards the more critical, even if less likely, threat.

IV. FINNISH FOREIGN AND SECURITY POLICY CONCERNS

A. POLICY CONTINUITY

As has been noted, the hallmark of Finnish foreign and security policy from the immediate post-World War II period to the present had been steadiness of purpose and continuity. Of course, there have been significant changes of emphasis over 40 years...

Beginning in the late 1950's, Finland under President Kekkonen began actively to promote the concept of Finnish neutrality, seeking Western acceptance of and Soviet acquiescence in the concept. For some years the Soviet leadership seemed to go along with Finland's promotion of its neutral status. However, beginning in the 1970's, the Soviets began to signal that Finnish neutrality aspirations should not be carried too far and reminded Finland of its obligations under the FCMA Treaty. The 1978 proposal by Soviet Defense Minister Ustinov for joint Soviet/Finnish military maneuvers was of course in total contradiction to a Finnish policy of neutrality. While Finland rejected the proposal, the incident showed the unimportance to the Soviet Union of Finland's neutrality aspirations. It is important to note, however, that Finland has not abandoned its pursuit of neutrality in the face of the Soviet Union's more restrictive approach to the concept.

Nor do we note any significant change in Finnish policy since Mauno Koivisto assumed the presidency. We have seen no direct evidence, to quote from the concept paper/term of reference, that 'Finland may be seeking greater latitude in selected defense and foreign policy matters which may have uncertain and unsettling implications for the Nordic Balance.' The end of the Kekkonen era appeared to offer at least surface possibilities for such change. Kekkonen in his final years seemed increasingly to cater to the Soviets, although maintaining a firm line on bedrock issues. He also was not above playing 'the Soviet card' against his domestic critics and opponents. Koivisto, a Social Democrat, was an overwhelming[ly] popular Finnish domestic choice for president. He has a more relaxed style and encourages more discussion and debate of national issues, including foreign policy, although he now has also had occasion to warn the Finnish media against treatment of foreign policy issues in a way that could be harmful to Finnish interests.

However, despite the palpably more open and relaxed Koivisto foreign policy approach and style, the most marked characteristic of his foreign policy to date has been its strict observance of the well-trodden Paasikivi-Kekkonen line. We see little likelihood that Koivisto will consciously or visibly test the limits of Finnish independence *vis-à-vis* the Soviet Union, particularly in the context of today's heightened international tension. In fact, one complaint voiced about Koivisto is that during his initial years in office he has not shown presidential authority and decisiveness, which might raise a question about his ability to deal firmly with the Soviet Union in a crisis. Such speculation about Koivisto and his will or ability to deal with the Soviets is thus far just that: speculation. While noted for his laid-back and low activity style, there is nothing in Koivisto's background to indicate he would be an easy mark for the Soviets. While we do not expect provocative probing of the limits of independence under Koivisto any more than under Kekkonen, we do expect that Koivisto will continue the policy of strong Nordic and Western ties to counter-balance the weight of the Soviet relationship. Moreover, we expect Finland to continue to strive to promote its neutral image, despite the USSR's coolness to the concept.

B. CONCERN OVER THE INTERNATIONAL CLIMATE

While GOF foreign and security policies have remained basically constant, the context within which the policy functions can change, and has changed, markedly. It is an axiom of the Finnish foreign policy establishment that Finland's foreign and security policy prospers during times of *détente* and suffers during times of superpower tension. For Finns the post-World War II high water mark for Finland was the CSCE summit meeting in Helsinki in 1975, which symbolized Finland's acceptance by superpowers, and all of Europe as an effective neutral state working for world peace. Finland has viewed the subsequent deterioration of US/USSR relations with foreboding, recalling that during earlier periods of East/West tensions, such as occurred over Berlin in 1958 and 1962, the Soviet Union tended to put pressure on Finland.

The INF issue between NATO and the USSR is an excellent if unhappy example of an international situation that goes straight to the heart and core of the all-important (to Finland) Finnish-Soviet relationship...[One] issue is, of course, the cruise missile over-flight question. Under the FCMA Treaty Finland is pledged to assure that Finnish territory will not be used in an attack on the Soviet Union. Finland is obliged to be able to repel any attack through Finland or to risk Soviet consultations regarding providing 'assistance' to Finland to repel an attack. A US cruise missile could cross Finnish territory at a low level on its way to the Soviet Union. What are Finland's obligations under the FCMA Treaty?

The GOF originally took the position that the current generation of ground launched cruise missiles (GLCM) does not pose a threat to Finnish sovereignty, does not require a military response, and hence would not be a proper subject for consultation under the FCMA Treaty. However, the Soviets promptly knocked down the Finnish interpretation in a 'Komissarov letter,' Komissarov being a pseudonym for unofficial pronouncements of authoritative Soviet positions. The Komissarov letter stated in no uncertain terms that the GLCM's do represent a threat to Finnish air space, do have to be defended against and would most certainly be a proper subject for consideration in terms of the FCMA Treaty....Foreign Minister Väyrynen immediately did an about-face and announced publicly he had meant all along that the current generation of cruise missiles are a threat to Finland and would be defended against...

Nevertheless, the cruise missile issue puts Finland squarely on the spot, and no amount of evenhanded neutrality will make it go away. This is a real problem for Finland, and while most Finnish authorities realize the necessity for the NATO dual track decision in response to unchecked Soviet deployments, the incident illustrates aptly why Finland get nervous when the superpowers are quarreling. This issue could yet come back to haunt Finland in the FCMA context.

C. THE CHANGING NORDIC CONTEXT

Finland is also concerned about East/West tensions in the Nordic area growing out of *inter alia* the Soviet military buildup on the Kola Peninsula and the NATO response in Norway. As indicated above, Finland does not consider the Kola Peninsula buildup to be aimed primarily at the Nordic area and consequently does not favor NATO response measures in Norway. In the Finnish military view, NATO countermeasures in Norway cannot hope to balance preponderant Soviet strength in the Kola Peninsula and thus only serve to raise tensions in the region. Again, the Finnish position can be best understood in relation to its FCMA Treaty obligations and the specter that military developments in the area displeasing to the USSR could result in invoking of the Treaty.

Finland's long-standing advocacy of a Nordic Nuclear Weapon Free Zone (NNWFZ) represents another point of continuity in Finland's Nordic policy. Again, the Finnish interest in a NNWFZ derives from a concern to avoid the development of any situation in the Nordic area which could serve as a reason for the Soviet Union to invoke the FCMA Treaty. The issue was first raised in the early 1960's by President Kekkonen, although the concept can be traced to a 1959 Soviet plan for a 'Baltic free of nuclear missiles.' The Finns revived the plan in 1972-75 and again in 1978, in that year holding bilateral consultations on the issue with the US, the Nordics and the USSR. The initiative foundered at the time owing to lack of interest by the other Nordics and the opposition of the US. The advantages to the Soviet Union of a NNWFZ—particularly one which in no serious way inhibits Soviet nuclear weapon activity in the Kola [Peninsula] or the Baltic—were and are obvious. After several years of mild, almost secondary support for a NNWFZ, Finland seems to have renewed its advocacy in recent months, amidst apparent movement on this issue on the part of the other Nordics and the Soviet Union.

What has changed in the current equation compared to 1978 is not Finland's support for a NNWFZ but the fact that the concept is beginning to find a more favorable and positive reception in important sectors of all of the other Nordic countries. While the other Nordics seem to have attached a number of conditions to the NNWFZ that are highly unlikely to be met, the fact remains that whereas before the concept was largely rejected out of hand, it is now treated as a proposal worthy of serious consideration. The Soviet Union for its part seems, startlingly, to be talking about in some way involving Soviet territory and Soviet ships in the Baltic. The Finns may be somewhat confused by these signals: there have been recent indications that the GOF wants to go slowly on next steps in the NNWFZ process, for example by keeping treatment of the issue at the Nordic foreign minister level where it is more easily containable.

It is clear in both of the above cases—Finnish concerns about NATO measures in Norway and advocacy of a NNWFZ—that acquiescence by the other Nordics in Finnish positions would alter the Nordic balance to the disadvantage of the West...Certainly, many Finns believe that the Nordic balance serves as a protection to the Finns *vis-à-vis* the Soviet Union. As recently as April 9 [1984] President Koivisto stated that 'it is not in the interest of any nation to alter the stable situation in the North.'

It is not clear, however, that there is unanimity of view among Finnish leadership on this issue. There seems in fact to exist a deep-seated Finnish ambivalence as to whether Finland's security policy is best served by a neutralized Nordic area or by a continuation of existing security arrangements. Some Finnish foreign policy figures appear to believe that a neutralized Nordic area, by completely removing NATO from the zone, would satisfy the Soviet Union that there is no conceivable security threat to it from the quarter and, thus, eliminate any Soviet motivation for invoking or threatening to invoke the military consultation clauses of the 1948 Finnish/Soviet Treaty. They argue that it would also isolate the Nordic area from any conflict between the rival East and West military alliances.

Other Finnish foreign policy leaders have on the other hand stressed that Finland favors the *status quo* in the Nordic area and that the existing security arrangements of each Nordic country have supported the stability of the entire Nordic area. While shying away from the term 'Nordic balance,' these Finns in effect endorse the concept. Left unspoken in this school of thought is the view—which we subscribe to—that fear of counter reactions in the other Nordic countries is a factor that importantly moderates Soviet policy towards Finland. Most Finnish foreign policy leaders, including former President Kekkonen, have expressed both views of the Nordic situation at one time or another, reflecting individual ambivalence on this question. In any case, those Finns who favor the neutralization of the Nordic area in principle are well aware that such a development is quite unlikely for the foreseeable future.

It does seem clear, however, that the idea of maintaining the Nordic balance through a super-sophisticated game in which Finland pushes one way while the other Nordics resist is not going to work much longer if the other Nordics stop resisting. In our judgement, continuation of this trend would constitute a great disservice to the interests of Finland, the other Nordics and NATO alike.

Washington found the embassy report to be useful. The report achieved all of the objectives I had hoped for: bringing the country team closer together and establishing a sense of an agreed assessment and policy priorities; educating the new generation in Washington agencies and the country team on some dimensions of recent Finnish history relevant to 1984; providing embassy input for the Nordic study underway in Washington; and establishing my credibility within the embassy as a qualified DCM. It was not often that one could achieve such multiple objectives with a single, albeit intensive and lengthy undertaking.

18

The Charms of Finland (II):
From Living on the Shores of the Baltic to Skiing the Finlandia Ski Race

There is a widely held belief in the Foreign Service that it is not a good idea to return to a country in which one has previously served, particularly if one had enjoyed the earlier assignment. The feeling is, don't press your luck; the second time around is unlikely to measure up to the first experience, and you will be disappointed and disillusioned.

My family and I didn't believe this and we were not disappointed with our decision to return to Finland. On the contrary. This time, however, we had to leave our oldest boy, Lane, behind at the American University in Washington, D.C. where he was enrolled in the International Studies Department. However, even Lane did not want to be left out of the experience, and with the kind assistance of the University of Helsinki, we were able to arrange for him to enroll at the University for a "semester abroad" for the 1985 autumn semester. He arrived in June 1985 after spring classes at American University ended and spent the summer with us as well before entering Helsinki University in the fall.

During the summer Lane was able to do odd jobs at the American embassy, including working for the motor pool during Secretary of State George Shultz' visit for the Tenth Anniversary meeting of Helsinki Conference. Lane took political science, history and economic courses at the University of Helsinki from professors who taught in Swedish, Finnish and (one) in English. We were proud that he received outstanding ratings from all of his professors. He not incidentally also had a marvelous time boxing at the Viipuri Boxing Club in Helsinki, learning skydiving, and hanging out with his Finnish friends and the U.S. Marine embassy security guards whose age he had now finally reached. Painfully aware of the passage of time, I recalled that during my first diplomatic assignment in Peru twenty-five years earlier and before getting married, it had been *I* who used to on occasion hang out with the Marine security guards!

Our second son, Carl, we re-enrolled at the local Swedish school, Mattlidens Skola. We also enrolled our daughter Vanessa, who had been too young for formal schooling during our first assignment, in the same school. She would have to repeat the experience of her brothers eight years earlier, learning Swedish from scratch.

We witnessed a wonderfully emotional and touching experience with Carl which in many ways summed up the attraction that Finland has had for our family. Magda and I personally escorted our fourteen year-old son to Mattlidens Skola in mid-March 1984 to meet with the school principal. He welcomed us back and said he would be more than happy to enroll Carl in school, even though it was late in the school year (how many times our children's education was interrupted during our diplomatic career and how well they took it in stride!). He said there were three different classes in which Carl could be enrolled and produced lists of the students in each section. Carl asked to look at the names of the students in the various classes. He quickly spotted one that had the names of most of the friends he knew when we had left Finland in 1979. He asked to be placed in that class, and the principal graciously consented.

The principal suggested we take Carl straight away to his classroom. Magda and I went along. As we interrupted the class and walked into it from a door at the rear, the students looked around and with astonishment saw Carl Cooper standing there. "Carl," they shouted, "is that you? What are you doing here?" There were such expressions of fondness, delight and friendliness on the part of the students that it almost brought tears to our eyes including Carl's! Once again, the cold and aloof Finns! Sure!!

The deputy chief of mission of the U.S. embassy has a beautiful home assigned to him or her, which was, like our earlier home, located in the stylish Helsinki suburb of West End on Kuninkaaniemi street on the banks of the Baltic. However in our case, we had to live for the first several months after our arrival in an apartment building on the corner of Siltatie and Ehrenströmintie near the embassy. It seems that a disastrous fire had ravaged the DCM home a couple of years earlier, and there had apparently been no hurry to get the home repaired. We had learned in Washington, however, that repairs and renovation were now well underway. Magda had the rare opportunity for a Foreign Service spouse of getting to choose furniture and express preferences for design and decorations for the DCM home that we had known from frequent visits during our earlier assignment. Meanwhile, we enjoyed living in the lovely in-town apartment with a great third-floor view of the Yacht Club and the South Harbor. Some of the smaller ferries, including the Soviet George Ots ferry, would pass through the narrow channel just in front of our apartment, giving a sensation of living in a lighthouse.

We finally moved into our new home in October 1984. It was (and remains) a beautiful house. A sprawling one-floor structure built originally by a large Finnish company as a kind of lodge, it had a spacious entry foyer, a large reception and dining area, a huge kitchen and a guest apartment and maid's quarters. The one previous weakness of the home had been that it lacked adequate bedroom space. But it's an ill wind that blows no good, and after the fire a large master bedroom was added to the end of the house facing the water with the residential island of Lauttasaaari visible off in the distance across the bay.

The property had a wide waterfront, even a sandy beach, and a jetty reaching out into the bay. And, treasure of treasures, there was a lovely sauna out-building just off the beach with a newly rebuilt interior including a wood sauna and a pine sauna anteroom. Before, during and after my day, many a Finnish politician, newspaperman, diplomat and, simply, friend, has spent some time, eaten some makkara (Finnish sausage) and drunk some vodka and beer in that lovely sauna! The setting of the house was so idyllic one could have believed himself miles from the nearest city, were it not for the traffic noise from an expressway (Länsiväylä) from the suburbs to Helsinki about a half mile distant. When Ambassador Rock Schnabel and his wife Marna arrived to Finland a year and a half later and we showed them the home of his Number Two, he asked me (maybe only half-jokingly) to explain how it was that I got to live in such beautiful surroundings while he had to live over the store! What the hell, the living conditions were rough, but *somebody* had to do it!

One of the nicest aspects of our return to Finland was the chance to renew old acquaintances and friendships. Upon moving into the refurbished DCM residence in September 1984, Magda and I gave a large "housewarming" party to which we invited the many Finnish, embassy, and diplomatic friends and acquaintances we had made both professionally and socially. Having learned to play the piano a little, I composed a simple song for the occasion and played and sang it for our guests. The lyrics read in part:

HOUSEWARMING

> We're having a housewarming
> -tupaantulaiset for you Finns
> We hope you will enjoy it, knock on
> the door and come right in!
> You are welcome guests in our new place
> It is of course a special case
> With waterfront and lots of land,
> And it all belongs to Uncle Sam!
> We are back again in Finland,
> And we couldn't be more pleased
> To see old friends, and make some new
> And spend such times as these,
> With all our friends who've gathered here
> From diplomats to financiers
> Not to mention politikkos

And Foreign Ministry oficios.
In our United States embassy
We all work very hard
To convince you Finns that we're OK,
That Ronald Reagan is our star.
He meets today with Gromyko
To tell him that it just ain't so
All those things the Russians say
That we're to blame in every way.
So, once again, terve' tulo [welcome]
It's nice to have you here
Let's raise our glass in a friendly toast
In a token of good cheer.
Too bad the weather's not so great
And it's only September 28!
We'll no doubt see you all quite soon,
Hopefully in this very room!

Well, no one ever said diplomats have to be good poets! But the little verses helped, I believe, set an appropriate tone for what was for us and we hope our guests a most enjoyable reunion.

That first summer in our new home we decided it would be foolish not to take full advantage of our seaside location and the presence of a jetty. So, we bought a boat to explore the gorgeous archipelago along the southern Finnish coast. It was a five-meter fiberglass boat with a small cuddy cabin and good canvas along with a fifty horsepower outboard motor. We got tremendous pleasure in cruising the waters and camping far and wide up and down the coast. This brought us into contact with another group of Finns with similar interests. We were also from time to time chased off islands that apparently were private property, until we gradually learned the rules and the proper protocol. The boat was fast and powerful enough to take the kids water-skiing, and our house once again became a magnet for Carl and Vanessa's school chums.

One of the primary responsibilities of a deputy chief of mission is to look after the morale of the embassy personnel, and this was a responsibility Magda and I took very seriously. We consciously tried to assure that all components of the embassy and their families had a sense of belonging to a team. Professionally, I tried to accomplish this team building in part, as noted above, by bringing everybody in on updating our assessment of Finland and U.S. interests. Socially, Magda and I tried to do this by making the DCM home a center of periodic off-hours activities for the embassy family. We consequently held a series of parties and picnics for embassy personnel, and we instituted an annual ski competition, which we staged, on the ice of the Baltic Sea in front of our home. I laid out courses over the ice and around a neighboring island and organized races for all age groups of kids and for the adults as well, giving "gold, silver and bronze" medals to the winners and food and drink and sauna to all. The embassy personnel seemed to enjoy it; I know that Magda, our kids and I did. Alas, the event did not survive our departure.

I've already confessed that my family and I had never skied before our first assignment to Finland but that we had enjoyed learning to ski, our limitations notwithstanding. I was impressed when we returned to Finland a second time to learn that Ambassador Nyborg had skied a couple of times in the seventy-five kilometer annual Finlandia ski competition (Finlandia Hiihto) from Hämeenlinna to Lahti. Now, I was pretty much reconciled to the fact that I would never speak Finnish as well as Keith Nyborg nor ski as well as he did. Nevertheless, I was determined that I, too, would one day participate in the Finlandia Hiihto. I wasn't ready to undertake that challenge in 1985, the first full winter of our second assignment to Finland, but I decided that I would make try to participate in the next and final opportunity, the Finlandia Hiihto of 1986.

It was not an undertaking that I entered into lightly. I had been running and jogging for some twenty years and liked it. I had over the years entered into numerous 10 K running competitions. I quite frequently would jog home to West End from the embassy in Kaivopuisto, a distance as I recall of some twelve kilometers. But to ski seventy-five kilometers is a challenge of an entirely different magnitude. I had but one objective in signing up for the Finlandia Hiihto: to be able to finish the "race" and not to embarrass myself in trying to do so. At age fifty, I thought that would be achievement enough. However, I realized that, given my limited skiing experience and my hopelessly faulty technique, even the simple goal of finishing would not be easy. I therefore began training already the previous fall, stepping up my running and jogging.

I participated in the September 29, 1985, 20 K Helsinki City half-marathon, finishing the thirteen and one/half miles as I recall in around two hours and ten minutes. As soon as the first snowfalls came in the Helsinki area, I began systematically logging skiing time at nearby ski trails. After the Baltic froze over it became even handier just to put on my skis next to our jetty and go skiing off over the ice for two or three hours at a time.

I received some excellent technical advice from my friend Kari Nars who, although an infinitely better skier than I, took me along to a couple of preliminary ski competitions to practice and to train. I would see him at the start of the competitions, and he would endure long waits at the finish line until I eventually struggled home. One such occasion was the Helsinki Capital City competition (Pääkaupunki Hiihto) of February 9. Fortunately, there was another Foreign Service Officer from the embassy who was also planning to participate in the Finlandia Hiihto, the Public Affairs Officer, Tom O'Connor, and we occasionally practiced together.

Finally came the big day, February 22, 1986. We gathered together with the thousands of other participants at the starting line near Lake Katumajärven outside of Hämeenlinna. We were expected to arrive at the starting line one hour before the scheduled 8:30 a.m. starting time. It was a bitter cold morning but not cold enough to warrant cancellation of the competition. Tom O'Connor and I had signed up together and had been issued starting numbers in the 7000 series, my own number being 7060. I learned later that the starting numbers of 7000 and over corresponded to the seventh and last category of the starting groups, the other categories of faster skiers starting ahead of us. That struck me as odd. Why should the fastest skiers start first? They were already the fastest. Why not give us slower skiers a fighting chance?

To my chagrin, I learned that the seventh starting group to which I belonged was categorized as the "Mustikkasopparyhmä" or the "Blueberry Soup Group," an appellation which baffles me to this day. What were they trying to tell me about my skiing skills? What did blueberry soup have to do with my skiing? To add insult to injury, this group was characterized in the program book as "hiihtäjät joille aika ei ole tärkein" translated in the program as "skiers for whom skiing time is not important." Well, of course skiing time was very important to me. It was only that there wasn't much I could do about it. I could only ski so fast, and that was it!

The sheer number of participants was staggering. The official program and results book of the event (issued a few weeks after the race was held) indicated that 12,100 skiers had signed the entry forms, and 10,301 actually participated. Everywhere one looked there were skiers. After the sound of the starting cannon boomed over frozen Lake Katumajärven, it took many minutes before those of us at the end of the masses of starters could begin to move forward. We were off! It became clear immediately after the first few strokes that the bitter cold weather had made the snow less slippery than would have been the case if it had not been so cold. The snow seemed to grab at each slide of the skies, cutting down the glide. Bad news for inexperienced skiers! Even more energy than normal would be required, and times would be slowed considerably.

Surely, the Finlandia Hiihto has to be one of the best-organized sporting events anywhere in the world. Every few kilometers along the seventy-five kilometer course there were refreshment stations where skiers could quench their thirst, eat nourishing snacks, get their skies re-waxed or go to the bathroom. First aid stations were also available at each stop. I had already learned from my previous cross country skiing experience that one should not wear too many layers of clothes, because no matter how cold it was, over-heating was more of a risk than becoming chilled—as long as one was vigorously skiing. I had put on thermal long johns, a flannel shirt and a ski sweater under a loose blue ski suit. In one particularly wise move, I had put on shoe covers to keep my feet drier and warmer. Already after the first few kilometers, my woolen cap, eyebrows and mustache became frosted with moisture from my breathing. Somewhere along the way, I don't remember how, I ended up with a different ski cap than I started out with. I think it was a promotional cap offered at one of the service tables along the way. At any rate it felt good to be able to put on a dry, warm woolen cap.

After the first two or three kilometers I settled into a steady, regular rhythm that I was reasonably confident I would be able to maintain. I noticed with dismay as I passed some of the electronic time checkpoints along the trail that I was progressing far slower along the course than I had done in previous preparatory competitions. It had to be the cold snow conditions that were slowing me down. For the first twenty or thirty kilometers of the competition, skiers kept passing me from behind. How far back must they have started, I wondered, to be still overtaking me this far into the competition? Then, gradually I began to notice that I was occasionally passing a skier here and there. So, I'm not the worst skier out here after all, I thought.

The hours passed. The course between Hämeenlinna and Lahti was rugged and beautiful. Finland's glacier-gouged terrain took us up one ravine and down another, time after time. The trail snaked through forests and glided by frozen lakes. I skied past the towns of Syrjäntausta, Lammi, and Kaunkorpi, stopping for refreshments at each station. A camaraderie among the skiers had quickly developed. It was less a competition at our level than a "happening" that we were jointly sharing. I was very favorably impressed by the literally thousands of Finns who, particularly near urban centers, stood by the ski trail to cheer on the participants. It didn't seem to matter to them that the leaders had sped by perhaps hours earlier. They cheered us slow pokes on, shouting encouragement.

Darkness fell, and I was still many kilometers away from the finish line. According to the regulations, skiers who had not arrived at various checkpoints by a certain time would not be allowed to continue. Slow as I was, I nevertheless was well ahead of those checkpoint limitations. Also, skiers who did not arrive at the Lahti finish line by 8:00 pm would not be considered as official finishers.

After many hours I began to reach the final way stations of the race located in the towns of Hollola, Hälvälä and, eventually, Tapanila. Only four more kilometers to go! My arms and back ached. My legs and feet felt like lead. By now it was past 6:30 in the evening. I had been out on the trail for over ten hours! The final segment of the trail led into Lahti and finally, into the impressive ski stadium in Lahti, which had been home to the 1978 World Ski Championships and which we had witnessed in our earlier assignment to Helsinki. Then, finally, the dramatic entrance into the stadium, a welcomed long, gliding downhill run past stadium seats, now empty, where hours earlier crowds had greeted the arrival of the Finlandia Hiihto leaders. And then the finish line! The time was just past 7:00 pm.

It was official. I had done it! My time: 10 hours 30 minutes and 45 seconds. The winner was Sweden's Örjan Blomqvist who finished in 4 hours 4 minutes and 10 seconds, a mere 6 hours 26 minutes and 35 seconds ahead of me. I finished at least two hours later than I had planned. But I finished. From the finish line we went to sauna, ate Finnish sausages (*makkara*), drank beer and relaxed. I found Tom O'Connor whom I had seen at the starting line but never again saw along the course. As it turned out, according to the official results I finished 8656 out of the 8820 who finished the competition. I preferred to think of it as finishing 8656 out of the 10,301 who started the race; almost 1500 skiers who began the competition did not finish. Of those who finished I edged out only 164, including Tom O'Connor who finished 8711 with a time of 10 hours 40 minutes and 23 seconds. I have looked at the list of skiers who finished behind me. A disturbingly high percentage of them were women! However, I noted that I finished ahead of four Americans (including Tom) three Brits, two Frenchmen, a Dutchman, a Czech, an Australian, an Austrian and a Japanese. The latter was the final official finisher with a time of 11 hours and 57 minutes.

For the next couple of days I could barely move. My muscles ached and in several places my skin had rubbed raw. But, you know, that is one experience I will always treasure. Although I have always tried before and since to stay in pretty good physical condition, that was the most physically challenging thing I have ever done—or ever will do. For me it was a once in a lifetime experience.

As DCM of the embassy, I found that my increased leadership and management responsibilities kept me inside the embassy more than when I had been political counselor. I was sort of the Mr. Inside man while Ambassador Nyborg and, later, Ambassador Schnabel took most of the trips. Consequently, I don't think that my Finnish language skills got quite back up to where they had been during my first assignment, although I continued to work hard at the language and probably actually expanded my vocabulary somewhat. It was my fluency that was not quite what I wanted, owing to insufficient opportunities to get away from the embassy and out into the country.

Nevertheless, it was most enjoyable to be able to fall back into many of my earlier routines, including my calls at the Foreign Ministry, now at a higher level, and my continued relationships with such key contacts as Jaakko Kalela, Max Jacobson, Jan-Magnus Jansson, General Aimo Pajunen, Harri Holkeri, Mikko Immonen, Paavo Lipponen and many others. I resumed my favorite practice of walking back from appointments through the Market Square on the South harbor. A particular pleasure was to be able to meet periodically with Jaakko Iloniemi, who by now had left the diplomatic service and was with Union Bank. During the latter part of my first assignment to Finland, Jaakko had been in Washington as the Finnish ambassador. Now that we were both back in Helsinki, we were able to have a most interesting series of luncheons as well as having each other and our spouses over for social occasions.

Ambassador Nyborg and President Koivisto had met from time to time for one-on-one lunches. Shortly after my arrival, Jaakko Kalela had suggested that it might be helpful if instead from time to time he accompany President Koivisto to the lunches and I accompany Ambassador Nyborg. This was accomplished and certainly helped me get a better grasp on President Koivisto's thinking.

Also at my initiative, I proposed to my Soviet Embassy counterpart, at the time a Mr. Tichtchenko, who was the real number two "diplomat" at the Soviet embassy, that we and our embassy political counselors get together occasionally for lunch. This we did on two or three occasions. He brought Soviet embassy political counselor Kostchev and I the U.S. embassy political counselor Paul Hacker. One day I was approached by another senior Soviet embassy official whose name appeared in our records as a KGB agent. He suggested that I meet with him for lunch. I advised him that my contact in Soviet embassy was my counterpart, Mr. Tichtchenko. At our next luncheon at the Soviet embassy, Tichtchenko let me know he had heard what had happened and expressed his appreciation for my insisting on maintaining contact with him.

On April 15, 1986 I had invited the foursome to get together again for lunch at my residence in West End. However, that morning I received a call from Tichtchenko saying that because of the U.S. air attack on Libya the preceding day, he had been ordered to cancel their participation in our scheduled lunch. He was most apologetic. The U.S. air attack had been taken in retaliation for Libyan responsibility in the bombing earlier in April of the La Belle discotheque in West Berlin, which according to American intelligence sources had been targeted at Americans who frequented the establishment. My assignment to Helsinki ended before another luncheon arrangement was made with our Soviet counterparts.

Our social life in Helsinki during our second assignment was if anything even more active and enjoyable than during our first assignment. We saw our friends the Brotherus, the Lönnfors, the Nars and others frequently. Kari Nars was at the time manager of the Bank of Helsinki and he kindly invited me and a group of other men, including the well known Finnish/Swedish author and celebrity Jörn Donner, up to the bank's ski lodge in Lapland one March weekend in 1985. We had a marvelous time. Also a celebrated wit and conversationalist, Jörn Donner was at the top of his form over the weekend. He had told us that as a change of pace he was writing a cookbook. One morning he cooked breakfast, including eggs, which were just awful. I commented dryly that we were certainly looking forward to his cookbook, provoking general hilarity on the part of the other guests and eliciting a wry smile from Donner.

Over ski week in 1985, Tapani and Lysa Brotherus had included us in plans to take the train up to a ski lodge near Pyhätunturi in Lapland. We took our son Carl and daughter Vanessa. The lodge belonged to some workers' organization and was simple, yet comfortable. We got in some excellent cross-country skiing. The Lönnfors had built a summer cottage in Snappertuna near Tammisaari, and we had the dubious honor of being invited to help them paint their new summer place one weekend. Of course, it turned out to be a hilarious experience. Later in the summer we helped Erik celebrate his 50th birthday at their summer place where, in that great Finnish tradition, he was surrounded on this momentous occasion by his family and many, many friends. For the one and only time in my experience, Per-Erik had such a marvelous time during the first half of his celebration that he was not able to be present for the second half!

Another much appreciated relationship we formed in Helsinki was with Kenneth and Tina Wrede who were among a small group of Finns who were very actively involved with the foreign diplomatic community. Every summer in their summer place on an island near Porvoo on the Gulf of Finland, the Wredes would invite ambassadors and a few other senior representatives from the diplomatic community together with leading Finnish foreign policy officials to a cook out on their island. It was always a marvelous occasion with good food, drink and conversation followed by a long walk through the woods to the beach and back. I think for some foreign diplomats it was one of the few occasions they had to get out into the Finnish countryside at the invitation of Finns. We were lucky enough to be included once again in a nostalgic return to this Wrede tradition during our visit to Finland during 1995.

In short our second stay in Finland was as interesting and enjoyable as the first, and the charms of Finland were happily reinforced in our minds.

19

A Glitch in Relations:
"Finland Can't Afford a Palme
Phenomenon"

On April 30, 1985, an event took place the repercussions of which underscored one of the primary themes running through this book. Namely, it was not always easy for Finland to walk the fine line that both assured the maintenance of good neighborly relations and mutual confidence with the Soviet Union while at the same time did not undermine confidence in the West regarding Finland's even-handedness and credible neutrality. The incident also illustrated the difficulty of keeping Finnish domestic politics and Finnish security and foreign policy in neatly separate and differentiated boxes.

Prime Minister Kalevi Sorsa, who was also party leader of the Social Democratic Party, delivered a speech on April 30 to a May Day-eve gathering of Social Democrats at the Käpylä Workers' House in Helsinki. In the speech, Sorsa sharply criticized United States policy in Nicaragua and then attacked President Reagan's Strategic Defense Initiative (SDI). As was all too usual in Finland, finding nothing critical to say about the Soviet Union which was at that time mired down in its war on Afghanistan, Sorsa instead chose to praise Soviet General Secretary Gorbachev's moratorium proposal on Euro-missiles. This was a position with which the United States was in vigorous disagreement and which struck at the very heart of the US/NATO dual track strategy for redressing the nuclear imbalance in Europe.

The sharply critical nature of Prime Minister Sorsa's remarks regarding two United States policies and his praise of a Soviet Union policy at odds with U.S. policy struck us in the embassy as being inappropriate and unbalanced. We were particularly annoyed that Sorsa would make such a speech shortly after we had arranged high level official meetings for him in Washington which he had visited wearing his hat as chairman of the Socialist International's Disarmament Committee. Despite having heard U.S. views on foreign and security policy issues from key American policy makers in Washington, Prime Minister Sorsa had made no effort in his speech to acknowledge United States' views on these issues.

Ambassador Nyborg was on the eve of departing for the United States on official consultations in Washington. I met with him before he left and proposed that we react sharply but discreetly to the Sorsa speech by formally raising it with the Finnish Foreign Ministry. He agreed, and we advised Washington of what we planned to do and were given the green light.

On May 3, 1985, in my capacity as chargé d'affaires of the embassy—now that Ambassador Nyborg had left for Washington —I called on the Foreign Ministry Under Secretary for Political Affairs, Klaus Törnudd. I was accompanied by the embassy political counselor. Embassy telegram "Helsinki 01953" of May 3, 1985 reported a full account of the meeting with the under secretary. The telegram was classified CONFIDENTIAL and went out over my name.

I prefaced my remarks to the under secretary by saying that the embassy had forwarded the text of the Sorsa speech to the Department of State and had not yet received instructions. However, I said that the embassy wanted the Foreign Ministry to be aware of our views and concerns. The text of the oral presentation I made on behalf of the embassy as reported in the embassy's telegram follows (I carefully read the text *verbatim* from the prepared talking points; I did not leave a copy):

—...I would like to refer to PM Sorsa's speech April 30 in the Käpylä Workers' House.

—the embassy has read this speech very carefully and has submitted the full text to Washington. We have asked for guidance on an appropriate U.S. response.

—Pending receipt of such guidance, I would like to say that the embassy's initial reaction is one of some concern that the speech is sharply critical and disparaging of the United States Strategic Defense Initiative and criticizes explicitly the policy of the United States Government in Nicaragua.

—The speech does not find anything to criticize in the policy of the Soviet Union and in fact explicitly praises [General Secretary] Gorbachev's moratorium proposal on Euro-missiles.

—The U.S. has very clear and well-known views about the growing Soviet and Cuban supplied military buildup in Nicaragua. We have very clear and well-known views about the desirability of moving away from a balance of terror based on nuclear weapons toward a more humane balance based on non-nuclear defense systems.

—We see no hint in the prime minister's speech that these U.S. views expressed to him very recently at very high official levels in Washington are taken into consideration at all.

—Moreover, these issues are either matters of direct controversy between the two superpowers as in the case of Nicaragua or the subject of delicate direct negotiations between the two as in the case of SDI and arms negotiations.

—We of course could make a detailed point-by-point rebuttal of the allegations contained in the speech, but will await Washington guidance before proceeding further.

—We have no idea how Washington will react to this one-sided public speech by the prime minister. It hardly seems the kind of speech one would expect to hear from the host government of the CSCE anniversary meeting scheduled to be held in less than three months time. I frankly do not discount the possibility that my government may choose to respond publicly to this sharp public criticism from the head of the Finnish Government, whatever hat he may consider himself to have been wearing when he made the speech.

—I might also note that we have studied and reported to Washington other recent public statements by very high-ranking Finnish Government officials. Of particular interest is Foreign Minister Väyrynen's speech before the Finnish National Defense Course March 27. We appreciated that the statement is very carefully worded, compared to more recent statements. However, in our view this statement also fails to recognize elemental facts concerning the U.S. SDI research program and reaches conclusions with which we certainly do not agree.

—In short…we must ask ourselves whether we are increasingly seeing a pattern in which the Government of Finland is taking selective positions on matters at controversy or under active negotiation between the U.S. and

Soviet Union, positions that are critical of U.S. positions and in praise of Soviet Union positions that are known to be unacceptable to the U.S. We fully recognize every country's right to express its own views and we welcome honest and objective criticisms and advice which we receive from time to time from all quarters, including from our allies. But what are we to conclude when criticism is public and seems to go only in one direction and when our best efforts to explain our positions are ignored? These questions are disturbing to the embassy.

Under Secretary Törnudd made no substantive response but noted that the prime minister's speech had been made in his capacity as leader of the Social Democratic Party rather than as prime minister and thus did not reflect official Finnish foreign policy which can only be authorized by the president. The embassy had already anticipated that ploy in my own presentation, and I advised the under secretary that we could not consider this to be a valid distinction. The prime minister is the prime minister and when he makes a public speech, we have to take his statements seriously.

Our *démarche* was not motivated purely by pique over Prime Minister Sorsa's unusually sharp criticisms. However as I explained in my presentation at the Foreign Ministry, we were concerned by what seemed to be a growing trend by Finnish officials to feel they could say whatever they wanted about Western or United States policy, while at the same time exercising self-censorship when it came to errant Soviet policies. For that reason I had deliberately included in my presentation a specific reference to a recent speech by Foreign Minister Väyrynen. We in the embassy considered our *démarche* to be a discreet shot across the bow in the hope that Finnish officials would be more careful in their public utterances. We had no intention of making the episode public, nor did Washington choose to raise the issue publicly, although the State Department did follow-up with the Finnish embassy in Washington and repeated its unhappiness with the Sorsa speech.

We were quite surprised, therefore, when the fact and substance of my May 3 *démarche* were leaked to the press, by whom it is not clear. The leak certainly did not come from the U.S. embassy, nor did anyone allege that it did. It was our speculation that U.S. unhappiness over the Sorsa speech was leaked to the media by

Center Party-oriented foreign ministry officials who would not be adverse to embarrassing the prime minister, Social Democrat Kalevi Sorsa. This was plausible inasmuch as the Finnish Foreign Ministry was at the time quite polarized politically between, primarily, Social Democrat and Center Party members and sympathizers. Foreign Minister Paavo Väyrynen was himself chairman of the Center Party and had very well known political ambitions to become president, as did Kalevi Sorsa. Therefore, it would not have been surprising that some Center Party supporter in the Foreign Ministry might have leaked the embassy's protest about the Sorsa speech to the media, conveniently leaving out any reference to the embassy's also complaining about a recent Väyrynen speech.

Whatever the source of the leak, it provoked a substantial and ultimately useful public and press debate about the Sorsa speech and the embassy reaction to it. An embassy telegram (Helsinki 02449 of June 6, 1985) classified CONFIDENTIAL reported the Foreign Ministry's official response to our *démarche* and provided a full account of the Finnish debate and the embassy's assessment of it. The embassy report stated that:

The Finnish MFA responded May 30 in predictable terms to the embassy and State Department remonstrations...to the GOF over the prime minister's May Day speech critical of USG SDI and Nicaragua policies.... The MFA's response to our *démarche* consisted of a non-paper (copy being pouched to the Department) which restated official Finnish positions on the current negotiations between the U.S. and USSR in Geneva and on the situation in Nicaragua. The restated positions are cautiously worded expressions of concern and hope for positive results in both problem areas. The non-paper proceeds to insist that 'statements expressing official policy should be distinguished from positions taken in the public debate in Finland on the level of the political parties. Such positions are not intended to modify the official policy, which is based on a wide national consensus, but rather to express the specific views of the party in question.'

[Chargé Cooper] responded to the MFA position by expressing continued satisfaction with Finland's official policy positions on the issues in question; while they do not coincide with U.S. positions they reflect concerns which are understandable from the Finnish perspective and which are couched in terms which take into account the U.S.' own concerns. The [Chargé] told the MFA official that, as we have previously stated, we do not see a valid distinction between when a high government official is speaking in an official capacity or in a party capacity. Therefore, we would expect that similar speeches in the future, if any, would receive similar responses from the USG.

The embassy telegram went on to discuss public reactions by President Koivisto and Foreign Minister Väyrynen to the incident:

Both Foreign Minister Väyrynen and President Koivisto were queried about this episode in recent television appearances. On May 21 Väyrynen told a TV interviewer that of course the prime minister has a right to his own views and to address some issues as a party leader rather than as a chief of government. He went on to point out, however, that on important foreign policy issues it is important that Finnish leaders speak with one voice and in a matter consistent with Finland's official policy. President Koivisto told a TV questioner on June 2 that the episode had perhaps been blown out of proportion and commented that had the embassy not called attention to it few people would have perhaps noted press reports of the prime minister's speech. He went on to note, however, that it is important that there be no question about Finland's neutral policy of maintaining good relations in all directions. A Finnish source has told us privately that both President Koivisto and Foreign Minister Väyrynen were concerned about questions concerning the even-handedness of Finland's neutrality that were raised by the Sorsa speech and public reactions to it.

The embassy of course had called attention (privately and diplomatically) to Sorsa's speech precisely because it did not appear to us to reflect the stated Finnish policy of maintaining good relations in all directions but, rather, seemed slanted towards the Soviet Union.

The embassy reporting cable of June 6, 1985 noted that there was extensive media reaction to the episode—more than twenty articles and editorials and various television commentaries. The telegram observed that:

Two or three of the articles and commentaries criticized the USG for attempting to muzzle the Finnish prime minister and Finns in general. This was, however, clearly the view of a small minority. The overwhelming media reaction was that (A) the Sorsa statement of April 30 was one-sided (B) such imbalance was inconsistent with Finland's policy of neutrality and effort to maintain good relations with all countries and (C) no meaningful distinction could be drawn between Sorsa's prime minister and party leader hats, when he is speaking publicly.

Several examples can be cited. The weekly newsmagazine *Suomen Kuvalehti* observed: 'It seems questionable to draw a line between official foreign policy and the views expressed by politicians and other citizens. The national interests may be in jeopardy if the politicians leave foreign policy to its own fate and presume the right freely to express their likes and dislikes.' The weekly went on to comment sarcastically 'it's not easy to applaud as consistent the fact that Sorsa first as prime minister labels Reagan a hopeless case and then, as chairman of the Socialist International Disarmament Group, travels to Washington to offer advice on disarmament.' It called 'illogical [that] Sorsa as May Day speaker for the SDP condemns the plans of one of the superpowers, but then as prime minister presupposes that the world has faith in the restraint and impartiality of Finnish foreign policy.'

The independent daily *Helsingin Sanomat* stated editorially that Sorsa expressed concern about disrespect for international treaties in his speech but that 'the value of the message is, however, diminished if he is in practice barred from expressing similar concerns in the case of other small countries.'

The embassy assumed that the editorial was referring to U.S. actions in Nicaragua in mentioning disrespect for international treaties and to Soviet actions in Afghanistan and Eastern Europe in referring to similar concerns in the case of other small countries. The telegram proceeded:

Regarding roles, the *Helsingin Sanomat* expressed doubt about the Foreign Ministry's position of distinguishing between remarks made by a minister in his capacity as party leader and in his official capacity. It stated that 'a government representative must naturally select the target for his remarks carefully and pay attention to his choice of words.' The newspaper went on to say that because of Prime Minister Sorsa's active role in the Socialist International and his position as a strong man of Finnish politics 'his statements are associated with the views of the Finnish Government even though one might not want that,' concluding that 'what is essential then is not the role in which an influential politician speaks but what he says.'

The Conservative newspaper *Uusi Suomi* in a short editorial titled 'Sorsa's Error' simply noted that Finland is not in a position to go around the world pointing out the mistakes of other countries because it cannot react consistently and in a balanced way in all cases. The paper pointed out former President Kekkonen's advice that Finland should act as a 'doctor' in world crises, not as a 'judge.' Regarding roles, *Uusi Suomi* said it is as easy for the prime minister to change his roles as for a tiger to lose its stripes.

In the roughest shot against Sorsa a *Helsingin Sanomat* columnist stated flatly that Sorsa's statements are in conflict with Finland's Paasikivi-Kekkonen foreign policy line and that the prime minister cannot claim special privileges in this area. [The columnist] said that whatever the differences between the U.S. and Soviet Union, both countries start from the assumption that 'political leaders make political statements.' Referring to Swedish Prime Minister Olof Palme's practice of criticizing in all directions, the columnist concluded that 'Finland cannot afford a Palme phenomenon.'

Meanwhile, Conservative MP Turre Junnila, a noted gadfly on foreign policy issues, has submitted a written question in parliament in which he presses the government for a position on Prime Minister Sorsa's 'anti-American statements' which he described 'clearly in conflict with the careful neutrality traditionally sought by Finland.' The government has not as yet answered the Junnila interpolation, but we are told by MFA sources that the response will be non-polemical and will hide behind the 'party leader' versus 'prime minister' role differentiation.

The embassy reporting telegram went on to discuss other dimensions of the Finnish debate over the episode:

There is little doubt that SDP and some GOF officials are not pleased that the embassy made an issue of the Sorsa speech (although they seem to accept that the leak to the news media did not come from the embassy). In addition to the formal MFA response, a couple of MFA officials have informally indicated regret that the matter has resulted in an embarrassing public debate. So have some SDP officials. Other MFA officials, however, have expressed private satisfaction that the embassy has held the prime minister accountable for his statements inconsistent with Finnish foreign policy. The division of opinion within the MFA is not surprising inasmuch as the MFA is rather sharply divided between SDP supporters and Center Party or at least non-SDP supporters. The former were unhappy over Sorsa's embarrassment; the latter believe it was very useful to call Sorsa on his speech. This latter view is also widely shared in non-socialist political circles. Moreover, whatever annoyance the SDP may have felt, relations between the embassy and SDP Party officials over the past few weeks have, if anything, improved.

Much of our private discussion on this matter with a broad spectrum of Finns focussed on why Sorsa apparently feels the need from time to time to speak out critically about the U.S. The consensus answer on this question is principally that Sorsa and the Finnish SDP are very much influenced by intellectual currents flowing in the Socialist International (SI) community, particularly by opinion within Swedish Social Democratic and West German SPD circles.

In addition to being influenced by SI views on disarmament and Central American issues, it has been pointed out to us that Sorsa often feels frustrated when he observes the Palmes, Brandts, Mitterands and Papendreous sharply criticizing one or another U.S. policy whereas Sorsa is constrained by Finland's foreign policy from speaking out, at least officially. It is speculated that Sorsa and his party advisers at times feel they are lagging behind their SI peer group on such issues. Some Finnish observers are increasingly concerned by SI influence on the Finnish SDP's foreign policy views in directions inconsistent with Finland's traditional emphasis on neutrality, low profile and restraint.

In addition to the SI factor, some more cynical observers see the occasional Sorsa speech critical of the U.S. as being aimed in part at his Moscow audience, noting that Sorsa had definite presidential ambitions following President Koivisto's probable second term. Finally, it cannot be denied that many Europeans, undoubtedly including Sorsa, are genuinely concerned about aspects of the United States SDI and Central American policies.

Obviously from the U.S. point of view this rationalization for Prime Minister Sorsa's speaking out against the United States does not stand the test of comparison with most other well known SI figures on one key measure: the others are free to sharply criticize the Soviet Union on any number of issues, and several often do. Finland's special geopolitical situation does not permit this. Therefore, if Finland's policy of neutrality is to be credible, it is proper from the point of view of Finnish national interest as well that Sorsa feel constrained from critical public statements about U.S. policy. Certainly, this is the principal conclusion which most Finns seem to have drawn from this episode. Ambassador Nyborg's protest to Sorsa in 1981 over a similar public criticism of the U.S. seemed to purchase a couple of years of restraint. We hope we will be as successful this time as well. COOPER

Thus the embassy wrapped up the episode. To be fair to Sorsa, however, he was hardly staking out new territory for Finnish leaders in criticizing U.S. policies and praising or echoing Soviet policy positions. Former President Kekkonen routinely spoke out against NATO and U.S. foreign, security and disarmament policies during his long presidency and favored policies known to be supported by the Soviet Union, always arguing, however, that he had reached these positions out of consideration of Finland's own national interests. Rarely, however, had Kekkonen been quite so blunt as had Sorsa in his April 30 speech.

One might also add to the telegram's observation that there were no doubt many sincere critics in Europe of U.S. policy on "Star Wars" and U.S. support for the "contras" of Nicaragua, including Prime Minister Sorsa. Indeed these two issues were the subject of bitter disagreement and debate within the United States. It therefore must have seemed quite normal to Prime Minister Sorsa to join in the criticism of the United States on these issues. In fact, several of the Finnish media reactions against Sorsa's speech were careful to point out that they did not disagree with what Sorsa said: they only disagreed that it was proper for Sorsa to speak out publicly on these issues while Finnish leaders were constrained from criticizing Soviet behavior.

The bottom line as far as the embassy was concerned was to lay down a marker that the Finns could not have it both ways: they could not maintain a credible policy of neutrality while criticizing United States policies and being silent on Soviet transgressions. At least, not without paying a price of diminishing the credibility of the even-handedness of Finnish neutrality. Indeed, as has been noted throughout this book, this was one of the horns of the "Finnish Dilemma."

One can never be certain of cause and effect, but we noticed what we thought was an almost immediate payoff from the U.S.'s vigorous reaction to the Sorsa speech. Nicaragua's president, Sandinista Daniel Ortega, visited Finland shortly after the Sorsa May Day speech episode and received a very cautious official reception in Finland. An embassy telegram classified SECRET (Helsinki 02079 of May 14, 1985) reported on a *démarche* I made as chargé d'affaires on behalf of the embassy under instructions from the State Department regarding the impending Ortega visit. A follow-up cable classified SECRET (Helsinki 02173 of May 17, 1985) assessed the results of the Ortega visit to Finland. I drafted and approved both telegrams. The May 14 cable reported:

The chargé called on Ambassador Jaakko Blomberg, Acting Director for Political Affairs of the foreign ministry, to present the requested démarche on Nicaragua in view of Nicaraguan President Daniel Ortega's forthcoming visit to Finland May 16. The chargé went through the talking points contained in REFTEL A in detail, underscoring the desirability that Ortega receive a message from Europe that peace in Nicaragua and Central America will depend upon practical and verifiable Nicaraguan actions to give real meaning to the Contadora Principles. The chargé expressed continuing USG concern that the Western European democracies seem reluctant to recognize the true nature of the Sandinista Government as again revealed late last year by Comandante Arce's secret speech, a copy of which was left with Ambassador Blomberg. The chargé expressed the hope that the GOF will convey to Ortega the concept that European support for the Government of Nicaragua will be linked to the latter's performance in living up to the Contadora principles.

With reference to the USG démarche last week to Finland regarding unbalanced criticism of U.S. policies by Prime Minister Sorsa (REFTEL C), [the] chargé said we expect that the Nicaraguans during the visit will engage in heavy anti-American rhetoric. He expressed the hope that GOF officials for their part will keep U.S. sensitivities in mind during the Ortega visit.

Ambassador Blomberg was essentially noncommittal on the substance of the *démarche*. He expressed appreciation for the U.S. views and the background information supplied. He said that he would assure that our concerns were brought to the attention of GOF officials who would be involved in the Ortega visit.

In the COMMENT section of the telegram I expressed the embassy's hope that the Finnish officials would demonstrate restraint in any public statements during the Ortega visit. In our follow-up cable of May 17, bearing the subject line "Nicaragua's President Ortega receives Cautious Official Reception in Finland," we were able to report that the Nicaraguan president had been received with considerable circumspection in Finland. Citing press reports, the telegram noted that although Ortega had met with President Koivisto, Prime Minister Sorsa and Foreign Minister Väyrynen, the only Finnish official to speak on the record about the visit was the foreign minister:

> Väyrynen said that the GOF officials reiterated Finland's line on the situation in Central America. Namely, that Finland supports a peaceful solution in the area based on the Contadora Principles and that 'it is regrettable that recent developments, such as a trade embargo have worsened the situation in Central America.' Regarding economic assistance, Väyrynen said specifically that Finland sees 'no need and no possibility' for increased development assistance to Nicaragua, because Nicaragua is already Finland's largest aid recipient in Latin America (70 million Finnmarks—approximately U.S. Dols 11 million—over the next three years) and aid to Nicaragua has grown faster than Finland's aid generally...

> Generally the press showed sympathy to a beleaguered Nicaragua, but there were several pointed references to the need for Nicaragua to be sensitive to its neighboring superpower's security interests just as Finland is sensitive to 'its' superpower neighbor's security concerns. President Ortega appeared for his part the soul of moderation and injured innocence, stating repeatedly that Nicaraguan Government policy is guided by the three principles of political pluralism, a mixed economy and non-alignment. He was very critical of U.S. policy but used for the most part unemotional, restrained language, claiming that Nicaragua only seeks to avoid confrontation with the U.S. and an overall solution based on Contadora Principles. He stated his satisfaction with expressions of political and economic support received in Finland.

The embassy cable ended with a somewhat self-satisfied comment:

The publicly expressed Finnish official positions during the Ortega visit were extraordinarily restrained and cautious and represented an absolute optimum result from the USG point of view given the circumstances and compared to statements by host governments in other capital cities on President Ortega's itinerary. There was undoubtedly a connection between earlier expressions of U.S. concern over unbalanced Finnish public statements and the highly judicious and cautious way in which the Ortega visit was managed by the GOF. COOPER

20

Shultz and Schevardnadze Hit it Off at the CSCE 10th Anniversary Conference: Shultz Takes a Liking to Helsinki

Nothing quite gains the attention of an embassy like an impending visit by a very senior U.S. government official. I had been in Helsinki in April 1979 for the visit of Vice President Mondale (the visit for which he was advised that the word "Finlandization" was not to pass his lips). The embassy had been thrown into a tizzy preparing for that visit.

An even more demanding challenge faced us in the embassy with the impending visit of Secretary of State George Shultz for the tenth anniversary celebration of the original Conference on Security and Cooperation in Europe (CSCE) meeting that had taken place in Helsinki in July of 1975. The secretary was bringing with him an enormous delegation, not only for the CSCE meeting itself but also for bilateral discussions that it was anticipated would be held with the Soviet Union.

By July 1985, hopeful signs had begun to emerge after a long cold spell in U.S./Soviet relations. Many factors had contributed to the cold spell. The Soviets had reacted negatively to the 1979 NATO "dual track" decision to begin to deploy countervailing allied intermediate range nuclear missiles in Europe unless the Soviet Union withdrew its SS-20 missiles which in the NATO view disrupted the nuclear balance in Europe.

The Soviets tried mightily from 1979 to 1983 to get the NATO alliance to rescind its decision, pulling out all of the propaganda stops and relying heavily on protests from "peace movements," left-wing parties, American "nuclear freeze" proponents and anyone who might help undermine NATO resolve. When this effort was ultimately (and narrowly) unsuccessful, the Soviets walked out of arms negotiations, saying they would not come back until NATO ceased its deployments. The Soviet invasion of Afghanistan in 1979 and the subsequent brutal impasse there had for its part produced a strongly negative reaction in the United States, as had Soviet complicity in the 1981 crackdown on Solidarity in Poland.

Moreover, the first few years of the Reagan administration were marked by a strong emphasis on building up the United States' military position in an effort to set the stage for "negotiating from strength" with the Soviets, a policy which was not fully appreciated by many outside of and even within the United States. The long illness of Brezhnev followed by sudden leadership changes in the Soviet Union 1982-1985 from Brezhnev to Andropov to Chernenko to Gorbachev also did not yield a situation in Moscow conducive to imaginative new thinking on arms control issues. And just when some elements in the Reagan administration, led by Secretary of State Shultz, were considering giving more emphasis to arms control (while at the same time being fiercely resisted by other factions within the administration) the Soviet shoot-down of KAL Flight 007 created more outrage and more bad vibrations. Also, throughout most of 1983 and 1984, the Soviet leadership seemed intent on doing nothing that might help President Reagan in his re-election bid, further dashing cold water on any significant steps towards negotiations.

All of these negative dynamics slowly began to turn, beginning with an invitation by President Reagan to Soviet Foreign Minister Gromyko to call on him at the White House on September 28, 1984 (the same day as my housewarming party in Helsinki, although I wouldn't want to make too much of the connection). The Soviet leadership had apparently given up the hope that Reagan would not be re-elected and had decided he was the one they would have to do business with for the next four years. That

White House meeting was the first time the Soviet foreign minister had been invited to the White House since the Soviet invasion of Afghanistan in 1979. The White House meeting and subsequent developments led to a successful Geneva meeting between Secretary Shultz and Gromyko in January 1985 in which they agreed to a framework for future arms talks. Shultz and Gromyko met again in May 1985 in Vienna and reached agreement in principle on holding a Reagan/Gorbachev summit meeting in Geneva in November 1985.

Throughout this period of serious tension in US/Soviet relations over arms control issues, the U.S. embassy in Helsinki, as U.S. embassies throughout Europe, was enjoined by the Department of State to forcefully put forward U.S. and NATO positions on the crucial arms control issues, not only with the government but with the media and political opinion leaders. Consequently, as DCM I organized together with other members of the country team a public affairs campaign to explain U.S. arms control positions. You have to believe me when I tell you that in Finland in 1985-86 this was a tough sell!

On November 8, 1985, in response to a request from the Department of State, the embassy spelled out in CONFIDENTIAL telegram Helsinki No. 5256 what we were doing and trying to do to inform the Finnish public. The message was drafted by the embassy public affairs officer Tom O'Connor (the other embassy skier) and myself. We reported that we had organized a coordinated program of bringing in arms control visitors from the United States, arranging briefings for parliamentary groups, think tanks, universities and the media, providing press information and delivering numerous speeches.

The embassy message, after explaining what we had been doing, went on to describe the tough audience that the embassy had to deal with in Finland:

> The general public in Finland, though quite well-versed on arms control, is not knowledgeable in detail about SDI [Strategic Defense Initiative]. However, they are susceptible to a gut feeling, strongly reinforced by Soviet propaganda, that SDI deployments may turn a dangerous page which cannot be turned back. Finnish government officials, because of their commitment to a neutrality which avoids taking positions on contentious East-West

issues, have generally been reluctant to take strong public positions on SDI. However, in his capacity as '[SDP] party chairman' Prime Minster Sorsa criticized SDI in strong terms last April. Following a vigorous embassy and Washington reaction, the prime minister has avoided speaking out on the theme since then. President Koivisto has voiced moderate skepticism regarding SDI on several occasions. Most media and academic commentators have been skeptical of SDI, using U.S. critics to bolster their cases...

The embassy concluded its report by observing:

We cannot honestly say that the above described mission efforts to increase understanding of SDI have resulted in visibly increased support of the SDI concept. However, we are convinced we have contributed significantly to a clearer understanding of what the U.S. intends with SDI and why we are advancing this program. There has also been a grudging acceptance, reflected in a few recent editorials, that at least SDI has brought the Soviets back to the negotiating table. The Finnish general and elite publics are now concentrating on Geneva to look for prospects for progress on arms control. The direction of attitudes toward SDI will be greatly influenced by whether progress is made or whether SDI is seen by Western media to be the major stumbling block, as the Soviets claim. On the broader arms control subject generally, we are convinced our efforts have contributed to a considerably improved understanding of U.S. positions and to a less uncritical approach to Soviet propaganda positions.

Meanwhile, while putting forward our best efforts on promoting U.S. arms control positions, preparations in the embassy went forward for United States participation in the tenth anniversary CSCE meeting. I was named the principal coordinator in the embassy for our preparations. This meant taking the lead in dealing with the Finnish Foreign Ministry officials responsible for organizing the event on behalf of Finland as the host government. Once again I had reason to be very favorably impressed by the organizational capabilities of the Finns in preparing such a massive undertaking as organizing a meeting of thirty-five strong-willed foreign ministers of the CSCE member countries.

More difficult than dealing with the Finns was handling the Washington contingents that poured into Helsinki in the weeks leading up to the CSCE meeting to assure that proper security, logistical, secure communications, lodging and other arrangements were being made in accordance with their often conflicting requirements. The security of the secretary of state is the responsibility of the diplomatic security bureau of the State

Department. Highly trained professionals, they often succumb to the understandable tendency—from their point of view—to subordinate everything to planning against even the most remote risk to the official they are responsible for protecting. They were only slightly less demanding in their single-minded purpose than are the secret service agents responsible for protecting the president of the United States.

Both organizations in their need to accept full responsibility for their charge have no qualms in quite undiplomatically running roughshod over the highly qualified (in the case of Finland) security elements responsible for security in the host country. The embassy was left to try to smooth over wounded feelings of the Finns who had been run over. While it happily did not reach such extremes on this occasion, I have personally been in situations where so-called "good will" visits by senior American officials to friendly countries have left behind a trail of "ill will" because of the excesses, rudeness and lack of manners shown by the visitors or, as is more often the case, their support staff.

Meanwhile, on July 3, the Soviet Union announced that Andrei Gromyko had been kicked upstairs to the ceremonial post as president of the USSR and was being replaced as foreign minister by Eduard Shevardnadze, who had been first secretary of the Communist Party in the Republic of Georgia. Thus, it was clear that the Helsinki Conference to be held July 30-August 1 would be Shevardnadze's first appearance as Soviet foreign minister at an international gathering. This news added to the drama and attraction of the event, and hundreds of representatives of the Western media were expected to attend. For the Finns (and for the U.S. embassy with regard to American correspondents) this heightened the importance of providing full support services and facilities for the members of the press who would be covering the event.

George Shultz later recorded in his memoirs of his years as secretary of state that at the first plenary meeting of the CSCE conference he had a member of his staff find out where the Soviet delegation was seated in Finlandia Hall and confirm whether Shevardnadze was present. When it was reported to Shultz that

Shevardnadze was indeed seated with his delegation, Shultz in his own words reported that:

> I set out down one aisle, across the front of the hall, and up the aisle leading to the Soviet delegation. As I proceeded, more and more delegates saw what was happening. The room quieted. When I reached his seat, we shook hands. He broke into a broad smile. There was a sense of relief and shared drama. We chatted in a friendly, open manner. 'I expect our meeting tomorrow to be constructive.' He reciprocated in a natural, easy way. No reservations. No guarded wariness.[1]

President Koivisto in his own memoirs commenting on this event indicated he had deliberately used his role as host to get the two superpower foreign ministers together informally during a working lunch and believes that he thus may have contributed to the holding of the first bilateral meeting between Shultz and Shevardnadze held at the U.S. embassy.[2] My own recollection is that, as was usual at such multilateral conferences, the U.S. delegation was expecting such a bilateral meeting, and we had been planning for it at the embassy. There is no doubt, however, that the informal settings provided the two delegations during the social functions arranged by the Finns contributed to a productive meeting.

The two foreign ministers met twice bilaterally. The first meeting was at the U.S. embassy. The embassy staff had made the administrative arrangements for the meeting but, again as is normal, neither the ambassador nor I were included in the meeting, which of course had little or nothing to do with Finnish subjects. Therefore, I could only stand in the embassy wings and watch the delegations enter the meeting room and, after several hours, watch them come out again. Secretary Shultz' delegation at the table consisted of Ambassador Max Kampelman who President Reagan, at Secretary Shultz' request, had named as overall coordinator of the "umbrella" disarmament talks agreed to by Shultz and Gromyko in Geneva; Ambassador Rozanne Ridgway, now assistant secretary of state for European affairs; Ambassador Paul Nitze, Secretary Shultz' disarmament talks advisor in Washington; Ambassador Arthur Hartman, U.S. ambassador to Moscow; and National Security Council Advisor Jack Matlock.

It was fascinating to watch the faces of the American delegation as they came out of the conference room following this first ever meeting with Foreign Minister Shevardnadze. They were smiling and ebullient. Immediately after the meeting, they made it clear that dealing with Shevardnadze had been like a breath of fresh air in comparison with previous meetings over the past two decades with the notoriously sour and unfriendly Gromyko with his heavy-handed "iron pants" negotiating tactics and general unpleasantness.

George Shultz noted in his memoirs that he had proposed using simultaneous translation at the meeting in the American embassy rather than the laborious and stilted consecutive translation that the Soviets had always in the past insisted upon, thereby in Shultz' view robbing discussions of any element of spontaneity. Shultz recalled that, to the dismay of Dobrynin and other advisors who wanted to keep Shevardnadze on a tight leash, the latter had readily agreed to simultaneous translation that in fact did greatly facilitate the discussions. (Shultz quotes Shevardnadze as agreeing happily that they had gotten eight hours of work done in four hours!)[3]

I queried Ambassador Ridgway about the CSCE bilateral meeting with Shevardnadze during my interview with her August 10, 1995. I asked her if I had been correct in noting in the faces of the American delegation after the first meeting in the U.S. embassy a look of elation and a sense that "this is a new ball game, that…you could see opportunities in dealing with Shevardnadze that had never been there with Gromyko." Ridgway confirmed that impression and went on to note that the delegation had been criticized by hard liners in Washington who thought they had actually seen

...a smile on my face at one point. It was a very difficult meeting for [Shevardnadze]. He was backstopped by all the old players, Kvitzinski, Dobrynin, and Kornienko; there they all sat, and I think [they had prepared him] for a Gromyko type role. That is, he had talking points that would have gone on for God knows how long. The first change came when he agreed that at the U.S. embassy we could use simultaneous translation. That right away made it very difficult for anybody to sort of lean toward the Gromyko way, because you know that the other side hears immediately what you are saying, so there is no need to speak for thirty minutes and then wait for a translation and pass notes, [etc]…But it added spontaneity. Shultz invited the spontaneity, while the Soviet team was trying to get Shevardnadze to read their notes and was jumping up and down, and trying to point him this way and that. He wasn't the kind of guy that they had trained under with Gromyko, and it was just very clear that you were going to be able to talk to him in a more natural fashion…Something was different in this [man's] demeanor and his willingness to engage across the table.[4]

Ambassador Ridgway noted in our discussion that the Soviet team had insisted at the second session of the bilateral talks, held the following day at the Soviet embassy, on reverting to consecutive translation. Shevardnadze did not like it, and all future meetings between Shultz and Shevardnadze used the simultaneous translation technique.

As we had expected, media interest in the CSCE meeting was intense. And there can be no doubt that, just as Shevardnadze had charmed the American delegation, he had also charmed the media. In fact the new boy on the block, from a public relations point of view, had to a considerable degree eclipsed Secretary Shultz and the U.S. delegation. Secretary Shultz, consistent with his unwavering policy (which ultimately paid off, I hasten to add) had caused considerable controversy with his formal speech at the CSCE plenary session by ticking off name by name, case after case of Soviet human rights transgressions and violations of the provisions of the Helsinki Final Act.

Finnish officials were dismayed by the confrontational tone of Secretary Shultz' speech, and I confess that I myself wondered about the wisdom of hitting the new Soviet team so hard even prior to his first meeting with Shevardnadze. Shultz came across as strident and over-focussed on human rights, and the media and his European critics accused him of missing an opportunity to give Shevardnadze (and Gorbachev) a chance to catch their breath before catching hell from the United States. At this stage of U.S./Soviet relations, it will be recalled, there was still considerable doubt among many about whether the United States was seriously interested in disarmament, and there was concern that the U.S. would use the human rights issue as an excuse for not moving forward on disarmament.

However, as Shultz' earlier speeches had made clear, he strongly rejected a diplomatic policy of "linkage"—the argument that the U.S. would not consider moving forward in one area if the Soviets were causing problems in another area. Yet he also did not believe that a single area important to U.S. and USSR relations— even disarmament—should dominate the relationship to the detriment of dealing with other important issues pending between the two countries. It was Shultz' consistent approach, which he believes contributed importantly to the ultimate success of the Reagan administration's Soviet policy, at every meeting with the Soviets to address *all* points of his four-part agenda: disarmament, human rights, regional conflicts and specific bilateral issues. While not holding one agenda item hostage to another, he strove for engagement and progress in all four areas.

In any case, I remember that at Helsinki even some veteran U.S. correspondents expressed the view that General Secretary Gorbachev and Foreign Minister Shevardnadze comprised a new Soviet foreign affairs charm team. The Soviet Union had a whole new lease on life with respect to the battle for public opinion, particularly in a Europe, where the Reagan policies were not yet appreciated. There was a clear sense that at Helsinki, Shevardnadze, the glamorous newcomer, had scored heavily with the Western media because of his charm, accessibility to the media and affability.

The CSCE Conference would not be the last we would see of George Shultz in Helsinki. He had liked the atmosphere in Helsinki. He had enjoyed the facilities and the opportunity to get together with his delegation and supporting team in a casual, unrushed atmosphere, away from the pressures of Washington. Consequently, the following November when the secretary led a U.S. delegation to Moscow to finalize preparations for the Reagan/Gorbachev Geneva summit later that month, the U.S. requested of Finland that the Shultz team be allowed to stop over in Helsinki for a day before proceeding to Moscow. The Finns were pleased to provide Secretary Shultz with the use of their new official guesthouse facilities for the November stopover. In fact this became a pattern that was repeated several times over the next few years.

President Koivisto in his memoirs observed that the Helsinki stopover visits were also very rewarding for him as well, because it gave him the opportunity to meet the leading disarmament figures who accompanied Shultz and to get frequent updates on pending policy issues. Koivisto properly gives Ambassador Ridgway with her Finnish experience considerable credit in convincing the secretary's party to stop over in Helsinki.[5]

Some on the secretary's staff for the November stopover had wanted the secretary to concentrate exclusively in Helsinki on preparing for the Moscow visit and not to meet with any Finns at all, including with President Koivisto. We in the embassy said this idea was absolutely unacceptable, and Rozanne Ridgway no doubt weighed in as well in Washington. As it was, the Shultz stopovers included no social events and usually only the one official call on President Koivisto and his key advisors. The stopover practice eventually led to President and Mrs. Reagan's May 25-28, 1988 extended stay in Finland and to President Reagan's memorable May 27 speech at Finlandia Hall.

In discussing the Reagan trip with Ambassador Ridgway during our interview, she underscored the importance of the Reagan stopover for Finland's interests. It was not only an opportunity for President Reagan to get a real feel for the country and its policies, but also it was a good experience for others who had accompanied him. She related that General Colin Powell

...had never been there. Powell did not know the details of Finland's history and the Winter War and Continuation War...We talked the whole way over the Atlantic. Yes [he was fascinated] and then he stayed on in important positions...in administration after administration. It made a big difference.[6]

I allowed as how "we haven't seen the last of Colin Powell yet." The Finnish connection indeed has continued to produce a Helsinki venue for fruitful high level meetings between senior American officials and their Soviet, later Russian, counterparts. On September 9, 1990, Presidents Bush and Gorbachev met in Helsinki at Bush's request for a seven-hour summit on the Persian Gulf crisis. And in February 1996, Secretary of State Christopher and Soviet Foreign Minister Primakov also met for talks in

Helsinki. On March 20-21, 1997, Helsinki was host to the Clinton/Yeltsin summit, which made significant progress on developing a long-term compact between NATO and Russia and on several important arms reduction measures. Most recently, Helsinki was a frequent meeting place for Russian, Finnish and American negotiators during the 1999 Kosovo crisis and war. Finnish President Martti Ahtisaari was credited with playing a key role in the negotiation to end the war.

~21~

From Nyborg to Schnabel:
The Issue of Political Ambassadors

By the time I arrived in Helsinki in March 1984, Keith Nyborg had already been the U.S. ambassador for two and one-half years—since September 18, 1981. It became a matter of some pride to Ambassador Nyborg that when he finally departed Finland in January 1986, he had been ambassador for four years and four months, longer than any other U.S. ambassador to Finland except Tyler Thompson who was ambassador for almost five years from 1964 to 1969.

As noted, Ambassador Nyborg was a political appointee who had not been drawn from the career ranks of the Foreign Service. As I understand it, he was recommended for the post by the Republican senator from Idaho. He had no prior diplomatic experience. Rather, he owned and ran a sizable ranch in Idaho, which he had named the "Finlandia" ranch.[7] Keith Nyborg was by no means without prior experience in, and knowledge of, Finland. As a young man he had served as a Mormon missionary in Finland. He had as a missionary developed a high level of fluency in the Finnish language. His language skills were such that he was used as an interpreter by the U.S. team during the 1952 Olympics. Some time after his missionary work in Finland had been completed, he had married Raija, a lovely woman from Finland.

Keith Nyborg is one of the nicest men I have ever met. He is one person I think of when I hear the term "Christian gentleman." I never heard him utter a word in anger or to act in any way that would intentionally hurt someone's feelings. He and Raija simply loved being the U.S. representatives to Finland, her homeland. I have stated above that prior country experience and language skills are rarely taken into account in the assignment of senior U.S. officials, particularly ambassadors. Nyborg was a notable exception. He knew Finland personally from his prior experiences in the country and he spoke fluent Finnish, the kind of Finnish that comes only to a person with high language aptitude who has been immersed in the language for a lengthy period. No American ambassador to Finland before or since came close to his language skills in Finnish, nor did I.

Ambassador Nyborg, however, had little knowledge of or background in international or European foreign policy and security affairs and issues. He seemed uncomfortable in dealing with such questions and was more than content to lean on his staff in handling these matters. For me as his number two, it was a marvelous opportunity to accept responsibilities that most career ambassadors would not have delegated to their deputies. Ambassador Nyborg, recognizing his own aptitudes and interests, gave his deputy chief wide latitude in organizing the work of the embassy and in carrying out policy instructions. He saw his role primarily as that of a "people-to-people" ambassador. With his fluent Finnish and his wife Raija, who of course is a native speaker, Ambassador Nyborg liked to travel around Finland, appearing before chapters of the Finnish American Society and other groups, showing the U.S. flag and expressing U.S. interest in the people of Finland. In this regard he was much like Ambassador Austad, although he did not share (and certainly did not envy) Ambassador Austad's flamboyance.

In my opinion, Ambassador Nyborg had a shrewd understanding of his strengths as an ambassador and chose deliberately to go to those strengths and to delegate responsibilities in other areas. These strengths included language skills, warm personality, a sincere interest in people, a caring attitude, and enjoyment of representing the United States. In his public speeches he would tend to stick to the light and humorous rather than to get too deeply into policy matters. As I say, this approach by

Ambassador Nyborg was good for me as his DCM because it gave me responsibilities and authority vis-à-vis my Finnish counterparts and embassy colleagues that I probably would not have had with a career ambassador.

On the other hand, I was aware that as deputy chief of mission, or even in the brief periods when I served as chargé d'affaires during Ambassador Nyborg's absence, a number two is always a number two. As such I could not deliver certain policy messages and positions as effectively nor represent the United States as authoritatively as could an ambassador experienced and knowledgeable in the substance of foreign policy. Nor could I carry as much weight in Washington in State Department and other official foreign policy circles as could such an ambassador. Unfortunately, and through no fault of Keith Nyborg—it was the president, after all, who named him as ambassador—we simply did not fully meet this requirement. Late in Ambassador Nyborg's tenure in Finland an article appeared in *Hymy* magazine which referred to me as the "real" leader of the American embassy. This caused me great embarrassment because I had always remained completely loyal to Ambassador Nyborg, but he was as always gracious and did not make an issue of the matter.

After his unusually long tenure, Ambassador Nyborg was withdrawn in favor of Rockwell A. Schnabel, who presented his credentials to President Koivisto on February 28, 1986. As had been widely reported in the press, Schnabel was included among a select group of Republican Party supporters who were said to have contributed $100,000 or more to the successful re-election campaign of President Reagan. He wanted to become an ambassador, and he was offered Finland. That's how things work. According to the information coming out of Washington in 1997, these days $100,000 would only buy you a night in the Lincoln room of the White House!

I had a marvelous relationship with "Rock" Schnabel, as smooth in fact as had been my relationship with Keith Nyborg. Often, newly named ambassadors are uncomfortable in inheriting deputy chiefs of mission who had been on the scene for some time and who had developed their own contacts and in-country reputations. To be fair, this is more often true of career ambassadors than of political appointees. Ambassadors from the career service are confident in their own knowledge and diplomatic skills and sometimes are skeptical that an inherited and well-entrenched DCM will automatically cede his or her own authority to the new boss. It was my experience that politically appointed ambassadors were normally more interested in having an experienced hand to assist them in the adjustment process than they are concerned about having a DCM that will not accept their authority.

We are trained in the Foreign Service to serve our ambassadors with complete support and loyalty no matter how they were appointed. No doubt this is not always the case, but it was certainly true of my personal experiences. In any case, my relationship with Ambassador Schnabel was based on a very concrete set of circumstances. Before his appointment was announced, I had already been offered a position in the State Department as director of the office of Northern European affairs and knew that I would be departing in the summer of 1986, only a few months after Ambassador Schnabel's assumption of the ambassadorship.

As director of Northern European affairs, I would be the senior State Department official with immediate day-to-day responsibilities for Nordic affairs including Finland. In effect, the U.S. embassy in Finland would be dependent upon me to support its positions in Washington. Thus, secure in my own future and representing no threat to Ambassador Schnabel's authority in Finland, upon his arrival I assumed the role of advisor and counselor who would assist the new and inexperienced ambassador in learning the foreign policy and diplomatic ropes. With his delightful sense of humor and unassuming but strong self-confidence, Schnabel readily accepted me as his temporary mentor and future Washington first-line contact with the State Department. We got along famously.

Ambassador Schnabel had been born in The Netherlands and had gone to the United States as a teenager. Remarkably, he spoke English without the slightest hint of a foreign accent. He had been a well-to-do investment banker in California whose wife Marna had her own very substantial family business. Lacking any direct experience in foreign and security policy matters, other than that which his European background may have contributed, Rock Schnabel nevertheless brought with him a sophisticated knowledge of international banking and financial matters. While in Finland he became to my knowledge a respected ambassador known for good judgement, particularly on commercial, financial and economic issues. As luck would have it, trade policy questions, particularly strategic trade, become important issues during his tenure, and he was able to put his experience to good use.

Notwithstanding my good relations with, and respect for, Ambassadors Nyborg and Schnabel—as well as for Mark Austad and Arthur Davis (in Paraguay) and other political ambassadors for whom I worked for during my Foreign Service career—I think it still has to be asked: Is this a wise way for the United States to choose its ambassadors? Are connections with Senators and political contributions the best criteria for selecting United States ambassadors? Not another advanced country in the world selects ambassadors in this way, at least not to the degree of the U.S. where, as noted earlier in this book, anywhere from between thirty percent to almost fifty percent of our ambassadors are comprised of political appointees. It is true that some outstanding figures from other walks of life have sometimes been named as U.S. ambassadors and have made important contributions. But if one looks back over the years at the politically appointed ambassadors to the Nordic countries, to be specific, one sees a considerable number of political ambassadors appointed by presidents from both political parties who really have lacked the background and experience to be ambassadors. At best they have had to depend on their professional staffs for support. At worst, some have been embarrassments and near-disasters.

Of course I am prejudiced, because for every political ambassador, that means there is one qualified senior career Foreign Service Officer who has been deprived of the opportunity to serve as ambassador after having proved his or her diplomatic and foreign policy skills over many years of a highly competitive career. It's great when you can be a DCM to a political ambassador because of the enhanced responsibilities and authority that situation sometimes brings. But many are the successful DCMs—and I include myself in that category—who end their diplomatic careers without having been able to apply their hard-earned career skills at the ambassadorial level.

Among other ills, the paucity of ambassadorial positions available to career Foreign Service Officers fosters an unseemly scramble among them for those few positions coming open, bringing out the worst in many of us as we maneuver for that ambassadorship. It seems to me that in addition to the personal and institutional costs, the generalized practice of appointing political ambassadors entails an indefinable cost overall to U.S. foreign policy and foreign policy making. While we should in the career service always welcome the healthy cross-fertilization that flows from having a certain number of highly qualified non-career officers, it is in my view pretty clear that the majority of political ambassadors fall short of that standard of excellence. Like the broader "spoils system" of the nineteenth century when most federal jobs were based on the patronage of the political party winning the last election, the spoils system in the appointment of ambassadors must also one day be eliminated.

Back to Washington as Director of Northern Europe

Returning to Washington from Finland was a logical and upward move from a responsible position in the field to an even more responsible—or at least a broader gauge—position in the State Department as director of the office of Northern European affairs in the bureau of European and Canadian affairs (EUR). My sizable office had first line responsibility for overseeing United States relations with ten countries of Northern Europe: the United Kingdom, Ireland, the "Benelux" countries of Belgium, the Netherlands and Luxembourg, and the five Nordic countries of Denmark, Finland, Iceland, Norway and Sweden. Today, there is no longer an office of Northern European affairs. Instead there is now an office of Nordic and Baltic affairs, a logical move reflecting the changed status of the Baltic countries and their proximity to the Nordic countries. The affairs of the Benelux countries, the United Kingdom and Ireland have been separated.

I reported to the assistant secretary of state for European affairs, Rozanne Ridgway, through one of her deputy assistant secretaries, Jim Wilkinson who also had supervisory responsibility for Southern European affairs and regional economic matters. Secretary of State Shultz had chosen Ambassador Ridgway as assistant secretary for European affairs in the summer of 1985 to replace Richard Burt who moved from that post to become ambassador to West Germany. Shultz recounts in his memoirs that Ridgway while U.S. ambassador to East Germany had come to his attention as an able and experienced career Foreign Service Officer (Burt was a political appointee). Shultz said he found Ridgway to be "creative, tough-minded and perceptive," and he personally chose her for this tough assignment. He noted:

...she was the first woman to head a regional bureau of the State Department, and her bureau...was at the center of important action. With noble features and steel-gray hair, her presence was commanding. The Soviets respected her stern diplomacy.[8]

Getting Ridgway confirmed in her new position, however, was not as easy as expected. Shultz records that President Reagan supported his choice:

...but we ran into trouble in the Senate with some of the Republican right, particularly Jesse Helms. Roz had been a presidential appointee in the Carter Administration. Would she support Ronald Reagan's policies? Could a woman handle this tough and demanding job? some Senators asked...I was advised on the political side of the White House that I should consider withdrawing the nomination. I would not, I made clear. Finally, the opposition faded away because they saw that they could not weaken my resolve. I was dug in on this appointment, and the president stuck with me. Roz was confirmed by the Senate on July 16 by a vote of 88 to 9.[9]

I had learned during 1985 that the Foreign Service Officer serving as director of the office of Northern European affairs, Marty Wenick, was due for transfer from that position in 1986. On one of Assistant Secretary Ridgway's visits to Helsinki in 1985, I expressed interest in succeeding Wenick in the Northern European affairs office, even though it would mean leaving Helsinki in 1986 rather than staying until 1987. Despite my own and my family's considerable reluctance to cut short our Helsinki assignment, I decided it was the best career move to make. I never regretted the choice, although as it turned out that the director's job did not lead to an ambassadorial assignment as I had hoped it might. In any case it was worth the gamble, and I was delighted to have the opportunity once again to work for Ambassador Ridgway.

Once again, Rozanne Ridgway with her decisive leadership and her collegial, inclusive approach to management and problem solving soon had EUR on track, more effective and influential than ever, in part because of Ridgway's close professional relationship to Secretary of State Shultz. Morale within the bureau soared, and it became a fun place to work, notwithstanding the lengthy hours and the difficult and complicated issues with which we daily battled. It was invigorating, because we knew that if we did our work well, we could make a positive contribution to U.S. policy formulation and implementation; we would be taken seriously. After all, that is why most of joined the Foreign Service in the first place.

The office of Northern European affairs had an interesting collection of countries and issues, and with Great Britain as one of our responsibilities, we were dealing with a major U.S. ally. The major challenge for our office in dealing with the U.K. was trying to stay abreast of the enormous breadth, depth and complexity of the relationship. And we were aware of the fact that Ronald Reagan and Margaret Thatcher had such a close and warm relationship that they often dealt directly with bilateral issues themselves. We had to scramble just to stay informed.

We also spent a great deal of time dealing with such highly complicated issues as international whaling which was a most difficult bone of contention between Iceland and the United States government. We were caught between heavy pressure from environmental groups to "save the whales," and Iceland's tradition of whaling which it felt no amount of international pressure should prevent it from continuing. We managed to keep the issue barely under control, but it reflects a fundamental difference in outlook, which persists to this day.

Another issue that arose from time to time was the question of U.S. naval visits to Nordic countries and the question of whether or not visiting U.S. navy ships carried nuclear weapons. Certain political groups in Norway, Denmark and Sweden demanded that no ship visits be allowed unless the United States was prepared to give assurances that the visiting ships did not carry nuclear weapons. It was fundamental and long-standing U.S. policy never to confirm nor deny whether any U.S. vessel was carrying nuclear weapons, and this led to some awkward diplomatic moments, particularly with Norway and Denmark.

A persistent issue that arose during my years as director of Northern European affairs was the question of export controls. During 1987, sensational press exposes revealed that the Japanese company Toshiba and a Norwegian company, Kongsberg, had evaded Western-agreed export controls and had jointly been responsible for shipping to the Soviet Union a highly sophisticated milling machine and related computer technology. The package of equipment and technology provided by the Japanese and Norwegian companies would permit the Soviets to produce propeller blades for their nuclear submarines which would be many times quieter than previous Soviet technology had been able to produce. This would make it much more difficult for Western anti-submarine units to detect the Soviet subs.

This problem was accentuated by expressions of outrage in the U.S. congress that companies in two allied countries were evading agreed upon policy and profiting from providing such equipment to the Soviets. It was extremely awkward for the Norwegians to be included in the wave of "Japan bashing" then, as later, popular in the United States. Through quiet, behind the scenes diplomacy, the United States and Norway were able to ride out this issue and take actions to avoid such cases in the future.

There was also a serious export control issue which emerged between the United States and Finland relating to submersibles built by the Finnish firm Rauma Repola for a Soviet "scientific research academy." Belatedly the U.S. became concerned that the submersibles would allow the Soviet Union to snoop around the ocean floor and perhaps interfere with sophisticated U.S. Navy communications equipment made famous by the novels of Tom Clancy. The State Department has not released any documents relating to this matter, but then-President of Finland Mauno Koivisto has written about it in some detail in his recent book, *Witness to History*.[10]

It was long-standing United States and NATO policy to try to prevent the transfer to the Soviet Union and its Warsaw Pact allies of highly sophisticated technology ("high tech" was the catch phrase) that could enhance their military capabilities. The policy applied not only to specific military technology—weapons systems, for example—but also to any advanced "dual use" technology, i.e., technology such as advanced computers, that might have legitimate civilian uses but which also could be used in military systems. The NATO allies had developed a coordinating mechanism "Cocom" which identified and listed technology to be denied to the Warsaw Pact countries and worked to assure that no allied country would convey to the East items included on the Cocom proscribed list. As the above reference to the Toshiba and Kongsberg scandal demonstrates, the Cocom effectiveness in preventing the shipment of proscribed technology to the East from NATO countries was imperfect at best. However, it did have the effect of greatly restricting the transfer of such technology.

The Reagan administration with, as President Koivisto noted, Richard Perle of the Department of Defense playing a key role had greatly tightened up U.S. policy in the export control area. The administration also addressed a long-standing concern of manufacturers and producers in the United States and other NATO countries. While they were expected to play by Cocom rules, producers in non-Cocom countries with advanced technologies — Sweden, Finland and Switzerland, for example—were not similarly constrained, at least not to the same degree. The U.S. therefore made an effort to bring other advanced countries into general conformity with Cocom standards. Thus, it was the objective to constrain not only NATO-originated technology but also advanced technology that may have originated in non-Cocom countries. To this end, difficult and complicated negotiations were held with several of the advanced, non-Cocom countries.

That was the context within which the Rauma Repola problem developed. The issue emerged while I was still at the embassy in Helsinki. Numerous visits back and forth between the United States and Finland were made as technicians and policy makers attempted to come to grips with the issue. The fundamental problem for Finland was, as President Koivisto points out, that the Soviets had already contracted for the submersibles and their construction had virtually been completed.

After initial efforts to solve the problem had not been successful, U.S. Ambassador Rockwell Schnabel was instructed by Washington to call on President Koivisto and deliver a strongly worded diplomatic note. Further, on May 29, 1986, Vice President Bush wrote a letter to the Finnish president urging that the Finns find a way to stop the submersibles from going to the Soviet Union. Assistant Secretary of State Ridgway visited President Koivisto in August 1986, and Koivisto describes in his book how he complained bitterly to her about the United States use of "blackmail" and "hostage taking" in the dispute. (The United States note delivered by Ambassador Schnabel stated that it was holding up approval of export licenses to Finland pending resolution of the problem).[11]

Ambassador Ridgway in my conversation with her in August 1995 remembered very clearly her meeting with President Koivisto that August day nine years earlier. She referred to Koivisto's correspondence with Vice President Bush, saying:

> Well, as you know, we used that correspondence at the time when the Defense Department wanted to cut Finland off from the whole of Western society because of the Rauma Repola submersible issue. I went that summer and saw him in Nantali. He told me that he had the impression that the United States was drawing a new border for the East-West conflict down the middle of the Gulf of Bothnia, and Finland was going to be on the wrong side. And he wrote a letter to Bush about this.

In his letter to Bush, quoted in his book, President Koivisto assured Bush that Finland had no intention to cause problems for world security. But he declared, Finland had to take care of its own security and preserve its position as a neutral country which is trustworthy and lives up to its commitments. He pointed out that Rauma Repola is a private company, which the Government of Finland could not interfere with, and even if it could, the government would want to act according to good trade practices and contractual obligations. In his strongly worded letter, President Koivisto defended the Rauma Repola contract and complained that the United States position can be seen as nothing less than a change in policy and a return to the past when neutrality was not considered as acceptable. The letter concluded that as long as Finland was not required to sacrifice its principles, it was prepared to continue to discuss the matter with the United States and noted that negotiations were underway with Rauma Repola.[12]

Finnish Foreign Ministry State Secretary Åke Wihtol led negotiations for the Finnish side. By that time I was in my new position in the State Department. U.S. negotiations were overseen by the then counselor of the department, Ed Derwinski. On the U.S. side an inter-agency task force was formed consisting of several government departments and agencies. I chaired numerous working level meetings of the inter-agency group as we sought to come up with approaches for use by Counselor Derwinski. Negotiations with Finland lasted for almost a year, including frequent trips to Washington by Ambassador Wihtol until an agreement was reached in the summer of 1987. The embassy of Finland under Ambassador Paavo Rantanen also played a key role in the successful negotiations.

Under the agreement, the submersibles were ultimately allowed to go forward to the Soviet Union in return for Finnish commitments and follow-up mechanisms which assured that henceforth Finland would adhere to Cocom standards and controls even for its own technology. At the same time, Finland would receive the same export rights as Cocom countries.[13]

Fortunately, not all of our relations with Finland were as problematical as the export control issue. I was pleased to have a most pleasant and productive relationship with the highly professional leadership of the Finnish embassy in Washington under Ambassador Rantanen and his "DCM," Minister Jaakko Laajava. The Government of Finland had the good sense to send the Washington-savvy Laajava back to the United States as ambassador in 1996. I always thought U.S. policy would have benefited from sending a former U.S. DCM to Finland back to Helsinki as U.S. ambassador. I even had one in mind! But, alas, that's not the way it's done in the U.S. system.

One of our most pleasant collaborative duties with the embassy of Finland in Washington was to help celebrate in 1988 the "National Year of Friendship with Finland" in commemoration of the 350th anniversary of the first Finnish migration to the New World. Prime Minister Harri Holkeri came to Washington on an official visit to help commemorate the occasion. It was good to see an old friend and valued discussion partner reach the high position of Finnish prime minister.

The year 1988 also marked the 350th anniversary of the first Swedish colony in the New World and, of course, Finnish settlers had been a part that same colony. This led to some interesting jockeying for position between the embassies of Finland and Sweden as to how to assure that proper attention was given to their own celebrations of this joint event!

Perhaps the major issue I dealt with during my period as director of Northern European affairs was dealing with the consequences of General Secretary Gorbachev's October 1, 1987 speech delivered at Murmansk and thereafter referred to as his Murmansk Initiative. Gorbachev's speech was a sweeping policy move that sought to put NATO and the United States on the defensive in the High North. He wrapped together a series of security and non-security policy initiatives in an attractive package which he sought to sell to his northern neighbors in a "just us Nordics" approach. He tried to contrast a supposed "commonality of interest" between the Soviet Union and the Nordics with aggressive NATO aims or, as Gorbachev put it, "the chilling breath of the Pentagon's polar strategy."

Gorbachev's initiative attracted serious attention in the State Department. As director of the office of Northern European affairs, I took the initiative in analyzing the implications of the speech and in proposing policy responses, working closely with other interested State Department offices and with other concerned agencies of the U.S. Government. All in all, the manner in which the State Department—through a process of inter-agency meetings, memoranda, exchanges of telegrams between Washington and the field and timely decisions—prepared U.S. foreign policy positions in response to the Murmansk proposal constituted in my opinion a rational and considered approach to foreign policy formulation. I was proud to play a significant role in that effort and to be commended along with other colleagues by Assistant Secretary Ridgway for my efforts.

~23~

Final Assignments,
the Making and Unmaking of an
Ambassador, and a Decision to Retire

My assignment as director of the office of Northern European affairs was for two years. Entering the second year in the summer of 1987, I began to investigate what career options for onward assignments might be available. One option would have been to stay in the Northern European job, which I enjoyed. However, a number of factors argued against doing that. First of all, I had reached an age (fifty-two) at which it was becoming clear that if I didn't make a decisive move soon, my chances of ultimately becoming an ambassador would slip away.

A second factor was that the costs of living in Washington were not permitting us to cover comfortably the expenses of our son Lane at American University and at the same time to prepare for the upcoming expenditures of Carl and Vanessa who would soon be reaching college age. We needed an overseas assignment. However, I had already decided that I would not go out again as deputy chief of mission. In my view I had proved I was chief of mission material, and I was not interested in acting again as a helpmate to another political ambassador.

It was quite clear that there were no realistic opportunities for my winning an assignment as ambassador in Europe in the foreseeable future. Few positions were coming open, most of which would go to political appointees, and any remaining posts would go to career officers senior to or more influential than myself. I was seriously considering leaving the Foreign Service to earn a separate income while drawing my Foreign Service annuity. I had been discussing with a private foundation the possibility of becoming an executive director of an exchange program that foundation managed. It looked promising, but I could not quite bring myself to decide to end my Foreign Service career at that stage. It would have also meant a move to New York City, which would have offset part of the financial gain.

Just as my discussions with the foundation were reaching a decisive stage, I was offered the position as chief of mission of the United States embassy in Grenada, effective the summer of 1988. The embassy since its establishment in 1983 had been headed by a senior Foreign Service Officer with the title of chargé d'affaires rather than ambassador. The basic reason for that fact was because the U.S. embassy in Grenada had been established as a response to a specific event—to deal with the consequences of the United States intervention in Grenada—and was not expected to be a permanent U.S. diplomatic post in the Caribbean.

I decided to accept that position. It would relieve the financial pressure. We could rent out our Bethesda home for enough to cover the mortgage payments and would be provided an official residence in Grenada. While the position in Grenada was not an ambassadorship, it did mean becoming chief of mission and my own boss. Also, the embassy in Grenada at the time was larger than a good number of U.S. embassies in small countries around the world. Moreover, it was engaged in very meaningful and constructive work: assisting Grenada in consolidating its democracy and rebuilding its economy and infrastructure after the 1979-83 Marxist-Leninist interlude that was ended by the 1983 United States intervention. So it was that I ended up as head of the American embassy in Grenada from 1988 to 1991. It was an unusual but quite delightful and productive assignment.

The Grenadians are a lovely people who—contrary to leftist mythology—had been dismayed with the Marxist experiment foisted upon them in 1979 by a *coup d'état.* A handful of young ideologues after seizing power had promptly allied their Peoples

Revolutionary Government (PRG) with Cuba and the Soviet Union. The PRG also installed one-party rule, closed down opposition newspapers and jailed its political opponents. The revolution collapsed upon itself in 1983, and the radical wing of the ruling New Jewel Movement (NJM) executed the more moderate but still committed Marxist prime minister, Maurice Bishop. More than ninety percent of the Grenadians welcomed the intervention of the joint United States-Caribbean military and police force that followed.

The intervention had been specifically requested by the Organization of Eastern Caribbean States, Grenada's neighbors, some of whom participated in the intervention force. Documents of the PRG and of the political bureau and central committee of the NJM captured by U.S. forces reveal the full extent of the PRG's involvement with the Soviet Union and Cuba and its ambition to carry the revolution to the other islands of the English-speaking Caribbean. The documents also reveal the cynical maneuvering of the PRG to pass itself off to the Socialist International as a Social Democratic movement, notwithstanding the PRG and their Cuban mentors' contempt for social democracy.[14]

The subject of Grenada is a complex and fascinating one, but to do it justice would require much more space than is appropriate for this book. Nevertheless, we should not leave the subject of Grenada without referring to the interesting dimension involving Finland, namely the vote in the United Nations General Assembly to condemn the U.S. intervention in Grenada. On November 2, 1983 the General Assembly voted on a resolution that "deeply deplores the military intervention, and calls for an immediate end to armed intervention and the withdrawal of foreign troops." The resolution was approved overwhelmingly by a vote of 108 in favor, 27 abstentions and 9 against.[15]

Finland voted in favor of the resolution. She was in good company. Many of the United States' closest allies, including the United Kingdom, also voted in favor of the resolution condemning the U.S. action. Nevertheless, Finland's vote received some criticism as constituting another deviation from the stated Finnish policy of not taking a stand on an issue at controversy between the superpowers. President Koivisto in his book *Kaksi Kautta* had little sympathy for critics of the Finnish vote:

In [UN] voting there are limited options, but it is possible to provide an explanation of vote in which one's true position could be put forward. Those people who have raised questions and otherwise indicated their dissatisfaction that [Finnish] officials had not wanted to give a special explanation to their vote now would want the Finnish side to start analyzing more thoroughly the exact degree of the two superpowers' depredations and to make comparisons. To what point now has the effort to stay clear of disputes between the superpowers led us?[16]

Nevertheless, Finland's 1983 vote on Grenada did in fact stand in sharp contrast to her vote in 1979 on another U.N. General Assembly resolution. Then Finland was among a handful of countries which did not vote in favor of a similar resolution condemning the Soviet invasion of Afghanistan (Finland abstained in that vote). It can be argued that military intervention for any purpose is always wrong and should always be condemned. But it can also be argued that there are qualitative differences between interventions. In the two cases in point, the qualitative differences could hardly have been more dramatic as to intentions and results.

The Soviet intervention was to impose a Marxist-Leninist government on the people of Afghanistan by force of Soviet arms, and it required the active engagement of a huge Soviet military war machine to maintain that government in office over the next several years. The United States intervention was to throw out an anti-democratic, one-party Marxist government that had come to power through a *coup* four years earlier and had now fallen into internal fratricide. Obviously, the opportunity to rid the Eastern Caribbean of a Soviet and Cuban outpost was not an inconsequential consideration for the Reagan Administration. Nevertheless, the effect of the intervention was to restore to the people of Grenada the right to choose their own government through democratic processes, which is exactly what happened in parliamentary elections in 1984, 1990 and 1995.

Finland's votes on these two issues, whatever the motivations, demonstrated the difficulty Finland had in implementing even-handedly its stated policy of staying out of issues at conflict between the two superpowers. It also underscored that when variations from this policy were considered convenient, they almost invariably revealed a Finnish willingness, as on various arms control questions, to take one attitude regarding Soviet positions and actions and a different and more critical attitude on U.S. positions and actions.

In September, 1990, while still chargé d'affaires of the U.S. embassy in Grenada, I was called to New York during the 45th General Assembly of the United Nations to serve as the U.S. delegation's senior advisor for Latin America for three months. During this temporary assignment I had the opportunity to lunch privately with the future president of Finland, Martti Ahtisaari, then a United Nations under secretary, whom we had known in Finland. I also met with Finnish Ambassadors Klaus Törnudd and Marjatta Rasi who were representing Finland at the United Nations.

In January 1991 I was reassigned from Grenada back to Washington D.C. to head up a Bush administration initiative to form an international support group for Central America. The initiative was called the Partnership for Democracy and Development in Central America (PDD), and I was designated the United States Special Coordinator for the undertaking. I officially reported to Deputy Secretary of State Lawrence Eagleburger, although in actual practice I coordinated the program directly with the assistant secretary of state for inter-American affairs, Bernard Aronson, and with Eagleburger's principal assistant, Kenneth Juster.

The essence of the program was to create an international support group bringing together the Europeans, Japanese, Canadians and the United States in a cooperative effort with the Central Americans to promote the consolidation of democracy and economic development in Central America. The idea was to seize the moment afforded by the end of dictatorship and civil war in Central America. For the first time in history, there were democratically elected presidents in all six of the Spanish-speaking Central American countries, in addition to the elected prime minister of the English-speaking country of Belize. The six presidents had established the joint goal of strengthening democracy and establishing a Central American common market.

This promising situation provided a solid regional basis for rallying PDD support for the achievement of agreed objectives in cooperation with the Central Americans.[17]

The idea was the creature of then Secretary of State James Baker and his immediate coterie of advisors. It was a good idea, and we made considerable progress in the years 1991-93. An inaugural meeting of some thirty countries was held in Costa Rica in April 1991. Follow-up plenary meetings of representatives of the same countries and of international agencies such as the World Bank and the United Nations were held in Ottawa, El Salvador and Tokyo in 1992 and 1993. Working groups were formed, together with the Central Americans, to develop specific ideas and projects in priority development areas identified in the PDD process. Programs were developed in the areas of administration of justice, a regional de-mining program and trade and customs reform. The U.S. helped fund and organize a regional trade and investment conference in Honduras in the spring of 1993.

However, the program began to founder over lack of political and economic support. As the United States foreign affairs budget tightened, it gradually became clear that not only would no additional U.S. resources be available for Central America, but that existing U.S. assistance levels dropped precipitously. The Europeans and Japanese from the beginning were suspicious that the United States' real agenda was to get them to commit assistance resources to Central America to compensate for an American resource draw down. I don't believe that was the initial U.S. intention, but as the developments demonstrated, U.S. economic assistance to the region did in fact begin to fall. There was also "donor fatigue" on the part of the other developed countries, which were unable to commit new resources to the Central American region. As the United States presidential elections approached, the Baker State Department all but lost interest in the PDD project.

I had proposed in a memorandum for the new U.S. administration that would be elected in November 1992—either a second Bush administration or a Clinton administration—that it build the PDD approach into an overarching regional Central

American strategy to energize U.S. policy in the region. It is not clear whether a second Bush administration would have supported the initiative. However, it became immediately apparent upon the election of President Clinton that his administration had no interest in using a program identified with the outgoing Bush administration as a center piece for its own policies. The new administration let PDD die a natural death by simply ignoring the initiative. It was clear from the outset that the PDD would last only as long as the United States provided leadership and support.

In the meantime, the Bush administration had decided to make me an ambassador. On October 7, 1992, I received a letter from the Director General of the Foreign Service extending congratulations to me on my "...selection as the next United States ambassador to Belize." I had been chosen by the Department of State and approved by President Bush, subject of course to completing necessary clearances (which I did) and to Senate confirmation. With my Spanish and Finnish language skills and long experience in Latin America and Northern Europe, Belize would not have been my first choice for an ambassadorship. However, I was pleased with my selection because it constituted recognition of my career of service and demonstrated my government's confidence in my ability to represent the United States of America as ambassador.

It was therefore a major disappointment to me when the Clinton administration, upon assuming office in January 1993, did not choose to reaffirm my assignment, preferring instead to send a political appointee as ambassador to Belize. I decided to give the process one more chance and accepted an assignment as director of the State Department office of Andean affairs. When in the next year's appointment cycle I was not chosen as ambassador, I decided to submit my resignation (actually early retirement) which became official in May 1994, following a three month temporary assignment as U.S. consul general in Guayaquil, Ecuador.

I was of course quite unhappy about the final outcome of my career and expressed my displeasure in the professional journal of the American Foreign Service Association.[18] However, I believed then, and continue to believe now, that the Foreign Service was a marvelous profession. Although I was not awarded an ambassadorship, I take great pride in my long Foreign Service career and am convinced that in South America, Finland, Central America and Grenada, I helped make a difference. Sometimes a rather important difference.

Part Three Notes

[1] George P. Shultz, *Turmoil and Triumph* (New York: Charles Scribner's Sons, 1993): 573.

[2] Mauno Koivisto, *Historian Tekijat* (Helsinki: Kirjayhtyma Oy, 1995): 170.

[3] Shultz, pp. 573-74.

[4] Cooper/Ridgway Interview Transcript, August 10, 1995.

[5] Mauno Koivisto, *Witness to History, The Memoirs of Mauno Koivisto, President of Finland 1982-1994* (London: Hurst & Company, 1997): 75. This is the English language edition of *Historian Tekijat*. In some respects the Finnish edition is more complete than the English version, and where significant I will cite the more complete version.

[6] Cooper/Ridgway interview.

[7] In the Finnish edition of this book I mistakenly misidentified Ambassador Nyborg's state of residence as Utah.

[8] Shultz, p. 689.

[9] Ibid., 572.

[10] Koivisto, *Witness to History*, pp. 85-89.

[11] Ibid., p. 86.

[12] Ibid., p. 88

[13] Ibid., pp. 88-89.

[14] U.S. Department of State, Department of Defense, *Grenada Documents: An Overview and Selection*. Washington D.C., 1984.

[15] Adkin, Major Mark, *Urgent Fury—The Battle for Grenada* (Lexington Books, MA, 1989): 319.

[16] Koivisto, Mauno, *Kaksi Kautta* (Helsinki: Kirjäyhtymä Oy, 1994): 118.

[17] See James Ford Cooper, "La Asociacion en pro de la Democracia y el Desarrollo en Centroamerica," in *La Reconstruccion de Centroamerica: el Papel de la Comunidad Europea*, Joaquin Roy, ed. (North-South Center, Miami, 1992): 403-06 for further background on the context and purpose of the PDD.

[18] James Ford Cooper, "Speaking Out," *Foreign Service Journal* (February 1994): 16-20.

PART FOUR

RETROSPECTIVE VIEWS AND ASSESSMENTS OF THE KEKKONEN AND KOIVISTO LEGACIES AND THEIR DIFFERENCES

Back to Helsinki: Re-examining Old Shibboleths with Old Friends

Upon retiring from the Foreign Service on May 4, 1994, Magda and I got into our car the very same day and headed for our new home-to-be, Punta Gorda, Florida. We had discovered this charming little town on the southwest coast of Florida some years earlier and had bought a lot in the residential area of Punta Gorda Isles where every house and lot is on a salt water canal with access to Charlotte Harbor and the Gulf of Mexico. We bought a boat and built a home on our lot into which we moved in January 1995.

Meanwhile, I picked up on a project that I had long been planning: writing a book-this book-about Finland. As already noted, in addition to drawing on diplomatic reporting of the United States embassy in Helsinki and on other U.S. government documents, I planned a research visit to Finland to interview Finns who had been my professional contacts during the 1970s and 1980s.

My objective in interviewing my former Finnish contacts was to get their views in 1995 on many of the events and issues that we had all worried and thought about during the Cold War years. I saw it as an opportunity for a thoughtful, retrospective look back on these matters from the perspective of time. Before travelling to Finland in May 1995, I compiled a list of Finns with whom I had dealt on a professional basis during my assignments to Finland. With the kind assistance of old friend Per-Erik Lönnfors, I was able to get the addresses of many of my former contacts and to mail them a memorandum suggesting interview topics for discussion.

Magda and I arrived in Helsinki in mid-May for a six-week stay. For the first three weeks we enjoyed the generous hospitality of our good friends, Ambassador Tapani Brotherus and his wife Lysa, who welcomed us into their home. After the Brotherus had to make preparations to close their home in connection with Tapani's assignment as ambassador of Finland to South Africa, we made arrangements with the assistance of university contacts of Pearl Lönnfors to rent quarters in the home of Pekka Heikkinen on Elontie in north Helsinki. Pekka proved to be a pleasant "landlord" as well as good company.

After arriving in Helsinki, I got in touch with additional former Finnish contacts and sent most of them copies of the memorandum of topics for discussion. The discussion paper identified a number of issues and questions that were relevant to my book's focus.

Specifically, I indicated an interest in discussing the following topics: Finland's position-taking on international and European security issues that seemed often to parallel Soviet stances and to be at odds with NATO/US positions; the effect of these positions on Western attitudes toward Finland; the degree to which President Kekkonen may have acquiesced in Soviet interference in Finnish internal affairs; the playing of the "Moscow card" in internal Finnish politics; President Kekkonen's handling of the Night Frost and Note Crisis episodes in the light of recent research finds in Soviet archives; whether the presidential power built up by Kekkonen had dangerously weakened the constitutional power of the other key political institutions of Finland; whether an atmosphere developed in Finland during the Cold War that encouraged a kind of competition among some Finnish politicians to gain favor with the Soviet leadership; the issue as to the degree of self-censorship in the media and academia; whether President Koivisto consciously followed a policy of playing down presidential power and restoring better balance to the constitutional system; and, finally, the relationship that Finland should currently be seeking *vis-à-vis* East and West.

The only criterion for my meetings that I tried not to deviate from—there were two exceptions—was that whomever I interviewed I must have known personally from one of my assignments in Helsinki. The exceptions were the U.S.ambassador to Finland in 1995, Derek N. Shearer, whom I had not met before the interview, and General Ensio Silasvuo, whom I knew only by reputation. All of my discussion partners are identified in the appendix to this book along with some descriptive comments. I was gratified by the courtesy and openness with which my requests for appointments were greeted. In the end, I was limited only by the constraints of time in my few weeks in Finland.

I recorded all of the interviews on my cassette tape recorder that (with the valuable assistance of Magda on some tapes) I laboriously transcribed when I returned to the United States. Two of the dialogues held wholly, or in part, in the Finnish language (with Aarne Saarinen and Juhani Suomi) were transcribed by a good friend in Florida, John Seton, a Finn who has lived many years in the United States and who is president of the Friends of Finland association in Sarasota, Florida. I am most grateful to him for the many hours he put into transcribing the Suomi and Saarinen tapes.

When each transcript was finished, I mailed it to my discussion partner asking that he or she review it and make any changes desired, even if the transcript was accurate but perhaps expressed something that the person wished had not been said. In each case I have fully honored the editing wishes of the persons interviewed, and several did in fact request extensive changes which I duly made. A handful of persons did not get back to me with their suggestions or comments. Inasmuch as I had received explicit approval from each interviewee before turning on my tape recorder, I considered my offer to edit the transcript as desired by the interviewee a courtesy, which I was pleased to extend. Therefore, in those cases where I received no responses to the transcripts sent for review, I have felt free to draw on any part of the interviews as recorded. I have retained all of the cassette tapes, should any questions arise.

Unfortunately, because of space limitations, I have been able here to draw on only a fraction of the lengthy discussions and have had to leave out some interviews completely, as interesting as they all were. The raw transcripts of the thirty-five interviews fill more than eight hundred double-spaced manuscript pages. They present individually and collectively a fascinating look into an extra-ordinarily wide range of often controversial issues important in Finland from the Winter War, through the Cold War period, and to current issues and the outlook for the future. Inasmuch as the views presented come from Finns who either participated in, or were observers of, one or more aspects of the events being commented upon, their retrospective judgements are significant in placing those events into perspective. The collection in my opinion constitutes a valuable "living oral history" of a vital period of the Finnish experience, and it is my hope after finishing this book to organize the transcripts for publication in a separate volume. In any case I have donated all of the transcripts, together with all U.S.G. documents cited in this book, to the University of Helsinki Library so that they will be available to other researchers.

In this book, however, I will be using only those interview observations most directly relevant to the main themes of this book. That means that a number of interesting topics, including discussions of issues current in the 1990s, are omitted as being outside of the scope of this book. I have made a conscious effort to represent contrasting views in order to assure as much objective balance as possible. In the selection and editing process I have made every effort to be fair and objective in citing individual remarks. I will regret it if any of those interviewed feel that I have not placed their individual comments into proper context. However, it would be only in a much more complete rendition of the interviews that full justice could be done in reflecting all of the nuances of the points of views put forward by my articulate and interesting interlocutors. I apologize to those whom I interviewed who are not cited in this book because of space considerations.

I have organized the relevant observations put forward by my discussion partners as well as my own assessments around two broad themes. These are presented below as Chapter 25 ("The Kekkonen Legacy: How Much was Really Necessary and How Much was Self-Serving?") and Chapter 26 ("The Koivisto Legacy: How Much Continuity and How Much Change?"). I have also cited where useful for additional background information a few of the recent publications on the Kekkonen or Koivisto years.

~25~

The Kekkonen Legacy: How Much Was Really Necessary and How Much Was Self-Serving?

In the very first taped conversation of my 1995 trip to Finland, General Ensio Silasvuo phrased—rather wryly and directly—one of the questions that I wanted to hear about from Finns. I was discussing with Silasvuo the evolution of the Paasikivi-Kekkonen line. I told the general my perception of the basic unofficial understanding with the Soviets after the wars which seemed to underpin the new relationship, namely that Finland would accept that the Soviet Union had legitimate security concerns about what happened in the area of Finland, and that in the other direction the Soviet Union should leave Finland alone internally to manage its own affairs without Soviet interference. General Silasvuo commented to me that:

> Unfortunately, the Soviets maybe did leave us alone in many cases, but there were many Finns who tried to use the Moscow card, that was Finland's problem.

I noted that use of "the Moscow card" was one of the themes I was looking at, and asked the general whether he felt it had become a big problem. He replied: "I must say that I hated this. My question is, was it really necessary to kiss their asses so much! I would like to make that question also to Kekkonen."[2] Former minister and former president of the Conservative Party, now Finnish ambassador to the United Kingdom, Pertti Salolainen, in our discussion phrased the question in very much the same way, although without the colorful metaphor. He asked rhetorically, and proceeded to answer his own question:

Well, I think that the basic question that we have to answer is, what was really necessary and what was not? I mean during the Kekkonen period. This is the core of the question...What was used only for internal power use? I think that the worst part of the Kekkonen era was that foreign policy was used for internal purposes.

This way of posing the question really does seem get to the core of the matter. The widely varying comments of the people I interviewed demonstrate that this is a highly subjective, controversial and emotional issue. I have organized various observations I received and my own assessments regarding the Kekkonen presidency under two general categories that, in fact, parallelled my 1979 assessment of the same issue: (1) The "Foreign Dimension," encompassing Finland's management of its relations with the Soviet Union, including position-taking on international and European security and foreign policy issues, acquiescence in Soviet interference in Finnish domestic affairs, and playing of the "Moscow card" against political opponents; and (2) The "Domestic Dimension," referring to the impact of Kekkonen's long period in office, the growth of presidential power at the expense of other constitutional players, and self-censorship.

Obviously, the line between these two "dimensions" is a fuzzy one; indeed, one of the central issues during the Kekkonen period is the degree to which foreign policy was used as a weapon in domestic Finnish politics. However, for analytical and organizational reasons it is useful to address them generally in separate categories, while conceding that they were in fact mutually overlapping and re-enforcing.

KEKKONEN: THE FOREIGN DIMENSION

Finnish Foreign and Security Policy Position-Taking

One aspect in Finland's management of relations with the Soviet Union was taking care to assure that Finland's positions on international security and foreign policy issues did not unnecessarily complicate relations with the Soviet Union. In my interviews I usually asked my discussion partners about this question, pointing out—drawing from my discussion paper list—that Finnish positions on security and foreign policy issues often seemed to be at odds with U.S. and NATO positions.

I asked whether such Finnish positions impacted negatively on U.S. and NATO positions or policies. Few interlocutors agreed that this was the case. A number of persons interviewed made the point rather effectively that Finnish positions had little impact on Western policy positions. Ambassador Max Jakobson felt that the effect of Finland's position-taking on Western policy positions:

...was not terribly important. They were the kind of positions you take on large international issues which are verbal in character and which never really affected the issue itself. They were of course meant to signal something about Finnish attitudes to this or that matter, but they didn't really affect any substantive issues between East and West. On some of the really basic problems I don't think we made any concessions that would have had a substantive effect. Let us say the German issue...It would have been different if we had actually recognized East Germany at an early stage. We did not do that kind of thing. We did take positions on some of the issues you have indicated, intermediate range missiles, first nuclear use, Afghanistan, Grenada...I don't say that all of these were right, I think some of them were unnecessary concessions...For instance, I thought it was a mistake to vote as we did on Grenada because I felt that the consistency of our policy would have required an abstention...But these are details. And they didn't really change anything.

Ambassador James Goodby commented on my concerns about Finland's position taking on international political and European security issues by saying:

I spent a long time in NATO and arms control before I ever got to Finland, and my basic attitude was that if they wanted to promote the Nordic nuclear weapon free zone (NWFZ), let them do it. It didn't make any real difference. What was much more important was that they develop a strong domestic economy....So far as the rest that was going on, I had bitter differences with Kekkonen over Afghanistan. After all, a small country on the border of the Soviet Union ought to be worried about what happened to another small country on the border of the Soviet Union! But he was completely indifferent to it. So I never did like that. But the rest of it did not cause any real problems for us.

It is also important, as pointed out by Ambassador Rozanne Ridgway among others, to keep in mind the context of the times in which the positions were taken. Ridgway noted:

The European left at the time was professionally anti-American, professionally anti-NATO, so it gets hard to distinguish how much of this was self-imposition by Finland of an unnecessarily leftist view in order to suck up to the Russians in areas they thought didn't matter, and how much of it was genuine and sharing the views of the European left...So it's a muddle. It's hard to pull out of it how much was Finnish/Soviet, how much was Finnish/Nordicism, and how much was Socialist International thinking, and so on.

However, she continued:

The only issue on which I'm really unforgiving was Afghanistan. Because from any analysis, Finnish national interest was not served by having that definition of the right of the larger border state to intervene in that fashion. Finnish membership as a respected member of the European left did not require that point of view, Finnish leadership in the United Nations international community, the rule of law, all of that, was not served by that position. There was nothing that was served by that. Maybe it became the culmination of all of these rather careless roads that people pointed to, but that one made no sense. And that coincided with my own opportunity to speak out at the February 1980 Paasikivi Society on what it meant to be a credible neutral. On the other positions on the international side, I think they were in fairly good company, whether that was their intent or not. I always felt reluctant to go in—other than on Afghanistan, where Finnish interests were not served—and pound the table. Because if the Finns got their analysis wrong, we were not going to be there to back them up.

I am prepared to concede the specific point made by these observers. It seems clear that Finland's positions regarding security and foreign policy issues, while troubling in some respects, did not importantly have an adverse effect on U.S. and NATO positions. This is primarily because Finnish positions were discounted as reflecting understandable Finnish sensitivity to Soviet Union concerns as well as its perspective as a Nordic country. Moreover, as I have observed in this book, a number of Finland's foreign policy decisions were defensible in their own right—such as on the Nordic NWFZ and cruise missile issues—and were well understood by the embassy and the State Department who recognized Finland's clear special interest and motivations. And Finland's position, for example, on the CSCE process—once it was understood in the West—came to be considered as a positive and constructive contribution to East/West relations.

It was also true, as Ridgway pointed out, that if the Finns got their foreign policy calculations wrong and ran into trouble with the Soviet Union, we would not be there to back them up. We told them as much in the 1940s and 1950s. At least this is true in a security sense. It should be noted, however, that both in the 1958 Night Frost Crisis and 1961-62 Note Crisis the United States advised the Finns we were prepared to provide economic support, if requested, to help offset Soviet economic pressure. Nevertheless, given that Finland did not fit under the Western security umbrella, Western diplomats in general shared Ridgway's diffidence about giving advice to Finland on security and foreign policy issues except in rare and extreme cases.

The foregoing observations notwithstanding, however, I continue to contend that Finnish positions on foreign and security policy issues which were frequently inconsistent with U.S. and NATO policy *did* cumulatively entail a cost to Finland. The cost was the degree to which the general pattern of Finnish positions contributed to the impression in the West that Finland was bending to pressures from the Soviet Union. Taken together with other perceived incidences of Soviet influence over Finland, these policy positions undercut in some measure the credibility of Finnish neutrality and contributed to the development of the Finlandization epithet. A good number of my Finnish interlocutors cited in this book share that opinion.

Ambassador Jakobson agreed that it was:

...bad from our point of view, [had a] bad impact on public opinion in Western countries, and led to the Finlandization question...In that sense it had some importance...And as I said, in some cases unnecessary as well. I would have thought that we could have avoided some of these positions, precisely for the reason that you mentioned. But of course there was always the argument, what does it matter, the damage was very intangible and difficult to assess what the damage really meant in terms of Finnish interests...

I pursued that point in a discussion with Simopekka Nortamo, long-time former editor-in-chief of the *Helsingin Sanomat*. Perhaps, I commented, the Finns didn't see any costs in the West in taking these positions, but they did have some effect on Finland's reputation and perhaps contributed to the Finlandization epithet. He observed:

> Exactly, and that was a very high price. And that was my special theme through all those years, that we have harmed our reputation. And it will take a long time to get it back. Last year [1994] when I wrote about joining the European Union, I said that this is just the step that will help us get back our reputation, but even this way will take a long time.

However, Per-Erik Lönnfors, until recently editor-in-chief and general manager of the Finnish News Service (STT), had a more relaxed view of the effect on Finland of its Cold War positions on international issues. He told me:

> I think they clearly reflected Finland's position as a neighbor to the Soviet Union. I think that the decisions and statements could have been made differently, but only marginally so. What I mean is that I don't think Finland lost very much if it took positions that took the Soviet interest too much into account. We lost some reputation, even some honor in some people's eyes, but Finland didn't lose on the interests side.

With respect to the question of whether Finland went too far in accommodating Soviet views in taking its positions, Lönnfors added that one needs to put this question into its historical perspective:

> I think one has to think of the fact that there had been two wars against the Soviet Union with the whole propaganda apparatus bringing up all the wars in the history between Finland and Russia and the animosity and all the negative aspects in the relationship between these two people, and soldiers killing each other. What Paasikivi and Kekkonen had to do was to turn around public opinion in Finland 180 degrees. In order to do that you have to conduct your own propaganda, and that from the outside can be seen as an exaggeration...

It was of course true that Finland had good reason for being especially sensitive to Soviet interests in taking their own foreign policy positions. However, it is also true that Finnish officials during the period under discussion would sometimes express surprise or disappointment if some of their actions seemed to be met with disapproval or unhappiness by their Western friends. As indicated in one U.S. embassy report cited above, perhaps the

Finns expected too much understanding from the Western countries. One can appreciate that the risk of this intangible and indirect cost in the West at decisive moments may have seemed remote and of little consequence when weighed against the more immediate and very obvious cost of the risk of incurring the unhappiness of the Soviet Union.

The "how much was really necessary" question runs as a *leit motiv* throughout this book. This trade-off was one of the perennial features of the "Finnish Dilemma" during the Cold War. But was it necessary in order to maintain an acceptable relationship with the Soviet Union to take so often positions that damaged Finland's reputation in the West? Finns disagree. On the one hand, as Per-Erik Lönnfors pointed out, Finland didn't lose much, perhaps only "some reputation, even some honor in some people's eyes, but Finland didn't lose on the interests side..." But as Jakobson indicated, once you started down that road, "where do you draw the line?"

There is no conclusive answer to this question. I can only say that it often wasn't clear to us in the embassy that these Finnish positions were always necessary. Most of us believed that Finland by the 1970s had more room for maneuver on international and European security and foreign policy issues than Finland took advantage of. And the failure to do so had the kinds of negative implications mentioned. At least, that is my assessment.

As will be discussed further when we evaluate aspects of the Koivisto presidency, it is also one of my contentions that the Kekkonen period was not exceptional in the area of Finland's position-taking on international security and foreign policy issues. In fact this cautious policy approach prevailed throughout the post-war and Cold War period under Mannerheim, Paasikivi, Kekkonen and Koivisto. It was a striking reflection of the fundamental change in Finland's foreign and security policy outlook resulting from the hard lessons learned from World War II. But it was not a cost-free policy. If in my view there was substantial continuity among Finland's Cold War years presidents on foreign policy positions, a separate question is whether there was a difference between Kekkonen and his predecessor (as well as his successor) in the way they dealt with the issues of Soviet intervention in Finnish affairs and the playing of the Soviet or Moscow card.

Here once again, as was to be expected, there were widely differing opinions among those interviewed about where truth lies. Honorable and honest people may hold contrasting views. The myriad views put forward by my interlocutors describing the same events reminded me of the English author Lawrence Durell's sequence of novels in the 1950s, referred to collectively as *The Alexandria Quartette*. In those novels various characters described the same events from their own perspectives, offering sometimes dramatically differing accounts. Looking at recent Finnish history and listening to its observers is much like that: truth takes on an elusive, changeable quality when viewed through the prisms of the various beholders. As most of my discussion partners readily conceded, these matters were highly complex with multiple motivations introducing a myriad of factors. It ultimately becomes a question of individual judgement.

At the heart of the matter—the nexus of all of the various strands of the phenomenon—was President Urho Kekkonen. The pivotal events, which clearly constituted the turning point in the development of the phenomena associated with the term Finlandization, were the Night Frost and Note Crisis events of 1958-59 and 1961-62. Dynamics were unleashed in those two crises that determined the development of the political culture that dominated Finnish politics and national life until the end of the Kekkonen period.

Retrospective Views on the Night Frost Crisis

One way I tried to get at this issue was to ask pointed questions in my interviews about the differences between the way Paasikivi had supported the Fagerholm I Government in 1948 and the way Kekkonen had failed to support the Fagerholm III Government in 1958 (the Roman numerals refer to the fact that Social Democrat K.A. Fagerholm was prime minister of three different Finnish governments or cabinets during the 1948-58 period). I suggested that perhaps the difference between the two presidents' management of these respective crises characterized the difference between the two statesmen in their approach to the question of Soviet influence in Finnish internal processes, such as deciding the composition of Finnish governments. This was also a point of comparison that has been found useful by other researchers of these issues.

I tried this approach with former Center Party Secretary and Alko Chairman Mikko Immonen. I pointed out that the Fagerholm government in 1948, like the later Fagerholm government in 1958, had come under heavy criticism from the Soviet Union. But President Paasikivi in 1948 had strongly defended the Fagerholm government against what he considered to be unfair criticism from the Soviet Union. And when the Soviets were attacking the government, Paasikivi wrote, according to the Paasikivi diaries:

> The Russians speak of Fagerholm's "third road" which they do not accept. For them there are only two roads: the communist road and the reactionary and fascist road. But we cannot go down either one of those roads, rather precisely the third road, our own Nordic country road, which at the same time fulfills our agreements with the Soviet Union. But no further.[3]

I noted that some people have observed that ten years later in a similar situation, the same prime minister was again getting criticism from the Soviet Union. But unlike Paasikivi, Kekkonen did not support Fagerholm. Immonen responded:

> First, of course, there were differences between Paasikivi and Kekkonen and their personalities and then in the periods and generations, and also in their behavior. For many reasons, personal reasons. I think there is [only] one common denominator and that was Fagerholm. But there was nothing else common in the situations of 1948 and 1958...There was not in 1948 any intention to change the basic political line because everybody felt it was a matter of survival to follow [Paasikivi]. But ten years later there were people who started re-thinking. Vennamo [Note: a populist rural political figure] came from Denmark...He started playing the strings in order to start changing our political line, a counter-Kekkonen line...Kekkonen believed that...[if] we had started at that time changing the political line, we would have destroyed the harvest which we have been [reaping] after the war. In that respect I don't agree with the argument that the situation was the same between 1948 and 1958....[For the Soviets] the Social Democrats were basically the Mensheviks and the Communists were Bolsheviks, according to Lenin's doctrines...It was...a distrust based on ideological reasons...The criticism of Fagerholm was a criticism of a government led by a Social Democrat in Finland.

I also asked former Social Democratic Party Chairman and Prime Minister Kalevi Sorsa about the contrast between the ways that Paasikivi and Kekkonen dealt with the Fagerholm government crises of 1948 and 1958, respectively, and whether these episodes shed light on the use of presidential power. Sorsa said he did not have personal knowledge of the events of that period but went on:

> Well, there certainly was a difference between the two presidents in their attitudes toward the Fagerholm governments. My conclusion after having read books is that Paasikivi clearly used the...Social Democratic government to stop the communist expansion. That is probably why particularly the communists in Finland but also the Soviet Union Communist Party were so basically negative towards the Finnish Social Democrats. Of course, and this was not necessarily the critical reason, but there was the old feud between the Social Democrats and the communists from the split between the Bolsheviks and Mensheviks.
>
> ...Kekkonen's attitude was, and he made it very clear, that he didn't consider Fagerholm's [third] government his own, and he [was] not standing behind it. Maybe he even plotted against it, but again it's difficult to know. He may have seen in Fagerholm's...government a power concentrated against himself and therefore was prepared [for] alliance with the Bolsheviks to disarm it...Maybe it should be explained...that Kekkonen already fought for his second term and that his main aim was against Fagerholm.

I asked Sorsa as a leading Social Democrat about his views as to whether the Social Democrats of the 1950s and 1960s—Tanner, Fagerholm, Leskinen, Pitsinki—were in fact unreliable on foreign policy grounds as has been charged by many Kekkonen defenders. Was it fair to say that Fagerholm and his contemporaries were not in accord with the fundamental Finnish policy of getting along with the Soviet Union? Sorsa answered:

> I would say that foreign policy was basically the weakness of Social Democrats of those times, it was so much a party of domestic policies, it did not really have a clear understanding of foreign policy and international politics. In fact, they didn't pay any attention to it. I remember having compared the writings of Kekkonen and Leskinen on foreign policy, and I was already then as a young man somewhat ashamed that our level of thinking on foreign policy was so much lower than Kekkonen's. Then, naturally one must admit that the so-called 'weapons brother' wing of the Social Democratic Party was leading the party, Leskinen, Väyrynen, Simonen, Tervo, Varjonen, and a few others. They were outright anticommunist and courageous in that, which made them also anti-Soviet.

I then asked Sorsa whether he was saying, as a number of other Finns have indicated, that President Kekkonen had some justification for using his power against Fagerholm and the Social Democrats? Did he have legitimate foreign policy and domestic policy reasons, for his attitude towards the Social Democrats? Or was it overuse of his power? Sorsa responded:

I think it was overuse. But, then, one must admit that political morals were different in those times. The parties played with foreign powers and did things which were not exactly acceptable. So, for an outsider as I then was...it is easy to condemn. But then, an historian probably should try to live in those times...

I queried former Center Party Chairman and Foreign Minister Paavo Väyrynen on the differences between Paasikivi and Kekkonen and their handling of the 1948 and 1958 Fagerholm government crises. Väyrynen disclaimed the expertise to comment on those historical events, which he did not participate in. He noted that Dr. Juhani Suomi has written on these matters and said he believed that Suomi's account, while perhaps somewhat pro-Kekkonen, was basically accurate. Väyrynen did say, however:

You have to remember that we had a very, very strong power struggle inside Finland, and Kekkonen's position was not at all strong in 1958.

I asked Väyrynen whether he thought that Fagerholm or the people behind him were opposed to the basic idea of having good relations with the Soviet Union, acknowledging that certainly the Soviets had indicated they did not believe that Tanner and Leskinen wanted to have good relations. Väyrynen commented:

It is very difficult to say. But the fact of life was that the Soviet Union felt like that. They had that opinion. And that was a fact and a reality. And secondly, I have understood that there was a basic difference in the field of foreign policy. Some people, and it was the right-wing socialists and conservatives, were willing to change the course of our foreign policy, to have less contacts and more thin relations with the Soviets and stronger ties with the West. I don't know how deep it was, but there was a difference of opinion, I think.

I asked long-time Presidential Chief of Chancery Jaakko Kalela about presidential handling of the early postwar political crises in Finland in 1948, 1958 and 1961. Kalela responded:

I have no first-hand knowledge and it has not been studied enough yet, but it is my thinking at least that in all these three cases...the Soviet reaction against Finland...showed a lack of confidence towards Finnish leadership, and all three cases...were connected with changes in the international situation, very fundamental changes...What they basically in both cases reacted to was...that Finland after a period of relaxation had...strengthened its ties to the West and was approaching Western economic organizations and Western integration...

Now, in the first case, Paasikivi chose to support the government... Basically he was afraid of a change of government leading to a renewed popular front government as we had had since the Second World War...While in the case of Kekkonen, this other Fagerholm government was basically anti-Kekkonen. There was clearly tension between the government coalition and Kekkonen...There was not very much danger that a change in government would lead to a stronger influence of the Communist Party directly on government policy. So he had freer hands than Paasikivi had ten years before. And certainly, he played his power game and just wanted to get rid of some of the politicians and get rid of this government which was basically an anti-Kekkonen coalition. But it certainly had its implications for the future. It doomed a similar coalition until Koivisto appointed another one in the mid-1980s.

[But] as a politician it [1958] was a situation of life and death for Kekkonen. If this coalition would have been in the government for four years, then Fagerholm would have been the prime minister and he or somebody else would have been a much more credible [presidential] candidate...And when you read Fagerholm's memoirs, there was openly the idea to push Kekkonen to the background...

I also raised with Jan-Magnus Jansson, former Swedish People's Party chairman and long-time editor-in-chief of *Hufvudstadsbladet*, my question contrasting Paasikivi's support for the first Fagerholm government in 1948 and Kekkonen's lack of support for Fagerholm's third government in 1958. Jansson made the point that from the very beginning Kekkonen had made it clear that he could not support the Fagerholm government in 1958:

Of course the only clear alternative would have been to use his power not to appoint the government, or to back up the government once he appointed it. And I think that even from his point of view when he disliked the government he could have done the latter, because if the government had been sitting about half a year or a year, it would have in any case for some other reason been dispersed. There was of course a very complicated factor of a purely internal nature, and this was the Tanner factor. Tanner was in prison during Fagerholm's first government. Tanner was the chairman of the Social Democratic Party during the third Fagerholm government, and one must always observe that the verdict against Tanner was very much in question. But anyway, he had been in prison for war guilt. Of course it was foolhardy of the Social Democrats to appoint him. But this was a difference.

I discussed the 1958 crisis with former Chairman of the Finnish Communist Party, Aarne Saarinen, and asked him whether in his opinion the Social Democrats and Fagerholm really would have threatened Finland's foreign policy and relations with the Soviet Union. Saarinen answered:

Indeed, it is true that the Soviet leadership, specifically, the Soviet Communist Party, felt a very strong distrust toward the leadership of the [Finnish] social Democratic Party. Certainly, Tanner, Leskinen, Pitsinki and those kinds of people were *persona non grata* to the Soviets; it was absolute. So then when the Fagerholm government was nevertheless named, it therefore meant the creation of distrust between Helsinki and Moscow.

Ambassador Jakobson considered the events of 1958 as critical in the evolution of Finland's post-war policies:

...the extent to which Kekkonen not only permitted but in a way himself brought Soviet influence into the domestic process is something I have [written about] and tried to analyze his reasoning for that. Fifty-eight was absolutely a turning point in this respect. It really in a way follows from his general concept of how relations with the Soviets had to be handled. You couldn't divide policy into compartments...foreign, policy, domestic policy, economic policy...everything was part of an overall process, and in order to make sure that the Soviets always understood and had confidence in the Finnish political process, they had to understand and be informed of any domestic changes...He believed, I think genuinely, that he could handle it...and on the whole he *did* handle it very well. But of course again you then come to this corrupting influence that this had on the whole political process.

In my dialogue with Foreign Ministry official and President Kekkonen's biographer, Dr. Juhani Suomi, I asked him a general question about Finland's foreign and security policy coming out of World War II and how it was applied by Presidents Paasikivi and Kekkonen. The question was whether Finland went further than was necessary in accommodating the Soviets, thereby unnecessarily feeding the Finlandization epithet. Suomi responded:

That is a big question, in that it covers a very long timeframe and we had very special problems...Very briefly, you quite rightly described that beginning; the first goal after the war was specifically to maintain our independence by whatever means possible...The FCMA treaty was agreed to, because it was thought that because distrust had led to war, if we could achieve trust, okay, let's do it by those [treaty] conditions, as long as we preserve our independence. Paasikivi and Kekkonen used sometimes the metaphor 'as long as we keep our head above water.' The idea was systematically to strive to achieve that, but then in Kekkonen's time a change occurred.

Having just cited Dr. Juhani Suomi, perhaps it would be appropriate at this juncture to relate some observations made to me by Suomi about U.S. diplomats, as well as to cite a number of references to the same subject that he has made in his multi-volume biography of President Kekkonen.

It is clear from Dr. Suomi's biography of Kekkonen, as well as from his statements to me, that he had a low regard for the professionalism of United States embassy diplomats in Helsinki, particularly in the 1950s and 1960s but also into the 1970s. Consequently, he believes that U.S. embassy reporting from those periods cannot be accepted as accurate or objective. He told me in our 1995 interview that U.S. ambassadors:

...did not know how to seek out information in the same manner as other countries in Finland. And now when these reports are seen, they are sometimes even a frighteningly one-sided group. And unfortunately, if you think of Finnish policy, they could have led U.S. diplomats astray. The reason was that many of those sources in fact were also in their own fashion playing politics. Often, they were at the time opponents of Finland's policy. They willingly put matters forward to the Americans in a very negative tone, hoping that through those reports [their views] could be carried to Washington in that manner. And that is in fact what happened.

Suomi said he could see from reports in the archives of the Swedish Foreign Ministry that Swedish diplomats were also concerned that the U.S. government was receiving faulty information from its diplomatic representatives in Finland. Suomi also was critical in our interview (as well as in the Kekkonen biography) of British diplomatic representation and reporting on Finland. He told me:

In relation to this matter the Swedes were really good observers, because in Finland there were only three states, which traditionally were good information gatherers and whose significance for Finland was large and for whom Finland's importance was also great. Those countries are Finland's fateful trio, Russia, Germany and Sweden. They sought out information from various places and of various points of view and then fused them together. This brings me back to my starting point, that not all of the reports to be found in the State Department are necessarily very objective.

I asked Suomi about British and Soviet reporting. He told me:

British reports were absolutely better than the Americans' but the British had periods in which an ambassador was, I would say, self-centered, in his own opinion very knowledgeable, and then it might happen that in fact the Brits would be led astray by the old habit that information would be picked up in NATO circles...But it is a fact that other British representatives were extraordinarily good diplomats, and above all, British intelligence was notably more realistic [than American]. However, you cannot compare the British with...of course the best [diplomatic reporting] material is found specifically from Sweden and then of course also from our Eastern neighbor.

I queried Suomi further, observing that it goes without saying that the Soviets had good contacts in Finland, but were their reports better and more accurate? Suomi answered that, while the Soviets had excellent contacts and "the best material," the problem was that their reports would be colored by ideological interpretation and by their desire to present themselves (the Soviet diplomats) in a good light, to show that they were making good propaganda:

And above all, the Russians had the problem that, although they had information sources their local representatives themselves colored the information because they wanted to emphasize their own importance. Those were Finland's problems in both directions.

I told Dr. Suomi that I have myself commented that the United States practice of often sending politically appointed ambassadors to Finland does not always yield a sophisticated top level of diplomatic representation. I insisted, however, that during my time and during the time of my career predecessors in the embassy— people like Ted Sellin, John Owens, Eric Fleischer, Paul Canney, Carl Clement, and my colleague and successor as political counselor Ward Thompson—we had good contacts with the Center Party, the Social Democrats, the labor unions. We sought and achieved quite good balance among our contacts and sources. In a revealing remark, Suomi said:

I don't really consider it as a problem whether contacts were balanced. That is not so important. In fact, politicians knew very little about our foreign policy. The problem was perhaps more that certain key government officials were missing from the group [of contacts]. Those who really had something to do with Finland's foreign policy.

Suomi then proceeded to discount the research done by Hannu Rautkallio, one of President Kekkonen's critics, who has researched Soviet files and discovered information damaging to Kekkonen. Suomi said Rautkallio is not considered in Finland to belong really to the "researcher team," that he depended on Soviet diplomatic reporting—not on Central Committee (read KGB) reporting—that he picks a sentence from here, a sentence from there, that he does not read or speak Russian, etc.

There are numerous further examples of disparaging comments by Suomi on U.S. and other Western diplomats in his exhaustive Kekkonen biography. Writing about the Night Frost episode, for example, Suomi puts forth his opinion that:

> For them [the Americans] Finland was a Moscow-controlled country, where developments could be used willingly as a basis for rejecting Soviet demands regarding Berlin.

Moreover, he added somewhat sarcastically that:

> Also, in Washington they had perceived growing Soviet pressure. A frightening prospect was presented: the Fagerholm government might before long dissolve, and in the succeeding government the communists might have seats. Therefore, they began to rush to prepare a broad assistance package.

Referring to Ambassador Hickerson's offer to Prime Minister Fagerholm of U.S. economic support and Secretary of State John Foster Dulles' advice that Finland ride out Soviet pressures, Dr. Suomi quotes President Kekkonen as saying:

> Dulles counsels to us are the stupid advice of a dilettante. Foreign policy leadership there is certainly in weak hands.

Dr. Suomi notes that President Kekkonen rejected sharply the aid offered against Soviet pressure. Kekkonen blamed "some Finnish group" for having put Ambassador Hickerson up to it.[4] Later, President Kekkonen bestowed further compliments on America's ambassadors to Finland:

> Of course Gufler is a hopelessly stupid man. But the USA has plenty of these! Hickerson is a dolt and Sessions, who was intelligent, didn't stay long.[5]

(I will comment on Suomi, and Kekkonen's, views about Western diplomatic competence reporting on Finland at the conclusion of this chapter.) Suomi's comments on Rautkallio provide a convenient segue into a look at retrospective views of the Note Crisis. First, however, I will summarize my assessment of Kekkonen, Paasikivi and the Night Frost crisis.

I believe that my thesis regarding the differences between the way the two presidents handled their Fagerholm Government crises is essentially valid. The precedent set when President Kekkonen allowed the Soviets in 1958 to veto certain parties and certain individuals from participation in government constituted a heavy blow to the Finnish political system. It was a clear departure from Paasikivi's position, expressed in 1948:

> Above anything else, we must hold tight to this, that we, that is the Parliament and the president, but not Moscow, decide which people will become members of government. If we surrender in this, then it means we are finished.[6]

This single act by Kekkonen—later re-enforced by the Note Crisis *denouement*, discussed below—led to a situation where there could not be a truly free play of political forces in Finland to determine which parties might form a government based on their parliamentary strength and their agreement on common programs. It led to a situation whereby the only road to political power and influence lay in currying favor with President Kekkonen and the Soviet embassy. It led to a situation whereby the Soviet Union and President Kekkonen would determine who were "good Finns" and who were "bad Finns." And it led to a situation whereby first the Social Democratic Party had to purge itself of "unreliable" leaders and begin a long, hat-in-hand transformation to render itself acceptable to President Kekkonen and to the Soviet Union. This humiliating migration was followed soon thereafter by the National Coalition (Conservative) Party, which, however, was never quite able to complete the journey during the Kekkonen presidency. It led, in short, to the phenomena associated with the term "Finlandization."

In my judgement there can be no doubt concerning all of the nefarious implications of the Night Frost Crisis resolution. At the same time, however, I see that there were some crucial differences between the 1948 government crisis faced by Paasikivi and the 1958 Night Frost Crisis faced by Kekkonen. As bad as the consequences of 1958 were for the Finnish political system, I understand President Kekkonen's dilemma. It is clear, for example, that Fagerholm himself was not the major problem. After all, only a few months earlier, in January/February of 1957, Prime Minister

Fagerholm at the head of his second government had undertaken a highly successful official visit to the Soviet Union. So successful had been the visit that Fagerholm brought home with him for the first time ever in a Finnish/Soviet communiqué explicit reference to Finland's "peace loving and neutral foreign policy," something that Kekkonen himself to that point had not achieved.[7] So, it is hardly credible that a Fagerholm-led government was the real issue.

It seems clear that a major precipitating factor in the crisis had been the defiant and head-strong action by the Social Democratic Party in naming Vaino Tanner as SDP chairman by a one vote margin over Fagerholm during their April 1957, special party congress. The same congress deepened the split between the pro-Soviet leaning Skogist minority of the SDP and the Tanner-led majority. The selection of Tanner as party chairman, whom the Soviets had insisted be branded as a war criminal and imprisoned, was waving a "red-flag," as it were, at the Soviets. According to Suomi, Fagerholm himself at that time realized that his own continuation as prime minister and Finnish relations with the Soviet Union would be made far more difficult with Tanner's selection as SDP party chairman.

As a number of interlocutors pointed out, including a number who were decidedly unsympathetic towards Kekkonen, the preponderant strength of the Social Democrats and the Conservative Party in the Fagerholm III government—notwithstanding the presence of Center Party cabinet officials including Virolainen and Karjalainen—meant that President Kekkonen would be dealing with a government politically hostile to him. And he was faced with a prime minister whom he had defeated in the 1956 presidential election by only the narrowest of margins in the electoral college. It was understood that Fagerholm, as prime minister, would be positioning himself to contest Kekkonen for the presidency in 1962.

Moreover, it is difficult to discount completely the arguments of Kekkonen defenders that there were elements among those opposed to President Kekkonen in the late 1950s and early 1960s who might have tried to change Finland's foreign policy. They might seek to "tilt" it—to cite a term used by Immonen in our interview—away from the Soviet Union and toward the West. Clearly, the "brothers-in-arms" spirit prevailing within the Social Democratic Party at that time was consistent with the possibility of a tougher foreign policy attitude toward the Soviet Union.

However, the experience of the Fagerholm I and II governments demonstrated that governments under Social Democratic Party leadership could maintain correct, if not particularly warm, relations with the Soviet Union. The selection of the Center Party's Johannes Virolainen as Foreign Minister was intended to convey to the Soviets that no foreign policy change would be forthcoming, although the Soviets obviously did not believe that Virolainen provided such assurance. Still, it is possible to believe that workable relations might have continued under a Fagerholm III government had President Kekkonen been willing to make clear to the Soviet Union that it was in fact the duly constituted government of Finland. And that he would permit no significant change in Finland's foreign policy.

However President Kekkonen, in his weak political position vis-à-vis the Fagerholm III government and with his own political future at stake, was, apparently, prepared to go all out to strengthen his own position. So he allowed the Soviets into the Finnish political process, redrawing the line that had been set by Paasikivi and Mannerheim.

In my interview with former Foreign Ministry official Paavo Laitinen he related a marvelous anecdote from a personal experience in 1958 which I think merits being cited for the insight it provides into the Kekkonen personality and attitude at the time:

> Maybe I should tell some personal experiences from this period. Because I was then in the commercial department of the Foreign Ministry, and Taneli Kekkonen was sitting in the same room as I, the son of the president. He is dead now. He was a very intelligent and analytical person. He was drinking a bit too much, but from an analytical point of view, he was one of the best diplomats we had...When the government was formed, he was telling me every day about the problems he had. His father-in-law was Fagerholm! Taneli was married to Fagerholm's daughter, Brita Fagerholm.

And he told me Kekkonen had been telephoning to Fagerholm asking him what was going on. And Fagerholm always told him that everything is all right, you don't need to worry, and put the receiver down. So he kept Kekkonen out of the political role from the beginning. Then you had a situation that there was supposed to be commercial negotiations with the Russians. I was there as a young secretary to organize the meeting between the Russian ambassador and the secretary of state. Then the Russians informed that they are not coming for the negotiations. So Kekkonen telephoned Fagerholm and asked what was happening, and Fagerholm answered that they are coming. He was just keeping Kekkonen out of the picture. And then things developed so that Karjalainen, who was minister of commerce, was given orders by Kekkonen to leave the government. And he left the government…

Then on the 6th of December 1958, I was at the Independence Day party as a kind of usher. Kekkonen came to me and said, Taneli is drunk, would you take him upstairs to our private rooms. I took Taneli up there because he was very drunk. We went up there, and he went directly to his father's bedroom. There was a small cabinet there, and he took out a cognac bottle. He took a huge glass and was just pouring it when Kekkonen walked in. Taneli got a little scared and said, "I am just pouring this for Paavo Laitinen." Kekkonen said let me help you, you're hands are trembling. Kekkonen poured a whole glass of some thirty centimeters in the glass and said to me in Finnish "bottoms up." And I was drinking that, and he was watching me very carefully, and I finished the whole thing.

Then we sat down, and Kekkonen funnily began talking about the political situation. Kekkonen said, "I say only one thing. I am determined to make sure that they in Moscow believe that I am in charge here in Helsinki." To me that was kind of a clear-cut case, that was his political will, and he wanted to act accordingly, whatever the situation was. I don't know how he had behaved or what he had said, but it was his clear political will that he wanted to show them who is the boss in Finland.

Thus, as Kekkonen told Paavo Laitinen, he was apparently determined at all costs to demonstrate to the Soviets that he was in full charge of events in Finland. It was the beginning of an extraordinarily close and unhealthy partnership—and a first step down a slippery slope. (By the way, Laitinen said that Kekkonen graciously provided a car and driver to take the unsteady Paavo and his wife Raili home.)

Retrospective Views on the Note Crisis

Regarding the Note Crisis, several of my interlocutors also had very decided views on that episode. Some were willing to consider recent information brought to light by Finnish researcher Hannu Rautkallio. In view of Dr. Suomi's disparagement of Dr. Rautkallio, I think a few observations are in order. Rautkallio has long been assessing Finland's foreign and domestic policies, drawing heavily, among other sources, on United States government and British government archives and diplomatic reporting. The great majority of the U.S. documents from the 1950's and 1960's that I reviewed for this book had earlier been obtained by Rautkallio either from U.S. archives or from his own FOIA request from the Department of State. However, the documents I cite from the 1970s and 1980s were not available when Rautkallio was doing his research. Relevant Rautkallio publications regarding the period from 1945 to 1956 are *Suomen Suunta* (Finland's Direction) *1945-1948*, and *Paasikivi Vai Kekkonen–Suomi lannesta nahtyna 1945-1956* (Paasikivi or Kekkonen–Finland as seen from the West 1945-56).[8]

In Rautkallio's book, *Novosibirskin lavastus: Nootikriisi 1961* (The Staging at Novosibirsk: the 1961 Note Crisis), published in 1992, he presents the gravest possible allegations against President Kekkonen. Based largely on research of Soviet Foreign Ministry files, he charges that Kekkonen was an active participant in a deliberate maneuver organized between him and senior Soviet authorities to force Olavi Honka out of the presidential race and thus assure Kekkonen's re-election.[9]

Rautkallio bases his conclusions about Kekkonen's actions on newly available sources from Soviet archives, where he found a wealth of new information. These included a memorandum written by President Kekkonen and passed to Soviet officials; memoranda of the central committee of the Communist Party of the Soviet Union regarding preparing the 1961 Note Crisis; directives from the central committee sent through the Soviet Foreign Ministry to the Soviet ambassador in Finland, A.V. Zaharov; the 1960-61 diaries of Ambassador Zaharov; reports by the assistant KGB

Resident in Finland J.V. Voronin; and a two hundred page report for the year 1961 written by the Soviet embassy in Helsinki.

Rautkallio argues that the documents prove President Kekkonen plotted with Soviet officials beginning in 1960 to assure his re-election and that Kekkonen was not a passive beneficiary of Soviet policy to guarantee his re-election but, rather, took the initiative in working out plans. The Kekkonen memorandum found by Rautkallio was written by the president, he believes, on September 2, 1960 and used apparently in a sauna meeting the same week during a visit to Helsinki by Soviet General Secretary Khrushchev. In it Kekkonen discusses in detail possible options in reaching a solution to the government crisis. A copy of the highly classified Finnish memorandum was apparently given by Kekkonen to one of the Soviet officials.[10]

Rautkallio found the document terribly significant evidence of President Kekkonen's conniving with the Soviets. I did not myself find that document particularly conclusive. What *is* in my view shocking about the memorandum, and the accounts put forward by Rautkallio and others, is their revelation of Kekkonen's extraordinarily close relationship with top Soviet leaders and embassy officials, especially KGB residents. President Kekkonen apparently discussed with these senior Soviet officials the most intimate details of the Finnish domestic political scene in a way that one would have thought unthinkable between a chief of state and representatives of a foreign government.

This extraordinarily close relationship between Kekkonen and the Soviet embassy was further underlined when Kekkonen provided to the Soviet ambassador exceedingly intimate details of his thinking on the Finnish domestic political situation in 1961. Rautkallio, quoting from Zaharov's diaries, says President Kekkonen related to Zaharov that:

"At some other time than the present, selecting a prime minister would be a quite untroublesome process. I could quickly name a new prime minister and the matter would end there...but this time I want to organize a little parliamentary show," said the president. "In Finland's situation, such shows are sometimes unavoidable."[11]

What a remarkable way for a Finnish president to speak to a foreign ambassador!

The most telling information presented by Rautkallio is his citation of a Soviet embassy report to the Foreign Ministry in Moscow covering 1961. Rautkallio quotes from the Soviet embassy report "Political Situation in Finland 1961" which he identifies as the embassy's annual report. He said the embassy report refuted the long-proffered official Finnish version that the Soviets did not believe Olavi Honka had much of a possibility of beating Kekkonen in the 1962 presidential elections. Rather, Rautkallio cites the Soviet embassy report as describing a plan the objective of which (quotes from Soviet report) was:

> "...the decisive weakening of the Honka alliance, to which end would be directed a blow consisting of the dissolution of Parliament and the holding of presidential elections and parliamentary elections at the same time.
>
> In order to do that the agrarian league (Urho Kekkonen) would need a convincing pretext for dissolving Parliament that would cover up the election maneuver. Our diplomatic note of October 30 would be used as the pretext."[12]

I have heard Rautkallio's findings disparaged by—in addition to Suomi—some other Finns who also argue that he is not a Russian expert and scholar and does not speak or read the Russian language and that he is considered to have a bias and to jump to conclusions. And that Soviet embassy officials had reason to deliberately exaggerate their role in the Note Crisis to make it appear to their superiors in Moscow that they were effectively manipulating the Finnish government when the reality may have been quite different.

I'm no Russian expert, but the information presented by Rautkallio—with whatever reservations one wishes to attach—surely has to be taken into account in evaluating whether President Kekkonen was prone to use his special relationship with the Soviet embassy and the leadership in Moscow as a weapon in Finland's domestic political competition. Does the information uncovered by Rautkallio in the Soviet files support or contradict the thesis that Kekkonen would use the Soviet card for his own benefit? Certainly, it is a significant piece of information that a 1962 Soviet embassy report describes the famous October 30, 1961 Soviet Note as a "pretext."

My Finnish dialogue partners had many interesting views of the 1961-62 Note Crisis from which I will cite only briefly. Mikko Immonen saw the political forces behind the Honka alliance as once again seeking

to start tilting more to the West. And Kekkonen's interpretation of the situation was certainly that it's not in the best interests of the country if there was a change. Many people hoped that we should have more and more possibilities to the West, but if we played the cards wrongly, the result would have been once again that there was less possibility, less elbowroom in the West. And I am personally convinced that Kekkonen all the time wanted to strengthen our position in both directions. There you see the difference between the political emphasis of the Social Democrat party of Leskinen [and] Pitsinki's policy and Kekkonen's policy.

I asked former Prime Minister Sorsa about the 1961 Note Crisis. Sorsa said he was in Paris at UNESCO during the note crisis and had been astonished over this development at a time when the Berlin crisis with which the Note was associated was already calming down. Sorsa commented:

I suppose that Kekkonen himself, being a superb politician, knew this play. He was a master at this. He played it for his own benefit, but also for the benefit of Finland. But the worst thing in it was that he...gave the example to much less masterful Finns, and from there followed something that can be called Finlandization. Because the president is the leader of all of us; he gives the example of how foreign policy is conducted. And what followed from his methods was that even during my time as prime minister there were well-known mainly Center Party politicians, but also in other parties, who thought that foreign policy was equal to *Tehtaankatu* [Note: a reference to the Soviet embassy on the street of that name], the Soviet Union, and that's it. There's nothing else! And that foreign policy could be done in covert discussions with *Tehtaankatu*. And I, upon understanding this fact, was really shocked. Members of my own government, reputed well-known people, but with no experience in foreign policy, they sort of talked about this as natural. And that was the dangerous side.

I queried former high-ranking Finnish Foreign Ministry official and ambassador to the United States Jaakko Iloniemi about the 1961-62 Note Crisis. Ambassador Iloniemi responded with a reference to my mention of the "Soviet card":

Regarding playing the Soviet card, I think Kekkonen did play it from time to time in order to influence Finnish domestic positions, and he used Soviet influence to boost his own position. The most remarkable was, of course, the 1961 "Note Crisis." In my view it has been established beyond reasonable doubt that Kekkonen was aware of the Soviet move and its intentions. This I consider to be Kekkonen's most controversial political act. Of course he had several purposes at the same time. The Berlin situation was also very tense in those days.

I asked Iloniemi about information coming to light in the Soviet archives. He responded:

I am very suspicious [about] diaries and other literary works by ex-agents of the KGB. I cannot understand why these professional disinformers should be taken seriously now that they make money by publishing books fashioned after demand for sensations. I am distrustful even in the case of embassy reporting, since there are good grounds to believe that such reports often misrepresented things in order to present the writers in a favorable sense. There has been much corruption in the Soviet system. I do not need these books in order to draw the conclusion that the accusations were, at least in part, well founded."

Jan-Magnus Jansson commented on the note crisis as follows:

Then you have specifically the 1961 Berlin crisis. That was of course mixed into the Note Crisis…I think I can say about this that we were under such enormous pressure that considerations of neutrality and so on were not very relevant. We had to save ourselves. Even if there were other aspects in [it], the note was in fact given, and we couldn't say, well, we don't care about this. We had to do something. But of course, there was clearly an internal domestic side of the note, and everybody knows it, and everybody knew it then…I was quite convinced, and I even talked with the Russian ambassador about it after the crisis, and he…clearly admitted that it had a domestic dimension. And of course it had, because Honka left his candidacy.

I am sure that Kekkonen knew practically that something would come. Juhani Suomi in his biography of Kekkonen mentions that [Finnish] Ambassador Wuori in Moscow warned the president that there was probably [going] to be an action from the Soviet side…It can't have come as a surprise when he was in Hawaii…I and people belonging to my group…wanted Kekkonen to be re-elected—because we considered Honka as absolutely incompetent. But we would have wished that he would have been re-elected without this intervention from the Russian side. We believe there was a majority for him…even without the note…But that is a hypothesis…We didn't hope for it, but we were prepared it would come. Kekkonen of course was also prepared, and perhaps it was like that, well if it comes, let me make the best of it. And he did…take advantage of it…But we were surprised by the form, the extremely hard diplomatically sensational form it took. We would have expected a speech by Khrushchev or something. A diplomatic note is very high in the hierarchy of measures that can be taken.

I asked Jansson about the school of thought with some documentary evidence that President Kekkonen perhaps had worked out the whole scenario of the note with the Soviet embassy and the KGB. He responded:

I'm not quite informed about these writings. You see, they are testimonies only of those Soviet functionaries and Communist Party people of the Soviet Union. And I would say that I wouldn't give full objectivity to the sources, because every functionary from ambassadors—if you permit me to say—to still more, Communist functionaries of the kind like Vladimirov and others, of course are interested in showing how important they were and how well they worked for their country. So I would take it with grain of salt...

Playing the Soviet Card

One of the interesting aspects of my interviews was the almost amusing way that representatives of the various Finnish political parties hurled back and forth the charge of acquiescing in Soviet interference in Finland's political affairs and of Finnish leaders playing the Soviet card. We have already noted how several observers have blamed President Kekkonen for bringing the Soviets into Finnish affairs and playing the Soviet card with vigor and not without skill. As Sorsa observed, the problem was that politicians other than Kekkonen did not have the same level of skill. Kekkonen supporters returned the charge. Paavo Väyrynen acknowledged:

It is true that during the Kekkonen period the Soviet Union was able to involve itself more in our domestic affairs, but it is not his blame, it was not Kekkonen's will that it should happen. It only was that when the Soviet Union had a very effective grip on our political parties, on our political life, they gradually were able to increase their influence. In my opinion Kekkonen was actually against this, and he was the guy who was very strictly maintaining our independence and fighting for our neutrality and fighting these pressures. Many times, almost all the political forces passed him on the left-hand side, so to say, [and] they were closer to the Soviet positions than he was. So to criticize Kekkonen for this is not justified.

Väyrynen was particularly critical of the Social Democratic Party's foreign and security policy, which he cited as an example of political parties passing Kekkonen on the left:

The Social Democrats after having left behind their right-wing past became the rival in the field of foreign policy, and they really had, so to say, a more leftist policy than was the Kekkonen line. And Kekkonen was obliged to some extent to be flexible towards their direction. There were many Social Democrats writing about this. One of the books referred to many times was the *Kaksiterainen miekka [Double-edged Sword]*, written by Jaakko Blomberg, and Jaakko Kalela was also involved. And they actually wrote about a defense community with the Soviet Union and Finland. They had ideas about the FCMA Treaty in a very strange way, very different from the Kekkonen interpretation. They thought we should prepare ourselves for an alliance with the Soviet Union in war time, and that's why we would not need that strong a home defense, that was the argumentation.

Sorsa described the development of the Social Democratic foreign policy line in somewhat different terms:

> What then happened towards the end of the sixties and especially in the seventies was that a new generation of young scholars interested in foreign policy problems came up, and it was this group of young men who put into question the then-Kekkonen policy, argued against it publicly, not always very wisely, but still they created real discussion, and then created an independent foreign policy stand for the party. And these were people like Jaakko Iloniemi, Jaakko Kalela, Jaakko Blomberg, and the Tampere group.

I noted that there were some controversial positions taken by these young Social Democratic foreign policy thinkers at the time. Sorsa said:

> We somehow happened to get just the cream of the young people interested in foreign policy at that time. I would also say that although they were very critical about the foreign policy line in the beginning, they finally proved very loyal and solid, so that even Kekkonen could make Jaakko Kalela his foreign policy advisor.... and from that time on the party has been one can say the leading party in international matters.

Current Finnish Prime Minister Paavo Lipponen also commented on Soviet influence in Finland and the playing of the Soviet card during the Kekkonen years. He spoke of his introduction into dealing with the Soviet Union:

> As a general comment...there was a whole sort of doctrine in the Ministry of Foreign Affairs, and I remember learning about this when I was a young party hand at the end of the sixties—beginning of the seventies. Ambassador Hyvarinen once lectured me—maybe he thought that I could still be saved!—...on the realities of relations with the Soviet Union. He had me to lunch, and for two or three hours we sat there. It was very valuable. What the designs of the Soviets could be. It was my assessment already at that time in the mid-1970s that the Soviet Union interpreted *détente* as a sort of tacit spheres of interest agreement and that Finland in a way would belong to their sphere of interest. Ustinov's suggestion of common maneuvers certainly comes from that type of doctrine. But that was really rejected right out of hand...But there really was this type of thinking, and I think many Finns were sort of deluded by *détente*. But I wasn't. It was a time of learning about things in international politics.

In response to questions regarding Soviet influence in Finland and the playing of the Soviet card, Lipponen commented:

Of course the dirtiest part of the post-war history was their [Soviet] involvement in our internal affairs. So there was a lot of cynical maneuvering; this liturgy was used in a power game in Finland. [Kekkonen] was the kind of politician who wanted to have everybody under his control, during his period. That changed completely when Koivisto became President...It was not only Kekkonen, there were a lot of people...using him against their rivals. It was a terrible system. There was a big risk of getting corrupted in that system. My party just avoided getting drawn into this type of business...

In my discussion with former Conservative Party Chairman and Prime Minister Harri Holkeri, he addressed one of my questions about whether President Kekkonen acquiesced in allowing Soviet influence in Finland. He said:

...In other words, was President Kekkonen too soft? Even this is always a question in Finland...Kekkonen was quite pragmatic towards the Russians. My personal opinion is that he was quite strong against the Russians...If we take for instance the so-called Note Crisis. It has been said that it was at Kekkonen's order. I do not believe that...When I was prime minister, I went through the archives: the Council of Defense was informed that something was coming already in August...There were certain signals already in advance, but Kekkonen went on the state visit to the United States, stayed there in Hawaii, and fulfilled his responsibilities according to the program and then the decision was made...

I reminded Holkeri that part of the solution to the Note Crisis was the clear expression by Kekkonen that his understanding with the Soviets depended on his own continuation in office. That caused the Honka alliance to fall apart. I noted that time after time it would be alleged that only Kekkonen could manage this relationship. Holkeri responded:

That is one of your key questions, okay. Let's put it first that way, since we had Kekkonen who had good relations with the Soviet Union, why not use him? Why not give him as a guarantee?

One Finn who absolutely earned his right to be heard in this retrospective look at Finnish attitudes towards policies followed by Finland during the Cold War, particularly during the Kekkonen years, is Georg C. Ehrnrooth, vilified along with Tuure Junnila as dangerously "unreliable" (i.e., anti-Soviet). After a general review of the themes of my inquiry, I asked Ehrnrooth about the issue of the playing of the Soviet card. He responded:

Well…I was most involved in [this] since the leadership, Kekkonen and his people, played this card especially against us. We were the only ones opposing him openly on many actions, starting already in 1956 and up to the very end of his many terms.

I asked Ehrnrooth whether he agreed that after the war Finland had to have a realistic reappraisal of its relationship with the Soviet Union because there was no longer any counter-force against the Soviets. He answered:

Everyone did, even those who voted against this Friendship Pact in 1948, even those had the same goal. They just were critical of the way this card was played. But it was always said by the majority group, the Kekkonen group, that we were against the goal, as you defined it. There is no evidence to prove such a thesis. But it was used in order to play the Soviet card and get rid of the opposition, which they were fairly successful in doing…

In summing up current assessments regarding the 1961-62 Note Crisis and the related issued of playing the Soviet card, readers will have noted that even some critics of President Kekkonen tend to believe that there were perhaps multiple causes of, and motivations for, the note crisis. From Kekkonen's point of view, he was faced with a worrisome challenge to his presidency by essentially the same two forces—the as yet unreconstructed SDP and Conservative Parties—that had challenged him during the Night Frost crisis. That the Honka alliance presented a serious threat to Kekkonen's election to a second term has been questioned by some observers. However, others saw the Honka alliance as having a powerful and broad political base, notwithstanding the lack-luster political reputation of Olavi Honka. In any case, Kekkonen was not willing to leave much to political chance. As Kekkonen loyalist Immonen pointed out to me in our interview, Kekkonen liked to be "200 percent certain."

Given what we know now about Kekkonen's astonishingly intimate relationship with the Soviet embassy, particularly with ambassadors and KGB residents, his ruthless use of power demonstrated time and again during his quarter-century presidency, and his and the Center Party's readiness to repeatedly play the Soviet card during that period, it takes a leap of faith in Kekkonen's dubious forbearance and dedication to democratic norms to believe that he did not have something to do with generating the Soviet note. Qualify how one might Hannu

Rautkallio's findings in the Soviet archives, can anyone really not believe that the documents are plausible and, at least, consistent with what is known of Kekkonen's way of acting?

My own impression is that in all probability the Note Crisis was at least in part a pretext ginned up by President Kekkonen and his closest Soviet contacts. The Berlin crisis, although already defused by Khrushchev's withdrawal of his ultimatum to the NATO allies, provided a sufficiently threatening security context to lend credibility to the note. Certainly, the U.S. embassy at the time took the Note Crisis at face value.

Given what we know now about how Kekkonen operated and given the information coming to light in the Soviet files, it seems to me that the burden of proof now falls on Kekkonen supporters to show that this was not a carefully prepared plan with the aim of assuring that Kekkonen would stay in office for another six years. Certainly, this would help account for why Kekkonen did not rally the country's political forces, including the opposition, behind a position of national solidarity going into his discussions with Khrushchev. Instead he chose to use the event to torpedo the Honka alliance and to present himself as the only person in whom the Soviets would have confidence enough to call off their demand for consultations.

Perhaps the nadir of the entire Kekkonen period was his maneuver in 1972-1973 to assure that he would be continued in office by a special law of the Parliament, as provided for in the constitution, without having to go to the trouble of standing for re-election. As in the 1961 Note Crisis, it was implied that his continuation in office was required in order to maintain Soviet confidence in Finnish leadership necessary to allow Finland to associate itself with the European Economic Community.

When it appeared that there was insufficient support for the special law in the Parliament in December 1972, Kekkonen threatened to resign, whereupon enough members of the Parliament fell into line. Kekkonen then graciously agreed to continue in office, and the law was approved by the necessary five/sixths majority in January 1973.[13] The episode was of major importance because it seemed to indicate a new level of arrogance, a ruthless use of the Soviet foreign policy card, and a lack of even minimal dedication to democratic norms. Kekkonen's actions in this matter lend credence to all of the other concerns normally voiced about him.

In defence of President Kekkonen, former Foreign Minister Väyrynen and others pointed out that some of his actions can be explained by the need to protect against the Social Democrats and others who were trying to pass Kekkonen on his left to develop their own special relationship with Soviet authorities. They have a point. Certainly the "new foreign policy" line put forward by young Social Democratic thinkers in the 1960s and 1970s went a long way in the direction of abandoning Finland's defense self-reliance.

These young Social Democrats went in the opposite direction of Kekkonen's search to avoid situations which might force Finland into consultations under the FCMA Treaty with the Soviet Union in war time. Instead, they seemed to favor Finland's drawing down its defense capabilities and relying on the Soviet Union for protection in war time. Moreover, there was a decidedly anti-NATO, anti-United States edge in many of the attitudes and positions put forward by young Finnish Social Democratic intellectuals in the 1960s-1980s, an attitude which we frequently felt and commented on in the American embassy. To be sure, this attitude was widely shared in the generally leftist mood of those years. Moreover, as noted in Chapter 17, Prime Minister Sorsa's 1985 May Day speech revealed a tendency by some Social Democrats to lash out at the United States on all kinds of issues. Meanwhile, it had been the Kekkonen policy to avoid such forays because they did not pertain to Finland's core interests.

The criticism of the Social Democrats for positioning themselves to develop close relations with Soviet authorities and to make themselves acceptable to President Kekkonen has, as I say, some validity. The same might be said of the Conservative or Coalition Party. However, it all comes back to the climate of the political culture that grew up under President Kekkonen. He had set the standard and the rules of the game. Any Finnish political party or party activist who had aspirations of influencing Finnish political developments—and isn't that why people go into politics in the first place?—had reached the only possible logical conclusion. They had to make their peace with President Kekkonen, and they had to curry favor with the Soviet authorities. They had to convince their "home Russian" Soviet embassy sherpas that they were reliable. It seemed as though a kind of competition developed among some Finnish political leaders to win the contest as "most favored" by the Russians. As Paavo Lipponen said, "there was a big risk of getting corrupted in that system." However, it is not clear that, as Lipponen asserted, his party was able to avoid getting caught up in that system.

KEKKONEN: THE DOMESTIC DIMENSION

The political climate and evolving political culture affecting the foreign dimension during the Kekkonen period also affected the domestic dimension, and anyone who was there could see it and feel it. The special exception law extending Kekkonen's term of office might well have been looked at within the domestic context, although to me it was more revealing for the exquisite subtlety of the indirect use of the Soviet card. The same climate prevailed with regard to the media and self-censorship.

As Max Jakobson noted in our interview, anyone can understand that in postwar Finland, given the precarious situation, a certain need for a sense of national responsibility on the part of the press might have been considered necessary. He observed:

Í always agreed that in a country [in our situation after the war] a responsible press would always have to consider what was in the national interest.

He added, however:

But again, where do you draw the line? I think the line was better drawn at an early stage which was a more dangerous period than in the seventies when the danger really was not there anymore.

For Simopekka Nortamo, self-censorship was a problem that caused grave damage to Finland's image overseas from which Finland has only in recent years been recovering. In 1991 Nortamo wrote a lengthy article in the *Helsingin Sanomat's* Sunday Magazine entitled "Finnish Self-Censorship."[14] Nortamo defined self-censorship broadly as meaning anything that inhibited, in some degree, journalists from playing their role, including examining foreign policy issues from various points of view. He said the main message of his article:

...was that we have to study at an academic level the whole phenomenon. We can't get rid of the memories of those years if we don't come clean...because also the phenomenon of self-censorship was sometimes very often more than people thought, but very often at the same time not the kind of thing that some people thought it was. When I referred to the foreign comment [about Finnish self-censorship] much of it was ill informed. Many articles were very sharp and very right in their purposes, there was everything in between, and some were just out and out crazy...But, I would say that the outside world had very good reason to be suspicious.

Per-Erik Lönnfors observed:

I think self-censorship as it came to be called developed slowly, and with emphasis on 'self.' Self-censorship [was] not censorship. The pressure was open, because Paasikivi openly called up chief editors and said they are writing stupidities. But that was his opinion. He didn't say you change what you write or else. He was trying in a legitimate democratic way to influence the chief editors. In my journalistic career I [was] never pressured; maybe I was too unimportant.

Then later, again with emphasis on 'self,' there was a much more subtle development. Partly towards understanding of the real national interest, partly trying to please Kekkonen or trying to become popular with the elite and the establishment...and in order to get information and to get invitations, and so on. It [was] a mixture of all those things. But during all those years, newspapers could write freely, and they were not pressured. In the self-censorship, I have not heard any arguments about pressure, government pressure against journalists.

When I asked Lönnfors about the press and President Kekkonen, he added:

You should keep separate the self-censorship with respect to Finnish foreign policy and the self-censorship with respect to President Kekkonen. Because this process of accumulating power got so far that it influenced journalists, and they got scared and there was such a network of power descending over the whole country that journalists got involved or they got pressured or subdued.

Lönnfors last remarks also introduced the issue as to whether President Kekkonen stayed too long and accumulated too much power—and the related issue of whether his long tenure encouraged the development of a distorted and subservient political culture in Finland. One of the most remarkable revelations of my interviews was the virtually unanimous view that, whatever good qualities and successes that one might attribute to President Kekkonen, he stayed too long and accumulated and used too much power.

I queried Paavo Lipponen on whether during the Kekkonen period an unhealthy imbalance developed between the power of the presidency and the other branches of government. Lipponen said:

> The fact, the mere length of the period of Kekkonen helped develop this kind of power system for the president, plus his personality and the Soviet card, everything, the nature of the Center Party—because it's a real power machine—and its power-centered way of thinking, all of this resulted in a very unhealthy system.

Lipponen recounted his experience in the autumn of 1975 when he was secretary of the Social Democratic Party group negotiating the formation of a new government. The negotiations were quite lengthy, and then President Kekkonen called all of the negotiating parties to the Presidential Palace and ordered the formation of a government of national emergency. Lipponen said:

> He pretty well ordered that you should form such a government, and he gave the alibi to the Communists...I stood there (I was the last in the line). I remember blood going up into my head because I was so angry that...these people, all the elite, the top democratic politicians, stand and take...orders from this man. It was really degrading.

Mikko Immonen regarding Kekkonen's long tenure in office noted:

> [It was] not only his [Kekkonen's] personal interest in hanging on but also there were real reasons for his continuation. But later on, when the security conference was over, then it was not wise—it would have been better for Kekkonen for his memoirs and for other things if he had refused in 1978. But then who were the politicians who asked him to continue? The Social Democrats! Because they were not ready. I can't blame Kekkonen in 1978.

I queried Harri Holkeri about President Kekkonen's use of power and whether he had arranged matters in such a way so that he basically was the only alternative if Finland were to have peaceful, good neighborly relations with the Soviet Union. Holkeri responded:

> You are right, if you are talking about the institution that formed around Kekkonen. But in that case you are talking about a team, not Kekkonen himself alone. He didn't have anything against being praised and being given that kind of status and importance. But there were people around him—now this I think is a key point in this issue—...who were using his friendship and loyalty for their own benefit...And those people quite often spoke for Kekkonen or behaved as though they had the truth given to them by Kekkonen. And what I'm criticizing Kekkonen for is that [he]...gave this possibility to too many people that they behave on his account. Some of these...persons...were brilliant. I could mention Karjalainen. He was brilliant in his mind, but weak in...character. I do not mean weak...towards the Russians, but weak in a social way.
>
> And so suddenly we had a very extraordinary unofficial political structure in Finland, besides the constitutional one. The master was the same, the president of the country, but there were some people who played together with Kekkonen who were able to keep the power against the public will. That is in my mind to a certain extent what happened during the long...Kekkonen incumbency.
>
> And now, what is my own explanation of...why my party was more than twenty years in opposition?...The reason was not Kekkonen but mostly the team around him, and of course it was power politics on the part of those parties who could get and unite together. But Kekkonen himself tried to tell me many times that it was not his work, believe it or not, he said. I said that I don't know, but I always said the question is not do I believe or not, but [that] we are in opposition, and I said...I'm trying to fight out of that.

When I raised with Kalevi Sorsa President Kekkonen's use of power, he responded:

> Yes, Kekkonen was certainly a president who used his powers to the extreme, maybe a bit over it at times. But not so that one could call him unconstitutional or that he would have had any idea at all to change the constitution. I think he still was a democrat. A very strong personality who believed that things happen best if everybody follows his beliefs.
>
> There was [also] this '*hovi*' or 'court' phenomenon. I don't really think that President Kekkonen wanted to have this court. It only is that when you stay and stay, it just forms around you and finally separates you from what's happening in the society. Again, I think it was a dangerous thing, but it comes from the fact that he had

those twenty-five years in power...[But] everybody reads...what researchers have found in their studies, but it doesn't disturb the people's trust in Kekkonen. People still think...he was good for the country, a great president...

Sorsa added that during his periods as prime minister he did not consider that President Kekkonen had unduly interfered with his responsibilities in running his government's domestic agenda.

I asked Paavo Väyrynen about whether he believed that somehow the Finnish political culture had changed in the sixties and seventies and that the rhetoric about good relations with the Soviet Union overwhelmed the more cynical attitude of the Paasikivi days. He responded:

Well, of course you should not generalize...I believe that Kekkonen all the time had the kind of Paasikivi thinking in his own mind. But many political leaders in Finland probably lost their basis of thinking and started to actually believe in...the rhetoric of foreign policy. It is very difficult to say—because all people were using the same kind of phrases—who really actually believed in them, and who had other ideas behind those phrases. For example, this young generation of the Social Democratic Party was very unrealistic, so to say. But in the Center Party I believe we had a relatively realistic position all the time. Of course inside my party we also had different opinions...[but] at least the people I know used to have realistic positions. And we were sometimes discussing the Soviet threat in a very concrete way, what to do if something would happen...But of course the left-wing Communists had another position, left-wing Social Democrats, maybe also some people in the Center Party.

I proceeded to ask Väyrynen whether the authority built up by President Kekkonen during his twenty-five years in the presidency grew to dwarf the constitutional position of the cabinet, the prime minister and the Parliament. Väyrynen responded:

In the first place you have to remember that powerful politicians in a certain position always over-shadow the other institutions. For example, Paasikivi as prime minister was a very strong leader also in the field of foreign policy. When he became president then he was a strong leader in that position and the prime minister was relatively weak. Kekkonen was strong as prime minister already, and then he became president and was strong in that position. But I agree with the basic argumentation, and that was the Koivisto line, to create a better balance between the institutions."

I asked Väyrynen whether in his view it was unhealthy for so much power to be concentrated for whatever reason and whether he thought that had become a problem in Finland. He said:

Yes, I can agree with that. But I did not support all the ideas of changing the constitution, because I believe that the constitution has been basically good, and Kekkonen was exceptional as a person, and his long period of service was an exception, so that as such the change of president would have created a better balance. And Koivisto, after having suffered as prime minister from this situation, tried to change this situation and balance the powers of the institutions. Now again we can see another trend. Ahtisaari has in some respects used more presidential power than Kekkonen did.

I discussed with Ambassador Jakobson the impact of President Kekkonen's consolidation of political power in Finland. He commented:

Certainly, the logic of Kekkonen's own policy led to a peculiar kind of institution. He was I think, genuinely convinced he was a man who could save Finland and the Finnish system, Finnish democracy and Finnish essential national interests, and that only he could do it. And he became more and more...self-sufficient in every sense of the word. Therefore, anybody who opposed him, criticized him [or] his...policy, was really...going against, something that was in the national interest of the country and had to be opposed, silenced...and so on. Of course it wasn't quite as total as I am describing it, but still this was essentially his way of operating.

...[Also] in order to be able to deal with the Russian leaders—and he very much personalized of course his whole policy—he had to be able to control government policy. He had to be sure that the government he appointed had to be the right kind of government...Again, this became a kind of mechanism that perpetuated his own power. Because he believed very strongly in his personal relationship with the Russian leaders, he had to be able to show them that he could deliver. If he promised something it had to happen, and therefore in order to be able to deliver he had to be sure he could really manipulate the government, and so on.

...This became a kind of system which, as you say, involved gradually the whole political system. But not everybody understood correctly what he was doing and this had a corrupting influence on the political life...Also, it distorted the normal parliamentary life, as you say in your report very well. This was one of the very important negative consequences...

Ambassador Iloniemi commented:

Regarding your question about Kekkonen's period of service, he served far too long in his high office. He was so skillful that he overshadowed others as a player. He used the prerogatives of his high office to the hilt with little respect for the constitutional division of labor between other institutions. He always made sure that no law was broken, but the intent of the law was often ignored. Much of the blame must be put on Finns...who...strengthened Kekkonen's hand by subservience. The Finnish political culture was immature, especially in the 1960s and 1970s...

With respect to your question about competition among politicians to curry favor in Moscow, to some degree that was true. It is important, however, to remember that most politicians could be honest to themselves in making gestures that were well received in Moscow. They believed that it was necessary for the maintenance of good relations with a superpower neighbor. Many sincerely believed that there were no alternatives to an attitude which, at least on the surface of things, was docile to Moscow. The above said is also true with journalists, authors, etc....The Russians made many efforts to include in the bilateral communiqués language which could be interpreted as an endorsement of self-censorship. Some forms of words came close to this. The diplomatic service, fully aware of the damaging effects of such expressions, fought...against these attempts with the acquiescence of Kekkonen.

As noted in U.S. embassy reports cited in Chapter 14, Jan-Magnus Jansson had written in 1980 a controversial article challenging the idea that was beginning to circulate of yet another appeal to President Kekkonen to stand again for the presidency in 1984. I mentioned this to Jansson who recalled:

Yes, I reacted then, and I think I was right to do it. Several people were very shocked at what I wrote. Of course you are right that with the lapse of years it was growing worse and worse...Three normal periods would have been the optimum, I think. Without the exceptional law it would have been so. Of course this would have meant that Kekkonen could not have been the host of the CSCE...[Also] as you remember, our relations with the EEC were at stake. I am told that he had said that the campaign of sixty-eight was so ugly, especially the behavior of the other candidates, Virkkunen and Vennamo, that he wouldn't participate again in such a campaign. But I think it is not an acceptable answer. And I think it was not dependent on the will of the Soviet Union...Of course the Soviet Union wanted Kekkonen to stay, but there would have been a normal election in seventy-four, and I cannot understand why that would not have been enough. The Soviets would have been very sure that he would have been re-elected.

Ambassador Ridgway also recalled the concerns she had felt over the some of the trappings surrounding the Finnish political culture of the 1970s. She commented:

To be a part of the elite, you had to assume a certain view and posture and all the rest. I told you that on the international side I never wanted to encourage the Finns to do something that I wasn't going to be able to support with my country if they got it wrong. But on the domestic side and all the rest, I could never get over it, the extent to which Soviet delegations paraded all over and...we were supposed to believe that somehow in their homes or in the forests...the Finns really knew what the score was and that this was all a charade. I think this was dangerous stuff. The Soviet delegations were always there, and they drank too much, and everybody knew that with a Soviet delegation you had to lock up your daughters and your booze. It was just awful, and I thought all of that was unnecessary.

I mentioned to the ambassador that a number of Finns had used that criterion "was it necessary" in looking back at those years. Ambassador Ridgway cautioned, however:

The Finns would be making a great mistake to say there was something to "Finlandization." Because the context in which the term was created—Franz-Josef Strauss, the German political left problem—the term implied something quite different. And it forgot a few things. Where I always started my discussions of where the Finns were at in their relationship with the Soviet Union, which you touch on only briefly in your paper, is that the Finns in a way have their own deterrence policy, based not necessarily on the current strength of their forces, but on their past willingness to fight the Soviet Union. They have the deaths...the cemeteries and a lost generation of young people, and I think...the Soviet General Staff...[and] military...had to take into account that the Finns would fight.

That was not a part at all of what Franz-Josef Strauss had in mind when he spoke of Finlandization. He may have been looking at self-imposed censorship, at a foreign policy that could get distorted on some kinds of issues, he may have been looking at their political elites, but he certainly did not take into account the fact that Finland had a deterrent policy based on its historic past. I don't know how to say what that's worth. But I think it's worth a lot. If the Soviet Union could get what it wanted, a quiet, non-threatening border, there was no reason at all to march into Finland which was not going to be easy. I never saw any evidence, Ford, when I was there that the capacity of the Finnish Army and the willingness of the Finnish Army had changed since 1939. As far as I was concerned, the Soviet General Staff knew that.

I responded that I completely agreed with that assessment and observed that most Finns today also believe that. I told her that the entire context of my book was how successfully Finland had managed its relationship with the Soviet Union. Finland's proven willingness to fight was a critical factor at decisive points throughout this entire period. The Finns had established the credibility of their willingness to fight. And their performance during the wars had won the Soviet military's admiration and respect, and they always knew that if they were to move into Finland it would be bloody and long. Ambassador Ridgway remarked:

Very long. Six hundred thousand mobilizable troops, it was not going to be a quick one. You could argue that Finland imposed upon itself in some areas, its press policy, distortion of the presidency, the Soviet role in local politics, all the delegations of trade unionists, that all of that were unnecessary and served an ignoble end. But it is not Finlandization, as Strauss intended to be understood.

I told the Ambassador that it was in fact to such phenomena that the Finns are referring when they use the term. I said the Soviet understanding of what the Finns could do constituted a bedrock, stabilizing influence. But this raises the question, how much accommodation with the Soviet Union was necessary?

There may have been nuances of differences between Ambassador Ridgway and myself in our retrospective look at Finland during the Cold War. However, there existed major differences between Ambassador James Goodby and myself in our respective views on the meaning of President Kekkonen's long tenure in office. Some of these differences have been revealed in Chapters 11 and 14 in our different assessments of Kekkonen reported to Washington in 1979 (mine) and 1981 (his). The following dialogue reveals some further differences as well as points of coincidence in our views.

I discussed with Ambassador Goodby the evolution of the political culture in Finland under President Kekkonen where it seemed essential that to prosper politically a Finn had to be on the good side of Kekkonen and the Soviet embassy. He responded:

Yes. If you were good at that relationship you prospered...There were a lot of reasons which went beyond party politics. I do not want to use the word "Finlandized," but there were a lot of Finns who prospered from that relationship. The thing that always troubled me more than anything else was the self-censorship. Because I can understand the catering to the Soviets and the other, but where they went too far was in censoring their own newspapers and media...And the politicians would warn that you shouldn't do this, you shouldn't say that. It was wrong. That was unhealthy, in my opinion.

I commented that another unhealthy dimension was letting the Soviets into the Finnish political game. The ambassador said:

Well, I guess you can make that evaluation, but I can kind of understand the playing of the Soviet card. I mean people tend to do that when you are up against a big neighbor. But the part I couldn't understand was self-censorship. That I would put at the top of the sins of that period.

I told Ambassador Goodby that I didn't know exactly how I would rank order the "sins of that period" as Goodby had put it.

But I was disturbed by the using of the argument—as was done by Kekkonen and people around him—that such and such a leader or party is not reliable on foreign policy grounds and that only Kekkonen and the Center Party could take care of the relationship with the Soviet Union. Goodby countered:

Well, that's right, but politicians are that way. Any politician is that way. That I consider as part of the game. If you can stand up and say, look Russia is important to us, it takes twenty-five percent of our trade, we get no protection from the West, we can count on nothing from that quarter, look what happened. And I can deal with them better than anybody else, if you don't support me the country will go to hell. If I were in that position, I probably would say the same thing. So, that I can understand.

The problem was, I noted, that such an approach divided Finns into good Finns and bad Finns, sometimes over very minor differences of views on how to handle foreign policy. I argued that coming out of the wars Finland had made a fundamental re-evaluation of its position in the world, which was understood and generally accepted by all serious elements of Finland's political structure. But both Mannerheim and Paasikivi had a very clear division in their minds which they expressed between doing everything reasonable to have a good relationship with the Soviet Union, and crossing beyond that to begin to internalize the liturgy of good neighborly relations with the Soviet Union. I suggested that President Kekkonen had blurred that line. Ambassador Goodby responded:

Well, that's right. But again, if somebody else had been in office they probably would have done the same thing.

I observed, however, that in fact this is something that Paasikivi had not done and Koivisto did not do. Goodby said that when he arrived in Finland as Ambassador in 1980:

Our whole preoccupation at that time was over Afghanistan, and my very first conversation when I presented my credentials to President Kekkonen was about three/quarters on Afghanistan. Finally, the President broke it off by saying we are not here to discuss that. And that was the end of that. And our relationship really wasn't all that cordial. I didn't see him very much, but I did make a point of seeing him every six months. I always had a long substantive agenda that I wanted to go over. I can't say that his responses made much sense to me, but still. I think you need to look at the politics of it. As you pointed out, the President needed to have some sort of card to offset the Social Democrats...I give Koivisto credit as an outstanding man, but he didn't need that at that time, because the politics of it were different. I took his point on the times and the politics being different and argued that nevertheless I felt there were some deep differences in personalities and approaches between these two men. President Kekkonen clearly was a man who thrived on power and enjoyed the use of power. Ambassador Goodby said:

Yes he did, and furthermore, I have to say I think he was one of those who really loved conniving with the Russians.

Ambassador Goodby asked me if it was my thesis that Kekkonen was largely responsible for Finlandization. I responded that I was trying at that point (August 1995) to keep an open mind but was leaning to the view that under Kekkonen a culture developed for which he has to accept most of the responsibility. Ambassador Goodby responded:

I guess I would come to a somewhat different conclusion, namely that the objective circumstances were such that such a culture developed, and there is no question that it did. But it probably would have developed anyway. I guess the only difference between us is that I would argue that was inevitable under the circumstances, and you would argue that Kekkonen had a lot to do with fostering it. You're probably right...[In any case] he didn't do anything to resist it.

To sum up my assessment of the domestic dimensions of the Kekkonen legacy, I tend to agree with President Kekkonen's critics, notwithstanding some of the points of views put forward by Kekkonen defenders and by Ambassador Goodby. In my opinion President Kekkonen's virtual domination of the Finnish political scene grossly distorted the balance of constitutional power in Finland and in some ways came close to making a mockery of Finland's democratic institutions. Some of Kekkonen's strongest supporters are prepared now to go at least part way down that road of analysis.

Even here, however, it is not an unmixed picture. For example, Koivisto and Sorsa, two prime ministers who served under President Kekkonen, have stated that during their periods they did not feel that Kekkonen overstepped the boundaries of interfering inappropriately with their governments, at least on day-to-day matters.

Nevertheless, while observers may not have been in complete agreement on how it happened and on how unhealthy it was, not a single interviewee would argue that this aspect of the Kekkonen era was a precedent that ought to be repeated. That is to say, I know of no Finn who would willingly see another Finnish president exercise as much power as did President Kekkonen. As happened in the United States after Franklin Delano Roosevelt's election to four four-year terms, the reaction in Finland as in the United States was "never again."

The beginning of the end of the "self-Finlandization" period— as some have called it—may have been in 1978 when soundings to once again continue President Kekkonen in office through an exceptions law as in 1973 foundered owing to insufficient support in the Parliament. The first indication that the old regime was losing its grip was when Prime Minister Koivisto refused to step down in the spring of 1981 despite pressure from a rapidly aging President Kekkonen and his "court" followers. Following one more unsuccessful effort by Center Party leaders on behalf of President Kekkonen in early September 1981 to force Koivisto out as prime minister, a seriously incapacitated Kekkonen had to withdraw on sick leave in September and submit his resignation as president on October 26, 1981. The Kekkonen era was over.

Ambassador Goodby and Ambassador Jakobson both in their own way touched on the age-old issue of, do the times make the man or does the man make the times? Jakobson concluded that there was a definite change in the way that Kekkonen dealt with the Soviets compared to Paasikivi. Goodby expressed his opinion that Kekkonen was just acting the way that any political leader would have acted in playing upon his effectiveness in dealing with the Soviets and using the Soviet card for domestic political purposes. My answer to Ambassador Goodby was that Kekkonen's predecessor did not play it that way—and neither did his successor. Also, treating the Kekkonen phenomenon as "just politics" overlooks the damage done to the Finnish political culture while that game was being played.

Before leaving the Kekkonen era, I believe it is instructive to return to Dr. Suomi's comments and those sprinkled through his biography of President Kekkonen. It seems to me that what Suomi is saying and writing is quite reminiscent of the times and of the political culture that I am exploring in this book. Apparently his position is that any diplomat or diplomatic report, British or American, or any researcher who is not in agreement with what Suomi believes is the correct interpretation of Finnish events during the Kekkonen period is inept, uninformed, poorly prepared or otherwise unqualified and should be ignored.

To me this attitude parallels the tendency during that period to brand any Finn who didn't toe the Kekkonen Line as, by definition, "unreliable" and not a "good Finn." The same tendency, it seems, was applied to foreign diplomats. You apparently had to be a Swede or a KGB agent to escape censure.

In his interview, Dr. Suomi seemed to be trying to discount U.S. diplomatic reporting on Finland as incompetent. He cited the U.S. habit of sending inexperienced political ambassadors, a point with which I agree. But also he said that in general our contacts were one-sided. When I contested that observation by pointing out the wide range of our contacts, he shifted his argument. It was not so much that we didn't have broad contacts, but that our contacts were mostly political and that Finland's foreign policy was far too subtle for most Finnish politicians to understand. One had to deal with the true practitioners of Finland's foreign policy, and he indicated that American diplomats lacked such contacts.

Well, if there was any institution with which the U.S. embassy had deep and constant contact, it was with the Finnish Foreign Ministry and with President Kekkonen's foreign policy advisors. In Chapter 6, I indicated my extensive Foreign Ministry contacts and can in fact point to perhaps a dozen meetings and luncheons with Dr. Suomi himself during my two Finland assignments. And my predecessors and successors maintained more or less similar levels of contacts. If Finnish diplomats did not level with us or, as in the case of the Ustinov incident, deliberately misled us, that speaks more to the Kekkonen approach to his management of foreign policy than to the quality of American diplomats.

In another exercise in ground-shifting, Suomi first praised Soviet (and Swedish) embassy representatives as having the best contacts, being the best informed and producing "the best material." Then, however, he discounted the "objectivity" of Soviet embassy reports and strongly criticized the Finnish researcher who discovered the reports in Soviet archives.

It seems as if President Kekkonen and Dr. Suomi could not accept as conceivable that a country like the United States, with its world-wide interests and its free-world and NATO leadership responsibilities, might have had legitimate cause for questioning any Finnish actions or positions. For Suomi, and apparently for Kekkonen, failure by American diplomats to duly record the unwavering infallibility of President Kekkonen's policies was clear evidence of American incompetence. Just a bunch of "dolts" (to quote Suomi's citation of Kekkonen) of which the United States had a plentiful supply.

One does indeed wonder, as Ambassador Goodby asked in our interview, did the Finns on the Kekkonen team ever ask themselves about the obvious disparity in the way Soviet and Western diplomats were treated? Or did they just not care?

26

The Koivisto Legacy: How Much Continuity and How Much Change?

Let us turn now to some retrospective observations and assessments regarding Mauno Koivisto's presidency. It is useful also to divide this examination between the foreign and domestic dimensions, using the same criteria as with our look at the Kekkonen period and again recognize the overlap between the two dimensions.

KOIVISTO: THE FOREIGN DIMENSION

Foreign Policy and Security Continuity
I have already suggested my general conclusion that as far as foreign policy is concerned. President Koivisto provided strong continuity to Finland's well-trod foreign policy line, with all of the minuses and pluses that such continuity implies. President Koivisto's recent book *Historian Tekijat,* later published in English as W*itness to History,* provides rich evidence of Finland's foreign policy continuity under his leadership.

It was a fascinating coincidence that Mauno Koivisto and George Bush were each at the peak—or in Bush's case often near the peak—of their respective national power for twelve years.

Koivisto for twelve years was president of Finland (1982-1994) and Bush served eight years as vice president and four years as president (1980-1992). During a good part of their ten-year overlapping period, Mauno Koivisto and George Bush engaged in extensive correspondence and they also had the opportunity at various times to meet face-to-face.

It was a revelation to me when I learned from President Koivisto's book that he had carried on such extensive correspondence with Bush. As the deputy chief of mission in Helsinki 1984-86 and as director of the office of Northern European affairs 1986-88, I was unaware of the extent and depth of their correspondence. President Koivisto's observations of events as they occurred and his correspondence with George Bush provide contemporary insights into Finnish perceptions of key international events, particularly developments in the East-West dialogue.

Koivisto indicates that his relationship with George Bush began when the vice president traveled to Finland in August 1983. President Koivisto used the occasion of his first meeting with Bush to outline Finland's view of its position coming out of World War II and to explain Finland's contemporary situation in the early 1980s. He emphasized Finland's belief that it should take care of its own problems and avoid leaving its problems for others to solve. Finland's own problems were under normal circumstances relatively small: the worst conflicts were those south of Finland, although serious confrontations between East and West could well weaken Finland's situation. Koivisto told Bush:

> The ongoing arms build-up and particularly the new missiles to be deployed in Europe do not in our view increase security, but instead reduce it. The nuclear powers already have more destructive power than they need.[15]

This was clearly a reference to the NATO "two-track decision" of 1979 that, unless the Soviets agreed in negotiations to withdraw the intermediate range SS-20 missiles which it had deployed in Europe beginning in the 1970s, NATO would proceed to deploy a similar number of countervailing intermediate range missiles. It was the NATO conviction that the Soviet SS-20 deployments had upset the balance of nuclear missiles in Europe. This position was central to NATO's determination to restore the balance of nuclear forces in Europe, preferably at the lower "track" level that would result from Soviet withdrawal of its SS-20s. It was NATO's position in the face of Soviet counter-arguments and protests from "peace groups" in Europe and the United States that to "freeze" nuclear weapons at their existing levels would lock in a Soviet advantage in nuclear missiles in Europe, a situation which NATO was determined to prevent.

After describing candidly Juri Andropov's deteriorating health condition, President Koivisto related to Bush that Andropov had assured him of his readiness to reach agreement to end the ongoing nuclear arms race as well as his determination to answer any challenge. Koivisto noted that when he had criticized the nuclear powers, including the United States, for going ever-further in the arms race, Bush responded by having one of his aides hand to Koivisto a paper which showed how the missile weapons balance had developed 1977-83. In this assessment, the number of Soviet Union missiles had grown, but NATO's numbers had remained constant. Koivisto observes in his book:

> According to the notes made at the discussion I replied politely that all balance calculations were fraught with the problem that there were already too many nuclear weapons in the world and that the adoption of any single missile increased nobody's security. According to my own recollection I was not that polite, but having glanced at the pamphlet handed to me by Bush, I said that this was the kind of propaganda material I did not yet have in my possession and that I would read it with great interest.[16]

Koivisto records that Bush laughed off his remark about "propaganda material," which Koivisto himself considered as not being particularly polite and did not return to the matter. However, it can be noted in *Historian Tekijat/Witness to History* that time and again the pattern would be repeated in the correspondence and meetings between Koivisto and Bush, particularly during the first years when at issue were nuclear arms negotiations between the Soviet Union and the United States. Koivisto would convey to Bush his own views or his understanding of Soviet views on arms control issues (which views were usually quite similar) and Bush would politely point out U.S. and NATO positions to a skeptical Koivisto.

In September 1983, Koivisto traveled to the U.S. on an official bilateral visit and to address the United Nations General Assembly. Before the visit he had decided that in his speech before the U.N. he would change Finland's official position on the "first use of nuclear weapons." The Soviet Union, its Warsaw Pact allies and many neutral and non-aligned countries had long sought a United Nations resolution banning the first use of nuclear weapons. Given the preponderant strength of the Soviet Union in conventional forces, it had long been a central strategic and tactical NATO position that the potential enemy should not have prior assurances from NATO that the latter would not be willing to use nuclear weapons. NATO wanted that question to be uncertain in the minds of Soviet military planners. As Koivisto notes, Finland had hitherto stayed out of that discussion because the superpowers were in disagreement over the issue. Koivisto's new policy meant that on another issue of importance to NATO, the Government of Finland decided for its own reasons to join the Soviet Union on the other side of the issue.

In Washington, Koivisto met with both Vice President Bush and President Reagan. Koivisto noted that before going to Washington he had received greetings from Moscow, and that Moscow had indicated it would be interested in receiving an evaluation as to whether the United States was seriously interested in trying to reach agreements with the Soviet Union in the negotiations under way. However, Koivisto states in his book that:

> I gained the impression that the United States was not seriously seeking mutual understanding with the Soviet Union.[17]

Therefore, President Koivisto after returning to Helsinki from the United States decided upon reflection not to send any message to Andropov, recording in his book that:

> Maybe they did not expect one, and if they did, and one did not arrive, they would draw the correct conclusion that no responsiveness was to be expected from the United States on the questions in dispute.[18]

Meanwhile on November 23, 1983, the United States, after failure to reach agreement with the Soviet Union on the INF issue, deployed its first intermediate range missiles in Europe in fulfillment of the timetable of the NATO two-track decision. The Soviets walked out of the talks. Koivisto records in his book that

Viktor Vladimirov—the KGB resident in Helsinki—called on him. He stressed to Koivisto that the neutral countries, Finland, Sweden and Austria, could play an important role in getting the talks underway again, based on a formula—under which the Soviets would have withdrawn some of their missiles from Europe—unofficially discussed between Soviet and American negotiators in Geneva. Vladimirov hoped that Finland would unofficially explore the idea with others, hoping also that it would not be pointed out that the exploration was at the Soviets' initiative.

On November 29, Koivisto wrote what was apparently his first letter to George Bush, stressing how pleasant and fruitful their meetings over the past year had been. He said that:

My letter concerns intermediate-range nuclear forces in Europe. The Soviets did as they said they would do. They behaved now just as they said they would behave. As a result we shall have a lot more missiles and warheads in Europe, and heaven knows where this development one day will end. It looks as though suitable conditions for the re-initiation of negotiations will not exist for a long time. When the Soviet Union says that they will not negotiate after the deployment of new missiles has begun, it means that they are unwilling to discuss the matter in any forum. It is argued that the Soviet Union will in any case return to the negotiating table. However, it looks as though any reference to such an argument tends to be regarded by the Soviets as disturbing or even poisoning the atmosphere.[19]

Noting that the United States and NATO wanted to continue negotiations at the same time that they are deploying missiles, and that the Soviet Union was ready to negotiate only if no additional missiles are deployed in Western Europe, President Koivisto floated the Vladimirov idea. He suggested that the only other option might be an exchange of views which, however, would not be called "negotiations." Koivisto said that, while there was not much Finland could do, he nevertheless offered his good offices in such case as they might be helpful. He then referred directly to the informal "park bench" negotiations between Paul Nitze and his Soviet counterpart, that Valdimirov had mentioned, as offering a possible way out of the impasse.

Bush answered the letter and agreed to send to Helsinki, as Koivisto had requested, a State Department expert who met with Koivisto and senior Finnish foreign policy officials to explain the U.S. position. In the meantime, President Koivisto had also discussed his initiative with a representative of the Swedish Foreign Ministry. Koivisto records that after seeing the U.S. official, he again met with Vladimirov who indicated the Soviet Union would maintain its position that the negotiations would not go forward.

Vladimirov called once again on President Koivisto on February 4, 1984 after returning from Moscow. The president records that Vladimirov said the Soviet Union would never return to the START arms negotiations and was prepared to walk out of the Vienna conventional weapons negotiations if the West tried to use those talks for propaganda purposes. Vladimirov told President Koivisto that if NATO's INF deployments were frozen, the various arms negotiations could go forward. Vladimirov told Koivisto that in the matter of arms control questions, the Soviet Union:

...counted the peace movement, the international Social Democratic movement and the neutral and non-aligned countries as the Soviet Union's allies.[20]

After the meeting with Vladimirov, President Koivisto once again wrote a letter, February 7, to Vice President Bush. He again passed along his assessment:

The impression that I have been able to form is the following: The Soviet Union will not return to the INF negotiations, unless their well-known conditions are met...

President Koivisto concluded that:

New negotiations on the nuclear weapons in Europe can therefore evidently be undertaken only at such a time when the present deployment programs have been completed–or the deployment has been discontinued. As I have understood the program on the NATO side will take at least another four years, and no information is available about the duration of the Soviet deployment program, a long period of deadlock and tension seems to lie ahead. The only way to move faster to a new starting point could perhaps be a halting of further deployment at an earlier stage. I am aware of the problems inherent in such a decision, but I wanted to mention it as a possible subject for further consideration and exchange of views.[21]

And thus proceeded the correspondence between Koivisto and Bush. It is clear throughout the meetings and correspondence between Koivisto and Bush that the latter highly valued their exchanges of information. However, time after time, as is recorded in Koivisto's book, he would advise Bush, as he did once again on May 22, 1984, that:

...I regret very much that a long period of deadlock seems to be ahead, unless a new starting-point could be found. In the foreseeable future, and however difficult to achieve, it seems to me that the necessary first steps would have to include a freeze on further new deployments of nuclear weapons.[22]

Later, relations began to improve between the United States and the Soviet Union after the rise of Gorbachev. Despite President Koivisto's frequently expressed concerns, the Soviets had come back to the negotiating table without NATO's making the unilateral concessions.

General Secretary Gorbachev in an October 19, 1985, letter to President Koivisto before the former's December summit meeting with Reagan, expressed the hope that it would be possible to reach agreement on intermediate range missiles without linking it to strategic and space weapons. Gorbachev said the Soviets had withdrawn a part of their SS-20 missiles and hoped this would lead to a response from the United States. Koivisto wrote Gorbachev November 25 congratulating him for the preceding week's summit meeting in Geneva. He said the meeting had led to an improvement in the international atmosphere and raised hopes for the lessening of world tension. Koivisto expressed support for Gorbachev's positions in Geneva:

We agree with you that the arms race should be prevented in space and stopped on earth. Reduction of the nuclear arsenals by 50 per cent as proposed by you and approved in principle at the Geneva meeting has the full support of the Finnish government. The same applies to the idea of reaching agreement on the speedy reduction of intermediate-range nuclear forces that have an immediate relevance for security in Europe.[23]

Koivisto expressed Finland's concerns over cruise missiles and support for the total elimination of nuclear weapons. He praised Gorbachev for his announcement of a temporary unilateral Soviet moratorium on nuclear testing.

On December 16, 1985, President Koivisto wrote Vice President Bush evaluating the same Geneva summit meeting. Describing his letter, he said he had asked whether:

Could *détente* continue even without progress in disarmament? I doubted that security would be improved merely by reducing a hundred-fold overkill capacity of nuclear weapons to a fifty-fold overkill capacity. I expressed skepticism about the clarity and consistency of American thinking, and was critical of the bellicose attitude over star wars.[24]

It is interesting that while only a few weeks earlier he had praised Gorbachev for the agreed objective of a 50 percent reduction of nuclear weapons, Koivisto wrote Bush that he doubted such a reduction would really increase international security. Yet he also made clear to Bush that he "warmly supported even small steps." Undiscouraged that events had proved his repeated predictions that the Soviets would never return to the negotiating table unless the United States made concessions on INF had been wrong, President Koivisto now criticized not only the United States' strategic defense initiative but also the logic and clarity of U.S. thinking on arms control matters.

In the embassy we used to complain sometimes about the tendency of some Finns and other Europeans to place the United States and the Soviet Union on the same "moral equivalence" plane, an "even-handedness" which we thought unfair to the West. It appears from President Koivisto's comments that in his mind the United States had a ways to go before it could rise to the moral level of the Soviet Union on nuclear weapons issues.

Vice President Bush responded on January 6, 1986, to President Koivisto's letter, once again patiently explaining the U.S. position on these issues and expressing confidence that the U.S. and USSR positions were coming steadily closer.

Immediately after describing the above exchange of letters with Vice President Bush, President Koivisto proceeds in his book to praise a new Gorbachev peace initiative:

> Mikhail Gorbachev sought to get arms negotiations moving forward by putting forward January 15, 1986 an arms reduction proposal. I commented on the proposal in my speech opening Parliament February 5: "From Finland's perspective the initiative is more than welcome."

Koivisto wrote Gorbachev on March 14, 1986, to congratulate him on being reelected party secretary in which "I encouraged him to continue his efforts to reach arms agreements." In his letter Koivisto stated *inter alia* that:

> I could not be more of the same view when you said: "we know only too well our country's responsibility for the future of peace, and therefore we cannot be of the opinion of those who would want to force mankind to accommodate to the nuclear threat and arms race."[25]

President Koivisto's books *Historian Tekijat/Witness to History* do not mention any further correspondence between Koivisto and Bush (except for an exchange of letters over the Rauma Repola submersible problem mentioned above) until September 1989. In between there had been several visits by George Shultz to Finland and the presidential visit of President Reagan in May 1988. The September 19, 1989, letter was the first correspondence since Bush had become president. President Koivisto offered his observations on developments in Eastern Europe and the Baltic states. In future letters, the two presidents exchanged views on further developments in Eastern Europe and the Soviet Union. By now, the advocacy tone in Koivisto's letters had substantially diminished, and the letters were primarily exchanges of information apparently much appreciated on both sides.

The next contact between Bush and Koivisto took place at the Helsinki summit meeting between Bush and Gorbachev held September 9, 1990. The summit offered further opportunities for discussions by Koivisto with both Bush and Gorbachev. The communiqué issued after the summit meeting pleased President Koivisto:

It said that a peaceful international order was not possible if larger states could swallow up their smaller neighbors, and Iraq was asked to withdraw unconditionally from Kuwait, permit the return of the Kuwaiti government to power, and release all hostages in Iraq and Kuwait. The declaration stressed the role of the United Nations and supported its resolutions on Iraq. If we ourselves had proposed or written the draft, it could hardly have been any different.[26]

Koivisto and Bush met once again, on May 6-8, 1991, when Koivisto made a working visit to Washington where they again compared notes on worrisome developments in the Soviet Union. They also discussed the Baltic nations:

Bush asked if the Soviet Union could grant them full independence, and I replied by referring to the ongoing debate in the Soviet Union on the meaning of sovereignty and said that the new union treaty was supposed to define the limits of the separation of powers. Externally, the independence question looked insoluble, because the Balts wanted international negotiations, and the Soviet Union insisted on the binding force of its constitution. Nevertheless, I said that I did not believe a negotiated settlement was impossible.[27]

The final communications between George Bush and Mauno Koivisto took place after President Bush lost the November 1992 election. Koivisto reports that he received "two warm-hearted letters" in January and February 1993 from Bush in which the latter expressed his appreciation for the dialogue the two had carried on over the years. Koivisto also made clear that he valued his good relationship with Bush. With the election of Clinton, it was the end of the Reagan/Bush/Koivisto chapter in the continuing saga of relations between the United States and Finland.

My own reading of the relationship was that it was a valuable one for both sides. It was also a measure of Bush's sincere interest in foreign affairs and dedication to building a better world, as well as to his lifelong habit of keeping track of important people and maintaining a world wide network of contacts. For Koivisto, it was obvious that the relationship with the vice president, who later became president, offered a unique opportunity to be connected to both of the super powers at a level where he might exercise some influence or at least provide advice and information.

It is clear from the foregoing that during the first few years—at least until 1986—the positions President Koivisto put forward to George Bush, particularly on delicate arms issues in negotiation between the Soviet Union and the United States, often seemed to parallel the positions of the Soviet Union. His book also reveals that on several occasions these policy suggestions followed closely meetings with the KGB resident of the Soviet embassy in Helsinki, Viktor Vladimirov (who was succeeded by Felix Karasev with whom President Koivisto also frequently met).[28]

There was of course nothing wrong with Koivisto assisting the two super powers in communicating positions to one another. Indeed, President Bush seems clearly to have understood that President Koivisto had special insights into the Soviet scene and valued the relationship even more for that fact.

However, a close reading of Koivisto's letters shows that he almost invariably gave more credence to Soviet disarmament positions than he did to NATO and United States positions even when the latter were conveyed to him by senior U.S. officials including Bush. This was particularly true on the INF issue.

Without the United States making the concessions advised by President Koivisto, agreement was ultimately reached contrary to his predictions. One wonders what went through the ever-gracious George Bush's mind upon receiving yet another missive from President Koivisto on why the United States should give up its position on intermediate range missile deployments!

A careful reader might also discern some significant nuances of difference in the tone of the president's letters to Bush—in the early years—compared to the tone of his messages to General Secretary Gorbachev. It almost appears that the Soviet Union was seen to be the real moral force for disarmament, and it was the policies of the United States and NATO that were seen to be threatening the world with nuclear extinction through their "unclear and illogical" thinking.

As major arms agreement were reached and as Soviet leaders became preoccupied with their growing internal problems, the character of the dialogue between the United States and the Soviet Union changed, and so did the nature of the dialogue between the United States and Finland. What had always been a useful and productive relationship, despite the points just made above, became even more fruitful as Koivisto and Bush discussed the declining Soviet economy and the plight of Eastern Europe and the Baltics. Again there can be no doubt, as evidenced by Bush's January and February 1993 letters to Koivisto, that Bush was grateful to the Finnish president for their long and cordial dialogue.

I believe the citations of examples from the Koivisto/Bush correspondence amply support my conclusion that Koivisto's foreign policy positions until deep into his presidency continued the Kekkonen and Paasikivi policy of reflecting extreme sensitivity to the foreign and security policy positions of the Soviet Union.

It is important to note, however, that in 1990 President Koivisto seized the initiative unilaterally to re-interpret drastically the 1947 Paris Peace Treaty and to in effect revoke the 1948 FCMA Treaty with the Soviet Union. These steps marked for all intents and purposes the end of the postwar era for Finland, and Koivisto wisely and courageously took the appropriate actions. Notwithstanding the weakened state of the Soviet Union, Koivisto prudently continued a cautious policy regarding the movement of the Baltic states towards independence until after it was recognized by the new leader in Moscow, President of Russia Boris Yeltsin, in August 1992. I liked Koivisto's laconic explanation of why he was behind the curve on developments in the Baltic: "They had better information than I on what was coming."[29]

In any case Koivisto was in good company in his caution. His good friend George Bush was also reluctant to get out in front of Moscow and Soviet President Mikhail Gorbachev with whom so much had been accomplished in the international arena.

Playing the Soviet Card

If there was continuity from Kekkonen to Koivisto in the foreign policy position-taking, I share the view proffered by most of the persons whom I interviewed that as far as permitting the Soviets to meddle in Finland's domestic political affairs and playing the Soviet card, there was a dramatic difference between the two men.

From the beginning it was evident that Koivisto brought a new approach to relations with the Soviet Union insofar as Finnish domestic politics were concerned. It certainly helped when it was made clear by the Soviets that Koivisto was not the man they preferred for the presidency. That honor was reserved for Ahti Karjalainen. Koivisto writes that he had a discussion about this with KGB resident officer, Viktor Vladimirov, who had returned on assignment to Helsinki:

> Vladimirov told me in the fall of 1981 in his own unique manner that he had not been sent to oppose my becoming president but rather to promote Karjalainen's selection.[30]

Already as prime minister in the spring of 1981, Koivisto had been asked "by some unfriendly journalists" about his relationship with the Soviet Union. As Koivisto recounted it: "I answered that there was not much to brag about."[31]

The Finns loved that answer, particularly since so many other Finnish political leaders were falling all over themselves to curry favor with the Soviets. The contrast was refreshing. As a young man, Koivisto had fought against the Soviet Union during the Continuation War, spending many months in units operating behind Soviet lines. He didn't have to talk about it—Finns knew. Mauno Koivisto's 1982 overwhelming election victory, a presidential candidate known not to be Moscow's favorite, was a message in and of itself. It helped to create a climate in which it was obvious that the Soviet Union would be expected to keep its distance from Finland's internal affairs.

In *Historian Tekijat,* Koivisto recounts various situations in which he was either approached by Soviet representatives or took measures that he believed warranted informing the Soviets about his plans. Of these occasions, two involved Soviet efforts to get the president involved on behalf of the embattled Stalinist minority wing of the Finnish Communist Party. The Soviet's alleged in each case that the struggle within the SKP was putting Finnish/Soviet relations at risk. In both incidents Koivisto conveyed his extreme annoyance, even anger, that he as the president of the Republic who maintained himself above partisan political questions should be approached on such an issue. After each incident Koivisto did speak with SKP Chairman Arvo Aalto—who had been singled out for criticism by the Soviets—about the Soviet concerns, even expressing annoyance that problems within the SKP were creating pressures on him from the Soviets. However, on both occasions it must have been clear to the Soviets that Koivisto was not going to involve himself on Soviet behalf in the internal affairs of the SKP.[32]

I am unaware of any instance where a Finnish political figure felt that Koivisto had used the "Soviet card" as an instrument to bolster his own position domestically, although there were efforts by others to use the card against him, particularly during the preview to the 1982 presidential elections. Several of the Finns whom I interviewed offered comments on the contrast between Kekkonen and Koivisto in the matter of playing the "Soviet card."

Pertti Salolainen had some very strong views about how the Conservative (National Coalition) Party had been victimized by the Soviet card during the Kekkonen period:

The Conservative Party was the one which was taken as a scapegoat, which had to suffer, so that the sun would look brighter...somebody had to be criminalized. And we were in the Conservative Party playing that role...Even the journalists...went along with this, even the *Helsingin*

Sanomat journalists who wrote [about] the "right-wingers" in the Conservative Party, who now at this moment turn out to be absolutely correct in their assessment, like Junnila and others. I mean what really happened was that, as some researchers have shown, the term "Finlandization" was in a sense very correct because the Russians and the KGB and the Russian sources via East Germany even financed the Center Party in internal struggles and Finnish presidential campaigns... Kekkonen and the K-Line went too far...

But what...the whole atmosphere led to...[was] that inside every Finnish party, there were people dealing with *Tehtaankatu* [Soviet Embassy], who were treated more favorably. And the big victory was if you were invited for the revolution cocktail party in the embassy. If you were seen there, then everybody knew that you were okay, you were in their good books. You had been either strong or subservient enough. But everybody had their "home Russian" (contact assigned by the Soviet Embassy). For instance I had my home Russian with whom I was discussing very frequently...But the question was, how you discussed with him, where you drew the line.

I suggested to Salolainen that Koivisto had not changed Finnish foreign policy and that he was conscious of the Soviet presence without, however, letting it get into Finnish politics. Salolainen noted: "Without using it internally. That was the difference between him and Kekkonen."

In my discussion with *Helsingin Sanomat* columnist Olli Kivinen, he also contrasted the Kekkonen and Koivisto periods. Regarding the Kekkonen period Kivinen observed:

The great unanswered question of course in dealing with President Kekkonen, who was the dominant figure, was why did we in many instances fall deeper under Soviet influence during the times in the sixties and seventies when things were basically already much easier than during President Paasikivi's time. That of course is the unanswered question. My answer—my theory, which of course is not proved at all by events then, but what I think did happen—was that in my opinion Kekkonen could play the game. But of course he played the game also for his own benefit and to strengthen his own position.

But then there were other politicians, small time politicians, in many parties who wanted to use this foreign policy line to benefit themselves and to attack others. And, I think their little thing got out of hand more or less, especially in the seventies, which I think can be considered to be sort of the low point of the whole history, because in all theory we should not have been in a situation where—and this is what I really disliked about that era—*Tehtaankatu* was given a veto right over the formation of governments in this country. That went by far too deep and...I think the explanation why perhaps was the personality factor which was seen quite visibly there.

Things changed when Koivisto became president. The whole era changed: the air changed and the whole situation changed. And the influence of the Russians, although the Soviet Union was still very much in existence, certainly did diminish. It didn't disappear of course overnight in the early eighties, but it clearly changed, while the general direction of the Soviet policy did not change.

I asked Kivinen whether he thought that Paasikivi and Koivisto drew the line on Soviet influence at a different place than Kekkonen. He responded:

I think you are absolutely right in that. Neither of them started using the Soviet card. On the contrary, they were very careful not to do that, and Koivisto for instance has made it absolutely clear time and time again that he wasn't willing. Of course, he couldn't change the line immediately overnight, but the general tone of the policies was exactly on that level, your first point on Finnish/Soviet relations, they went on their steady road, but what really changed was the use of these policies for personal benefits and of course, some of the Center Party people, some of the Conservative Party people did use it even after that. So it died down rather slowly, but it did die away. And of course it finally ended only after the collapse of the Soviet Union. It started to fall to pieces with the new policies of Gorbachev...Koivisto was not a gamesman, he played a completely different game. I've never been anti-Kekkonen. I think he did a good job in this first field that you mentioned, general foreign policy, but I did not like his way here at home.

Jukka Tarkka, author, columnist, member of Parliament and a leader of the Young Finns political party, expressed similar views in our discussion:

I think that from an internal point of Finnish policies the most dangerous time was the seventies when the Soviet Union had a very strong hold on Finnish internal affairs...Almost all important Finnish politicians were very submissive...helpful and very cooperative with the Soviet officials. From that perspective, the Soviets had infiltrated the Finnish society very deeply and on a very broad scope. That threat was more dangerous, because that was a mental threat, a question of national morale and national identity. It was very dangerous.

President Kekkonen played that card very effectively. He quite ruthlessly used foreign policy as a tool for his domestic policies. This was the most negative point about President Kekkonen's work as a statesman. Of course, he was a great statesman and he served the country very well, but in this regard he was wrong and it was very dangerous. [The effect] can be felt even now. It became part of our political culture. This is one of those points why we Young Finns think we need a new political culture; we must get rid of that kind of thinking. But I am afraid it will be a very slow process, because it is more or less a question of generations.

I asked political scientist and former Docent at Turku University, George Maude, about the difference between Presidents Kekkonen and Koivisto with respect to the Soviets' mixing into internal Finnish affairs. He commented:

Well, if I start with Koivisto, obviously the fact that he was elected at all, because he wasn't the boy they wanted, and the fact that the Center Party didn't even pick the boy that they [the Russians] wanted—in spite of Väyrynen's policy of supporting Karjalainen, the Soviet-backed candidate—can be interpreted in two ways. First, that Väyrynen played this Finlandization card and the Soviet Union was willing to go along with this as far as we know, and the stuff that is coming out seems fairly reliable...But...the system in Finland simply wasn't having it, so a change was already occurring there before the breakup of the Soviet Union. I think the election of Koivisto was a very healthy thing from that point of view.

Prime Minister Lipponen contrasted the attitude of President Koivisto in dealing with Soviet influence in Finland to that of President Kekkonen by saying: "What Koivisto really did was to clean off all this kind of behavior that was overly subservient."

One telling event that speaks to the new approach to Soviet interest in Finnish affairs was the way the Government of Finland handled the important Finnish decision in 1989 to begin negotiations that would lead to eventual Finnish membership in the European Union. The Soviet Union was simply advised via a memorandum, given to KGB resident Felix Karasev, explaining why Finland felt it necessary to join the European Union. It assured that "preservation and development of the good and trusting relations between Finland and the Soviet Union would remain Finland's priority."[33] With that assurance, as far as I am aware, Finland went about its negotiations without the Soviet Union—admittedly much weaker and, indeed, in its final stages—raising objections.

The exercise of Soviet influence in Finnish affairs and the use of the "Soviet card" were over. As Kivinen put it, when Koivisto came in, "The whole era changed: The air changed and the whole situation changed."

KOIVISTO: THE DOMESTIC DIMENSION

Balance of Political Power Redressed

I asked the Chancellor of Turku University Jaakko Nousiainen whether he thought that President Koivisto consciously set out to redress the balance of political power in Finland. Nousiainen explained that Koivisto had been influenced in his views of the presidency by Abo Academy professor Sven Lindman who favored a limited presidency and a dominant Parliament. Nousiainen said of Lindman:

His idea was that a combination of presidentialism and parliamentary government is somehow strange. His point was that presidentialism in Finland can serve only one purpose. The president's role should be restricted to be a regulator of the parliamentary machinery. It means that he is active when the parliamentary machinery is in difficulties. So important presidential powers are cabinet formation, dissolution of Parliament...appointment of higher civil servants.

Koivisto was Lindman's student, and he got this idea from Lindman...I have heard him say that Lindman's idea of the presidential role appealed to him. And the other factor was his experience from Kekkonen's time. When he was prime minister from seventy-nine to eighty-one. This was the time when the president was already ill and still people let him understand that the president wants this or that, and nobody knew what his office chief Perttunen was doing, and there were various intrigues to force Koivisto to resign.

I asked Nousiainen whether in his view Koivisto's policies were needed and healthy and were they successful. He answered:

Certainly. Partly this is a personal view, and also a political view because I support parliamentary government, West European parliamentary government. But we must say that all of this that happened, the strengthening of the prime minister's role or the cabinet's role, was not the result of the president's action. Partly, he only went along with [it]...I mean the political situation in Finland changed. The rivalry between parties had calmed down. From the beginning of the eighties we have had the strongest, long-lasting majority cabinets. They sit through four year electoral periods, and this was a development independent of the president.

Others were more emphatic that President Koivisto deserved the credit for restoring a better balance to the political institutions in Finland. Salolainen said simply: "He brought back democracy to Finland, parliamentarism and democracy. People don't understand how important he was after Kekkonen."

I asked Kivinen for his views on whether Koivisto intentionally set out to reduce the mystique of the presidency and to balance constitutional powers. He answered:

Well, I think he was quite honest in my opinion in trying to strengthen the power of the Parliament especially, and also the government. But this of course was a very difficult thing and it took a long time. I don't know whether his interest also slightly waned on the way! Perhaps it's fair to say that you could see some waning of his interest in that direction, not a major one but a minor one. And of course it has changed even since. I think some of his things were watered down in the end, partly because many parties were against them, and many presidential hopefuls were against as well. But I think he was honestly for it until the end really. But then I think this whole way of piecemeal renewing of the constitution is not a good thing.

Addressing the same question, Jukka Tarkka responded:

I think it was his purpose and that is what he really did in a very logical way, and I do feel it was very important for our political institutions. It is interesting, even if it goes beyond the scope of your study, that President Ahtisaari now is trying to build again a strong presidency, which according to my view is contradicting the general trend in our society. And I'm afraid that his motive is pure lust for power. It's dangerous. So he is kind of reversing the direction of Koivisto.

I asked Max Jakobson for his views on the Koivisto legacy in the area of the accumulation of presidential power as had been seen under President Kekkonen. Jakobson answered:

Well, of course the power of the presidency [under Kekkonen] became in a way completely distorted in relation to all of the others, this is a very good point you made in the report you sent me, and once Koivisto came in this distortion, this aberration was removed.

I wondered whether this was a matter of deliberate policy by Koivisto. Jakobson answered:

I think so. It was never really articulated clearly, but he has said it—you know he is a very difficult person in that respect—but he has said it in rather enigmatic, oblique phrases…And he said before he became president: he said you must not expect me to play the role of a hero, implying that he was not going to be the man who deals with every problem and solves every problem as Kekkonen had, and so on, but he was very careful never to criticize directly Kekkonen, always talking very respectfully about Kekkonen, the great president.

I queried Jakobson as to whether in his opinion the accumulation of presidential power under Kekkonen had reached unhealthy proportions. He said:

Very unhealthy. Afterwards, it has to be said that it all passed very painlessly, it all changed painlessly. There was no great crisis. Thanks to Koivisto. I think he very wisely changed things without actually making any great declarations of principle about it, which could have caused a lot of debate and emotional problems and so on. He just did it gradually without any ostentatious gestures. I think it was very wise...[He did it] by example, and just by letting things happen, rather than trying deliberately and demonstratively to change things. Did he do it instinctively, I don't know, but obviously he knew in what direction he had to go.

Most observers, including those cited above, agree that Koivisto did take a very different approach to power than President Kekkonen. Koivisto seems to have attempted to redress the balance of power between the president, the government, the Parliament and the political parties.

To be sure, he was not averse to using power when necessary. Three of the persons I interviewed directly felt the impact of Koivisto's presidential power.

I asked former Conservative Party leader and former Speaker of Parliament Ilkka Suominen about differences between President Kekkonen, who some Finns today described as semi-dictatorial, with Mauno Koivisto. Koivisto, I noted, was considered by many as having entered the presidency to try to redress the balance of power among the constitutional players. Suominen's answer surprised me:

I think the only difference between Koivisto and Kekkonen in the use of power was that Kekkonen formulated a 'court' around him, and with the consent or without the consent of Kekkonen this court became the dictator...Koivisto never built a court around himself, but he had exactly as much power and he used exactly as much power, as I well know from 1987, as Kekkonen. The only point is that he developed a system with which he tried to tie the hands of his successor. He didn't tie his own hands, but he formulated a policy trying to tie the hands of his successor, which...Martti Ahtisaari now has strongly opposed.

Suominen said that the only presidential power to be really affected was that no longer can the president dissolve the Parliament. He said he and Koivisto had had an argument about this through the press when he had been Speaker of Parliament. He continued:

So Koivisto is not right, I am not right, but both are right. There is no one hundred percent this or hundred percent that. But this was the only way that presidential powers were reduced by President Koivisto. And he was ruthless with his power...He had a great deal of influence on the prime ministers, on both prime ministers that I know intimately, Harri Holkeri and Esko Aho. They were his keen followers, and every wish of the president came through, through the prime minister. Kekkonen's main interest was foreign policy. Koivisto's main interest, I think, was monetary and economic policy, which he guided through the Bank of Finland. He had a keen interest in and good knowledge of foreign policy, I'm not denying that at all, but he sort of did it as his duty. He had far more many near-crashes than Kekkonen had in far easier times [for Koivisto]. One was the mutiny in 1991 when Gorbachev was practically thrown out...In the independence of Estonia we were...a little bit too slow.

In the chapter on the Kekkonen legacy above, Paavo Väyrynen credited Koivisto with attempting to redress the balance of power between the presidency and the other constitutional powers. However, Väyrynen also noted that Koivisto was not a stranger to the use of presidential power. He commented:

One of the comments I have made concerning Koivisto's time, on the other hand, is that in the government formation of 1987 he used presidential power more than Kekkonen ever did in forming a government. Because actually there was a genuine will of the majority of the Parliament to form a bourgeois government, and he used his power to change that fact.

I asked Väyrynen whether Koivisto was showing presidential anger because the bourgeois parties sought to form a government without proper consultation with him. He responded:

That's what he said, but I believe that in any case there was this plan. We tried to prevent it, and that's why he was angry. The Social Democrats had a plan and we tried to prevent it, but he was more powerful. And what he was angry about was that he was compelled to show his own role in the game. According to his own character, he would have liked to play in the background and let it appear to happen by itself.

Another Finnish political figure who expressed to me some sharp views about President Koivisto and his use of power (as well as about President Kekkonen) was former minister of defense, 1994 presidential candidate and current UN Balkans peacekeeping official Elizabeth Rehn. She had some personal recollections about the Kekkonen years:

My approach certainly would not be as someone who was an expert on those earlier issues, because I was not involved in politics then. My views are more from that of the good normal citizen, about how she felt about all of this, and then jumping into politics on the state level in seventy-nine. I don't know if you know, but I was very much in opposition to President Kekkonen. I never voted for him because I thought he was much too much a 'dictator' for Finland.[34] And when I was asked in seventy-eight to be a candidate for electorship, I just said I absolutely cannot be an elector for

President Kekkonen because I can't look at his 'dictatorship' in a positive way, and I believe he is too old and that he should not be the president any more. And there was hell about this!

But when I was elected as a Member of Parliament, in some of my interviews there were questions about how can I now act when I have been so much in opposition to President Kekkonen, and I said that I really believe that you should be frank, and I still said that he is too old, he has taken too much of the power, and that is not good for democracy. I must say that when he became ill, after that I did not say a bad word about President Kekkonen, and I have even in some way [revised] my opinions, because now that I knew so much more about where we were standing and where we were going, I believe that he created a good basis for us to go on...But I was more furious about the fact that all those who took power through Kekkonen's 'dictatorship,' that they were really pressing the internal affairs of Finland so strongly. All those skiing behind him.

I asked Rehn about the shift from Kekkonen to Koivisto and the differences that brought in some of the areas we had been discussing, such as his low profile. She responded:

I believe it was absolutely the only right thing to do, in the beginning. But then people, you know how people are, first they are in opposition to too strong power and are longing for a low profile, but then they are longing for someone who will be a father for them again. So the criticism of Koivisto grew of course because of his very low profile during his period that he should have been stronger. And then, when he was strong, it was perhaps not on the right issues.

He didn't like the criticism that came to him. I appreciate Koivisto very much. I like his sense of humor. We had very, very good talks together, until one certain moment when I was both the prime minister and the foreign minister one summer. It was in the beginning of the Yugoslavian conflict, and he was never too much for refugees, and he decided that we should introduce visas again for Yugoslavian people, and there should be a refugees meeting in Geneva with Mrs. Ogata of UNHRC, and a governmental conference about all of the problems arising in the former Yugoslavia.

I said that I'm am not prepared to introduce or propose this for the government because I believe that it's the wrong time and that we should have some understanding for those people. And he became furious because he thought everything was okay with me and that I would be obeying him. And then Mr. Väyrynen came back from his vacation and showed the responsibility that someone should show, and there was really a mess...So it was presented and it went through, and I made my amendment or reservation in the government.

Koivisto could never forgive me for that...He didn't receive me any more for private talks. I was very often present when new ambassadors were leaving the letters of accreditation with him, but it was just announced to me that I should not be the one to be there. I understood he didn't want me present...I don't think that he is angry with me anymore, but he was very interesting in that way that he couldn't forgive people...So, you should be careful when you get the power of the presidency.

Obviously, therefore, there are examples of President Koivisto using presidential power but, unlike President Kekkonen, behind the scenes. Nevertheless, most observers gave President Koivisto very high marks for, as put most dramatically by Pertti Salolainen, having "brought democracy back to Finland, parliamentarism and democracy." It is of course far too early to pass historical judgements on the recently completed Koivisto period. It would be my guess, however, that historians will also give full recognition to Koivisto for having returned the country to a more normal and practical democracy, in contrast to his predecessor. It seems to me that after Kekkonen, Finland desperately needed a man of Koivisto's character, personal history and temperament to deflate the image of an imperial presidency and to restore Finnish faith in a kind of work-a-day democracy.

Certainly, for a foreign observer, the openness and more relaxed atmosphere in Finland that I saw in the mid-1980s, compared to the tense, liturgy and slogan-ridden Finland of the 1970s, was already a dramatic change. The collapse of the Soviet Union put that whole era to an end.

I shall close this chapter with an anecdote told to me by Ilkka Suominen:

[My wife] Riitta and I received an invitation which we thought to be 'the usual one'...to the November 1991 celebration of the Great Soviet Revolution in the Soviet embassy on *Tehtaankatu*. When arriving at the embassy, we noticed it to be completely dark. The gate was open and the main entrance, by which the usual 'leather coat chap' stood, was lit by a lonely lamp.

Inside the embassy we were led through the dark and empty banquet hall into the ambassador's private quarters on the third floor. It turned out to be a very small dinner party instead of the huge usual reception for around a thousand people, as you yourself will remember so well.

The Finnish side was represented by President of the Republic Mauno Koivisto [and Mrs. Koivisto], Prime Minister [and Mrs.] Esko Aho, Foreign Minister Paavo Väyrynen, and Chief of the President's Office Jaakko Kalela with his wife. From the Soviet side we were hosted by Ambassador Boris Aristov...and Mrs. Aristov....Other Soviet participants were Minister

Counselor Felix Karasev, Head of the Party Line in the embassy [and two or three other Soviet diplomats].

The conversation was mainly small talk, but also a lot was devoted to political events, the failed coup in Moscow only two months earlier, the actual takeover by Boris Yeltsin which was already going on. Towards Christmas time that year the Soviet Union was then [to be] finally declared 'dead.' The historical phase was in the air throughout the dinner, but it became quite tangible when Ambassador Boris Aristov gave his speech. It was full of Slavonic emotion—not far from tears, I should say —containing sad and dark speculations and implications of what would happen to the relations between our countries. He also [related] the history of good relations and the importance of President Mauno Koivisto's role in maintaining and fortifying those relations.

As the president himself very seldom reciprocates speeches at dinners, if no head of state is present, he gave this answering duty to me—I was Speaker of Parliament at the time. [He told me] "Ilkka, say something pleasant." Naturally, I obliged. As I only had the time of Boris Aristov's speech to think it over, I realized that I could not join in the tune of mourning and sorrow. Frankly, I do not remember what I said exactly, but I do recall laughter at two or three points, so I suppose it was not too bad.

We did not stay long—Mauno Koivisto never did—and at home Riitta and I sat and discussed for a while. And we realized how historic this evening had been. We had attended a wake for the Soviet Union.

27

An American Diplomat's Parting Thoughts and an Appreciation of Finland

What is one to make of all of the foregoing? Has this book captured the essence of the Finnish reality during some of the Cold War years? I have sought to present the United States' understanding of Finnish politics and policies in the Cold War period. Also, I have tried to describe U.S. and NATO policies within whose context we in the State Department and embassy viewed developments in Northern Europe. U.S. diplomatic reporting from Finland during the Cold War years is cited, including a number of reports that I wrote or supervised during the 1970s and 1980s. The views on key issues of two American ambassadors and a number of prominent Finns who participated in or were observers of developments in Finland have been presented. And I have presented my own assessments of the Kekkonen and Koivisto legacies.

My views are based on my diplomatic experience as a senior U.S. official in Finnish affairs, both in Helsinki and Washington, on research conducted in writing this book, and on my fascinating interviews with key Finns. I make no claim to a "definitive" judgement on these matters nor to have exhaustively researched the growing literature in this field.

In the final analysis, these judgments of complex issues are often subjective and personal matters. As we have seen, intelligent and honest persons can look at the same events and reach quite opposing conclusions about what they meant. One of the most important lessons I have gained from writing this book has been that there is not necessarily a single *truth* in complex matters, and that it is wrong to discredit those who do not agree with your view. As Jakobson has written, paraphrasing Henry Kissinger, "the difference between a patriot and a knave" in certain situations "is a very thin line."

Indeed, I believe that one of the most unhealthy dimensions of the Finnish political culture during the 1960s and 1970s was the penchant during the Kekkonen years to divide Finns into "patriots and knaves," "good Finns" and "bad Finns," or "sheep or goats," to use Timo Vihavainen's phrase.

Also, I wish to reiterate a principal conclusion of this book that may have been lost sight of in the dizzying swirl of conflicting opinions presented above. This is that Finland, initially against great odds, was in fact highly successful in managing its postwar foreign and security policies, particularly its relations with the Soviet Union, in such a way as to maintain its independence, Western values and a measure of credible neutrality.

This accomplishment represents a towering achievement for Finnish statesmanship and leadership and stands in marked contrast to what might otherwise have been the case. As noted in Chapter 4, many observers would not have believed in 1944, in 1958 or even 1962 that Finland would be able to succeed in maintaining its independence. Finland's postwar and Cold War leaders— Mannerheim (briefly), Paasikivi, Kekkonen and Koivisto—deserve much credit for this outstanding achievement. This book and my assessments of individual developments discussed throughout it need to be interpreted within the context of that overall success.

That success does not, however, gainsay the fact that within its parameters a number of phenomena could be observed—important phenomena—which have merited and have been receiving considerable attention by contemporary observers and, increasingly, historians. The contemporary and historical interest concerns the fashion in which Finland pursued its objectives and the perceived implications—negative and positive—of some of the phenomena. That, of course, has been the general focus of this book.

Leaving this book behind is almost as sad as leaving Finland behind, as we did upon completing diplomatic assignments in 1979 and 1986. This book has been another journey to Finland. Working on it has brought a flood of memories of our years there. Going over embassy reports that I had prepared and checking my old appointment calendars, I had vivid recollections of private luncheons, parties, special people I had met, embassy colleagues now gone, embassy problems to be resolved, etc. Researching books and articles in Finnish sparked a resurgence of my Finnish language vocabulary, suffering still (or again!) from a concentration on specialized political and foreign affairs subjects which will do little good the next time I find myself in Stockmanns. Revisiting Finland in 1995 and being able to see old friends and interview former Finnish colleagues was almost like a third diplomatic assignment to Finland—the final "political report." The doors were still open, the "dour" Finns still resolutely refusing to conform to their assigned image.

Incidentally, many readers may rightly wonder why on earth I am reassessing Finnish politics and policies while America is replete with its own grievous political, social and economic problems. Why don't I concentrate on my own country's problems and leave Finland alone? Well, this was what I was trained to do and enjoyed doing for thirty-four years in the diplomatic profession. There are some 270 million Americans daily expressing their opinions about U.S. problems. Additionally, most of the world makes a habit of telling the United States what's wrong with it, including not a few Finns! But how often does an American get to write about a country like Finland?

The Helsinki that Magda and I saw in 1995 is not the Helsinki of 1976 or 1986. Little things and big things have changed. The people on the streets are different. There are more dark and swarthy foreigners: in yesteryear it was an oddity, in today's Helsinki it is commonplace. That's mostly for the better—a too homogeneous society can breed complacency and arrogance. A more diverse society reminds one that the world is complex and that ethnic and racial problems are more complicated when faced at home than they appeared when they were someone else's problem. Yet, and this goes for my own country as well, we cannot solve the problems of the underdeveloped world by bringing their citizens in ever-increasing numbers into our own countries.

There were in the summer of 1995 more cultural events and "happenings" going on in downtown Helsinki than I remember from before. That's good! Never have I seen the Esplanadi with more life than in May and June of 1995. More outdoor cafes! Helsinki was almost Mediterranean in this aspect. The Kappeli—where I began this book over an "olutta" or beer—is now only one of many. How delightful! More bicycle paths from the outskirts go all the way downtown. That's good! An even more impressive public transportation system in the Helsinki metropolitan area than I remember from before. That's good! Of course, in 1995 we were dependent on public transportation—no embassy drivers this time! But, objectively speaking, Helsinki has done an extraordinary job, compared to most world capital cities, in minimizing personal automobile traffic on downtown streets and maintaining a pleasant, friendly atmosphere and character. Congratulations are due to my good friend Juha Sipilä for his work as executive director of the Helsinki Metropolitan Authority.

More graffiti. That's bad! In fact I don't remember any graffiti during my earlier years in Helsinki. There must have been some, but nothing on the scale that could be seen everywhere in 1995. Someone has conveyed to the youth of Helsinki that graffiti is okay, maybe even an art form. Isn't it rather environmental pollution! I hope the phenomenon is a temporary one.

A new opera house. I don't know! It's a great facility, but as seen from Mannerheimentie, I just don't know! Better hockey! Finland has in recent years established itself among the leading world hockey powers. Numerous Finns have made their way to the National Hockey League, including the rugged Esa Tikkonen whom I saw play Finnish league hockey in the mid-1980s, hockey Hall of Famer Jari Kurri, and current perennial scoring champion Teemu Selanne. In international World Cup hockey, Finland has progressed from being usually a second tier country to become 1995 World Champions, beating Sweden in Stockholm. In both

1998 and 1999 Finland reached the World Cup championship finals only to be edged out and finish second.

Infinitely more variety on Finnish TV and radio has certainly helped to break down Finnish insularity by exposing Finns to an extensive menu of European and international (often American) programming. That's good, I guess. Certainly, it has removed the Finnish people from the danger of being subjected again, as they were during the Cold War days, to one-source bias and propaganda. In a way, though, I kind of missed the sense that I had in the 1970s that everyone was watching the same program I was watching. There was a kind of town-meeting atmosphere about the TV of those days, as furious as I would often get at some of the propaganda.

Sign of the times: "The NOKIA Sugar Bowl" game in January 1997 in New Orleans for the American collegiate football championship of the 1996 season. A quintessentially American event, with one of the largest TV audiences of the year in the U.S., sponsored by the Finnish company NOKIA. That's good!

More unemployment. That's bad! It is a frightening effect of globalization of the world economy. In Europe, social and economic policy has maintained high wages of the employed at the expense of unemployment figures reaching double-digit figures. In the United States flexible social and economic policies have permitted wide-spread economic rationalization and company down-sizing which has maintained and even improved U.S. economic competitiveness—with a resulting boost in employment and an unemployment rate in only the 4-6% range. However, the process until very recently resulted in essentially flat wage rates over the past twenty years as many higher paying production jobs have been lost to lower wage countries with U.S. employees being shifted to often lower-paying service industry jobs.

Somehow, Europe, Japan, Canada and the United States have to cooperate in figuring out a way to assure that the economic globalization process does not ratchet down wages in our countries toward the level of the lowest wage countries. Because Finland cannot afford its high unemployment rates, and the United States cannot afford stagnating personal incomes.

We all worked hard in our own way to assure that Western values would ultimately prevail over the anti-democratic and anti-humanistic values of the Soviet system. We cannot now ourselves fail our own values and countenance an increasingly unjust world divided into the haves and have-nots and domestic societies similarly divided into those prepared to participate in the modern information society and those who are left behind both educationally and economically. This is a particularly difficult problem for America. But the demographics affecting the welfare state are as applicable in Europe as in North America.

With the end of the Cold War, we need to develop a new foreign policy "vision" that will give our peoples a new sense of purpose—beyond commercial advantage—in constructively engaging in the broader world on the eve of the new millennium.

The Finnish people have much to offer in this new worldwide challenge. The Finns have in the past disproportionately to their numbers contributed to the world of the arts, industry, design, sports and culture. There is every reason to believe that the name Finland will continue in the future to be associated with quality, sensibility, quiet courage—yes, *Sisu* (courage or guts)—patience and social justice. For the Cooper family, Finland will always be associated with, in addition to those qualities, crisp cold ski trails, endless summer evenings, sparkling waters, and above all, friendship, loyalty and good fellowship. A nation with these qualities has little to fear from the future. After all, look at what it has come through in the past!

Part Four Notes

1 Readers wishing some information regarding the persons interviewed are encouraged to refer to the Appendix.

[2] General Sisasvuo's dry sense of humor was evident in several parts of our interview. In an interesting discussion of the Winter War, I asked him about the Soviet use of Mongolian troops in the Battle of Suomussalmi. The General responded, "Yes, they had hoped these Mongolians would be fast on skis. They were mistaken."

[3] Cited by Timo Vihavainen, *Kansakunta Rahmallaan* (Helsinki: Otava, 1991): 42.

[4] See Juhani Suomi, *Kriisien aika, Urho Kekkonen 1956-62* (Helsinki: Otava, 1992):180-181.

[5] Ibid., p. 242.

[6] Cited by Vihavainen, op. cit., p. 43.

[7] Juhani Suomi, *Urho Kekkonen 1956-62,* p. 75.

[8] See Hannu Rautkallio, *Suomen Suunta, 1945-1948* (Savonlinna: Weilin & Goos, 1979) and *Paasikivi Vai Kekkonen—Suomen lanesta nahtyna 1945-1956* (Helsinki: Kustannusosakeyhtio Tammi, 1990).

[9] Hannu Rautkallio, *Novosibirskin lavastus: Noottikriisi 1961* (Helsinki: Kustannusosakeyhtio Tammi, 1992).

[10] Ibid., pp. 13-15 discuss the Kekkonen memorandum.

[11] Ibid., p. 92.

[12] Ibid., pp. 111-112.

[13] Martti Haikio, *"A Brief History of Finland,"* op. cit., pp. 82-86.

[14] Nortamo, Simopekka, "Suomalainen itse-sensuuri," *Helsingin Sanomat Kuukausiliite,* No. 17 (August 24, 1991): 14-28.

[15] Koivisto, *Historian Tekijat,* p. 95 (phrase in quotes). *Witness to History,* p.35 (not in quotes).

[16] *Witness to History,* pp. 35-36.

[17] *Historian Tekijat,* pp. 102-4. This phrase does not appear in *Witness to History.*

[18] *Witness to History,* p. 41. *Historian Tekijat,* p. 104. The original Finnish language word "vastaantuloa" is translated in *Witness to History* as "concession." I think the meaning is closer to willingness to move closer or "responsiveness."

[19] *Historian Tekijat,* p. 119. The version in *Witness to History,* p. 51, differs slightly.

[20] *Witness to History,* p. 56.

[21] Ibid., p. 57.

[22] Ibid., p. 60.

[23] . Ibid., p. 76.

[24] Ibid., p. 77.

[25] *Historian Tekijat,* pp. 187-88. The above two citations are not included in *Witness to History.*

[26] *Witness to History,* p. 156.

[27] Ibid., p 193.

[28] 28 After the collapse of the Soviet Union, Koivisto sent a message to Felix Karasev in January 1992 that his successor would no longer have access to the presidential palace. Ibid., p.214.

[29] *Historian Tekijat.,* p. 10.

[30] Kaksi Kautta, p. 21.

[31] Witness to History, p. 1.

[32] Historian Tekijat, pp. 139-145.

[33] Witness to History, p. 226.

[34] I asked Minister Rehn if she was comfortable using the terms "dictator" and "dictatorship" in referring to President Kekkonen. She said, well, maybe the terms should be put in quotation marks.

APPENDIX

Interviews

This appendix provides a brief description of the Finns and other persons (including U.S. ambassadors) whom I interviewed in 1995 for this book and who are cited in this book. It also briefly identifies the other persons whom I interviewed for this book but whom I did not cite owing to space constraints.

The descriptions of individuals in this Appendix are not intended to constitute *curricula vitae* with exact dates and records of positions held—that information can be obtained from the appropriate sources. Rather, the descriptions are intended to put my discussions with those interviewed into the context of the positions they held and the relationships that we enjoyed as well as to convey a few personal impressions.

The subjects are listed in alphabetical order, except that I start with the current prime minister of Finland, as of this writing, Paavo Lipponen. I am without exception most grateful to all of those who participated in this interview process.

Persons Interviewed and Cited in This Book

1. Prime Minister Paavo Lipponen

Paavo Lipponen certainly has come a long way from when we first met in 1976. At that time he was planning secretary of the Social Democratic Party. He immediately became one of my most valued and appreciated political contacts. I think this was because of his evident sincerity and seriousness of purpose.

Exhibiting already in those early days his deep voice and deliberate manner of speaking, Lipponen nevertheless had a quick and subtle humor and was an entertaining interlocutor. We would meet for lunch every few weeks, and he and his wife were dinner guests at our house on various occasions. Lipponen had somehow gained the reputation in the United States embassy as a far-left Social Democrat. However, even in our first contacts with I found him to be principled yet pragmatic, and certainly never dogmatic. The same could not be said of all of his party colleagues and for a number of Social Democrat academicians who frequently tended to adopt in those years an anti-NATO and anti-U.S. attitude.

We also met from time to time when I came back to Finland in the mid-1980s, but since I was not dealing directly so much during those years with political parties, our contact was less frequent. In the summer of 1995, after not having seen Paavo Lipponen for several years, it was an honor and certainly most gratifying and pleasant on a lovely June morning to be received in the Kesaranta residence assigned to the Finnish prime minister. As with all of the other interviews, the interview was requested, granted and tape-recorded as a part of my research for a book on the way Finland dealt with certain political, foreign policy and security issues during the Cold War years.

2. Georg C. Ehrnrooth

Georg Ehrnrooth, together with Dr. Tuure Junnila and a number of others, was one of those considered outside the pale during the long years of the Kekkonen presidency. Many Finnish observers even today would argue that Ehrnrooth was in fact an opponent of the "Paasikivi-Kekkonen" line of maintaining good relations with the Soviet Union and hence represented a threat to those relations. Ehrnrooth argued then, and now, that this simply is not true: he claims he supported the Paasikivi foreign policy line and that it was Kekkonen himself who deviated from the Paasikivi line by taking an overly obsequious attitude towards the Soviet Union and allowing that country to interfere shamelessly in Finland's internal affairs.

In our interview, Ehrnrooth discussed these issues and defended his positions, feeling very much vindicated by developments since the departure of President Kekkonen. Particularly in recent years, many observers who were silent have stepped forward to criticize the Kekkonen years on many of the same grounds that Ehrnrooth used during those years he was vilified.

Honesty compels me to record that Ehrnrooth was not taken seriously by most officials of the American embassy during the Cold War years. He was considered to be too strident and as lacking an appreciation of the precariousness of the Finnish situation vis-à-vis the Soviet Union. Even when we were criticizing the Kekkonen administrations in our own reports, we tended to think that Ehrnrooth exaggerated in his criticism of Kekkonen.

One important embassy officer, Robert Houston, who was deputy chief of mission in the mid-1970s and who was in that position when I arrived at post in 1976, took a position quite close to that of Ehrnrooth. As a result he was regarded with considerable skepticism by official Finland, within the embassy and by the State Department. These voices in the wilderness deserve recognition today for having been more alert to the excesses of the Kekkonen years than others. Yet, I would still argue that they over-dramatized the situation and failed to grasp fully the game within games that the Finnish leadership was knowingly playing.

I used to meet with Ehrnrooth from time to time during my assignments to Helsinki and always found him an intelligent, gracious and provocative interlocutor. He certainly has earned the right to be included in any survey of what Finns thought about Finland during the Cold War.

3. Ambassador James E. Goodby

James Goodby, a career United States Foreign Service Officer with the Department of State, was named United States ambassador to Finland in 1980, replacing another career officer, Rozanne L. Ridgway, as ambassador. Ambassador Goodby arrived in Finland in March 1980, presenting his credentials to President Kekkonen in April. As noted above, Ambassador Goodby asked me in late 1980 to serve as his deputy chief of mission but was himself replaced by a political appointee before my appointment was made.

Ambassador Goodby, one of the State Department's leading Europeanists, NATO specialists and arms control experts, went on to be named as the United States ambassadorial representative at the CSCE Disarmament Conference held in Stockholm in 1983, and from there to other senior assignments. He served during the Clinton administration as a senior arms control specialist in the Department of State with the personal rank of ambassador. Ever since his posting to Finland, Ambassador Goodby has maintained a lively interest in Finland.

4. Harri Holkeri

When I first called on Harri Holkeri in the offices of the National Coalition, aka the Conservative Party, a few weeks after my arrival in Finland in 1976, he was already the young chairman of the party. He had acceded to that position with the untimely death of Juha Rihtniemi in 1971. As with Paavo Lipponen, I could not have known then that I was dealing with a future prime minister of Finland. This was particularly so in the case of Holkeri, inasmuch as his party was in the midst of its long period of opposition from which it would not emerge until 1987 when Holkeri would be named prime minister.

The parliamentary elections of 1979, which resulted in important gains for the National Coalition Party, propelled Holkeri more centrally into the national limelight or, more aptly put, into the bright lights of television studios. It was with pleasure that years later in 1987 I was able to meet the recently named Prime Minister Holkeri at a reception offered by Ambassador Paavo Rantanen at the Finnish embassy in Washington.

With respect to our interview in his Bank of Finland office Helsinki in May 1995, I found it interesting that Holkeri considered it fitting to begin with a long introduction describing Finland's recent history. He apparently felt that my questions had some negative spin regarding the Kekkonen period, and he wanted to be sure that I was properly aware of the Finnish context. Of my interviews, his was one of the more sympathetic to, and under-standing of, President Kekkonen, the man who seems to have been largely responsible for keeping the National Coalition Party in seemingly eternal opposition.

5. Ambassador Jaakko Iloniemi

When I arrived in Finland in 1976, Jaakko Iloniemi was director of the Foreign Ministry's political department. He was soon thereafter promoted to under secretary for political affairs and, a year or so later, appointed as ambassador of Finland to the United States, a position which he filled with distinction, ably abetted by his charming wife Leena. He was undoubtedly one of Finland's most brilliant and influential diplomats of the Cold War period. As the newly arrived political counselor at the American embassy, it would be unusual for me to establish a professional relationship with the high-ranking Iloniemi. But he graciously permitted to me to do so, and we met periodically in the late 1970s until his assignment as ambassador to Washington. We resumed our professional relationship upon my return to Finland in 1984, by which time Ambassador Iloniemi had left government service to assume a senior banking position. To the great pleasure of Magda and myself, we also had frequent social contact with Jaakko and Leena during this period.

In the course of his assignments in charge of political affairs in the Foreign Ministry, Ambassador Iloniemi had both great responsibilities for Finnish foreign policy as well as frequent very close contact with President Kekkonen. I therefore consider his striking observations on the Kekkonen years as highly authoritative and revealing of the spirit of the times.

6. Mikko Immonen

Mikko Immonen was secretary of the Center Party during my first assignment to Helsinki. He was my best and most frequent interlocutor from that party, and we met frequently both in his party headquarters as well as at lunches and, from time-to-time, hard-fought but good-natured tennis matches. Mikko and his wife Ilona were dinner guests at our home on several occasions, and we also had the pleasure of being invited to their home, a not too frequent gesture by Finnish politicians. Immonen had worked both as a journalist and a diplomat before becoming an official in the

Center Party, and he understood the importance of keeping interested foreign diplomats well-informed about his party and its programs. Mikko would later move on to become chairman of the state alcohol company ALKO before retiring from that position a few years ago.

A die-hard Agrarian League/Center Party and Kekkonen loyalist, Immonen is an articulate and vigorous spokesman and defender of the historical outlook of that political grouping. He was particularly insistent on the Center Party and Kekkonen's perception of the 1960s that Social Democrats and the Honka Liitto candidacy represented real threats to Finland's policy of good relations with the Soviet Union. This view and the attitude surrounding it provided the rationale for President Kekkonen and his supporters to go to great lengths to assure—by "two hundred per cent" as Immonen puts it—that persons or parties not completely supportive of Kekkonen's foreign policy views not be given access to political office and power.

In his opening comments during our discussion, Immonen referred to how important Kekkonen and the Agrarian League had been to his father personally and to his father's generation. This gave some insight into the highly personal nature of the background and formation that individual Finnish political leaders bring with them as they go about their business. I guess that explains why so many good Finns can hold such differing views of the Finnish political reality, past and present.

7. Ambassador Max Jakobson

Ambassador Max Jakobson is undoubtly better known and respected in governmental and academic circles outside of Finland than any other Finnish public figure, with the possible exception of Finland's presidents. This has been true for at least twenty-five years, since Jakobson was Finland's ambassador to the United Nations and at one time a candidate for UN secretary general. Jakobson is widely read and respected for his analyses of European political and security issues and for his explanations of Finnish policies to the outside world. When I arrived in Finland during my first assignment Jakobson was the managing director of "EVA,"

Finland's private sector umbrella and research organization. From that position he played a key role in popularizing and promoting understanding of Finland's private sector which, as in many parts of the world, had come under attack in the 1960s and early 1970s. He was one of the leading figures in the development of the "consensus" spirit of the Finnish political, economic and social dialogue of the late 1970s and 1980s.

As a foreign policy and political analyst, Jakobson knows few peers. Therefore, it was highly gratifying to me as a relative neophyte to Finland in the late 1970s to be able to establish a professional relationship with Ambassador Jakobson. This resulted in frequent meetings and lunches during both periods of my assignments to Finland which I considered extremely valuable in advancing my knowledge of Finland's politics and foreign policy. Having been a key player in the development of Finland's policy of neutrality, it was always interesting to hear his assessments of how Finland was faring in its relations with the Soviet Union and the West in the 1970s and 1980s. Ambassador Jakobson has written extensively about Finnish foreign and security policy developments during the Cold War. In our discussion he expressed pointed views about what Finland did correctly during those years and where Finland and Finnish leaders in his view made mistakes.

8. Dr. Jan-Magnus Jansson

Dr. Jan-Magnus Jansson's long political and journalistic career made him a significant actor and observer during virtually the entire postwar and Cold War period, giving him a unique perspective on many of the most important developments during this critically important era of Finnish history. Once again, I was fortunate and privileged to be able to establish contact with Dr. Jansson early during my first assignment to Finland. We developed a pattern of periodic meetings either in his *Hufvudstadsbladet* office on Mannerheimentie or at one of several agreeable downtown Helsinki restaurants. In the embassy he was considered one of our most valuable interlocutors because of his political and journalistic importance as well as for his unusually close political connections in several directions which made him an extremely well-informed observer.

In his numerous years as editor-in-chief of the prestigious *Hufvudstadsbladet* newspaper and chairman of the Swedish People's Party, Dr. Jansson displayed an intelligent balance and a dispassionate calmness as events developed and could be counted upon to give an objective view of matters in progress. In our interview, he provided insights into the Kekkonen years and the Koivisto period. Generally sympathetic to President Kekkonen, he nevertheless expressed full awareness of the excesses of the Kekkonen period. Jansson's views were interesting, well-expressed and thoughtful, even when one does not fully agree with him.

9. Jaakko Kalela

Jaakko Kalela is surely one of the most extraordinary political figures in the Western world, from the point of view of the positions he has held for more than two decades under three Finnish presidents. I know of no other Western political figure who has acted, first as foreign policy advisor and, subsequently, as chief of staff to several presidents over such a long period of time. It is as if Henry Kissinger and Bob Haldeman were one person and were in the same positions for President Clinton in the 1990s as they were in the 1970s under President Richard Nixon!

It was obviously very helpful that I was able to have a close, professional association with Jaakko. And it was a large personal bonus that Magda and I were able to maintain a friendly personal relationship with Jaakko and his wife Aira, who was and is a first class professional in her own right. Jaakko Kalela and I met frequently, usually in his office, sometimes in nearby restaurants during both of my assignments to Helsinki, and had many long *tour d'horizon* discussions on matters of current interest. We knew in the embassy that Jaakko had come from what we considered to be the intellectual left-wing of the Social Democratic Party, and we certainly did not agree with all of his international views. We often wondered what kind of advice he was giving to his presidential masters. Certainly, our views on a number of nuclear arms and arms control matters were far apart. However, I invariably enjoyed our discussion meetings and always found him willing to hear our arguments. And it was certainly important to the embassy that we be able to deliver our points of view directly to the president's senior advisor.

With Kalela, as with a number of my other interlocutors, I was struck by the candor with which Finnish officials are now prepared to look back on the Kekkonen years and to look objectively, sometimes critically, at some of the practices of those years.

10. Olli Kivinen

Olli Kivinen was, with the possible exception of Per-Erik Lönnfors, the Finnish journalist with whom I had the most professional and personal contacts during my two assignments to Helsinki. An astute observer of international and European affairs, Kivinen always had a well-informed view that he was prepared to put forward forcefully. That is what has made him an interesting and provocative columnist for the *Helsingin Sanomat* over the past twenty-five years.

In our frequent luncheon and social meetings, we would have spirited discussions on all sorts of issues, including the state of the United States, its society and its politics, areas where Kivinen was frequently quite critical. In between my assignments to Finland, Kivinen came to Washington to cover the U.S. presidential elections of 1980, and we renewed our acquaintance and our discussions. Olli did not greet the election of Ronald Reagan with enthusiasm.

As with a number of the Finns that I interviewed in 1995, it is clear now that there were many features of the Kekkonen years with which Kivinen did not agree at the time, but which only in recent years have become matters that one can discuss openly and publicly. His judgement today is that Finland in the 1970s fell deeper under Soviet influence at the very same time that the country was moving toward closer integration with the West. He attributes this seeming anomaly to President Kekkonen's personality and influence and to the lesser politicians who were only too quick also to play the Soviet card. This general phenomenon of recognizing and openly discussing these dangerous trends only well after the fact is, in my view, itself a telling commentary on the mental state of the Finnish body politic during the 1960s and 1970s.

11. Paavo Laitinen

My wife and I became friends with Paavo and Raili Laitinen early during our first assignment to Finland. He had been a Finnish diplomat for many years, but by the time I arrived in Finland he was an officer with the Union bank. Because of his professional background, I always found him well informed on matters of the day. I became aware during my visit to Finland in 1995 that Paavo had some interesting insights into Finland during the 1960s and had some specific experiences and anecdotes to relate which add to the fabrics that comprise the web of what makes Finland what it is today.

12. Per-Erik Lönnfors

Magda and I count Per-Erik Lönnfors and his wife Pearl among our closest friends in Finland. As a professional contact, he was most valuable because of his wide experience both as a Finnish diplomat and a journalist. As a former diplomat, who had served as press officer in the Finnish embassies in Washington and Stockholm, he understood the function of diplomacy and the information needs of an embassy political officer. As a journalist he was well informed about both foreign and domestic Finnish affairs. Pearl was from the United States, partly of Chilean background and a fluent Spanish speaker. This meant that she and my wife Magda, who was born in Chile, had a great deal in common. As sometimes happens, therefore, what began as a professional relationship matured into a warm friendship that has endured over the years. It was most fortunate for me in my trip to Finland in 1995 that Per-Erik was general manager and editor-in-chief of the Finnish New Agency in which capacity we had a most interesting and wide-ranging discussion.

13. George Maude

While I was in Finland the first time I read George Maude's, *The Finnish Dilemma,* which impressed me greatly for the way in which it dealt perceptively with many of the key dimensions to Finnish foreign and security policies of the day. It was my intention as political counselor of the American embassy to maintain contact with academics writing on Finnish politics and foreign relations. I got in touch with Dr. Maude and over the course of years we had a number of interesting conversations. On one occasion he invited me to address his political science students at the University of Turku about United States foreign policy, and I recall a most lively afternoon of tough questions and spirited give-and-take.

Upon embarking upon my project of writing a book about Finland during the Cold War, I naturally turned to George Maude, traveling to Turku to engage him in a discussion and elicit some of his up-to-date views.

14. Simopekka Nortamo

As managing editor of the *Helsingin Sanomat* from 1971-1976 and editor-in-chief from 1976-1990, Simopekka Nortamo was one of Finland's most important and influential postwar journalists. I met periodically with Nortamo during both of my assignments to Finland and always found him a most interesting interlocutor. Not infrequently during those days, I would raise with Nortamo on behalf of the embassy some complaint over what we in the embassy would perceive as "lack of balance" in the Finnish media in its treatment of the Soviet Union and the United States. What I usually got in response was a spirited defense from Simopekka of the fairness of whatever treatment I was complaining about, as Nortamo would dutifully and energetically play his institutional role of defending the *Helsingin Sanomat*.

I would not have guessed then that many of the kinds of concerns we were expressing about Finnish media practices were also nagging at Nortamo. He later came out, long after my departure from Finland, with a scathing indictment of "self-censorship" and "Finlandization" in the Finland of the 1960s and 1970s. Simopekka had further thoughts on these and other controversial Finnish subjects in our interview in the spring of 1995.

15. Chancellor Jaakko Nousiainen

I mentioned in chapter one that the first book I ever read on Finland was *The Finnish Political System* by political scientist Jaakko Nousiainen. I had met Dr. Nousiainen on a few occasions during my assignments to Finland, and I certainly wanted to include one of the leading scholars on the Finnish political system and presidency among those Finns I would consult for my book project. Now chancellor of the University of Turku, Dr. Nousiainen's observations on the use of presidential power under President Kekkonen and President Koivisto are, therefore, most authoritative as well as interesting.

16. Elizabeth Rehn

I first met Elizabeth Rehn during my second assignment to Finland when she was a member of Parliament for the Swedish Peoples Party. She was a dinner guest at our home on a few occasions. She was later to serve from 1990 to 1995 as Finland's first woman minister of defense, and still later won world-wide attention as candidate for the Finnish presidency in 1994, losing to now-President Martti Ahtisaari in a close race. Her name shows up in current Finnish public opinion polls as a strong candidate for the presidential elections to be held in the year 2000. In our interview she discussed with characteristic energy and candor her impressions of the Kekkonen and Koivisto years, her achievements as minister of defense and her presidential campaign.

17. Ambassador Rozanne L. Ridgway

I had been in the American embassy in Helsinki for less than a year when Ambassador Ridgway arrived in Finland, replacing Ambassador Mark Austad who had left some months earlier after the inauguration of President Jimmy Carter. Austad had been a political appointee of the Ford administration. Ridgway was a career Foreign Service Officer, and the first woman to serve as U.S. ambassador to Finland (and only woman to date). Ridgway brought many refreshing changes to the embassy, including a collegial approach and a willingness to work closely together with her entire staff.

As noted in the text, Ambassador Ridgway went on to even higher positions in the Department of State, eventually becoming the first woman to serve as an assistant secretary in charge of the pivotal bureau of European affairs. It was my good fortune to work for Ambassador Ridgway twice more after Finland, once when she was counselor of the Department of State in 1980-81, and as director of Northern European affairs when she was assistant secretary for European and Canadian affairs. After retiring from the Department of State, Ambassador Ridgway has been president and then co-chair of the prestigious Atlantic Council as well as serving on the boards of directors of several key United States companies and corporations. I am most honored and grateful that Ambassador Ridgway was willing to write the foreword to this book.

18. Aarne Saarinen

Aarne Saarinen was the long-time chairman of the Finnish Communist Party (SKP for its initials in the Finnish language). This book describes how he and other "liberals" within the SKP fought a continuing battle over several decades to establish the independence of the SKP from the Communist Party of the Soviet Union and to commit the SKP to working within Finland's democratic political system. The book also relates my successful efforts to establish an overt relationship between the U.S. embassy and the SKP, including with Saarinen himself.

It was gratifying, therefore, when Aarne Saarinen agreed to meet me in June 1995 as a part of my series of interviews. He received me in his simple, but book-lined quarters at the retirement home where he lives in north Helsinki, a simple man of the people, now as during his party days. He still has his strong deep-pitched, deliberate speaking style which had always renewed my faith in my ability to understand spoken Finnish, and he could still figure out from my sometimes tortured Finnish what I was commenting on or asking. The views he expressed during the interview impressed me as those of a man most understanding and generous towards former friends and antagonists alike, of a man, in short, at peace with himself and his life's work.

19. Pertti Salolainen

Pertti Salolainen was a highly popular young member of Parliament from Helsinki for the National Coalition (Conservative) Party when I arrived in Finland for my first assignment. He became one of my first political contacts in the party. That professional relationship deepened into a lasting friendship with Pertti and his wife Anja who were quite often dinner guests at our home, during both of our Helsinki assignments. By my second assignment 1984-1986 it was clear that Salolainen sought the leadership of his party. He had competed for it in 1983 and lost to Ilkka Suominen. By the time of my second tour in Finland, the Conservative Party was still in opposition, notwithstanding President Koivisto's rise to presidential office and the widespread belief that "general" foreign policy considerations were no longer a factor in keeping the party out of government. Salolainen was subsequently to gain the chairmanship of the Conservative Party and to serve as minister for foreign trade after the conservatives finally became a part of government. He is currently serving as Finland's ambassador to the United Kingdom. Salolainen during our interview had some very pointed comments about life in the National Coalition Party during the Kekkonen years and about rivalries within the party.

20. General Ensio Silasvuo

During my diplomatic assignments to Finland I had known General Silasvuo only by his reputation as a leading figure in international peacekeeping efforts with the United Nations. However, my friends Lysa and Tapani Brotherus know General Silasvuo quite well and described him as a charming conversationalist with fascinating experiences to relate. Lysa arranged with General Silasvuo to receive me. In fact it was my first appointment in the round of interviews. The general and his wife greeted me at their charming apartment on Castreninkatu with a lovely view overlooking Helsinki. Mrs. Silasvuo had prepared cakes and coffee and then left the general and me to our discussion. It was indeed a fascinating conversational excursion over the years from the Winter War right up to the crisis of the 1995 UN peacekeeping operation in Bosnia. The charismatic general enlivened the conversation with his dry wit and deft phrases.

21. Kalevi Sorsa

As a three time prime minister, three time foreign minister, and long-term chairman of the Finnish Social Democratic Party, Kalevi Sorsa has been one of Finland's three or four most influential political leaders of the past quarter-century. Disappointed to date in his presidential aspirations, Sorsa remains ready in the background in his newer role as senior statesman. Sorsa had first arrived onto the national scene when, as Social Democratic Party secretary, he was selected as foreign minister in the Paasio minority Social Democratic government in 1972, becoming prime minister of a majority coalition government later the same year. Upon my arrival in Finland in 1976, the Social Democratic Party of which Sorsa was by now chairman, was out of government. However, he returned as prime minister of his second government in 1977.

I cannot claim that Sorsa was a close contact of mine in the embassy. As prime minister much of the time, he was understandably somewhat beyond the reach of a political counselor. My more frequent SDP contacts were with Party Secretary Ulf Sundqvist and Planning Secretary Paavo Lipponen, as well as with numerous members of Parliament. However, I did call on him on a few occasions, and met him numerous times at luncheons or other affairs arranged by the ambassador at the embassy. The same was generally true of my second assignment to Helsinki when once again Sorsa was prime minister during the entire period of my 1984-1986 assignment, and my primary SDP contacts remained with my old Social Democratic friends, and with Erkki Liikinen, by then secretary general of the party.

It was therefore with great pleasure that I learned that former Prime Minister Sorsa would meet with me in his Bank of Finland office in June 1995. Not only that, but when my tape recorder turned out to have malfunctioned during the latter part of the interview, Sorsa graciously agreed to receive me once again on a separate trip I made to Finland in late September of the same year. As the only person ever to have served as prime minister under both Presidents Kekkonen and Koivisto, Sorsa has a unique perspective on comparisons between the two men and their leadership styles, as well as on many other issues and subjects of interest.

I feel a little sad that Chapter 19 must deal in some detail with the controversy following Sorsa's 1985 May Day speech. In all of my contacts with him he had been unfailingly gracious and was, as I mentioned, most generous with his time when I interviewed him in 1995. However, the 1985 May Day incident and its aftermath provide a cameo glimpse into some of the characteristics of the Finnish political culture of that period which I think is instructive.

22. Dr. Juhani Suomi

Juhani Suomi was one of my early contacts in the Ministry for Foreign Affairs when I arrived in Finland in 1976, and we maintained a periodic professional relationship throughout my two assignments in Finland. An expert on Soviet affairs in the foreign ministry, he was among those career foreign ministry officials identified with the Center Party, just as Jaakko Blomberg, Jaakko Iloniemi and others were identified with the Social Democratic Party. Politicization in the Finnish foreign ministry is an interesting phenomenon. In the United States, the State Department is politicized at the top, in the form of political appointees being brought into senior State Department positions and the many politically appointed ambassadors all of whom clearly owe their jobs and their allegiance to the political party and president then in power. The career officers of the United States Foreign Service on the other hand are almost totally independent of even informal political partisanship, although some officers may be perceived as being "liberal" or "conservative". In Finland, and in some other countries, such as Sweden, diplomatic officers are sometimes even selected or recruited with a view of their known political party preferences. I am not sure this is always healthy.

In any case, in our meetings Dr. Suomi demonstrated his knowledge not only about Soviet affairs, but perhaps even more importantly, his good feel—from a Center Party perspective—for domestic partisan Finnish politics and its influence on foreign policy. Subsequent to my assignments in Finland, he has become quite famous for his masterly and exhaustive series of volumes in his ongoing biography of President Kekkonen. His work is absolutely essential to any researcher who would wish to write about this subject. So, in addition to reading extensively from his biography of President Kekkonen, I sought him out as a part of my series of interviews. He received me in his office in the political department of the foreign ministry, and he generously gave of his time for the interview.

In Chapter 25, I have been critical of some Dr. Suomi's comments to me and some quotes from his biography of President Kekkonen that in my opinion reminded me of the negative dimensions of the political atmosphere in Finland during the 1960s and 1970s. Dr. Suomi publicly criticized me in Finland after the appearance of the Finnish edition of this book, even claiming he was misquoted. I was able to demonstrate from copies of the audio tapes and transcripts of our interview that my citations of him are completely accurate. I regret that Dr. Suomi took offense at my comments, which nevertheless I stand by as statements of my opinion. Be that as it may, I nevertheless believe that the opinions Dr. Suomi expressed to me in our interview constitute a very important perspective on the issues that I raise.

23. Ilkka Suominen

I did not meet Ilkka Suominen during my first assignment to Helsinki 1976-79, when Harri Holkeri was chairman of the National Coalition (Conservative) Party. But I got to know him quite well during my second assignment when he was by then chairman of the party. In fact we spent the better part of a week together during an embassy trip to which we used to invite and escort high level Finnish politicians and journalists on a so-called "NATO" tour. The idea was to expose influential Finns to the thinking of the Western, primarily U.S., delegations to the various European arms control and security entities. On one trip in 1985, the group consisted of Ilkka Suominen, Erkki Liikinen, Per-Erik Lönnfors, Simopekka Nortamo, Embassy Public Affairs Officer Tom O'Connor, and myself. These trips were invariably interesting, not the least for the interaction among the Finns, whom we always tried to select from different backgrounds.

The Conservative Party under Suominen's leadership took pains to invite embassy officers every few months to a sauna to discuss political events of the day. All in all, we had a most agreeable relationship. Suominen's views are particularly interesting with respect to the operating styles of Presidents Kekkonen and President Koivisto.

24. Jukka Tarkka

When I served in Finland, I knew Jukka Tarkka as a columnist with the *Helsingin Sanomat,* but he was not one of my principal contacts there. Consequently, I know him less well than many of the others whom I interviewed. I have read many of his columns and a couple of his books, most notably *Presidentin ministeri* and *Suomen kylma sota.* Tarkka subsequently embarked on a political career, becoming a co-founder of the Young Finns Party and was elected as a member of the Finnish Parliament in 1994, where he received me for our interesting and wide-ranging interview. Tarkka was not re-elected to Parliament in the 1999 elections.

25. Paavo Väyrynen

Paavo Väyrynen, three-time Finnish foreign minister, former chairman of the Center Party, and past (as well as possibly future) aspirant to the Finnish presidency is one of Finland's best known and more controversial political leaders. During my diplomatic assignments to Finland I frequently had occasion to meet with Mr. Vayrynen, usually with one of my ambassadors or with official visitors from the United States. During my first assignment, he was one of Finland's youngest ministers and was considered a protege of President Kekkonen. As one who has himself been criticized for his alleged use of the "Soviet card" well into the 1980s, Väyrynen argued in his conversation with me that it was not the Center Party or President Kekkonen who were playing the Soviet card. Rather, he said, it was the other Finnish political parties who were trying to curry favor with the Soviets by taking more conciliatory positions on foreign and security issues than the Center Party. Former minister Väyrynen has himself written extensively about several of the issues discussed in the transcript, and his writings perhaps give a more complete background on his views. However, this book records his spontaneous views put forward during the interview. Väyrynen currently serves as a member of the European Parliament.

Persons Interviewed for this Book but Not Cited

1. Ambassador Derek Shearer, United States ambassador to Finland 1993-1997
2. Ambassador Åke Wihtol, former Finnish Foreign Ministry state secretary
3. Admiral Jan Klenberg, former commander, Finnish Defense Forces
4. Ambassador Jaakko Laajava, current ambassador of Finland to the United States
5. Jaakko Laakso, member of parliament of the Leftist Alliance, former editor of the Stalinist Finnish newspaper *Tiedonantaja*
6. Rafael Paro, editor-in-chief of *Hufvudstadsbladet*
7. Juha Sipilä, general manager of the Helsinki metropolitan area cooperative council
8. Aatos Erkko, CEO of Sanoma Osakeyhtio, parent company of the *Helsingin Sanomat*
9. Kari Nars, senior counselor of Finnish Ministry of Finance and recognized European monetary advisor and expert
10. General Aimo Pajunen, former Ministry of Defense chief of chancery

Index

CPSIA information can be obtained
at www.ICGtesting.com
Printed in the USA
FSHW012331120319
56300FS